613, 2

Child
and Family
Development
Implications
for Primary
Health Care

Child
and Family
Development
Implications
for Primary
Health Care

DEBRA P. HYMOVICH, R.N., Ph.D.

Professor of Nursing
School of Nursing
University of Colorado

ROBERT W. CHAMBERLIN, M.D.

Associate Professor of Pediatrics
University of Rochester Medical Center

With a contribution on school-age children by
SANDRA DALE, R.N., M.S.
Assistant Professor of Nursing

PHILIP R. NADER, M.D.
Associate Professor of Nursing

University of Texas Medical Branch—Galveston

McGRAW-HILL BOOK COMPANY
New York   St. Louis   San Francisco   Auckland   Bogotá   Hamburg
Johannesburg   London   Madrid   Mexico   Montreal   New Delhi
Panama   Paris   São Paulo   Singapore   Sydney   Tokyo   Toronto

This book was set in Optima by Port City Press, Inc.
The editors were David P. Carroll and Abe Krieger;
the designer was Joan E. O'Connor;
the cover drawing was done by Jennifer Leah Barron
and designed by Jane Moorman;
the production supervisor was Robert A. Pirrung.
R. R. Donnelley & Sons Company was printer and binder.

CHILD AND FAMILY DEVELOPMENT: Implications for Primary Health Care

1 2 3 4 5 6 7 8 9 0   DODO   8 9 8 7 6 5 4 3 2 1 0

Library of Congress Cataloging in Publication Data

Hymovich, Debra P
Child and family development.

Bibliography: p.
Includes index.
1. Child development. 2. Family. 3. Children—
Care and hygiene. 4. Family—Health and hygiene.
5. Sick children—Family relationships. I. Chamber-
lin, Robert W., joint author. II. Title.
RJ131.H94   362.7'8'10422   79-9450
ISBN 0-07-031650-3

NOTICE

Medicine is an ever-changing science. As new research and clinical experience
broaden our knowledge, changes in treatment and drug therapy are required. The
editors and the publisher of this work have made every effort to ensure that the
drug dosage schedules herein are accurate and in accord with the standards
accepted at the time of publication. Readers are advised, however, to check the
product information sheet included in the package of each drug they plan to
administer to be certain that changes have not been made in the recommended
dose or in the contraindications for administration. This recommendation is of
particular importance in regard to new or infrequently used drugs.

To Jonathan, David, and Jennifer Barron
For sharing so much of their young lives with me
and
To my mother, Lillian Hymovich,
For keeping the parents' perspective in focus

DEBRA P. HYMOVICH

To my daughters Ann, Martha, Sue, and Mary
Who taught me so much about growth and development
and
To Ida, who shared with me the joys and sorrows of
raising a family for so many years

ROBERT W. CHAMBERLIN

CONTENTS

CONTENTS

CONTENTS

Foreword

A Gusii child in Africa traditionally grew up with his own mother, but sharing his father with many other mother-child households. A Tibetan child grew up knowing one mother but many fathers; a child in the Kaingang culture grew up where men and women formed a group marriage and co-parented all the children. Israeli children in modern kibbutzim grow up in communal settings. Children in North America may grow up in the typical nuclear family with one mother and one father, or in one of the many newly emerging family forms.

Whatever form it takes, however, the family, like war and music, is one of the few "cultural universals" anthropologists have been able to document. People of all times and in all parts of the world have recognized that without some form of family life there would be no way to allow children to grow up to become functioning members of their societies. Wolf children have been known, orphanages have been tried and "throw-away" children have existed, but their development only makes it more clear that families are the necessary prerequisite to normal, healthy development of children.

Spiro (1949), in his ethnography of the Ifaluk, showed us how clear the importance of the family has always been to people everywhere. He describes the attitude of these Micronesian people toward their children saying, "To isolate the (child) would be to commit a major atrocity, for if he is left alone 'by and 'by he dies, no more people" (pp. 89–94).

FOREWORD

In view of the fact that lay people have always recognized the obvious importance of the family, it may seem surprising that professional recognition of its importance is relatively recent; and even currently, it is often not appreciated clinically. This phenomenon may not, however, be quite as surprising as it first appears. We, as professionals, know that even dealing with an individual is exceedingly complex. The recent upsurge of the concept of holism, i.e., that a person, although composed of an infinite number of parts, remains a whole that is clearly, but amazingly, much more than the sum of its parts, attests to this appreciation. If the experience of dealing with an individual is this complex, how much more complex the experience of dealing with a family unit. Fear of the complexity of such interaction has probably been responsible for the resistance of many clinicians to using this concept. Even the research related to the family is much less definitive than that related to the individual.

At first glance, the theoretical and research work available on the topic has seemed disparate and nonapplicable to many clinicians. It is here that one of the major strengths of the work of Drs. Hymovich and Chamberlin and their contributors lies. Their ability, not only to compile and synthesize the theories and research related to families, but also to apply these to clinical interactions of the health care provider is one of the most outstanding features of this book. Their ability to interweave a very in-depth knowledge of individual maturation with knowledge of family dynamics and to apply this to the common everyday problems of families of typical and exceptional children is truly a remarkable feat. Surely this book will be one of the professional turning points that will help us, as clinicians, to utilize more fully the information available to us from the theoreticians and researchers—information that may previously have appeared somewhat inaccessible or inapplicable.

It is indeed a privilege for me to introduce you to what I am sure you will find an excellent source for understanding not only the interplay between individual and family maturation, but the relationship of this interplay to the health of individuals, families, and societies. It is also a pleasure for me to extend to the authors the appreciation of both the nursing and medical professions for an invaluable resource book for the theoretician, the researcher, and most of all, for the clinician.

Marie Scott Brown, R.N., Ph.D.
Associate Professor of Parent-Child Nursing
University of Colorado

Foreword

If one wants to help children, help families! This theme has been behind much of child development work for the past generation, but has too seldom been put into practice. Part of the reason for this lack is the absence of a sound teaching guide that melds knowledge of research in child development and family development with clinical application. This book aims at such integration. It blends the world of theory and practice in a way few other books do. Written by clinicians—nurses and pediatricians, who continue to straddle the worlds of research and practice—it will find major usefulness among clinicians. The material ranges widely, presenting specific clinical guidance for management of families of children with conditions as disparate as respiratory infections and cerebral palsy to obesity and family crises. It includes age-related developmental needs of well children, all the while keeping the family focus, as well as the interrelated needs of individual children growing up in families.

Dr. Hymovich, a nurse-clinician, and Dr. Chamberlin, a pediatrician, and their colleagues, have each studied child development at the research level. But they remain clinicians rather than primarily research workers. The authors' theoretical framework is eclectic, using the synthesis of the major developmental themes of the past half century: psychoanalytic, psychosocial, crisis-stages, cognitive, temperament, and learning theory.

Family development has yet to achieve such eloquent or multiple theoretical frameworks as individual child development. The authors describe the family function approach that characterizes much of the family literature. They acknowledge the very large role played by economics, jobs and culture, in family and child life. But this book is essentially a one-on-one clinician-child or clinician-family therapy book, rather than a book on social policy. Few nurses or pediatricians have delved so deeply into the developmental literature and yet continue to apply this information as well as these authors. Families and children will be the better because of this work.

Robert J. Haggerty, M.D.
Professor Public Health and Pediatrics
Harvard School of Public Health

Visiting Professor of Pediatrics
Harvard Medical School

Preface

Professionals who have frequent and continuing contacts with parents and children are in a strategic position to influence child and family development. This book is written to provide these professionals with basic knowledge of child and family development and guidelines for using this knowledge that can be applied in primary health care settings.

We have selected those areas of child and family development that seem most relevant for clinical practice. It is our goal to present basic concepts, principles, and facts that seem particularly pertinent for the health care provider. It is our intention to provide the reader with developmental knowledge that can be immediately applied in the clinical setting.

Each chapter presents a four-pronged approach: individual development, family development, the effect of selected variables on development, and clinical applications of developmental knowledge. The concept of developmental tasks within each stage is used as an organizing framework for presenting basic aspects of biological, social, emotional, and cognitive development from pregnancy through middle childhood. Common topics are included for each stage so that their evolution can be followed longitudinally across stages as well as cross-sectionally within a given stage of development.

Since it would be impossible to cover, in depth, topics related to all variant forms of individual and family development, we have chosen to mention only those areas that are fairly common in the United States and to provide the reader with selected references regarding each topic. Rather than cover these areas superficially, we have used them only as examples. Topics that are easily found in other sources are mentioned but not covered in depth.

In addition, the implications of common illness patterns and behavior problems of each stage of development are presented. Reactions to chronic and fatal illness and to hospitalization at each stage of development are explored, along with the effects of central nervous system dysfunction and other developmental disorders on developmental sequences.

Finally, some approaches to parent education in the primary care setting are examined, as is a broader look at some aspects of communication between parents, children, and health care providers. Although we recognize that many clinicians provide care for adolescent clients, it was not feasible for us to include that age group in this edition.

It is important to stress that research evidence related to both child and family development is incomplete and does not provide us with definitive guidelines. A review of the literature discloses that there are more articles that describe general clinical impressions or several cases rather than systematic research. As far as possible we have tried to stay close to original data sources so as to better document what is and is not known.

This book is not intended to be a cookbook of "how to's," nor is it designed to provide only the "whys." Rather it is a blend of concepts, theory, and clinical application. It is our hope that this book will provide readers with a selection of the evidence that is available, encourage constant questioning of our behaviors and suggestions, and stimulate further research to fill in the gaps of our knowledge.

ACKNOWLEDGMENTS

This book could not have been completed without the assistance and support of many people. We would like to thank Susan McCabe, Madeline Schmitt, and Jean Miller for their reviews of selected sections of the manuscript, as well as the students who offered many useful suggestions. Appreciation is also expressed to Gloria Hagopian and Sarah Rothrey for their assistance with some of the tedious details.

We are especially grateful to Elizabeth Tong for her cheerful assistance in obtaining photographs, and to the many families who were willing to let us photograph them. We appreciate the willingness of Susan

McCabe, Marie Brown, Barbara Adams, Judy Igoe, and Larry Tonzi to share many of their photographs with us. We are also grateful to the many publishers who gave permission to use some of their materials.

Appreciation is expressed to Robert Haggerty, M.D., whose broad outlook on pediatric care in an age of specialization was a source of inspiration and encouragement. We also wish to acknowledge the fine cooperation of Sandra Dale, R.N., and Philip Nader, M.D., in preparing much of Chapter 5, and their contributions to Chapter 1.

We wish to acknowledge the cheerful and sympathetic help of Natalia Cueto, whose patience with multiple revisions and incomprehensible handwriting is much appreciated. We are especially grateful to Connie Martin for her perfectionism in typing and proofing the entire manuscript and for making it possible for us to meet our deadlines.

Debra P. Hymovich
Robert W. Chamberlin

Child
and Family
Development
Implications
for Primary
Health Care

ONE

Introduction to Child and Family Development

A s the twig is bent, so grows the tree. Many theories and investigations regarding human development validate this old adage, while others indicate that human beings also have some measure of control over their own destinies. This pliant twig can develop in a variety of ways, some of which are healthy and some of which lead to illness. A person's development determines his or her being at any given time and influences that individual's biological, psychological, and social reactions in current and future situations.

Because of their long-term contact with new families, primary health care providers are in a strategic position to assist families in achieving optimal development of all members. The purpose of this book is to aid the health provider in this task. To do this we shall attempt to review what is known about child and family development at different stages and make practical suggestions about how such knowledge might be used in the delivery of primary health care.

This chapter provides the practitioner with an overview of concepts, principles, and theories of individual and family development, factors affecting development, and the way in which this information can be applied in the clinical setting. These concepts and principles and their application will be expanded upon in each of the succeeding chapters.

The term *growth* refers to structural changes within the individual,

FIGURE 1-1   by Debra Hymovich

while *development* indicates an increase in complexity and function that results in new characteristics and/or abilities of the individual. In this book, these terms are expanded to include the structural changes within the family (growth) and increasing complexity of family functioning (development).

INDIVIDUAL DEVELOPMENT

Principles of Development

Several principles of growth and development are useful in understanding an individual child's progress. Human development follows a predictable pattern. Evidence of this pattern can be seen in physical, cognitive, and behavioral development. There is general agreement among child developmentalists that growth in the pre- and postnatal individual proceeds in a *cephalocaudal direction.* Examples of this principle can be seen in the fetus, where the brain develops prior to the limbs, and in the child, where control of trunk muscles occurs prior to control of the legs. Growth also proceeds in an outward direction from the central axis of the body to the periphery. This *proximodistal* principle is evident in utero where the limb buds develop from the trunk, and the phalanges from the limb buds. In the weeks following birth, infants can be seen using their arms before using the whole hand, and later the fingers to grasp objects. *Differentiation* proceeds from the simple to the complex and from the general to the specific. The development of a complex human infant from a single cell is evidence of this process in utero. We see the infant progressing from generalized movements of the entire body in response to most stimuli prior to voluntary movement of individual body parts.

The concept of *critical periods* in human biological development applies also to embryonic growth, where the most rapidly growing tissues are particularly sensitive to any change in conditions. The extent to which this concept can be applied to postnatal development, particularly in relation to behavioral areas, has still not been clearly demonstrated, although evidence suggests that such sensitive periods do exist. It appears that these periods are of longer duration in humans than in animals, and that learning can and does take place at a later time but is a slower and more difficult process (Havighurst, 1972; Scott, 1972). Klaus and Kennell (1976) postulate a sensitive period in the mother-infant bonding process, while McGraw (1943) identified the existence of critical periods for optimal learning of motor skills in the human infant.

A final important principle is related to the *uniqueness* of each individual. Although all people follow a predictable pattern of development, each person develops in a style that is uniquely his or her own. There is impressive evidence from a number of studies suggesting that infants differ from birth and that they maintain these differences over time (Bell and Harper, 1977; Kessen, et al., 1961; Thomas et al., 1968). These individual differences are due partly to differences in heredity and partly to environmental influences. Some of the variables influencing the uniqueness of growth and development are described in another section of this chapter.

Theoretical Frameworks

It is possible to view human development from a variety of theoretical perspectives. We have selected several frameworks for brief presentation here because they have provided the basis for some of the research regarding child and family development as well as selected aspects of clinical practice. These theories are expanded upon in subsequent chapters. The reader who wishes to further explore these, or other theoretical frameworks, is referred to references such as Baldwin (1967),

Erikson (1963), Gale (1969), Hall (1954), Havighurst (1972), Maddi (1976), Maier (1969), and Pervin (1975).

We have not attempted to critique these theories but, rather, to present their major components. Since we have found no single theory to be useful in all situations, a developmental task framework is used throughout the book in an attempt to synthesize a variety of approaches for use in assessing and intervening with individual family members.

PSYCHOANALYTIC THEORY

Sigmund Freud is generally considered the founder of the psychoanalytic (psychosexual) theory of personality development. The basic tenets of this theory are presented below.

The total personality is said to consist of three major systems: id, ego, and superego. The *id* is the most primitive structure of the personality and is the primary source of one's instincts or impulses. Its function is to release psychic energy (libido or life force) in order to relieve tension and find pleasure (pleasure principle). The pleasure principle is fulfilled through impulsive motor activity and through image formation (wish fulfillment). The young infant who cries when hungry and begins sucking before the nipple is present is said to be controlled primarily by the id.

As the child interacts with the environment, the *ego* is formed. The ego, or executive of the personality, mediates between the id and the later-developing superego. It is governed by the reality principle and is capable of postponing the discharge of energy until an appropriate and acceptable means of satisfaction is available. For example, the hungry child learns to ask for food and to wait while it is prepared.

The *superego,* a product of the child's socialization (rewards and punishments), is the moral or judicial branch of the personality. This is formed primarily in the family where the child is interacting with the parents. It includes the internalization of values, customs, and beliefs representing the ideal, rather than the real, state. The ego ideal corresponds to a child's conceptions of what parents consider morally good, while the conscience corresponds to the child's ideas of what parents consider morally bad and for which the child is punished.

Personality develops as the individual learns to resolve tensions stemming from biological growth processes, frustrations, conflicts, and threats. *Anxiety,* a major concept of psychoanalytic theory, is said to play an important role in both the development and functioning of the personality. Anxiety, or fear, may be objective, neurotic, or moral. Objective anxiety has its roots in the external world and is a realistic source of danger, while neurotic anxiety resides in the id and is a fear of being overwhelmed by an uncontrollable urge. Moral anxiety stems from the conscience of the superego and is experienced as feelings of shame or guilt.

One's personality has generally developed by the end of the fifth year of life by learning to respond to four major sources of tension: physiological growth processes, frustrations, conflicts, and threats. The two methods by which the individual learns to resolve tensions are through identification and displacement. The process of *identification* involves incorporating the qualities of another into one's own personality. During the early years, children generally identify with their parents, and, as their world expands, they find other people in the environment with whom to identify. The process of *displacement* occurs when the original object is inaccessible to the individual and energy must be channeled to a substitute object. The form of the displacement will depend upon how closely the substituted object resembles the original one and the sanctions and prohibitions imposed by society. A displacement that represents a higher cultural achievement, such as painting, is called a *sublimation*.

When tensions become excessive, the *defense mechanisms* come into operation. These mechanisms are essentially unconscious means devised by the ego for distorting reality in order to reduce stress or anxiety. Commonly used defense mechanisms include: (1) *regression,* reverting to an earlier level of development; (2) *fixation,* remaining, temporarily or permanently and to varying degrees, at a certain level of development without progressing; (3) *projection,* attributing responsibility or feelings to another person rather than to the self; (4) *rationalization,* finding a justifiable excuse for a given action to make it more acceptable; (5) *repression,* barring an anxiety-producing object or event from registering itself in the conscience; and (6) *reaction formation,* substituting one instinct (such as hate) with its opposite (love) to keep the real feeling out of awareness.

The psychoanalytic concept of the *unconscious* means that there are mental processes and phenomena of which the individual is unaware. Related to this is the principle of psychic determinism; that is, no behavior occurs purely by accident. Behaviors such as gestures, slips of the tongue, and forgetfulness are said to be caused for some unconscious reason.

In psychoanalytic theory the adult personality has its roots in the early experiences of the child. Consequently, these early childhood experiences have a lasting effect on the individual and are important in determining that person's subsequent behavior.

Development proceeds through a sequence of stages based on the region of the body (erogenous zone) that is the primary source of libidinal pleasure and gratification. The principal erogenous zones are the mouth, anus, and genitals. Personality is shaped by socialization in these three vital organ systems of the body. Socialization involves feeding, weaning, elimination and sexuality training. The *oral stage* of infancy is so named because the primary source of libidinal pleasure is centered around the infant's mouth; this pleasure comes from sucking and eating. This stage can be divided into two substages: the first substage is called the oral-dependent phase and is characterized primarily by the activity of incorporation or taking in of food that is offered. The second, or oral-aggressive, phase begins about the time the infant is weaned, and includes biting activity.

The *anal stage* begins sometime around the second year of life when the child's source of pleasure shifts from the mouth to the anal region of the body. During this stage the child must learn to postpone the pleasure that comes from relieving anal tensions. The child learns to regulate two mutually conflicting activities: retention, or holding on, and elimination, or letting go. The manner in which toilet training is managed during this stage is believed to have a major influence on the child's later personality.

The *phallic stage* (early genital stage) of personality development corresponds with the preschool years. The child's source of libidinal pleasure now shifts to the genital region, and the child becomes curious about sex differences and the origin of babies. According to Freudian theory, the penis is considered a valuable possession by boys and is envied by girls, and its lack is often viewed by girls as a defect. A major male concern during this stage is the castration complex, a fear of mutilation or loss of the penis. Another feature of this period is the development of the Oedipal complex, in which the child focuses love and attention on the parent of the opposite sex and wants to displace or remove the parent of the same sex. This is often referred to as the Electra complex when speaking of the girl's love for her father.

During the elementary school years, the child enters the *latency stage* of development, during which Freud believed there is a period of relative sexual quiescence. It is the period when the child is involved in learning the skills, values, and roles of the culture. By the end of this stage, a person's basic personality structure is said to be established.

As young people reach adolescence, they enter the *genital stage* of development. There is a reactivation of the sexual drives that had been quiescent during the previous stage. This stage differs from the earlier genital stage (phallic stage) in that the adolescent's choice of a love object is no longer incestuous and the adolescent becomes more altruistic toward this love object.

Today there are various psychoanalytic (neo-Freudian) schools founded by others such as Carl Jung, Alfred Adler, Karen Horney, Harry Stack Sullivan, and Eric Fromm. Although it is not possible to explore each school of thought separately, it should be kept in mind that they diverge from Freud's original conceptualizations largely by focusing on the social determinants of personality that interact with sexual development.

PSYCHOSOCIAL THEORY

Erik H. Erikson expands upon the psychosexual framework of Freud to include the adult years as well as the sociocultural variables influencing development. While Freud emphasized development as closely tied to achieving control over id impulses, Erikson's focus is on the autonomy of the ego and development of personality through active involvement with the environment. Libidinal energy is seen as a force directing the individual's development. An important concept in Erikson's theory is that of mutual regulation; that is, individual family members grow and develop together, with each person influencing the development of the other.

Erikson describes the life span from birth through senescence as consisting of a sequence of eight stages. Inherent in each stage is a developmental crisis, or turning point, when there is a period of increased vulnerability to, and heightened potential for, mastering a particular psychosocial task. Specific dichotomies are utilized to describe the central task occurring at each stage, emphasizing the need to cope with the tasks rather than to simply pass through each phase. If there is successful resolution of the developmental crisis, the individual is ready to move on to the next phase; if resolution is unfavorable, later development becomes more difficult. A problem is never completely resolved; rather, its resolution is dominant during a particular stage, but it reemerges at various points to be further resolved.

The developmental crisis to be resolved during infancy (birth to 12 to 18 months) is the establishment of basic *trust* while overcoming a sense of basic *mistrust*. This basic sense of trust is developed as physical and emotional needs are met by the infant's care takers. The quality as well as quantity of the mother-infant relationship is an important determinant of this sense of trust, especially in the feeding situation.

During the toddler years, the child, who has just learned to trust his or her mother, now learns self-trust to become a self-willed and autonomous person. While developing a sense of *autonomy*, the toddler tries to resolve feelings of *shame and doubt*.

The central task of the preschooler (3 to 6 years) is to develop a sense of *initiative* that enables the child to plan and carry out activities. At the same time, the child is learning to overcome feelings of *guilt* for things he or she would like to do. This guilt is caused partially by the Oedipal conflict and partly by the rigidity of the developing superego.

Erikson identifies the central task of the school-aged child as the development of a sense of *industry* while overcoming a sense of *inferiority*. This is the age when productivity becomes important as the child learns the basic tools of the culture. Children who receive recognition for their efforts continue to develop a positive self-concept, while those children who believe they are unable to master tasks develop feelings of inferiority.

The predominant task during the adolescent years is that of developing a sense of *identity* rather than one of *role diffusion*. The development of identity begins during infancy when the baby first recognizes its mother and later itself as an individual. Identity includes an integration of all previous identifications and self-images and includes positive, as well as negative, conceptions of oneself. Role diffusion implies a certain confusion about one's place in the world and hence uncertainty as to appropriate behavior.

The young adult seeks to develop a sense of *intimacy* with persons rather than develop a sense of *isolation*. The hazard of isolation is the inability to expose the self by sharing it with another in mature friendship and love.

The majority of adult years are devoted to the task of establishing a sense of *generativity*, which essentially means productivity and satisfaction with what is produced. At the same time, the adult is trying to avoid the hazard of *stagnation*, characterized by self-absorption, lack of productivity, and a competitive attitude toward others, including one's children.

During the later years, the individual's final developmental task is the achievement of a sense of *integrity*, indicating the development of a self-concept with which one is satisfied, and pride in one's creations (children, work, or hobbies). If people have not successfully resolved earlier tasks, they may look upon their lives with *despair*.

COGNITIVE THEORY

Jean Piaget's theory focuses on the cognitive aspects of development. His assumption is that personality evolves from a composite and interrelationship of affective and intellectual functions. From studying normal children, Piaget has come to view development as an evolutionary process with a series of sequential phases and subphases. The goal of human behavior is to achieve near-biological, affective, and mental equilibrium.

Piaget's approach to development focuses on the evolution and function of the intellectual structures of the mind. The basic framework of development consists of the schema (organizational structure) and of adaptation. The formation of *schemata,* which encompass internalized thought processes and overt motor behavior, enables the child to adapt to, and organize, his or her environment. The schema adapts through the two invariant processes of assimilation and accommodation. *Assimilation* is the process whereby the person integrates new environmental stimuli into already existing schemata, while *accommodation* involves the modification of existing schemata or the formation of new schemata for stimuli that do not fit into the existing structures. Optimum cognitive growth requires a relative balance (equilibrium) between assimilation and accommodation.

Piagetian theory is based on the concept that development follows a definite sequence of invariant stages and that each of these stages has its own unique characteristics. Although Piaget suggests an approximate time frame for each stage, he points out that there is no specific age at which each stage begins. The variability in this timing is based on individual differences, cultural expectations, and experiences. His framework consists of four major stages, each of which is characterized by a different process of thought. Each stage represents a range of organizational patterns that occur in a definite sequence.

The earliest form of thinking occurs in the first period, or *sensorimotor stage,* that begins at birth and lasts until the child is approximately 2 years old and is beginning to use language. During this early period, the child's functioning depends primarily on sensory and motor experiences. That is, the infant assimilates and accommodates to the world through actions and sensations (feelings, seeing, tasting, hearing). Self-expression and communication with others is through motor activities. The child moves from purely reflex behavior to beginning concepts of object permanence, time, and space. The baby begins to differentiate between cause and effect and can intentionally make things happen in the environment.

From approximately 1½ or 2 to 7 years of age, the child progresses through the stage of *preoperational thought.* The functional change occurring at this time is the appearance of symbolic functions and the acquisition of language. Behavior is no longer guided only by sensory and motor events but also by mental representations and internal thoughts. This stage is characterized by egocentrism; that is, the child's acquisition of language is characterized by the child's inability to view situations and things from any perspective other than his or her own. The preoperational child has not yet developed the concepts of reversibility or conservation. For example, if these children are shown two balls of clay of equal size and then they see one ball rolled into a sausage shape, they will say that one ball has more clay than the other and deny they still have the same amount. This absence of conservation can be accounted for by the fact that children reason from the configuration rather than the transformation. They see the final stages and compare these, forgetting the transformation because they do not know how to reason about it. Preoperational thought is also characterized by centering; that is, the child concentrates attention on one detail of a situation without taking into account all aspects of the event.

The period from about 7 to 11 years of age is referred to as the stage of *concrete operations.* It is called concrete because the child is able to solve problems based on observable objects or actual events already encountered but cannot yet apply this logic to primarily hypothetical or verbal problems. Children's thinking becomes more logical and systematic; it is no longer limited to their own perceptions, and they learn to see events or situations from several perspectives. They can apply logical operations, such as classifying, serializing, conserving, and reversing, to solve problems involving concrete objects and events.

At about 11 or 12 years, the child begins the fourth and last period of intellectual development, the stage of *formal operations.* The child becomes capable of reasoning on the basis of propositions or hypotheses, not merely on the basis of concrete objects. Young adolescents are learning to think about their own thoughts and to solve complicated abstract problems. At this stage, the individual is less interested in the content of the thought than the form of relationships within it, thus enabling an understanding and appreciation of such things as satires, proverbs, and analogies. By the time the adolescent is about 15 years old, the cognitive processes are those of an adult.

LEARNING THEORIES

Learning theories place heavy emphasis on the side of the environment in shaping behavior. These theories are based on the belief that behavior is primarily the result of the continuous formation of connections between environmental stimuli and responses. Behavior is viewed as the outcome of learning and is believed to occur as the result of an internal state of imbalance or need, called a drive (such as hunger). Behavior that is reinforced is strengthened, and behavior that is ignored or punished is weakened. Behavior is learned by association with a stimulus, a process that is said to be the same at all ages. Consequently, in stimulus-response theory, development is not subdivided into stages as it is in psychosexual, psychosocial, and cognitive development theories.

Stimulus-response theory is based on the concept of conditioning. Conditioning occurs when one or more stimuli (S) have become associated with one or more responses (R) through repeated association with each other. Behavior is learned through either classical or operant conditioning.

In *classical conditioning* (S-R), a neutral stimulus is paired with a stimulus already known to elicit a response (conditioned stimulus). The conditioned stimulus and neutral stimulus must be presented at approximately the same time (principle of contiguity) in order for the neutral stimuli to become conditioned. In Pavlov's classic experiment with dogs, he conditioned the salivary response to occur in response to the sound of a bell by pairing the giving of food with the ringing of the bell. Eventually the dog salivated on hearing the bell though no food was presented.

In *instrumental (or operant) conditioning,* the organism learns to manipulate the environment in order to produce a desired response. Skinner notes that many behaviors are "emitted" by an organism that cannot be attributed to a specific stimulus. He calls this operant behavior because the responses operate on the environment. Through operant conditioning (S-R-S), there is an increased probability that an emitted response will continue to recur under the same conditions. The desired response is reinforced when it occurs; this reinforcement may be either positive (presentation of a stimulus) or negative (removal of an aversive stimulus). Thus, the presentation of a positive reinforcer or the removal of a negative reinforcer are similar to rewards, while the removal of a positive reinforcer or presentation of a negative reinforcer are punishments. Praising a child (positive reinforcement) or refraining from nagging (negative reinforcement) are examples of parental activities that may increase the child's good behavior, while restricting the child to the house (removal of positive reinforcer) or spanking (presentation of negative reinforcer) are examples of punishment that serve to decrease the child's misbehavior.

The number of responses the learner emits in a given period of time depends upon the *schedule of reinforcement* employed. Reinforcement can be either continuous or intermittent. Continuous reinforcement involves reinforcing every response, while intermittent reinforcement may be delivered according to a time interval (one reinforcement per given unit of time) or a ratio interval (one reinforcement after a specific number of emitted responses). Ratio and interval schedules of reinforcement can be either variable or fixed.

CHILD AND FAMILY DEVELOPMENT

A variety of *reinforcers* may be rewarding to a particular individual. There may be some concrete reward, such as candy, or social reinforcers, such as praise, a smile, or a hug. What is reinforcing for one person may not be reinforcing for another; therefore, reinforcers must be tailored to the individual. Tokens may be given to a person for making the desired response. When a certain number of tokens have been accumulated, they may then be exchanged for the actual reinforcers.

The techniques of *shaping* are used to teach an individual complex acts. Shaping involves rewarding responses that come closer and closer to the desired behavior, until finally the desired response is achieved and reinforced. People can be conditioned to discriminate between similar stimuli so that they respond to only one particular stimulus. They can also learn to generalize their behavior in the presence of stimuli other than the original stimulus used.

It is also possible to *extinguish* behavior by ignoring undesired behavior. Skinner has found that punishment does not result in eliminating certain responses but only in suppressing their rate. Behavior that is only rewarded part of the time is likely to be continued even in the absence of that reward. Therefore, consistency of management is important regardless of whether one is trying to reinforce or extinguish behavior.

From the viewpoint of *social learning theory,* much of what a person learns occurs vicariously, through observation and imitation of others (Bandura and Walters, 1963). Bandura and his colleagues have found that children will imitate models who are aggressive, stingy, altruistic, and helpful. They are more likely to imitate models similar to themselves, those who are rewarded, who appear to be prestigious, or who are in control of resources (Bandura, 1971).

According to these theorists, childhood personality patterns develop primarily through imitation of parental models and other significant persons. To Bandura, the term imitation (or modeling) is synonymous with what others call identification. It involves the direct copying of certain behaviors, thus acquiring the other persons' mannerisms and style, as well as accepting their values and beliefs. Through the identification process, children develop a conscience, acquire sex-role behavior patterns, and learn to behave as adults. For example, children learn sex-typed behavior in the same manner they learn other types of behavior, through a combination of reward, punishment, and observation. Sex-role differentiation usually begins right after birth when the baby is given a name and pink and blue identifications are used in the nursery. Following this, direct indoctrination includes distinctive hair styles, clothing, "sex-appropriate" toys and recreational activities, and parental reactions

INTRODUCTION

to sex-role behavior. In addition, the child models (imitates) parental behavior and is rewarded for sex-appropriate behavior and discouraged from behavior considered inappropriate (Bandura, 1969).

DEVELOPMENTAL-MATURATIONAL THEORY

This theory, most closely associated with the work of Arnold Gesell and his colleagues, indicates that many of the phenomena observed in children are related to the unfolding or expression of innate tendencies within the child as he or she matures. Typical behavior and thinking patterns are described for each stage of development, and though environmental influences are recognized, they are given less importance in the overall scheme of things than these innate tendencies (Knoblock and Pasamanick, 1974). Development of the mind, body, and personality is the result of one's genetic inheritance. Environmental factors do not generate developmental changes, they merely support, inflect, or modify the behavior (Gesell and Ilg, 1949). The family is seen as a cultural workshop for transmitting the social inheritance. A democratic household is said to foster a way of life that respects the individuality of the growing child (Gesell and Ilg, 1949, p. 4).

Gesell has provided us with the ages-and-stages approach to child guidance. Each age and stage has characteristic behavior patterns. Physical maturation and neurological development precede behavior. Behavior represents all of a person's reactions, whether reflex, voluntary, spontaneous, or learned.

From studies of a large number of children, Gesell and his colleagues developed a set of norms to indicate when motor, adaptive, language, and personal-social behavior patterns typically appear in children from birth to 16 years (Gesell and Amatruda, 1945; Gesell and Ilg, 1949; Gesell, Ilg, and Ames, 1956). Periods of equilibrium and disequilibrium are seen along the developmental continuum. The degree of this equilibrium and disequilibrium varies widely among individuals. As with any stage theory, it is important to remember that (1) different children may pass through the sequence of stages at different rates; (2) each stage is named for the process that has most recently become operative, even though others may occur at the same time in their original form; and (3) each stage is marked by the formation of the total structure that includes its predecessors within the necessary substructures.

The first 5 years of life assume greatest significance in early learnings from the family and are believed to form a deep and lasting impression on the individual. By age 5, the child's physical and mental makeup is fairly clear, and later developments are primarily variations of the child's well-established characteristic reactions.

INDIVIDUAL DEVELOPMENTAL TASKS:
THE APPROACH USED IN THIS BOOK

A developmental task is "a task which arises at or about a certain period in the life of an individual, successful achievement of which leads to happiness and success with later tasks, while failure leads to unhappiness in the individual, disapproval by the society, and difficulty with later tasks" (Havighurst, 1972, p. 2). Developmental tasks are conceptualized as arising from three sources: physical maturation, cultural pressures, and personal values and aspirations. Tasks may arise from any one of these factors alone or, as in most cases, from a combination of these three factors. At least four interrelated operations are involved in an individual's assumption of each new developmental task: (1) perception of new possibilities for behavior, (2) formation of new self-concepts, (3) effective coping with conflicting demands, and (4) motivation to accomplish the next stage of development (Duvall, 1971).

People face many tasks during their lifetimes and, as yet, no one has attempted to identify all these tasks. Tryon and Lilienthal (1950) identified 10 categories of "ever-changing" tasks from birth through adolescence. Duvall (1977, pp. 172–175) expanded these to specific tasks of the adult through old age. These 10 ever-changing tasks are:

1 Achieving an appropriate dependence-independence pattern
2 Achieving an appropriate giving-receiving pattern of affection
3 Relating to changing social groups
4 Developing a conscience
5 Learning one's psychosociobiological sex role
6 Accepting and adjusting to a changing body
7 Managing a changing body, and learning new motor patterns
8 Learning to understand and control the physical world
9 Developing an appropriate symbol system and conceptual abilities
10 Relating one's self to the cosmos

The particular manner in which these tasks are accomplished by individuals at various stages of development is not universally applicable because, as the definition applies, these tasks are partially determined by the culture. The specific age-related tasks identified by Havighurst are appropriate for children growing up in the United States but might be inappropriate in another society.

Developmental tasks serve as guidelines that enable individuals to know what is expected of them at a given age in their society. They also provide a framework for care takers to follow in helping their children develop and for care givers who are assessing child development and guiding parents.

We have tried to synthesize these ten ever-changing tasks into five tasks that can provide a framework for application by clinicians working with children and their families. The five tasks that will be used throughout this volume are:

1 Developing and maintaining healthy growth and nutrition patterns
2 Learning to control one's body satisfactorily
3 Learning to understand and relate to the physical world
4 Developing self-awareness and a satisfying sense of self
5 Learning to relate to others

The way these tasks are accomplished at various stages throughout childhood and adolescence and their implications for practice are specified in the following chapters.

FAMILY DEVELOPMENT

Just as the individual can be viewed from numerous theoretical perspectives, so too can the family be studied from a variety of conceptual frameworks. Theory development and research related to the family is still in its infancy, and many gaps in our knowledge still exist.

As with the theoretical approaches to individual development, we have found no single theory to be useful as a guide for clinical practice. Here, too, we have selected the developmental task framework as a possible means of synthesizing a variety of approaches for assessing and intervening with families in clinical practice.

This section provides the reader with an overview of family structure, functions, and roles. This is followed by a brief discussion of three theoretical approaches for viewing the family: systems, interactional, and developmental. The reader who is interested in further study of these and other theoretical approaches is referred to Duvall (1977), Howells (1971), Hymovich and Barnard (1979a,b), Kantor and Lehr (1975),

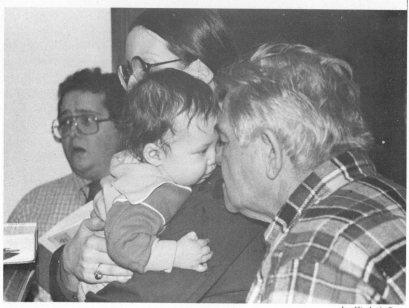

FIGURE 1-2   by Elizabeth Tong

Kenkel (1973), Nye and Berardo (1966, 1973), and Rapoport, Rapoport, and Strelitz (1977).

Family Structure

Family structure varies from the traditional nuclear family to single-parent, three-generation, dual-career, and communal family forms. It is becoming increasingly common for individuals over the life cycle to move from one family form to another. For example, a traditional nuclear family may become a single-parent family for a variety of reasons, or married children may move into or out of the homes of extended family members (Sussman, 1979).

NUCLEAR FAMILIES

The traditional nuclear family consists of husband, wife, and children living in a common household. Some families form part of a large extended family structure, while others may form a more isolated unit.

EXTENDED FAMILIES

The extended family, composed of two or more nuclear units living in one home, generally consists of an older parent couple with their child's spouse and children. This family form is more common among lower-class ethnic groups in America. Upper-class extended families often own joint property with a cluster of houses, although they do not live in the same household (Smart and Smart, 1976).

COMMUNAL FAMILIES

American communal families vary according to structure, membership, location (urban, rural), degree of religiosity (religious, nonreligious), amount of political involvement (political, apolitical), size, stability, economic base, family living styles, demands made upon their members, degree of openness (open, closed), social and political organization (authoritarianism to egalitarianism), and child-rearing and sexual practices. Ramey (1972) indicates that about the only generalization that can be made about communes is that they consist of cooperating groups of people who have a commitment to their group. The communal family may consist of more than one monogamous couple and their children or a household of adults, all of whom are "married" to each other (group marriage), and their offspring, with all adults acting as "parents" to all the children. According to Skolnick (1973, p. 143),

> The communal movement represents part of the counterculture revolt against the prevailing ethics of middle-class American society. The middle-class life style is perceived as sexually and sensually dulled, cold and manipulative, exploitive rather than generous, devoid of community and brotherhood, and finally, endangered with a perversely destructive rationality. Communal ideology rebels against all of this.

DUAL-CAREER FAMILIES

In March 1969, nearly 52 percent of intact American families had another family member (usually the wife) in addition to the husband working outside the home. This proportion was 11 percent higher among nonwhite families than white families. Mothers entered the labor force for a variety of reasons, including the need or desire for additional income, career goals, boredom at home, and because of a labor shortage in certain occupations (Sussman, 1979).

SINGLE-PARENT FAMILIES

In 1974, approximately 16 percent of families with children under 18 years of age in the United States were headed by only one parent, with nearly 95 percent of these single parents being women. The most prevalent and increasing reasons for single-parent families are divorce or permanent separation. In addition, an increasing number of unwed mothers are choosing not to marry but to keep and rear their children. There are also a number of single men and women who are adopting children. In these single-parent families, one adult performs the functions usually shared by two people.

Family Functions

In 1938, Ogburn proposed seven major categories of functions performed by the family for its individual members, the family as a unit, and/or society. These are tasks to be performed by the entire family group and may be divided among the family members or shared by them. These functions are economic (production of goods and services), protective, religious, educational, recreational, affectional, and status giving. Others (Nye and Berardo, 1973) suggest socialization as a better term than education because it covers much of the child's informal learning. Other activities recently suggested include sexual and therapeutic functions.

Many of these functions (education, religious training, economic production, protective) are now shared by others in the community. Duvall (1977, pp. 114–116) indicates that there are at least six nontraditional family functions emerging. These functions are giving affection, providing personal security and acceptance, giving satisfaction and a sense of purpose, assuring continuity of companionship, guaranteeing social placement and socialization, and inculcating controls and a sense of what is right.

Position and Roles

The position a person occupies within a system is referred to as "status" (Parsons, 1955). Positions based on characteristics of an individual such as age, sex, and religion are one's ascribed status, while those based upon what one is able to do, such as occupation, reflect an achieved status. In relation to the family, position refers to a family member's location in the family structure. This refers to positions such as wife-mother, husband-father, son-brother, or daughter-sister.

Each position within society, and in the subsystem of the family, has an associated set of norms or expectations that specify the behaviors associated with it. These behavioral expectations are related to the concept of role. In our society, spouse and parent roles are undergoing changes. According to Rowe (1966, p. 204):

> Each position contains a number of dominant and recessive roles related reciprocally to at least one role in each of the other family member posi-

INTRODUCTION

by Elizabeth Tong

FIGURE 1-3

tions. Typical roles for adults in the family are mothering, expressing affection, disciplining, home-making, and providing financial resources. Children's roles include, among others, sharing household responsibilities, studying, consuming, and taking part in recreation.

Family roles are learned as individuals interact with one another. Parental roles evolve and change over time as parents develop with their children. Child and sibling roles change at various phases of the life cycle. In two-parent families, husband-wife roles must become complementary and reciprocal if family unity is to be maintained. The obligations of the wife to carry out the housekeeper role and the family obligations to kin are becoming more of an option than an obligation.

Husband, wife, and spouse roles that are currently accepted by sociologists include those of housekeeper, child care, child socialization, provider (for husband), and a sexual role for the wife. Nye (1974) suggests that three new roles are now present in the American family. These are sexual, therapeutic, and recreational roles. The therapeutic role is one of providing assistance to another in solving any problem bothering that person. The recreational role is viewed "as a set of responsibilities incumbent on occupants of a position to facilitate the recreational resources and activities available to others" (p. 240).

Roles have been conceptualized as expressive (person-oriented, emotionally supportive) and instrumental (task-oriented). In the past, the expressive role was generally considered to be that of the wife-mother, while instrumental role functions were usually performed by the husband-father. Benson (1968) indicates that although mothers may be generally more expressive than fathers, their role tends to be both more expressive and more instrumental in relation to the children. Males are expected to combine both instrumental and expressive qualities in their roles as husband, father, and breadwinner.

Theoretical Frameworks

SYSTEMS APPROACH

Families can be viewed as systems composed of a number of subsystems. A system may be defined as a complex of elements in interaction with each other (von Bertalanffy, 1968). Systems may be described as open or closed. Family systems are "organizationally complex, open, adaptive, and information processing systems" (Kantor and Lehr, 1975, p. 10). Open systems exchange matter and energy between themselves and the environment, while closed systems have tight boundaries, exchanging information only within themselves. System boundaries limit their exchange of information (communication with the various elements outside their boundaries). Family systems interact to varying degrees with other social systems such as the occupational, educational, religious, economic, legal, and health care systems. Each of these systems has a tremendous effect on family functioning. For example, the economic system determines the level of living and the religious system influences philosophy of life, while the legal system affects responsibilities of the family, community, and state.

The elements of the system are tied together in a meaningful whole through their relationships with each other. Three interacting subsystems exist within the family—the family-unit, interpersonal, and personal subsystems (Kantor and Lehr, 1975). Activities involving one subsystem will at the same time interact, either competitively or cooperatively, with at least one other subsystem. Systems obtain information from the environment through a feedback process. They are capable of self-regulation in order to maintain a "steady state," that is, to keep a balanced relationship among their elements (family members).

INTERACTIONAL APPROACH

The interactional approach views the family as an everchanging "unity" of personalities. Concepts such as position, role, reference group, adaptation, and communication are component parts of this framework. In fact, there are some who call this role or action theory rather than inter-actional theory. It is based on the premise that we live in a symbolic as well as physical world and are stimulated by and stimulate others through symbols. Equally important is the belief that interaction cannot be completely understood by objective means but rather must be viewed in terms of the perceptions the participants have of one another in the social-stimulus situation.

Emphasis is on the interpersonal relationships of family members as they communicate with each other. This approach implies a process in which the family is in a constant state of flux rather than in equilibrium. Interaction is always a dynamic process involving the continuous testing of the concept one has of another's role (role taking). Reiss (1971) indicates that family interaction patterns develop over time and are determined by how the family views the culture transmitted by reference groups important to them.

With this approach, the family is viewed as a relatively closed system of interaction. Research based on this framework has been related to family communication patterns, decision-making and problem-solving characteristics, responses to crises, and marital and family harmony and conflict.

DEVELOPMENTAL APPROACH

The developmental approach attempts to synthesize compatible concepts of other frameworks in order to view the family as it changes over time. Usually, it refers to changes taking place in nuclear families over time. The framework incorporates the internal functioning of family members in addition to family participation within the community. Conceptually, the family is viewed as a "unity" of interacting personalities (Burgess, 1926) and as a semiclosed system (Rodgers, 1973). Important components of this approach are the concepts of the family life cycle, positions, roles and norms, and developmental tasks.

Family Life Cycle   The family cycle, or family career (Rodgers, 1973), is a useful frame of reference for looking at family life over time because it emphasizes the dynamics of family interaction as they shift and change. This cycle has been divided into stages determined by the amount of transition required in the family by specific events, generally based on changes in plurality patterns. Various authors have attempted to delineate these stages into as few as two divisions (expansion and contraction) to as many as 24 phases. Duvall (1977) identifies eight stages in the family life cycle based on the age and school placement of the oldest child. Although this sequence may be clear-cut in one-child families, it would obviously have to be modified for families with more than one child. She believes a family goes through a particular phase with the first child and then, to some extent, repeats that phase with other children. Rodgers (1962) attempted to deal with the complexity of this issue by developing a 24-phase classification based on both the oldest and the youngest child in the family.

Family Developmental Tasks: The Approach Used in This Book The concept of developmental tasks of the family unit emerged in 1950 and has been explored in depth by Evelyn Duvall. A family developmental task is identified in much the same way as an individual developmental task. It "is a growth responsibility that arises at a certain stage in the life of a family, the successful achievement of which leads to present satisfaction, approval, and success with later tasks—whereas failure leads to unhappiness in the family, disapproval by society, and difficulty with later family developmental tasks" (Duvall, 1977, p. 177).

Duvall (1977) lists the eight basic tasks common to all American families, regardless of social class and subculture, as (1) physical maintenance; (2) allocation of resources; (3) division of labor; (4) socialization of family members; (5) reproduction, recruitment, and release of family members; (6) maintenance of order; (7) placement of members in the larger society; and (8) maintenance of motivation and morale. Values are transmitted by the manner in which developmental tasks are achieved as they arise. She has also delineated certain stage-critical tasks that occur when the family is assuming new responsibilities growing out of rapid changes at given points in the life cycle. For example, a stage-critical task of the newly married couple is to establish a mutually satisfying marriage, while a stage-critical task of the family with a school-aged child is listed as encouraging the child's educational achievement.

Clausen (1968) suggests seven generic tasks (aims, activities) to be accomplished by parents if their children are to be successfully socialized in any society. Along with each of these aims is a corollary task or achievement for the child to master. Clausen indicates that parents need to be somewhat successful in carrying out these tasks if their children are to survive and become competent enough to be considered acceptable to their parents and others. These tasks are to (1) sustain and nurture their infant; (2) train and channel physiological needs; (3) provide teaching, training, and opportunities for the child's psychomotor, cognitive, and social skills; (4) orient the child to the world; (5) transmit cultural values and goals; (6) promote interpersonal skills; and (7) set limits. Corollary

INTRODUCTION

tasks for the child are to (1) accept nurturance, (2) control expression of physiologic impulses, (3) learn what is being taught, (4) develop a "cognitive map" of his or her world, (5) develop a sense of right and wrong, (6) learn to take another's perspective, and (7) develop ability for self-regulation.

We believe that for the clinician working with families, there are practical implications that can be derived from using a developmental task approach. From a practical standpoint, it is important to use a framework that has the capacity to encompass the variant family forms as well as the traditional nuclear family. Consequently, we have reformulated family developmental tasks into a conceptual framework that appears more useful for clinical application.

The tasks, as we have revised them and as they are used in this book, are as follows: (1) meeting the basic physical needs of the family, (2) assisting each family member to develop his or her individual potential, (3) providing emotional support and communicating effectively with all family members, (4) maintaining and adapting family organization and management to meet changing needs, and (5) functioning in the community.

MEETING THE BASIC PHYSICAL NEEDS OF THE FAMILY   This task includes functions such as providing shelter, food, health care, and clothing for the family members, as well as allocating resources to meet the family needs for facilities, space, and material goods so that individual needs can be met.

The economic cost of child rearing is usually considered to have two components (1) "direct maintenance cost," the actual amount of money spent for items such as food, clothing, education, and so forth; and (2) "opportunity cost," that income which the wife (generally) foregoes by staying home to raise the children (Espenshade, 1977, p. 33). Considering all the possible sources of variation in raising children (type of residence, region, food, cost level), Espenshade estimated that in 1977 the expense involved in raising a child to the age of 18 years in the United States ranged from $31,675 (low cost, rural, North Central), to $58,255 (medium cost, rural, West). Comparable figures for 1969 were $19,360 to $35,850. Expenses for the firstborn child tend to be about twice that of a second child. Expenses for second and third children are about equal. As income rises, more of the family's total savings tend to be used for children.

ASSISTING EACH FAMILY MEMBER DEVELOP HIS OR HER INDIVIDUAL POTENTIAL   This task includes the individual development of the parents

CHILD AND FAMILY DEVELOPMENT

as persons as well as the parental role of socializing the children and of helping them to develop their individual interests and talents. To accomplish this task, family members need to be aware of their own and each other's potentials and limitations. Inherent in this task is the provision of emotional support for one another. Because providing emotional support is such a key element in family interaction, we shall discuss it separately.

PROVIDING EMOTIONAL SUPPORT AND COMMUNICATING EFFECTIVELY WITH ALL FAMILY MEMBERS   In our culture, the major proportion of need satisfaction occurs within the family. Each individual has needs to be met; therefore, need gratification cannot be focused on any single family member. Caplan (1959) stresses that adults as well as children have emotional needs. They, too, need to love and be affectionate as well as to be loved; they need to be controlled as well as to control others; and they need the gratification of being part of a group where they can feel free to relax and be secure.

Adults also have need for personal achievement in both material and spiritual matters. Caplan indicates three concepts that are important to need satisfaction: perception, respect, and gratification. The extent to which the family perceives the individual's needs as essential will determine the extent to which these needs are met. Second, the extent to which each family member is respected as an individual is important. In fact, there may be times when it is not possible to gratify the needs of a particular family member; however, it is still important that their needs be perceived and respected.

This task includes a means of communication and interaction among family members; administering sanctions (positive and negative) to maintain order within the system; and establishing and refining a philosophy of life. This subtask serves as a basis for decision making and methods of meeting individual and family crises.

While the size of the family increases arithmetically, the complexity of family relationships increases more rapidly. According to the law of family interaction, the addition of each person increases the number of personal interrelationships within the family in the order of triangular numbers (Bossard, 1945, p. 292). To find the number of interpersonal relationships within the family, the following formula is used:

$$X = \frac{y^2 - y}{2}$$

where X = the number of interpersonal relationships
    Y = the number of persons

INTRODUCTION

Thus, for a family of three, there would be five relationships, and for a family of five the number of relationships would increase to ten.

Family interaction is modified by a number of variables that influence parental practices (Stolz, 1967, p. 162). Characteristics of the parents that include both temporary conditions (i.e., fatigue, illness, being busy) and more stable tendencies (i.e., relaxed, tense, anxious) influence how they raise their children. In addition, the parents' interaction with each other influences each other's behavior.

Spouse relationships   Most parents talk over with each other what they should do in certain situations and come to mutual agreement. About two-thirds of parents say discussion ends in mutual agreement; when it does not, usually the mother's opinion tends to prevail (Stolz, 1967, p. 172).

The power relationship between husband and wife tends to be a colleague rather than companionship role for most managerial and professional couples. The spouses are not equal in decision making; rather, the husband is involved in most decisions with the wife making fewer family decisions alone. In the lower-middle-class family, husband and

FIGURE 1-4

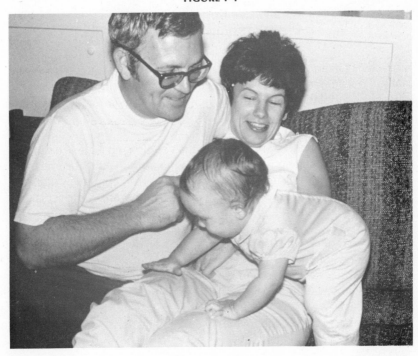

FIGURE 1-5   by Debra Hymovich

wife interact as equals. The men tend to be in blue-collar supervisory- and craftsmen-level jobs and lower-level bureaucratic and quasiprofessional jobs. Husband and wife are apt to both participate in child rearing but maintain a traditional division of labor in other areas (Aldous, 1969; Rainwater, 1965).

Today, emotional compatibility of the couple is an issue. Continuing trust between the parents is essential in maintaining an intimate emotional tie. Each partner must also believe in the other's commitment and understanding. When loss of faith or respect for one another occurs, the relationship is vulnerable to disruption (Weiss and Pexton, 1970).

Parent-child relationships Each generation has different rights and responsibilities. Parents are expected to guide, nurture, and teach and to give of themselves as their child grows. It is expected that children will be dependent upon adults and be free to invest their energies in development (Lidz, 1976)

Parents are called upon to modify their interactions according to their child's motivations (likes, wants, desires); level of maturity; temporary condition of child (e.g., ill, injured, sleepy, hungry); abilities (intellectual, motor, and artistic); physical characteristics (size, sexual development, and physical defects); individuality; sex; and ordinal position. Both mothers and fathers emphasize that their interaction with one child tends to affect their interaction with a second child more than their subsequent behavior with the same child (Stolz, 1967).

Relationships with extended family Grandparents remain closer to members of the nuclear family than do any other relatives. Aunts and uncles, followed by cousins, are next closest (Robins and Tomanec, 1962). The child's tie between the nuclear family and the extended family is the tie between adult couples and their parents. Grandparents often provide financial aid and emergency assistance, give constructive advice and encouragement, and provide a wide range of services, such as baby-sitting (Moss and McNab, 1961; Sussman and Burchinal, 1962).

As children reach middle age, they may be giving financial assistance to their aging parents as well as to their young children. Max Kaplan

FIGURE 1-6

by Debra Hymovich

(1960) indicates that the positive role of grandparents within the family is defined largely by the needs of the nuclear family, not by the interests of the extended family.

Generally, it is the wife who bears the major burden of communication between nuclear and extended family, and it is usually the parents of the wife who give more frequent assistance to the couple than do the parents of the husband (Adams, 1964).

Although geographical distance does not mean that kin no longer help each other, it does mean that the actual exchange of services is reduced. Routine tasks are no longer intermeshed, nor can kin routinely rely on one another (Weiss and Pexton, 1970).

Sibling relationships   Most theories of family interaction focus on spouse relationships and the influence of parents on their children's psychosocial development. Sibling relationships generally are seen as products of the children's interaction with their parents rather than relationships among the children themselves (Bank and Kahn, 1975). Research related to sibling interaction is sparse. At this point, about the only generalization that can be made is that sibling relationships are highly complex, with the children taking on a variety of different roles when interacting with one another. Among these many roles are those of model, protector, companion, care taker, and provider of services, as well as pest, enemy, and rival. According to Pfouts (1976, p. 200), "Interaction among siblings is more likely to be stressful and volatile than that in most other relationships because the sibling relationship is so firmly rooted in ambivalence. Love and hate are the two sides of the sibling coin."

MAINTAINING AND ADAPTING FAMILY ORGANIZATION AND MANAGEMENT TO MEET CHANGING NEEDS   This task primarily involves the division and reorganization of labor among family members. All families designate particular jobs or roles to their individual members. ". . . the healthy family perceives the individual's needs and abilities, and also the needs of the family and balances these. In this way it establishes an equilibrium" (Caplan, 1959, p. 42).

"Although the family division of labor may be complex, the most common social expectation is that the father figure will supply the raw materials for family and social survival, while mother's more characteristic duty is to prepare them for immediate use" (Benson, 1968, p. 46). This traditional division is still apparent today although fathers are usually helping prepare family resources for consumption while mothers serve as reserve (income) producers. Some evidence points to the emergence of a more egalitarian marriage pattern (Devereux et al., 1962; Elder, 1964; Johannis and Rollins, 1959).

FUNCTIONING IN THE COMMUNITY   This task necessitates family decisions concerning the amount and type of involvement they wish to have in community organizations and activities. To a great extent, a child's knowledge of and feelings about the community are determined by the family.

The form of services available in the community affects children and their families. Among the many services needed and usually provided are those for health, recreation, education, and religion, and social agencies for those needing special facilities.

THE EFFECT OF SELECTED VARIABLES ON DEVELOPMENT

The rate and pattern of development is influenced by a variety of complex interrelated factors occurring within the individual, the family, and the environment. Examples of how some of the many variables affect the developing person are discussed in this section. It should be remembered that each of these factors is closely interrelated with the others, and it is often difficult to differentiate any single cause as having a direct influence on development. There is general agreement that both heredity and environment (nature and nurture) contribute to one's growth and development.

Individual Variables

HEREDITY

One's genes and chromosomes are responsible for determining characteristics, such as sex, race, and a variety of chromosomal and genetic aberrations. Besides variations in physical characteristics, one's genes and chromosomes are also responsible for determining susceptibility to certain diseases and congenital defects that can have profound effects on family and child development. Studies of twins demonstrate that genetic factors are largely responsible for both body proportion and fat disposition and probably play an important role in determining differences in patterns of male and female growth (Sinclair, 1969). There is some indication that how much a child eats and how the food is utilized may be genetically determined [DHEW (HSM) 72-8130, 1972; McCracken, 1962; Mayer, 1966; Withers, 1964].

SEX

Many investigators have shown sex differences in the timing of growth, with physical maturation occurring earlier in girls than in boys (Karlberg et al., 1968; Tanner, 1970). The sex of children also influences parental behavior, as evidenced by some reasonably consistent differences in the ways parents react toward boys and girls (Bell and Costello, 1964; Korner, 1971). Differences in handling are apparent from the first use of pink and blue blankets at birth to the custom of who pays the marriage expenses for the young adult. Just how pervasive is this rearing atmosphere is brought out in the studies of gender development by Money et al. (1955a,b) showing that regardless of a child's genetic sex, he or she develops the behaviors and mannerisms of the sex of rearing, and attempts to change this after age 2 are extremely difficult.

Women have repeatedly been shown to be more sensitive to inter-personal relations than men and to be more responsive to group norms. Boys tend to be more "thing-centered" and girls more "person-centered" (Benson, 1968, p. 22).

AGE

There are many typical age-related growth and illness patterns as well as behavioral and developmental characteristics. Age also influences family patterns as parental roles change with each new stage of child development. Some examples of the effect of age on development are as follows:

1 The most rapid growth periods occur during fetal life, infancy, and adolescence. There is evidence to suggest that postnatally, a child's susceptibility to nutritional deprivation is greater during these periods of most rapid growth than during other periods (DHEW, Ten-State Nutrition Survey, 1972).
2 Infancy is believed to be the period when the foundations for basic trust (Erikson, 1963) and attachment (Klaus and Kennell, 1976) take place.
3 Responses to events such as separation, illness, and hospitalization vary at different ages.
4 Parents report that the energy demands of child rearing differ with the developmental level of the child (Howell, 1973b).
5 Parental age is also an important variable. The adolescent mother interacts differently with her first baby than does a mother in her mid-thirties who has had great difficulty getting pregnant.

INTRODUCTION

FIGURE 1-7

by Debra Hymovich

TEMPERAMENT

Thomas et al. (1968) have described temperament as the behavioral style of the child. Nine characteristics were identified as being relatively stable across time and useful in describing how one child differs from another. These characteristics are as follows:

1 Activity level: The amount of motor activity of the child.
2 Rhythmicity of biological function: The predictability or unpredictability of the infant's cycles (i.e., sleep-wake) and patterns (i.e., eating, toileting).
3 Reaction to new situations: Approach-withdrawal.
4 Adaptability: If the initial reaction is one of withdrawal, how long does it take for the child to adapt?

5 Threshold: The strength of a stimulus necessary to set off a reaction.
6 Intensity: Given a response, how intense is it?
7 General overall mood: Whether this is generally a happy or fussy baby.
8 Distractibility: Given an activity or response, how easy or difficult is it to get this child interested in something else?
9 Attention span and persistence: In general, how long the child attends to an activity once engaged in it and if distracted, whether he or she returns to the same activity in a persistent way or goes on to something else.

They found children with certain clusters of these temperament characteristics that resulted in characteristic behavior patterns.

"Difficult children" were found to have irregular biological functions, intense negative or withdrawal reactions to new situations, slow adaptation to environmental changes, and a predominantly negative mood. About 10 percent of the children in their sample of over 100 children were identified as difficult children. The demands they placed on their parents were great, and unfavorable parental attitudes were noted to develop in reaction to nurturing a difficult child.

"Easy children" were observed to have regular biological rhythms, a positive mood, low or mildly intense reactions, rapid adaptability, and a positive approach to new situations. The majority of children in the sample fit into this "easy child" cluster and were able to adapt to a wide variety of child-rearing practices.

A third category, the "slow to warm up children," were similar to the difficult child in terms of withdrawal reactions to new situations, slow adaptability, and predominantly negative mood, but their response to frustration was generally of mild intensity compared to that of the difficult child. Instead of having screaming temper tantrums they were more likely to go off and pout in the corner. This often presented problems to their parents because of their initial withdrawal responses and slow adaptation to new situations.

Other temperamental clusters influencing reactions to environmental situations are the "high activity level–short attention span children" and those who show persistence in their actions and have difficulty shifting to new activities.

Parents indicate that their child-rearing practices are influenced by their children: by their behavior, their perceived characteristics, and their response to parents' methods (Stolz, 1967, pp. 175–176). Behaviors of children that influence parents' responses to them include aggression; orderly living (clean, neat, noisy, and so on); eating, sleeping, and toileting habits; dependency; fear; curiosity; sex problems related to immodesty, sex play, and masturbation; dependency (in general, parents respond more to dependent behavior they disapprove of); fears and anxiety; and happy or unhappy behavior (Stolz, 1967). Parents also report they are more influenced by what a child wants, likes, or is interested in than by what a child does not want, dislikes, or is not interested in. Of the mothers and fathers interviewed by Stolz (1967), 100 percent and 92 percent, respectively, reported being influenced by the child's wants and interests, while 90 percent of the mothers and 69 percent of the fathers indicated being influenced by dislikes.

NUTRITIONAL STATUS

Results of animal studies clearly indicate that malnutrition affects both physiological and psychological development. Factors influencing these effects of malnutrition include the specific nutrient involved, as well as the timing, severity, and duration of the malnutrition and the characteristics of the disorders themselves. Human data are more difficult to interpret because of the variety of other variables accompanying the malnutrition. Among these variables are varying degrees of poverty, educational deprivation, diminished social stimulation, and less-well-integrated family units. There are some data to suggest that many children who have been severely malnourished during infancy suffer from physical and cognitive retardation (Osofsky, 1969).

Data from the Ten-State Nutrition Survey [DHEW (HSM 72-8/32)] have shown that the educational level of the person buying and preparing the family's food is related to the nutritional status of children under 17 years of age.

HEALTH STATUS

One's physical, emotional, cognitive, social, and spiritual health all have an effect on individual growth and development. Family physical, emotional, and social health are also important variables, not only on the individual's but also on the total family unit's development.

Illness The effect of illness on a child's development will vary with the condition's severity and duration. Minor short-term illnesses generally do not retard growth rate in well-nourished children; major diseases may cause slowing followed by a "catch-up" growth when the disease has been cured (Tanner, 1970).

Illness may affect any member of the family (parent or child), but its

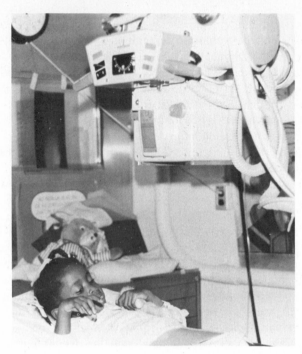

FIGURE 1-8   by Debra Hymovich

effects are felt by the entire family. When illness occurs, some of the tasks and roles of the sick person must be reapportioned among other family members or left undone. The amount of stress the illness places on the family depends upon a variety of factors, including the duration of the condition, resources available to the family (human and physical), and the family's developmental stage (Craven and Sharp, 1972).

ACUTE ILLNESS   An acute illness, lasting only a few days, may temporarily disrupt the family routine and resources. If the family has been able to cope relatively well with other such acute situations, the impact of this illness may be relatively short. Temporary adjustments in family function- ing may be made, but their effects generally are not long lasting. A mother may lose a night's sleep; a sibling may miss some extracurricular activity; a mother or father may find loss of work to be only an inconvenience. On the other hand, to a low-income family where employment is precarious, this may become a difficult burden. Obviously, the needs of these two families will differ.

INTRODUCTION

CHRONIC ILLNESS   While the terms disease, illness, disability, and handicap are often used interchangeably, Pless and Pinkerton (1975) distinguish conceptually between these terms. The disease, or illness, is the condition or pathophysiologic process which is the biological underlying substrate (e.g., diabetes, cerebral palsy, hemophilia, renal disease). The disability it produces is the immediate direct behavioral manifestation of the illness (e.g., walking with a limp, a swollen painful joint after trauma, shortness of breath). The handicap is a socially determined limitation of performance in specific activities (e.g., being unable to compete in athletics).

The incidence of chronic illness is estimated to be somewhere between 5 and 10 percent of the population. There is increasing evidence that these chronically disabled children and their families can be considered at risk for psychological sequelae and/or management problems (Pless and Pinkerton, 1975). Chronic disease may affect physical growth, although in some cases it is difficult to separate this effect from that of accompanying malnutrition (Tanner, 1970).

The measures of family impact are still rudimentary, and most studies are retrospective and suffer from all the limitations involved in such studies. These studies, primarily descriptive, have nevertheless contributed to our understanding of the impact of a variety of chronic illnesses on disabled children and their families. The majority of these studies have based their findings on interviews with only one member of the family, usually the mother. One notable exception is Burton's study (1975) of children with cystic fibrosis. She interviewed both parents and all children over 9 years of age, and observed all family members regardless of age.

Among the findings of these studies are the potential for childhood chronic illness to precipitate increased stress and family disruption (Barsch, 1968; Howell, 1973; Mattsson, 1972; Rutter et al., 1970); family disintegration as evidenced by disrupted marriages (Holt, 1958); and the arrest of normal family growth (Farber, 1960). More recently, it has also been recognized that family life can be strengthened as well as weakened by such adversity (Bergmann, 1965; Jabaley et al., 1970).

Since the family is a complex network of interacting personalities, the impact of chronic illness on the family unit is equally complex. The family may, both directly and indirectly, influence the child's adjustment and well-being, while the child, in turn, may have a profound effect on other family members. Stresses imposed by the child's condition may underlie many of the symptoms presented by other family members (Kellner, 1963). For example, dormant guilt feelings of parents may become manifest during periods of increased stress as migraine headaches, peptic ulcers, or episodes of marital disorganization.

Parsons and Fox (1952) predicted two main effects of childhood illness on other family members; first, that mothers would find it more difficult to meet the demands of their husbands for care and affection, and, second, that sibling rivalry would be accentuated. These theoretical formulations have been largely supported by studies looking at the impact of diabetes (Crain et al., 1966) and cystic fibrosis (Meyerowitz and Kaplan, 1967) on family functioning. Parents described the impact of cystic fibrosis in terms of decreased time to be with their spouses, communication problems, and the loss of time and energy for recreational activities. In a recent study on the Isle of Wight (Rutter et al., 1970), parents of children with chronic physical disabilities reported similar difficulties. Other problems included financial burdens, changes in housing or sleeping arrangements, loss of time from work, loss of sleep, curtailment of family activities, resentment on the part of siblings, and disruptions in the mother's daily routine (Kendall and Calmann, 1964).

Some researchers (e.g., Gath, 1972; Hewitt et al., 1970) point out that many families of chronically disabled children are more alike than different from other families and that the magnitude of problems they face have been exaggerated in the literature. The Newsons (1976, p. 44) point out that the basic requirement of these parents is "to enable them to 'adjust' and 'accept' and 'resolve their guilt feelings': they want to be treated like ordinary people who have a highly practical problem," rather than as those in need of psychiatric help.

Farber's studies of families with a severely retarded child indicate that the normal family life cycle is arrested. For example, as siblings grow and develop, they eventually catch up with and surpass the retarded child in terms of their social and mental development. Consequently, their roles are constantly being redefined as this age gap increases. The role requirements of parents also change from parents who eventually see their children become autonomous, and leaving home to parents who must continually care for their retarded child.

Among the problems faced by parents of chronically disabled youngsters are those of uncertainty, chronic sorrow, stigma, and a "burden of care" above that faced in other families (Rutter et al., 1970).

Whether individual or family coping is the focus, commonalities in coping strategies have been noted across illness conditions. As part of their conceptual framework, Moos and Tsu (1976) have defined seven categories of adaptive tasks and an equal number of categories of coping skills which they believe are abilities that can be taught and used flexibly over situations. They emphasize that specific coping techniques are either adaptive or maladaptive depending upon the appropriateness of the situation in which they are used. These coping skills are: (1) denying or minimizing the seriousness of the condition, (2) seeking relevant information, (3) requesting reassurance and support, (4) learning specific illness-related procedures, (5) setting concrete, limited goals, (6) rehearsing alternative outcomes, and (7) finding a general purpose or pattern of meaning.

Hamburg (1974) emphasizes the importance of social support systems in the coping process across the life span, indicating that family support can effect smoother transitions. Evidence of the importance of strong familial relationships in coping with chronic illness has been found in studies by Burton (1975), Litman (1964), and Robertson and Suinn (1968). In a study of 20 children with cystic fibrosis and their mothers, Tropauer et al. (1970) found familial support to be crucial for adaptation. They noted a carry-over to the child of emotional disturbances in the parent. Kaplan and colleagues (1973) found that the coping strategies of parents strongly influenced the coping of their leukemic child. They also found that discrepancies between the coping strategies of parents created adaptive problems for their children.

Moos and Tsu (1976) maintain that family members and friends, as well as the patient, use the same types of coping skills in crises that affect all of them. However, this has not always been supported by the data. For example, Mattsson (1972), in a review of the literature on long-term physical illness in childhood, found contrasts in the coping behaviors of children and parents. He delineates the importance of cognitive processes for both in mastering distressing emotional reactions caused by illness. Coping strategies for parents of leukemic children (Friedman et al., 1963) were found to include shock and disbelief for some, but intellectual acceptance was more common. Other coping strategies included active seeking for hope-sustaining beliefs, resolving the problem of responsibility, searching for meaning in the tragedy, and anticipatory grief. Most parents found their religious beliefs to be comforting.

Kaplan and his colleagues (1973) indicate that coping tasks vary significantly from one illness to another, citing the differences in tasks faced by parents of prematurely born infants and parents of children with leukemia. Their studies show that the coping of parents of leukemic children may be adaptive, maladaptive, or discrepant. Discrepant coping occurs when parents take opposing positions concerning the diagnosis. This discrepancy may lead to poor communications, interruption or prohibition of collective grieving, and weakened family relationships. This is

similar to the model proposed by Drotar and colleagues (1975) to describe the adaptation of parents to the birth of an infant with a congenital
malformation. Their study of 20 parents suggested that asynchronous
parental reactions often caused temporary emotional separation of the
parents. Asynchronous reactions were defined as different time durations
of the parents in relation to each stage of the grieving process.

Children with a history of an illness or accident from which they
were not expected to recover may be considered vulnerable by their
parents and destined to die during childhood (Green and Solnit, 1964).
Parents of these children had difficulty separating from their children and
setting disciplinary limits for them. Many parents reported their children
slept poorly; however, it was found these parents frequently woke their
child at night. The parents tended to be overprotective, overindulgent,
and solicitous, and their children were overdependent, disobedient, irritable, argumentative, and uncooperative. The children were also characterized by bodily overconcerns and school underachievement.

One or more of the following factors predispose the child to this
vulnerable reaction: (1) the child was born with a congenital anomaly;
(2) the child is firstborn to older parents who were childless for many
years; (3) the child was premature; (4) the child had an acquired handicap (i.e., epilepsy) or, (5) a previous life-threatening illness; (6) the physician predicted the fetus might die during pregnancy; (7) mother had
postpartum depression following the child's birth; (8) the parents are no
longer able to have additional children; (9) conscious, strongly ambivalent feelings toward child were present in a parent; (10) there was an
unresolved grief reaction related to the death of another child, a spouse,
or some other close relative; (11) a hereditary disorder was present in
family; and (12) there was an emotional need in the mother to find
something wrong with the child.

Examples of the potential effects of chronic illness on family developmental tasks are presented below.

Meeting the basic physical needs of the family   The economic functioning of
the family can be greatly disturbed by the presence of a handicapping
condition (Kew, 1975). Among the potential expenses are those for travel
(to and from hospital, clinics, and so forth), changes in the home
(adaptations, moving), and special supplies (e.g., food, clothing,
equipment). The financial demands of chronic illness may necessitate
changes in the employment status of one or both parents. The father may
need to obtain a second job; the mother, who had previously been unemployed, may have to find a job to supplement the family income, or the
employed mother may find it necessary to quit her job and remain at

home. The special equipment, foods, and medications can be a drain on family resources (McLean et al., 1968; Rutter et al., 1970).

Housing arrangements may need to be altered to facilitate care of the chronically ill child. It may be necessary for the family to find new living accommodations, either because of the special needs of the child or for financial reasons. Special day-care facilities and educational needs may also be an added financial burden.

Assisting each family member develop his or her individual potential   Child-rearing practices toward the disabled child and toward the able-bodied siblings are usually altered. The roles and relationships of parents and children change throughout the family life cycle. These relationships may be altered, however, when a disabled child is present. For example, Farber's research (1968) points out that the family's life cycle may be interrupted or even completely arrested by the presence of a retarded child because that child may never assume the roles expected of someone of comparable chronological age.

The presence of a disabled child in the family is likely to affect the siblings socially through curtailment of social activities and reluctance to invite friends to their home (Kew, 1975). School performance may deteriorate and somatic complaints increase (Pless and Pinkerton, 1975). Adolescents become concerned about their own future and meaning of their sibling's condition to them.

Providing emotional support and communicating effectively with all family members   The diagnosis of a handicapping condition in the child represents a crisis for the entire family. The family lives with chronic stress, or, in Olshansky's (1962) terms, "chronic sorrow." At various points in their life cycle, new situations arise that have the potential for producing a family crisis. By definition, a crisis of relatively short duration, in which the total lifetime of the handicapping condition is 4 to 6 weeks, cannot be considered a crisis; rather, there are a series of crises at various stages in the life cycle.

"The parents' capacity to remain relatively stable while in the middle of minor or even major changes and adjustments of life-style seems to be a crucial element if the equilibrium of the whole family is ever to be retained" (Kew, 1975, p. 143). The ability of different parents to maintain their stability differs in both manner and degree. Criteria for maintaining family equilibrium include: (1) defining the handicap in a realistic way and understanding the true nature of the handicap; (2) freely communicating their reactions, both positive and negative, to what has happened; (3) making joint decisions concerning readjustments to the crisis; and (4) making readjustments and reorganizations that take into consideration the needs of all family members (Kew, 1975).

Berggreen (1971) investigated the families of 20 multihandicapped children and found a variety of effects on the parents. Of the fathers, 15 percent are in mental hospitals, 10 percent are addicted to alcohol, 10 percent are divorced and have no connection with their families, and another 15 percent play very little active part in the family. Of the mothers, only 25 percent were described as normal; 50 percent were described as depressed and tired or nervous and overprotective; 25 percent have physical ailments; and one mother (5 percent) is receiving psychiatric help. Of these marriages, 25 percent were classified as unstable and 10 percent ended in divorce.

Parental relationships: When a crisis occurs, role complementarity between family members breaks down. "Some parents may be unfamiliar with the roles required of them, having had no experiences on which to 'pattern' their responses, or they may have failed to identify the particular roles that are required; alternatively they may have insufficient resources for playing a required role, or simply be unwilling to do so" (Kew, 1975, p. 58). Others may feel the role is incompatible with their newly acquired role of mother.

A number of studies of parents of chronically ill children indicate that many parental relationships are strengthened by their sick child's problems. In one study, couples who felt their relationship was strengthened said they were united in the process of working out solutions to their common problem. Those parents who felt their marriage was weakened believed it was because the majority of the mother's time was occupied by the ill child (Sultz et al., 1972).

Parent-child relationships: Factors affecting the adjustment of siblings include (1) the nature and degree of the handicap; (2) the age of the sibling(s); (3) the sex of the sibling(s); (4) the size of the family; (5) the birth order (Farber, 1968)—children closest in age to the handicapped child are more prone to disturbance than children considerably older or younger; (6) religion (Zuk, 1970); (7) substitute parent figures; and (8) the personality (Burton, 1975) of the sibling.

Differential treatment by parents of handicapped children and their able-bodied siblings has been documented in a number of studies (Berggreen, 1971; Davis, 1963; Kew, 1975). It has been shown that able-bodied children often react to this imbalance in discipline in a variety of ways, including jealousy (overt or disguised) and attention-seeking behavior (disruptive behavior, temper tantrums, clinging).

Parents may react to siblings in very different ways. They may over protect, and encourage the children to excel, or treat them as "high-class china" in an effort to ensure that they are perfect and remain so. Or, they may respond by making the handicapped child the center of family life (Berggreen, 1971; Kew, 1975). "The prospects for normal siblings seem to be worst in families in which there are only two siblings or when other siblings are of much the same age as the handicapped child. The normal child must then compete with the handicapped child for parental affection and attention" (Berggreen, 1971, p. 19). It can be very difficult for parents to cope with the questions of their other children at a time when they are scarcely able to cope with their own emotions.

Maintaining and adapting family organization to meet changing needs Illness in the family means that some tasks and roles of the sick member must either be assumed by others or go undone. The amount of stress the illness places on the family depends upon their resources, such as available money to buy services and number of extended family members available to help; and other characteristics such as the developmental stage of the family and how many of the members' needs are met solely within the family (Craven and Sharp, 1972). If a parent becomes ill, another source of stress is whether another family member is capable of assuming the role functions of the ill person, for example, the provider role.

Central Nervous System Dysfunction As well as having effects similar to that of any chronic illness on family and child development, central nervous system (CNS) dysfunction appears to carry an added burden by increasing the susceptibility of persons to environmental stress and strain (Rutter et al., 1970). Thus, while there is no specific syndrome of behavior characteristics related to brain damage (Paine et al., 1968; Rutter et al., 1970; Shulman et al., 1965), there is an increased incidence of behavioral disorders in general.

Besides increasing susceptibility to stress, CNS dysfunction may show itself as either retardation in motor development (normal function but delayed attainment) or actual dysfunction (reduction or distortion), or both. With reduction, there is decreased resistance to passive motion, poor postural adjustments, and decreased spontaneous activity. There may also be decreased or absent reflexes. There is often increased resistance to rapid passive movement of extremities, or there may be dyskinesia with discoordination of movement, changes in tone, and involuntary movements. If these affect muscles of the tongue and the pharynx, difficulty in swallowing may result. There may be increased resistance to slow, passive movement of the extensor muscles of head, arms, and trunk, with poor head control and grip. With older children there may be evidence of ataxia or tremor. Knoblock and Pasamanick (1974) discuss these in great detail in their recent revision of Gesell and Amatruda's *Developmental Diagnosis.*

Severe Emotional Disturbance   Psychotic or severe neurotic disturbances have their most profound effect on the social development of the child and on family interaction patterns. Studies of the children of schizophrenic parents indicate various manifestations of psychopathology in 25 to 45 percent of the children. These take the form of either severely withdrawn or acting-out patterns of behavior. Studies by Kanner (1943) and Bender (1942, 1947) of children diagnosed as "autistic" or "schizophrenic" describe marked deviations in language development, communication skills, and the ability to form attachments with other persons.

Environmental Variables

SOCIOECONOMIC AND CULTURAL

Family structure and functions, child-rearing beliefs and practices, food preferences and eating habits, concepts of health and illness, and use of lay healer and folk medicines all vary across different subgroups. The primary health care worker needs to be aware of these differences in order to successfully bridge this cultural gap and to integrate scientific medicine with traditional care patterns.

It is difficult to separate culture from socioeconomic status as variables affecting development. For example, poverty among Spanish surname families is greater than twice that among white families, and the per capita income is less than for nonwhites as well as for whites (Sebastian, 1972). The Mexican-American population is largely an immigrant group from the lower socioeconomic population (Samora, 1966), and the problem appears to be self-perpetuating. About one-third of the two-parent black families and about two-thirds of the female-headed black families are living in poverty (Moynihan, 1965). Thus, behavior and attitude differences often result from a mixture of influence of both subculture and low socioeconomic status. Therefore, it is hazardous to attribute any of these differences to ethnicity by itself.

Socioeconomic Status   Powell and Powell (1974) summarized demographic data related to socioeconomic status and conclude that "the most handicapping, disabling condition in childhood is poverty itself. Those at greatest risk are the nonwhite, namely, the black, the central city ghetto dweller, the rural dweller, large families, families with one parent and families headed by a parent of low educational achievement" (p. 145). According to Osofsky (1974), many, if not all, of the racially related differences in mortality are socioeconomically determined.

Being poor, uneducated, and a member of a minority group increases substantially the possibility of having a complication of pregnancy in general and a low-birth-weight baby in particular (Abramowitz and Kass, 1966; Birch and Gussow, 1970; Miller et al., 1974).

Continuity of medical care for infants and children exists for 60 percent of the white middle class, but only for 25 percent of minority group middle class, and 10 percent of minority group lower class (Mindlin and Densen, 1969).

Social class, as measured by education, has been found to be predictive of different child-rearing styles (Kohn, 1963; Yarrow et al., 1962). It is correlated with, though not necessarily the cause of, high-risk pregnancies and differences in child-rearing practices and beliefs.

Studies in the United States, Switzerland, and Scotland have shown that boys in the upper classes are taller and heavier than their counterparts from lower classes (Krogman, 1972, p. 142; Tanner, 1970). Conjugal role organization also differs according to social class, with lower-class black and white families having more segregated role functions than middle-class families (Aldous, 1969).

Socioeconomic status appears to influence nutritional status (DHEW, 1972) and body size (Tanner, 1970), as well as attitudes toward body size (Goldblatt et al., 1965). Family income is also related to diet. In families with an income of over $10,000, the incidence of poor diet is 9 percent, while in families with an income of $5000 to $7000, it is 18 percent, and with an income under $3000, the incidence is 36 percent. Lack of education in these families also contributes to poorly balanced diets (Perkins, 1977).

CHILD-REARING BELIEFS AND PRACTICES   Numerous studies have shown that differences in educational levels and socioeconomic backgrounds affect the attitudes and child-rearing practices of parents (Chillman, 1966; Hess and Shipman, 1965, 1967, 1968; Kohn, 1963; Yarrow et al., 1962). Working-class parents tend to use more physical punishment, ridicule, and behavior restrictions. Middle-class parents tend to be warmer, use love-oriented discipline, and be more permissive (Becker, 1964; Pearlin and Kahn, 1966; Prothro, 1966). Creativity also has been shown to be affected by amounts of control and nurturing. Heilbrun (1971) found that sons who had high-controlling and low-nurturing mothers were less creative.

CHILD AND FAMILY DEVELOPMENT

Kohn (1969) hypothesized that parents of different social classes emphasize different values when socializing their children. He suggested that because of differing occupational requirements and realities, blue-collar parents are more likely to emphasize conformity to external standards while white-collar parents stress the development of internal standards of conduct. A study by Gecas and Nye (1974) of 210 couples in the state of Washington found that in disciplining their children, middle-class parents tended to be more verbal, more likely to use reason, and less likely to use physical punishment than the blue-collar parents. The white-collar parents, and parents who had a college education, were more likely to have different responses depending upon whether a child accidentally or intentionally broke an object than were blue-collar parents or those who had a high school education or less. Kohn's study (1969) of 200 white-collar and 200 blue-collar families in Washington, D.C. indicated that the father's occupation had an important influence on parental values related to child rearing. Although there was considerable similarity between the choices of middle-class parents and working-class parents there were some noteworthy differences. The middle-class parents tended to stress happiness, curiosity, and dependability, while working-class parents stressed obedience, neatness, cleanliness, and the ability to defend oneself. The middle-class parents emphasized factors that go with autonomy or self-direction (happy, curious, dependable) while working-class parents stressed factors that go with conformity or general obedience. Yarrow and his colleagues (1962) found that college-educated mothers stressed more independence training of their children and indicated more sensitivity to their needs than did high school–educated mothers.

Wright and Wright (1976) found a clear trend toward increased self-direction in both blue-collar and white-collar parents between 1964 and 1973. Mothers in the middle and higher socioeconomic classes are less inclined to regard "obedience to parents" as a virtue as compared with mothers in the lower class or with fathers in general (Kantor et al., 1958; Kohn, 1950; Sewell, 1961).

Other reports regarding social class differences indicate minimal difference in the affective elements of mother-child interaction (Bayley and Schaefer, 1960; Tulkin and Kagan, 1972) and larger differences in verbal interaction and cognitive stimulation (Levine et al., 1967; Tulkin and Kagan, 1972). There are data to support the notion that lower-class mothers do not believe they can do much to influence their child's development (Minuchin et al., 1967; Tulkin and Kagan, 1972).

Conjugal role organization also differs according to social class, with lower-class black and white families having more segregated role functions than middle-class families (Aldous, 1969).

Social class and economic status can affect language development, sex-role preference, and personality development (Burchinal et al., 1958; Deutsch, 1965; Hall and Keith, 1964). A recent review of the data shows that though there is probably some correlation between social class and the use of physical punishment, there is some question as to the strength of the correlation. Race may affect use of corporal punishment independent of social class. The data on the use of corporal punishment do not substantiate the ideas that physical punishment in childhood leads to adults who commit homicide or physically abuse their children (Erlanger, 1974).

Subcultures   In the United States the main subcultures are black, Spanish-speaking, and various tribes of American Indians.

BLACK FAMILIES   Anthropomorphic evidence indicates a different body build for American and African black individuals than for American and European white persons. The black person has a more slender, linear build, while the white build is more lateral and stockier (Krogman, 1972,

FIGURE 1-9

by Elizabeth Tong

p. 149). Compared with the white population, blacks have higher birth rates, do not use birth control as faithfully (Kiser, 1962), have almost triple the white infant mortality rates, and have 4 times the rate of maternal mortality (Powell and Powell, 1974). The black illegitimacy rate is nearly 8 times that of the white rate, with a ratio for blacks of nearly one illegitimate birth for every four legitimate births. Even when income is taken into account, the black illegitimacy rate is higher (Reiss, 1971).

The modern family is subjected to unique stresses and strains. Even when socioeconomic status is held constant, the stresses imposed on the black family are qualitatively different from those of the white family (Billingsley, 1968; Davis and Havighurst, 1953; Dollard, 1973; Rainwater, 1966). Blood and Wolfe (1960) reported that 20 percent of 554 white families and 44 percent of 108 black families were classified as wife-dominant. At the same social status level, the white husbands were more powerful in their marriages than were black husbands.

Urban-rural differences are also noted, with a higher percentage (86 percent) of black rural families with children being headed by men than in urban areas (77 percent). These differences are not noted in white families. Looking at income alone, 64 percent of the black families in the lower income bracket are headed by men, compared with 93 percent in the higher income bracket (Billingsley, 1968).

Statistics indicate that in 1968 the black person did not earn quite 60 percent of what the white individual did and that on the average the white person had 2 or 3 more years of education. The unemployment rate for blacks is twice that for whites. About one-third of the husband-wife black families and two-thirds of the female-headed black families are living in poverty. For whites, the comparable rates are 9 and 30 percent, respectively (Moynihan, 1965).

Chillman (1966) has described eight interlocking factors of poverty that are closely related to one another and perpetuate each other into a cycle of poverty. These factors are: (1) poor physical and mental health, (2) low income, (3) chronic underemployment and unemployment, (4) low educational attainment, (5) the cultural patterns of poverty, (6) poverty environment, (7) large families, and (8) broken families. The black family is at high risk for each factor. "The survival factors for black people in America have been (1) the family as a center of life, with an extended kinship system, (2) the primacy of the mother-child relationship, and (3) religion and, more recently, (4) the civil rights movement" (Powell and Powell, 1974, p. 146).

Divorce and separation rates are higher among black families than white families and associated with this are more black families without a male head (Moynihan, 1965; Reiss, 1971). Of black children, one-third live in broken homes, while about 10 percent of white children do so (Moynihan, 1965). In 1965, Harrington found that the black slum child was more likely to experience an unstable home than a white child.

In 1966, 75 percent of black families had annual incomes rated as inadequate ($8000 for a family of four was considered adequate), 15 percent had critically low annual incomes (under $2000), and 40 percent had poverty incomes (under $4000) (Joint Commission on Mental Health of Children, 1973). This means that the majority of black parents lack the financial resources to provide the basis for the healthy growth and development of their children. Billingsley (1968) estimates that about 50 percent of the black families can be classified as lower class, 40 percent as middle class, and 10 percent as upper class. These classes are based on an understanding of the black social structure rather than on the class categories that are relevant for the white population.

In a recent review of the literature on the psychosocial development of black children, Taylor (1976) feels that the emphasis placed on social and cultural influences has exaggerated the black child's psychological vulnerability. The variables of lower racial status, poverty, "broken" family structures, and poor school performance may not affect the black child in the same way as the white child. The insulated environment (racial isolation) establishes barriers to assaults (prejudice) on personal worth. Black children also tend to use other black children, not white children, as reference. The most crucial variable in the black child's level of self-esteem was the attitude of significant others (parents, siblings, friends, teachers) toward the child. This appeared to be stronger than in white children. Significant others are in the immediate community, family, and subculture, and it is their response or the child's perception of their response that affects the psychosocial development of the black child (Taylor, 1976). This could pose problems when the black child is bused out of the familiar environment and away from significant others.

The grammar of the black English vernacular differs from that of standard English (Labov, 1970); consequently, black children who must operate with standard English are handicapped.

SPANISH-SPEAKING FAMILIES Research on Mexican-American families has been described as inadequate, and full of stereotypes (Boulette, 1977). Furthermore, there is a great deal of heterogeneity among members of the same as well as different Hispanic groups. Many of the characteristics attributed to Spanish-speaking families are the result of poverty rather than cultural differences. Beliefs about the causation of disease that are clearly culturally related can be readily identified (Martinez and Martin, 1966). Culturally determined differences in family and child development are harder to separate from those related to poverty. This mix of economic and cultural factors is apparent in a study of California families with Spanish surnames (Acosta and Aranda, 1972). In this study it was found that these families were larger than white and nonwhite families, with about one-quarter consisting of six or more persons, compared to 10 and 18.6 percent, respectively. Family members were also younger (70 percent under 35 years of age), had a lower educational level (about one-half had completed less than 8 years of school), and had lower incomes than the other groups.

The combination of poverty, migration from outside the United States, and physical and language characteristics that readily distinguish them from the dominant native-born white or black Americans leads to a number of family characteristics that could influence both child and family development. These characteristics include: isolation or segregation in low-income ghettos, absent fathers, and removal of children from school to act as interpreters or to take care of the younger children (Boulette, 1977). As with other families in poverty, these multiple stresses have the potential at least for producing types of family dysfunction that lead to child abuse and neglect.

Some of the problems in acculturation experienced by Puerto Rican women are described by Torres-Matrullo (1976).

AMERICAN INDIAN FAMILIES   Although it is dangerous to generalize from the few studies of particular tribes to the state of all American Indians, there do seem to be some common themes. In general, the health problems appear to be similar to those of any minority group of low socioeconomic status; i.e., poor nutrition; greater incidence of infectious disease, particularly gastroenteritis, suppurative otitis media, and tuberculosis; and more psychopathology (Wallace, 1972). However, there are some unique features as well. Early socialization is often undertaken on physically isolated reservations so that there is considerable culture shock when the child enters the school system of the dominant white culture. The child becomes caught between two cultures, and there are increasing problems of poor achievement and acting out (Saslow and Harrover, 1968).

FAMILY SIZE

Family size may influence development in a number of ways. For example, in families with more than one child, siblings play a role in the socialization process. An older sibling may serve as a role model, companion, or competitor, while a younger child may help the older one to feel more grown up. Children without siblings are likely to be less skilled in later relations with peers and to be more adult-oriented. Clausen (1966) suggests that in larger families more demands are made for self-care and that firstborn children tend to have greater responsibilities than in small families. Hawkes and colleagues (1958) found that children in small families tend to rely on their parents for emotional security, while children in large families also find security in their relationships with one another.

Studies of growth rate have shown that children from larger families have a more rapid growth rate than children from smaller families (Krogman, 1972, p. 143), and that children of large families tend to be smaller and lighter than children of smaller families (Tanner, 1970).

Family size influences relationships in a number of ways. First, it determines the number of interactional systems within the family. Second, family members have their own interests and needs and, therefore, make different demands on the other family members. The composition of the family also makes a difference. For example, the wider the age range, the greater will be the difference in interests and values. This is especially true in three-generation families.

Oral methods of discipline and verbal reasoning tend to be used more often in small families than in large ones. Bossard and Carter (1958–1959) found that parents of small families employ a wider range of disciplinary techniques than do parents of larger families. As family size increases, parents tend to be less flexible and more authoritarian and to rely more frequently on strong child-rearing controls.

FAMILY STRUCTURE AND HOME SETTING

Birth Order and Ordinal Position   The child's position within the family structure contributes to personality development and coping modes. Each child will occupy a different position in the family and will therefore view childhood differently than does his or her sibling. Adler feels that the position occupied is important because of the child's striving to achieve superiority (Dreikurs, 1953).

There is some evidence to suggest that birth order affects birth weight (Salber, 1957), parent-child interaction (Clausen, 1966; Koch, 1960), achievement and eminence (Schacter, 1963), and social behavior (Sampson, 1962; Schooler and Scarr, 1962).

Firstborn children have also been found to be more affiliative and dependent than their siblings (Adams, 1972), exhibit more susceptibility to social pressure, and be more sensitive to tension-producing situations (Bradley, 1968). While found to be more self-confident, they have also

exhibited more nervous habits and shown a slower recovery from emotional upsets than siblings (Koch, 1956). Risk-taking behavior does not
appear to be influenced by ordinal position; however, children from
small families have been found to accept fewer risks (Jamieson, 1969).

According to Adler, the eldest child needs to maintain superiority
and retain love of parents, particularly the mother. The second child
responds from the position of inferiority and a need to successfully compete with the eldest for parental attention. The second child is always
trying to catch up. The youngest child is always the "baby," usually
pampered and cared for by the older siblings and parents. The middle
child has to cope with being neither the privileged elder nor the special
baby, but squeezed somewhere in between (Dreikurs, 1953).

Ordinal position appears to play a definite role in the developmental task of gaining knowledge. From Adler's observations, it would
seem that social interaction, self-control, and self-esteem are also influenced by the internal strivings and competition that occur as a result
of ordinal position.

Home Setting   Three types of home setting influence parents' behavior:
the physical plant of the house and yard, certain activities in the home
(routines, special occasions), and people in the home (absence of parent,
presence of visitors). Settings outside the home also influence parental
expectations and behavior with their children. Of special note were
neighborhood settings (i.e., traffic, streets, construction sites); public settings (stores, restaurants, public conveyances); visiting in other people's
homes; recreation settings; and school settings (Stolz, 1967).

Parents identify five behavior settings in their home, neighborhood,
and community that influence their behavior with their children (Stolz,
1967). Dangerous situations are emphasized most, followed by the time,
weather, occupational life of parent (i.e., work hours, kind of work, near-
ness to home), and degree of importance to parents.

Communal Living Arrangements   Several articles are available on observations of children living in communal family situations (Eiduson et al.,
1973; Johnston and Deisher, 1973). Neither of these are in any sense
controlled observations, but they do point to some interesting hypotheses that can be investigated with scientific rigor. Perhaps the most
striking observations in these articles are the wide differences between
communes in their approach to child rearing. It is obvious that all communes are not alike, and any sweeping generalizations are hazardous.
There are, however, some common themes that run through a number of
these alternate styles of living that provide experiences for children significantly different from those found in the isolated nuclear family. One of

these is the greater development of a peer culture at an early age with less dependence on adults. This greater exposure to peers of all ages and many different adults appears to lead to a greater self-reliance and the development of more mature social skills at an earlier age than most traditionally raised children. More contact with adult males is another difference that may have implications for future development.

Another area of difference is the whole approach to sexuality, with frequent exposure to nudity in both children and adults and few inhibitions about body exploration, including sexual intercourse between young children.

Maternal Employment   The frequency of having a *single parent* (usually the mother) or *both parents working* is increasing. In 1960, 88 percent of all children under 18 lived in families with both parents present, but by 1975, this proportion had decreased to 80 percent (Norton and Glick, 1976). It is estimated that 14 percent of all white children live in single-parent families. In this country, over 40 percent of mothers with children under 18 years of age are employed (Waldman and Glover, 1972).

The age of the child is a major factor in determining the percentage of mothers who work and the proportion of time they work. The older the child, the more likely the mother is to be employed full time. This is true for both white and black mothers, although a higher proportion of black mothers work in all child-age categories. Nearly one-quarter of the employed mothers are single parents who are usually the only income-producing adults in their families (Waldman and Glover, 1972). About 9 percent of the families have working mothers because the husband and/or father is unable to earn an adequate income (Keyserling, 1972).

In March 1974, 30 percent of all married women from intact families with children under 3 years of age were working. Of mothers with children under 6 years, 33 percent were employed, and 51 percent with children between 6 and 17 years were working. Of these women, two-thirds were employed full time. For single mothers, 45 percent with children under 3 years were employed (86 percent full time), while 54 percent with children under 6 years and 67 percent with school-aged children were working (80 percent full time) (Bronfenbrenner, 1976).

Factors increasing the probability that a woman will work have been summarized by Howell (1973b). They are: (1) having older rather than younger children, (2) husband's income low rather than high, (3) mother's education high rather than low, (4) high rather than low labor market value of woman's employment skills, and (5) the mother's ideology about her place in the world of work. An important consideration for parents is the availability of proper substitute care. Such care is not read-

CHILD AND FAMILY DEVELOPMENT

ily available in many areas and is a major reason for mothers not working (Brooks, 1964). Ruderman (1968) found that mothers with very young children were the least satisfied with child-care arrangements.

In considering the subject of working mothers, a multitude of variables need to be taken into account, including: (1) how long she has worked, (2) what hours are worked, (3) whether she works at home or elsewhere, (4) whether the family is intact or broken, (5) family size, (6) socioeconomic status, (7) place of residence, (8) age of children, (9) ethnic background, (10) educational level (Wallston, 1973), and (11) family interaction processes, such as the husband's attitude toward his wife's work (Howell, 1973b). In addition, personal factors, such as the woman's achievement orientation, ambition, and sex-role ideology that may relate to self-selection need to be considered (Siegel and Haas, 1963).

Evidence from recent studies indicates that maternal employment does not result in harmful effects to the young child provided adequate substitute care is available (Caldwell et al., 1970; Mace, 1961; Rabin, 1965; Rabkin and Rabkin, 1969). Results of studies of its effects on the school-aged child and adolescent have been inconsistent, although the child's sex may be an important factor in this age group (Frankel, 1964; Hoffman, 1965; Nye and Hoffman, 1963; Spargo, 1968; Yarrow et al., 1962). Orden and Bradburn (1969) found that maternal employment increased sociability between husband and wife and was correlated with reports of increased marital happiness by both spouses. It has also been shown that if both parents are satisfied with the wife's employment status (working or nonworking), the marriage tends to be happier than when disagreement is present (Ginsberg, 1966; Nye, 1963). Generally, women who enjoy their work also enjoy their parenting role, while mothers who are dissatisfied with their work are more likely to be unhappy or dissatisfied with their mothering role (Howell, 1973b). Studies indicate that usually marriages with working mothers are reported, by both spouses, to be as happy as other marriages (Blood, 1965; Nye, 1965; Orden and Bradburn, 1969).

Numerous studies refute the claim that children of working mothers are particularly likely to become delinquent or develop some form of psychiatric disorder (Douglas et al., 1968; Rutter et al., 1970; Yudkin and Holme, 1969). In fact, West (1969) indicates that in some instances children of working mothers may be less likely to become delinquent. There is no evidence that children suffer from having several mother figures so long as stable relationships and good care are provided by each (Moore, 1963). Day care need not interfere with normal mother-child attachment (Caldwell et al., 1970).

Yarrow and others (1962) studied 50 working and 50 nonworking middle-class mothers in Washington, D.C. These two groups had similar definitions of the accepted female role in marriage and attitudes toward their performance in carrying out their roles. Although employment itself had little relationship to child-rearing patterns and adequacy of mothering (such as limit setting, sensitivity to child's needs, warm and satisfying mother-child relationship), some differences were noted regarding mother-role satisfaction. The mothers in both groups who were satisfied with their present roles did equally well in their mother roles, but, for those mothers who were dissatisfied, those who remained at home did a poorer job as mother than those who went to work. The working, college-educated mother planned more time with her family on weekends, while the high school–educated mother increased her control over the children and gave them more responsibilities for doing things around the house. Yarrow's work indicates that working or not working is not the key to how a mother carries out her mother role, but that her satisfaction with what she is doing and her educational level are more important factors. These women were motivated to work or not work primarily as a means of achieving certain family and child-rearing goals or for self-fulfillment. Among nonworking women, reasons included "love of mothering" (48 percent), a "duty to mothering" (39 percent), or a desire for freedom or an easier life (15 percent).

Few differences in child-rearing patterns were noted in college-educated employed and nonemployed mothers. The high school–educated mothers who were working indicated they had firmer control over their children, assigned them greater responsibilities, and delegated the stricter disciplinary role to the father more frequently than the nonworking mothers. The working, college-educated parents indicated more planned, shared activities with their children than the nonworking parents. Maternal employment appears to bring about different kinds of familial adaptations depending on the value systems of the particular subgroup involved.

Social, familial, and personal factors are important in determining the mother's success in her dual roles (Yarrow et al., 1962).

Employed mothers and fathers report that the energy demands of child rearing differ from the energy demands of work, and vary with the developmental level of the child (Howell, 1973b).

FAMILY VALUES, GOALS, AND CHILD-REARING STYLES

The relative attention that parents, and subsequently their children, place on various aspects of their life and development is closely related to their values and goals. The child's values emerge during the process of socialization (Ackerman, 1958). When marriage occurs, the values of the two individuals merge and are redefined for the new family. This new family then socializes its children according to its unique values.

Family Orientation   The family's value orientations serve as a basis by which the family lives and makes decisions. Farber (1960) identified three types of family orientations. The *parent-oriented* family is one in which the parents' goals and aspirations take precedence over those of the children, and family life is built around the personal development and achievement of parent and child. In the *child-oriented* family, family life is centered around the needs and desires of the child. Important values to this family are participation in community activities and economic security. Parents in a *home-oriented* family focus their attention on favorable interpersonal relations within the family. More emphasis is placed on family life than on community participation.

Child-Rearing Patterns   There is little research describing parental values and what parents hope to accomplish through child rearing. One notable exception is the Stolz study (1967) of parental values. Stolz analyzed over 4000 value statements made by 39 families. Parents valued three primary roles for themselves: to educate, to provide emotional security, and to control their children. Beliefs about punishment were mentioned 4 to 5 times more often than those about reward. Other parental values included providing for nurturance, economic support, and using outside resources. A larger percentage of parents valued a closely knit family. As with other studies, parents in the lower socioeconomic class or who were less well-educated valued orderly living and economic values.

Child-Rearing Styles   In a review of the child-rearing literature some years ago two main ideologies about family life and child rearing were identified, and these are still prominent in the lay literature today (Chamberlin, 1965). These are outlined in Table 1-1.

In general, the "authoritarian," "strict," or "directive" approach emphasizes a sharp dichotomy of parental roles and unquestioning obedience to parental authority by the children. The parents see the child as having a tendency to develop bad habits that will get out of control unless they suppress them and keep the child headed in the right direction.

The "democratic," "accommodative," or "permissive" ideology emphasizes overlapping parental roles and a child-rearing approach whose goal is to help each child develop his or her full potential. The

INTRODUCTION

TABLE 1-1

Comparison of "Authoritarian" and "Equalitarian" Ideologies Concerning Family Structure and Roles

"Authoritarian" ideology	"Equalitarian" ideology
General family structure and the marital relationship	
Hierarchal conception with father as head and the wife and children subservient to him. Marital relationship based on conformity to the sharply dichotomized roles of husband and wife.	Decentralization of authority with greater equality between husband and wife and overlapping of roles. Marital relationship based on mutual respect, companionship, and commonness of interests.
Roles of husband and wife	
Husband's behavior should conform to the masculine stereotype, i.e., "The 'real' man is master in the home, a good provider, and firm disciplinarian, one who tolerates no weakness in himself or others. His predominant personal traits are ruggedness, determination, assertiveness, and willpower."	The husband and wife roles are flexible and overlap. The husband may help out with some of the housework; the wife may hold an outside job. A wider range of male and female behavior is acceptable.
Wife's behavior should conform to the stereotype of femininity. ". . . the sweet, submissive, normally controlled woman who knows and keeps her place in the home."	
Role of parents	
Emphasizes firm discipline and obedience to authority with attempts to suppress inappropriate sex-role behavior or behavior that does not fit in with conventional values.	Emphasizes individual development with less pressure for conformity to conventional values and specific sex-role behavior.

SOURCE: Reprinted from *Clinical Pediatrics*, 1965 4,151 with permission of J. B. Lippincott Company, Philadelphia, Pa.

child is seen as having the basic capacity to learn and mature without excessive pressure or protection, and parents see their main role as one of guidance and encouragement.

These ideologies become translated into different child-rearing styles according to how the parents respond to common behavioral situations arising with their young children. The authoritarian or strict

parent usually has more rules defining what is and what is not acceptable behavior and is more liable to respond to rule violations with some
kind of physical or psychological punishment (the scold, spank, yell
approach). The accommodative or permissive parent tends to ignore
more behavior and is more likely to respond to transgressions by trying
to reason with the child about why the behavior is unacceptable and/or
by finding mutually acceptable alternatives ("rational discipline").

These rather striking differences in approach appear to produce surprisingly few significant differences in the behavior of the children subjected to them, at least in the early years. In a recent longitudinal study
following a group of children from age 2 into first grade there were no
significant differences in the behavior of children raised by these two
different styles on any of the measures indicating malfunctioning either
at home or at school (Chamberlin, 1978). In other words, there was no
evidence to suggest that the relatively more permissive style was producing large numbers of "spoiled brats" or that the more strict style was
producing large numbers of either overly inhibited or overly aggressive
children.

Baumrind (1966, 1971) distinguishes an "authoritative" approach
from an authoritarian one, describing a combination of high control and
open communication as the style more likely to be related to preschool
children with behavior patterns described as "assertive, self reliant and
self controlled." However, this is a cross-sectional study and the correlations are only modest, suggesting that they would be considerably
weaker in a prospective longitudinal study.

In his review of the consequences of patterns of parental discipline,
Becker (1964) provides some evidence that different child behaviors occur depending upon the interaction of parental restrictiveness-
permissiveness with the degree of warmth or hostility. Studies have also
shown that inconsistent or erratic discipline is related to antisocial behavior (Andry, 1960; Bandura and Walters, 1959; McCord et al., 1959).

In general, none of these studies has shown consistently strong relationships between any one style of rearing and any specific type of child
behavior. This has led investigators to shift from looking at effects of
parents on children to how parent and child characteristics interact over
time (Sameroff and Chandler, 1975).

Specific Training Procedures Psychoanalytic theories implicated specific
child-rearing practices, such as early weaning or coercive toilet training,
as having pervasive long-term effects on personality development, but
reviews of research by Orlansky (1949) and Sears (1943) have found little
objective evidence to support this hypothesis.

INTRODUCTION

The effect of other training procedures on aspects of child development is an interesting if unresolved subject. Evidence of effects is largely based on the demonstration of deficits that arise under conditions of global deprivation and their prevention or amelioration with specific training procedures. There is also some evidence to support the idea that specific skills or talents can be developed through training procedures that are started at any early age in the nondeprived child.

PROVIDING COMPENSATION FOR ENVIRONMENTAL DEFICITS There are a number of studies of institutionalized children indicating that specific training procedures can improve functioning. For example, Dawe (1942) spent 50 hours on weekends over a 3-month period in an orphanage viewing and discussing pictures, reading poems and stories, taking children on trips, and verbalizing simple observations. She found that children stimulated in this way significantly increased their vocabulary and sentence length when compared to unstimulated controls and had an average gain of 14 points in IQ compared to a loss of 2 points in the controls over the same time period.

Certainly the most dramatic result of intervention is that reported by Skeels and Dye (1939). They found 25 children ranging in age from 7 months to 3 years in an orphanage with few attendants and low stimulation. All the children showed marked retardation, with a mean IQ of 64. Thirteen were transferred to an institution for mentally retarded women with mental ages of 9 to 12 years. These people played with the children, cared for them, and gave them much attention. At follow-up 2 years later, it was found that the transferred groups had made extraordinary gains in IQ, with a mean gain of 32 points, while the 12 children remaining in the institution had a mean loss of 21 points. A further follow-up when the children were all adults revealed that the experimental group had a median of twelfth grade education and had average or better achievement in terms of education, occupation, income, family adjustment, intelligence of children, and contribution to the community. In contrast, the other children had a median education level of third grade; one had died in a home for the retarded, four others were still in an institution, six were working as unskilled laborers, and one was self-sufficient at a middle-class level (Skeels, 1966).

A number of children reared in ghetto environments, particularly those from large families, have also been shown to be behind their small-family, middle-class peers in some aspects of verbal and social development. Specific interventions through either training the parents or working directly with the child have shown significant increases in verbal ability and various measures of IQ, and so on (Barnard and Douglas, 1974;

Schaefer, 1972). In one study by Irwin (1960) it was found that reading stories and talking about them to children for only 15 or 20 minutes a day significantly increased the vocabulary and speech production of these children.

The most dramatic of the home intervention studies is that in Milwaukee carried out by Heber and Garber (1975). Here, mothers with IQs below 80 were identified as "high risk" for raising children with familial-cultural mental retardation. An intensive intervention program was started for a group of 20 of these children when they were between 3 and 6 months of age. This consisted of transporting them to a special infant education center where they spent 8 hours a day, 5 days a week, on a year-round basis, receiving emotionally supportive and intellectually stimulating types of interaction from specially trained neighborhood para-professionals. By 18 months of age significant differences were found in the language and developmental quotients for the experimental group when contrasted with the controls, who were home-reared in traditional ways. By 5½ years of age there was a mean difference of 31 IQ points (122 versus 91) between the experimental and control groups.

Critics of this approach point out that as soon as the stimulation stops, these gains begin to erode, and after exposure to several years of school, there is no difference between stimulated and control groups. This suggests that these children would have been just as well off without such a program. More recent studies, however, indicate that these gains can be maintained if extra stimulation is both provided at home and continued on in the school (Bronfenbrenner, 1975).

DEVELOPMENT OF SPECIAL TALENTS IN THE NONDEPRIVED CHILD   Fowler (1962) reviewed many of the studies describing the early backgrounds of children with exceptional talents. He found that many children who were precocious in reading, mathematics, and musical abilities received intensive stimulation from an early age. He has also found little to support the notion that early stimulation is harmful emotionally. In fact, the evidence available suggests that most of these children function in an above-average way socially as well as intellectually. The problem with interpreting these studies is that these training procedures occur in a matrix of other events as well. Many of the parents in these families had considerable talents themselves, and what part modeling plays in the development of the children is unclear.

DEVELOPMENT OF MOTOR SKILLS   Some knowledge is also available about the effects of early training on motor ability. In an effort to study when the immature nervous system of the infant becomes responsive to practice efforts, McGraw (1935) began training one of a pair of twins in motor skills such as climbing, jumping off heights, swimming, roller skating, and riding a tricycle, and comparing the age of attainment of these skills with the other twin who served as a control. The training of the first twin commenced at about 1 month of age. At 22 months, the control twin was also given an intensive training period over 2½ months of these same activities to see if he could learn them just as well in a shorter period of time when the nervous system was more mature.

The trained twin learned these skills at a considerably earlier age than the untrained twin. And even though the untrained twin learned most of the skills in a shorter time period at age 2, he was less muscular and coordinated than the trained twin both at age 2 and at another follow-up period at age 6.

In a cross-cultural study, Super (1976) found that the motor precocity of African infants as compared to American infants, was seen only in certain areas (age of sitting, standing, and walking) and was directly related to specific efforts by their parents to teach these skills. It is also clear that motor development can be delayed under rearing conditions that severely restrict opportunity to practice a given function. Buhler (1930) reports a study comparing the motor development of a group of Albanian infants who were kept swaddled almost continually during the first year of life with infants raised without such restraints. She found the swaddled babies showed distinctly less spontaneous motor activity, coordination, and general body mastery than the others. In a study by Dennis (1941) in which two twins were taken from cribs only for feeding and bathing, neither had learned to sit up alone by 1 year of age and they would not support their weight on their feet. Spitz (1945) and Dennis (1960) report similar delays in motor development for children raised in institutions providing only custodial care of children.

STRESS AND CRISIS

The term *stress* applies to a broad variety of situations causing disturbance of equilibrium or homeostasis. Events that are stressful to one individual or family are not necessarily perceived as stressful by another. A variety of events occurring throughout the life cycle of every individual or family may create stress and emotional strain and set in motion a series of adaptive mechanisms that lead either to mastery or nonmastery of the situation. Examples of such situations include marriage, childbirth, and death (Lindemann, 1944). From a biological perspective, "stress is the consequence of the rate of wear and tear in a biological system" (Selye, 1959, p. 660).

The terms crisis and stress are often used interchangeably. Stress actually denotes three different sets of phenomena: (1) a stressful event or situation, (2) an individual's state when responding to the stressful situation, and (3) the relationship between the stressful stimulus, the person's reaction to it, and the events to which it leads (Rapoport, 1965).

Stressful events that may precipitate family crises have been classified by Hill (1965) according to (1) the source of trouble (intrafamilial, such as nonsupport, mental illness, alcoholism; or extrafamilial, such as floods, war, bombings, tornadoes); (2) the effects on family configuration [such as the addition (birth) or loss (death, divorce) of a family member]; and (3) the type of event, that is, whether it changes family status (i.e., sudden impoverishment or sudden wealth) or creates conflict among family members regarding their role conceptions (i.e., families with adolescents) (Burgess, 1947).

Whenever stressful events occur that threaten an individual's sense of biological, psychological, or social integrity, some degree of disequilibrium results and the possibility of a crisis exists.

Caplan (1964) defines crisis as an "upset in the steady state." It is a period of *disorganization* when an individual or family is overwhelmed with a problem that cannot be solved by their usual coping mechanisms (Fink, 1967; Miller, 1968a). During this period family members are seeking new problem-solving patterns for coping with the situation.

While new situations are being worked out there is the danger that tension may be reduced for the family as a group but that this may occur at the emotional expense of one or more individual members, either by neglect or by exploitation of their individual needs. This places a large burden on parents to lead the family effectively through the crisis.

As the family finds new solutions for solving the disruption it begins to *recover* from the crisis. Things begin to improve, and new routines are established.

The level of *reorganization* reached by the family and each of its members may be greater than the degree of organization prior to the crisis. Changes in parent-child relations may be precipitated by the crisis, especially in families that are not well integrated (Angell, 1936). A crisis may be viewed as a turning point (Rapoport, 1965). If it is managed well, it can become a growth-producing event for the individual and family. If the family is not able to cope well with the event, they may emerge from it in a weaker state.

Examples of the effects of various crises on family functioning over time are nicely illustrated in a longitudinal study of 46 families over a

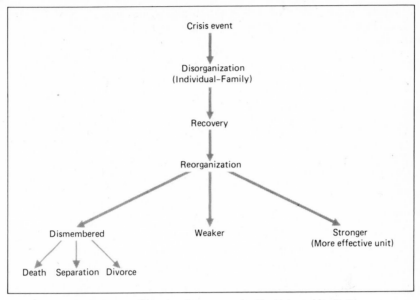

FIGURE 1-10 Effect of crisis event on family. (*Adapted by D. P. Hymovich, Pediatric Nursing, 1976.*)

2-year period by Koos (1950).

Illness When illness is present it has an impact on all members of the family. When illness occurs it is likely to be a situation for which the family has had little or no time to prepare and which presents problems to them as they attempt to cope with it. Depending upon how the family interprets the situation, it has the potential of becoming a crisis event or of being resolved with relatively little disruption in family functioning.

Children with both acute and chronic illness are subjected to many emotionally stressful situations. The psychological threats associated with a single acute illness are usually less harmful and of shorter duration than those associated with long-term illnesses. However, some psychological effects of sickness are unavoidable even if the child remains at home. Some form of feeding, sleeping, or behavior problems are likely to occur. In his study of the emotional effects of illness, Prugh (1953) found no relationship between the nature of the child's illness and his or her psychological reactions. But he did find a definite correlation between the child's previous emotional adjustment and reaction to the stressful experiences of illness. The child's age is a significant factor influencing reaction and adaptation to illness (Langford, 1961).

The effect of illness on siblings has received little attention. These children are likely to become fearful that they too will become ill with their sibling's disease. The magical thinking of young children may lead them to believe they caused their sibling's illness and to fantasize about what is happening to their hospitalized brother or sister. They may become angry at the disruption in their lives caused by the illness.

Hospitalization   A variety of factors are related to the way a child handles the stresses, anxiety, and tensions associated with hospitalization (Langford, 1961). These include the child's age and personality development,

> . . . his past ways of dealing with new and different situations, the immediate emotional surroundings of his illness; the nature of the illness, its acuteness, severity and duration, the type of symptoms; the degree of discomfort involved in diagnostic procedures, including the type of anesthesia and its administration; the meaning of illness in general to the child, his pre-existing feelings regarding health and disease, his specific fears and fantasies; attitudes of his family toward illness in general and the particular illness; the children's relationships with physicians, nurses, and other hospital personnel, their attitudes and feelings about children, the nature of the hospital setting, its policies and practices; the ability of the parents to visit; the type of preparation the child has had for the specific experience. (pp. 669–670)

No relationship was found between the child's previous emotional adjustment and reaction to the stressful experience of illness (Langford, 1961).

Death   Rubin Hill (1965) views death as family dismemberment. Kaplan (1968) indicates that individuals must accomplish certain psychological tasks in the resolution of a crisis, such as death. The family must also accomplish certain tasks as a group. Thus, death, as a crisis-provoking event, affects the intrapsychic adjustment of the individual as well as the family unit.

Goldberg (1973) suggests three tasks to be resolved by the family following the death of one of its members. The first is to relinquish the memory of the deceased, so the family, while still respecting and cherishing the person's memory, can make decisions based on its present needs. Second, intrafamilial roles need to be realigned as death creates a change in the composition of the family group. Redistribution occurs in regard to both the instrumental and socioemotional functions of the family. The family also has to revise its relationships with the organizations and institutions comprising the social system external to the family.

For a child, the loss of a parent can disrupt the identification process, particularly sexual identification. The critical variables include the age of the child, the extent of pathological problems in the parents, the social and educational environment, and the amount of stress (Lewis, 1974).

The effect of a sibling's death on a child undergoes transformation and evolution as the living child continues to develop. Many factors other than the child's age will influence his or her response to the death. According to Cain et al. (1964, p. 741):

> . . . the determinants of children's responses to the death of a sibling were found to include—the nature of the death, the age and characteristics of the child who died; the child's pre-existing relationship to the dead sibling; the immediate impact of the death upon the parents; the parents' handling of the initial reactions of the surviving child; the reactions of the community; the death's impact upon the family structure; the availability to the child and the parents of various "substitutes"; the parents' enduring reactions to the child's death; the major concurrent stresses upon the child and his family; and the developmental level of the surviving child at the time of the death.

It appears that children tend to suffer from a sibling's death in proportion to their parents' ability to cope with their own ambivalent feelings and to understand those of their children. Because of the variety of variables involved, it is very difficult to make general statements which will apply to any single individual or family.

Family Disorganization and Conflict   Pavenstedt (1967) has provided a detailed look at the effects on child development of exposure to home environments characterized by continual disruptions and stress. Since this study deals with preschool children, it is discussed in detail in Chapter 4.

Wife battering is not a new phenomenon, although we still have little information concerning its current incidence and prevalence. Such abuse is common in all ethnic groups as well as all socioeconomic and educational levels (Gingold, 1976) and is not related to age or length of time the woman has been married or living with the man (Martin, 1976). Wife beating during pregnancy is especially common (Gingold, 1976).

These women experience loss of self-esteem and loss of a sense of security and of trust in their partners. In addition, these women are fearful of leaving their husbands (Martin, 1976).

Van Stolk (1976) suggests there may be a relationship between wife battering and child abuse because she has found that men who abuse their wives also beat their children or that a man beats his wife as she is attempting to protect her children.

Family dysfunction may lead to overt cases of child abuse and neglect. Many cases of abuse arise from a single or multiple series of family crises. While most child abuse is reported in the lower socioeconomic groups, this may be due to the fact that the poor are more likely to utilize reporting institutions. Neglect has been described as occurring during periods of economic and/or situational stress, breakdown of the nuclear family, parental depression, and other pathological conditions. In both neglect and abuse, parental needs are a priority (ten Bensel and Berdie, 1976).

Separation and Divorce In discussing the association between separation experiences and deviant behavior, Rutter (1971) suggests that it is the family discord accompanying such separations rather than the separation itself that is important, because it is the tension and disharmony within the family that adversely affects the child. Studies of intact families show that when disharmony is present in the homes, boys are more likely to become deviant than boys in harmonious homes. The longer the family discord, the greater the likelihood of antisocial disorders; however, these harmful effects are not necessarily permanent. If the child later lives in a harmonious home, the risk of antisocial behavior decreases. Family discord alone can be considered an independent variable because it is also influenced by what the child brings to the interaction situation, such as sex and temperament attributes.

Rutter (1971) suggests three possible mechanisms to explain why and how family discord interacts with a child's temperamental characteristics to produce antisocial behavior. First, there is evidence that parental supervision and disciplinary approaches toward their delinquent boys differ from that of other parents (Craig and Glick, 1965; Glueck and Glueck, 1962; Sprott et al., 1955; West, 1969). Second, in line with the experimental studies of Bandura (1969) and coworkers that indicate children readily imitate other people's behavior, it may be that family discord provides the child with a model of aggression, inconsistency, hostility, and antisocial behavior that is copied. Or, perhaps without a warm, stable relationship with their parents, the children do not learn how to get along with others, and these difficulties in interpersonal relationships are the basis of antisocial conduct.

Social Deprivation In terms of social deprivation most of the studies have been concerned with the effects of institutional environments that provide adequate physical care for the children in them but little else. Early reports by Spitz (1945) and Dennis (1960) focused attention on this issue, and a more recent study by Provence and Lipton (1962) has carefully documented the effects of such environments on early development (see Chapter 3).

INTRODUCTION

Day-care settings for young children and school settings for older ones are other examples of institutional environments where children spend a large part of their time. A careful study by Minuchin and others (1969) documented surprisingly few differences in the learning and behavior patterns of children exposed to different school environments. Day-care environments vary widely (Keyserling, 1972), but this has yet to be systematically explored except in terms of maternal-child attachment. In these studies, no differences in attachment were shown between home-reared and day care–reared children (Caldwell et al., 1970; Kearsley et al., 1975). However, both the day-care settings in these studies were comprehensive in scope and emphasized social and intellectual development as well as custodial care.

Finally, there is evidence that hospital environments, particularly obstetrical services and premature infant nurseries, influence mother care-taking behavior and the early development of the child by routines that foster or interfere with early mother-child contact and stimulation (Klaus and Kennell, 1976; Scarr-Salapatek and Williams, 1973).

MASS MEDIA

Over 96 percent of American homes have one or more television sets. Frequent viewing begins at about the age of 3. In one reported survey,

FIGURE 1-11

by Elizabeth Tong

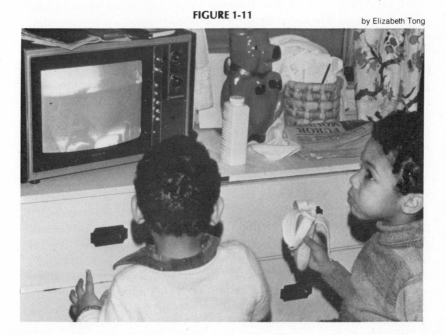

preschool children were estimated to watch television an average of 30 hours a week (Siegel, 1974); in another survey, up to 54 hours a week (Somers, 1976). This means that by the time of high school graduation, children will have spent some 15,000 hours viewing television (Kaye, 1974).

What are the effects on the child of this heavy exposure? As one person so aptly put it, "all television is educational; the only question is what it is teaching." Content analyses of shows during prime times for children have shown a heavy emphasis on crime and violence. Studies by George Gerbner show that 8 of 10 television shows contain violent episodes, and these occur at about the frequency of eight per hour. One authority estimates that the average American child will have viewed the killing of over 13,000 persons on television by age 15 (Siegel, 1974; Somers, 1976).

What is the effect on children of this massive long-term exposure to violence? Two major Federal Commissions have tried to answer this question. The first, set up by President Johnson in 1968 under the leadership of Dr. Milton Eisenhower, was composed of 13 distinguished public and private citizens, including judges, lawyers, senators, congressmen, a psychiatrist, a priest, and an author. After reviewing all the data they came up with an unequivocal report stating they thought that children do learn to behave aggressively from watching television and that observed violence stimulates aggressive behavior rather than acting like a cathexis to prevent it, as advocated by some (Somers, 1976).

The second committee, set up in 1969 by the then Secretary of Health, Education and Welfare, Robert Finch, consisted of 12 behavioral scientists. Five of these, however, were employed by or had close ties to the television industry. In addition, the networks were allowed to exercise a veto over prospective members and did so for seven. This eliminated such persons as Prof. Albert Bandura of Stanford University, whose research has consistently shown that children model behavior they have observed (Somers, 1976). Given these circumstances it is not surprising that this group came up with an equivocal answer of maybe yes and maybe no.

In a more recent review of studies on the effect of television on children, Rothenberg (1975), a child psychiatrist, felt there was sufficient evidence to conclude that children do learn how to behave aggressively by watching television, and if practiced at least once these learned responses lasted over long periods of time.

Certainly there can be no doubt among advertising firms that television affects children's behavior. In one study, 87 percent of the mothers interviewed reported that their preschool children asked for food items advertised on television, and 91 percent said their child asked for an advertised toy (Siegel, 1974). Since much of the food advertised is sugar-coated and packaged for eating while viewing, it seems likely that this would have some effect on the incidence of dental caries and obesity, but as yet there is no documentation of this. Kaye (1974) believes that the relentless stimulation of a child's desires through advertising provides an education in greed as well as gluttony.

Most research on the effects of television viewing has concentrated on how the medium directly affects the child and not on how the medium is used by the American family. Researchers have assumed that television has equal stature with the family as a socializing agent. The role of the family as mediator has been neglected. Interpersonal communication patterns are important variables in identifying the effects of television (Abel, 1976). Abel found that families who placed a high emphasis on family relations and on interpersonal communication appeared to be sensitive to and in control of their children's television viewing. In addition, the child was aware of and responsive to parental viewing preference. The family communication network was noted to be a definite influence on children's viewing.

OTHER

Studies have indicated that the season of the year influences growth, with growth in height being more rapid in the spring and growth in weight faster in the autumn (Tanner, 1970). Season of the year and the geographical environs also affect types of accidents and illnesses likely to occur; for example, drownings in the summer and in environments close to water and ski injuries in the winter in mountain areas. Conditions such as streptococcal infections and rheumatic fever have seasonal fluctuations; the higher incidence being in the winter and spring months (Vaughn and McKay, 1975).

CLINICAL APPLICATIONS

Health care workers can use their knowledge of child and family development in a number of ways. They can provide emotional support to parents and help them meet their own needs and those of their children and to develop knowledge of themselves and their family. In addition, by educating parents about child and family development, primary health care personnel can relieve much parental anxiety about normal developmental deviations and family developmental needs and changes; they can decrease areas of parent-child conflict around typical stage-related behaviors, and help parents provide the child with an environment of emotional support and cognitive stimulation. They can screen for developmental lags and, when indicated, set into motion remedial efforts. They can help parents avoid developmentally related health hazards such as nutritional deficiencies, accidents, and ingestions, and common contagious diseases such as measles, whooping cough, or polio. Finally, application of this kind of knowledge can help minimize the traumatic effects on the developing child of such events as hospitalizations, chronic health problems, brief and prolonged separation from parents, and family dissolution and disruption.

In this section we attempt to give an overview of how this might be done, and in later chapters to provide specific examples for each developmental stage. For some of what we advocate, we can provide documentation of effectiveness. Other recommendations are based on clinical experience with little proof of effectiveness other than clinical impression, with all its known fallibilities.

Using Theory in Clinical Practice

Theoretical frameworks serve the purpose of bringing together general principles that can be used for solving specific problems and for making predictions about specific behavior and events. These theoretical principles can be useful to parents as well as to professionals, and have been applied in varying degrees in child development literature for parents. However, they must be used with caution, recognizing that our current

FIGURE 1-12

by Elizabeth Tong

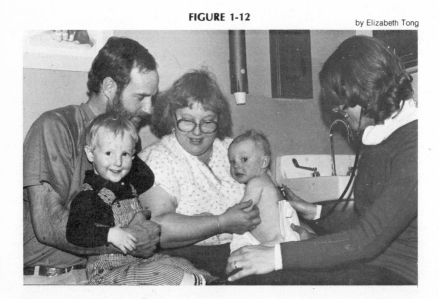

INTRODUCTION

theories and supporting research have proved to be inadequate for those constructing blueprints for parents to use in bringing up their children (Nye and Berardo, 1973). A special problem is one of developing presumptions from untested or erroneous theories. Bruch (1954) indicated that many experts who deal in parent education have a limited or distorted knowledge of psychoanalytic theories and consequently may make inappropriate suggestions. Le Masters (1977) has also indicated that experts have created problems for parents based on unrealistic expectations, particularly in terms of behavior. This has led many parents to feel inadequate and guilty.

> All this does not imply that there is no role for the expert, only that it is a more modest one of communicating relevant facts and suggestive theory-material that is frequently very useful to parents but that does not provide the basis for a blueprint that all parents should follow. Because each child is somewhat different and each parent somewhat different, prescriptions that instruct the parent in how to rear his child are inappropriate and will be even when the behavioral sciences are mature. (Nye and Berardo, 1973, pp. 402–403)

Theoretical beliefs are important, however, in that they influence advice given by professionals or accepted by parents. For example, if we believe that 2½-year-old children are unmanageable due to growth patterns (developmental-maturational theory) we are likely to ignore such behavior until further growth occurs; on the other hand, if we believe this behavior is learned and therefore can be changed (behavior theory) we may try to modify it.

Yates (1975) indicates that parents can be helped to use theory through teaching them the four steps of the experimental method: observation, hypothesis making, testing, and evaluation. Knowledge of theory may be useful in predicting some of the short-term and long-term outcomes of specific parental practices, in helping to prevent problems before they occur, and in helping to solve problems that do occur. Perhaps one of the most obvious points brought out by these various theories is that there are widely variant approaches to rearing children and there is no "right" way. The multiple interrelated factors affecting development also help us to see that an approach that works for one family or child may not work for others.

Stone and Church (1973, pp. 243–245) suggest several principles that need to be considered by parents who are trying to regulate their young child's behavior. First, parents must recognize the need to set limits and exert some control over their developing child until the child learns to exercise his or her own judgment. Second, developmental timing is a necessary consideration. Havighurst's concept of developmental readiness and the concepts of developmental-maturational theory are important here, in that it can be very frustrating to both child and parent to expect behavior of which the child is not yet capable. On the other hand, there is danger in not expecting enough of the child and perhaps holding the child back or denying experiences necessary for development (overprotecting, babying, infantilizing). It may sometimes be difficult to know whether a child is ready for new learning. One way to find out is to teach something but be prepared to stop if the child is not ready. Third, parents should recognize the principle of gradualism, that is, not pushing the child into something too rapidly, and then watching the child for feedback. To some extent, the child's temperament will indicate the degree of abruptness that can be tolerated with each new transition. Fourth, parental self-confidence is necessary in that parents must be able to act decisively and feel secure in their own decisions. They need to be able to differentiate between actual needs of the child that must be met versus childhood wants that may or may not be gratified. A final principle is one of avoidance of moralism; for example, the toddler is too young to comprehend moral issues such as generosity or truthfulness, but rather we can convey such ideas in our manner of approach and by the use of words such as "gently" or "easy" when manipulating vulnerable objects.

Psychoanalytic theory has been included in this book primarily because of its historical contributions to more recent theories and because it has been a major influence in child-rearing practices. Several recent reviews of the psychoanalytic literature (Eysenck and Wilson, 1973; Kline, 1972; Zigler and Child, 1973) indicate there is little empirical evidence to support the usefulness of this theoretical approach to child rearing. Psychoanalytic theory "has consistently failed over the years to produce positive evidence of its predictive powers; thus it is in a highly vulnerable position" (Eysenck and Wilson, 1973, p. 393). Its major contribution may be to help us realize that the behavior we see in our clients is internally motivated and we often need to determine the source of that behavior in order to be most helpful. Parents can be helped to understand that expectations need to be geared to their child's developing ego and superego.

Erikson's psychosocial theory is useful in helping us understand the growth and development of the parents with whom we are working, as well as their children, and to focus on the contributions of environment to development. The importance of trust as a basic component of interpersonal relationships is a valuable concept for us when establishing meaningful relationships with our clients.

The cognitive theory of Piaget is useful in providing guidelines for communication with children that can be used by professionals and parents alike. By understanding how children view their world, we are in a better position to understand their behavior and to provide them with age-appropriate experiences and information. Perhaps one of the most valuable contributions of this framework is the importance of sensory stimulation in the early years.

The principles of the social learning theories are increasingly evident in child-rearing literature for parents and professionals. These principles provide concrete guidelines for modifying behavior, and they have been applied in rearing both healthy and abnormal children. Although research related to behavior modification approaches can be criticized because of a variety of design weaknesses, there is increasing support for the value of including parents as therapists in modifying their children's behavior and, consequently, their own behavior.

Developmental-maturational theory provides guidelines for parents and professionals to use in assessing the child's current stage of development, particularly physical development. Because of the wide variability of individual behavior, they should not be considered as standards to which the child must conform. The use of demand rather than rigid schedules is advocated by proponents of this approach. As with the other theories, it contributes to our understanding that expectations need to be geared to the child's maturational level. This is basically the concept of developmental readiness described by Havighurst.

The concept of individual and family developmental tasks provides another dimension in that it enables us to look at the interrelationships of the various individuals within the family as well as with the family as a unit. Within each of these tasks are components of other theoretical frameworks. We see this approach as a helpful way of synthesizing the useful principles for practice. The way in which this synthesis can be applied is described in this section and in the clinical application sections of each of the succeeding chapters.

The developmental framework, although not yet fully researched, appears to provide the clinician with useful guidelines for working with children and their families. Consequently, this book emphasizes the developmental processes of families and their members. Such an approach facilitates synthesizing knowledge of the individual with that of the family. These tasks must be accomplished in such a way as to meet the biological and cultural requirements, as well as individual aspirations and values.

The lives of individuals and families can be viewed as developing along a continuum. We may enter this continuum at any point, such as at the birth of a congenitally deformed baby, during the infant's early stages of development, or when any member of the family seeks health care. Once we have become a part of this continuum, we need to look at all its dimensions, that is, at each member as an individual and interacting with others, and at the family unit as a whole. Knowledge of these stages of development helps us to better understand the tasks they may be facing, the possible reasons for their behavior, and their potential needs. This knowledge can then be used to plan intervention strategies and to measure the outcome of our therapeutic interventions.

Basic Functions of Provider-Client Encounters

The four basic functions of clinical encounters are as follows:

1 Providing emotional support
2 Assessing the strengths and weaknesses of individual and family functioning
3 Providing education
4 Making specific recommendations or prescribing specific treatments

The amount of time devoted to any one aspect of a visit will be determined by its nature (i.e., acute illness, health maintenance, chronic problems). These four aspects are discussed in the following sections along with a more detailed look at ways of helping families weather the crises of acute and chronic illness, hospitalization, and death.

ESTABLISHING SUPPORTIVE RELATIONSHIPS

Approaches to Relationships In 1956, Szasz and Hollender described three models of professional-client relationships. In the *activity-passivity* model, the professional is active while the patient is passive; with the *guidance-cooperation* model, the professional "tells the patient what to do" and the patient is compliant; and in the *mutual participation* model, the professional helps the patient understand the problem and his or her role in its management.

We agree with others (Hansen and Aradine, 1974) who advocate the use of the mutual participation model as a means of facilitating increased client involvement in primary care and a more effective problem-solving approach to care. They stress the importance of client and family participation in the problem-solving process. Although we believe this is an important goal to strive for, we also recognize that the approach used should be compatible with the desires of clients.

Basically, the problem-solving process consists of four steps: assessing, planning, intervening, and evaluating. To accurately define a mutually agreed upon problem requires adequate assessment of all relevant data. Once the problem is identified, mutually agreeable goals and a treatment plan can be formulated and implemented. Evaluation of outcomes of this care is based upon the goals that have been set. The family should be helped to make informed choices when alternative actions are possible. To make such choices, they need to be provided with the information concerning the benefits and risks of each option.

Guidelines for Establishing and Maintaining Supportive Relationships Studies of client-professional relationships indicate that attitudes, beliefs, and behaviors of the clients and professionals are at least as important as the professional's knowledge and competence in determining outcomes (Charney, 1972). The research of Korsch and colleagues (1971) identified the following communication barriers: interrupting parents with advice or questions, leaving the room while parent is still talking, and ignoring feelings and concerns. A correlation was found between compliance with instructions and the mother's expressed satisfaction with the doctor's behavior (Korsch and Negrete, 1972). Freemon and others (1971) found that doctor-patient communication was facilitated when the physician was friendly, expressed solidarity with mother, took some time to discuss nonmedical social subjects, and gave the impression of offering information freely without clients having to request it or feeling excessively questioned.

Melvin Kohn (1969) suggests that because most social scientists have middle class–oriented values, they do not adequately understand the values and goals of the working class. He suggests that working-class parents are as concerned as middle-class parents about their children. He believes it is necessary to view these goals from the working-class perspective rather than judge behavior from a different perspective.

Although we suspect the ability to form trusting and supportive relationships with another person is related at least in part to how much emotional support the health care worker received in his or her own upbringing, there are certain things that can be learned that facilitate such a relationship. Among these are:

1 Introducing oneself to child and parent.
2 Addressing parent and child by name.
3 Providing support, praise, and reassurance for those areas being handled well to bolster the parents' self-respect and morale. On the basis of their studies, Korsch and Aley (1973) recommend emphasizing the parents' own ideas and resources in formulating plans for

intervention and whenever possible encouraging and supporting the approach originating from the mother.

4 Allowing expression of the parents' ideas and concerns about their child and themselves. Parents need to know you are available when they want you and that you are willing to listen and guide them without condemnation or annoyance. A warm relationship needs to be established between the health provider and the family; an atmosphere in which parents can feel free to ask their questions and talk openly about their anxieties, disappointments, and resentments, and express feelings of guilt, anger, loss, and rejection.

5 Using vocabulary that is clearly understood by each person.

6 Focusing on parental needs and concerns in addition to the needs of the child.

7 Being available by telephone in times of stress.

8 Listening carefully and giving the individual time to respond to questions.

9 Establishing agreement with the family regarding problems and priorities for action.

10 Providing information when appropriate.

11 Viewing the situation from the perspective of the client.

12 Being actively involved in communicating with school-age children regarding their own health and health care needs.

Generally, it is the mother with whom we have the most contact; however, the same principles of support apply to the father or other person (e.g., grandmother) who accompanies the child on health visits or has responsibility for that child's care at home.

Guidelines for facilitating communication include:

1 Asking open-ended questions, such as, "Do you get any help in caring for the children?" "How do you manage?" "How do you blow off steam?" "What worries you about this?" "Why does it worry you?"

2 Making the problem "universal," with statements such as, "Many parents have these problems." "We see this all the time."

3 Using the parents as resources by use of questions such as, "What do you think is the problem?" "What have you tried?" "Why do you think it didn't work?" "What would you like to try now?"

4 Suggesting parents write down their questions when they think of them to refer to when calling or meeting with you.

5 Being aware that obvious overt behavior can be misleading; therefore, exploring the meaning of such behavior facilitates understanding.

6 Repeating explanations may often be necessary. Parents may seek this

INTRODUCTION

repetition through their repeated questioning. Parental anxiety decreases the accuracy with which parents perceive their situation and leads to misunderstandings, especially to misinterpretations of verbal communication. Generally, the more anxious the individual, the greater the distortion of reality, and the greater the difficulty in communicating.

Bridging Cultural Gaps   One of the barriers to utilization of modern health services in general and preventive health services in particular is the cultural gap that often exists between consumer and provider. Different beliefs about causation and treatment of illness, diet during pregnancy, and ways of relating to authority figures may interfere with communication and compliance with prescribed regimes (Jellife, 1956; Scott, 1974).

Some of the problems of delivering medical care to Spanish-speaking persons from other cultures have been documented by Saunders (1954). A discussion of how different theories of causation of disease complicate providing care to Puerto Rican families is provided by Harwood (1971). Treatment of the common cold is an example.

The Puerto Rican mother gets very upset when a child gets a cold because she believes that it will start a chain reaction leading to bronchitis and pneumonia. However, providing reassurance and symptomatic treatment for this requires some knowledge about the Puerto Rican's "hot" and "cold" theory of disease. This theory is based on the belief that health is a state of balance among the four humors of the body—blood, phlegm, black bile, and yellow bile. Illness is thought to result from the imbalance of these humors, which leaves the body too hot, too cold, too dry, or too wet. To cure the illness and balance the humors, a cold disease such as an upper respiratory infection must be treated with a hot remedy. If the health provider recommends cold fluids such as orange juice or milk instead of hot ones such as tea the mother will be dissatisfied and not return.

The use of lay health aides recruited from the culture being served and trained to translate treatments based on scientific medicine into culturally acceptable forms is one way to bridge this gap (Chamberlin and Radebaugh, 1976; Hoff, 1969; Wise et al., 1968).

Some types of psychosomatic problems are better handled by traditional folk medicines than by "scientific" medicine. Martinez and Martin (1966) describe some of these encountered with families of Mexican descent. Torrey (1972), in a review of cross-cultural psychotherapy, concludes that as long as the therapist and client are in the same belief

TABLE 1-2
Assessment of Individual Developmental Tasks

Task	Useful information
Maintaining healthy growth and nutrition patterns	Growth rate (height, weight, head circumference)
	Nutritional status (subcutaneous tissue thickness)
	Eating behavior
	Immunizations
	Illness patterns
	Accidents
Learning to control one's body satisfactorily	Use of large and small muscles
	Activities engaged in
	Independence in self-care
	Accomplishment of developmental milestones
Learning to understand and relate to the physical world	Cognitive development
	Sensory and cognitive stimulation
	Moral development
	Concepts of health, illness, death, time
	School achievement
Developing self-awareness and a satisfying sense of self	Self-concept
	Perceptions of body image
	Temperament characteristics
	Gender identity and behavior
Learning to relate to others	Communication skills
	Dependence-independence
	Attachment-separation
	Sexuality
	Interactions with parents, siblings, peers, others

system, the results obtained in terms of relief of symptoms are about the same regardless of the approach used.

ASSESSMENT

The second major role of the health provider is making an assessment of the strength and weaknesses of the individual and the family. Specific assessment related to each of the individual developmental tasks is found in Table 1-2.

INTRODUCTION

Health The usual history, physical examination, and skin and laboratory tests should be performed.

Growth and Nutrition A dietary history about the amount and kinds of food intake and the presence or absence of pica, and basic measures of height, weight, head circumference, and dental development are made.

Development and Learning Knowledge of normal patterns should allow the health worker to estimate the child's developmental age in terms of the five major task areas presented. More formal testing with the Denver Developmental Screening Test (Frankenburg, 1975) is also a possibility. Estimating the quality and quantity of cognitive stimulation provided by the mother is also part of this assessment.

Child Behavior and Parent Response Here an attempt is made to get some idea of the child's basic temperament pattern, what his or her behavior is like during a typical day, and how the parents are responding to it. From this information one can ascertain the "fit" or "lack of fit" between the type of child and the child-rearing style adopted by the parents.

Family Development and Functioning Assessment of family development should include: How satisfied the mother is with her current balance between being a wife, mother, and individual; how much time she has away from the children; whether she plans to work; and so on. For example, there are times when the mother's needs seem to take precedence over those of her baby, or when, because of personality difficulties, she becomes anxious in caring for her infant. She may need help in accepting her needs and feelings so as not to feel guilty about them (Lidz, 1976). She needs some time away from the child in order to pursue her own interests but may need help in realizing this.

Whether need to be aware of the potential that a wife is being battered by her spouse. These women may give us clues by statements indicating things have been rough or difficult lately. Physical signs such as bruises, fractures, or lacerations may be possible indications of battering (Gayford, 1975).

Sibling reactions to the infant and the father's role in care taking are also ascertained. Recent events such as moves, illness, and so on, are explored in terms of their effects on family functioning. The role of grandparents and support systems for the family may also be explored.

The family developmental task framework can be used to guide us in locating the stage of development for any particular family, thus providing us with some information as to whether they are about on schedule,

CHILD AND FAMILY DEVELOPMENT

TABLE 1-3
Assessment of Family Developmental Tasks

Task	Useful information
Meeting the basic physical needs of the family	Family satisfaction with: housing, food, clothing, health, community, health care, financial situation Resources available, used, needed Seek and accept help when needed
Assisting each family member develop his or her individual potential	Satisfaction with accomplishment of developmental tasks Extent to which each family member is accomplishing his or her individual developmental tasks Parental understanding of needs of each family member Availability of resources needed for each family member to accomplish tasks Adaptation of approaches to developmental level of each member Extent to which each member's tasks support or conflict with those of others
Providing emotional support and communicating effectively with all family members	Satisfaction with relationships Relationship between family members Communication patterns Decision-making patterns Expression and sharing of feelings Stability of marriage (e.g., wife abuse) Relationships with extended family Individual family member's temperament, personality, cognitive level, self-concept How individual needs for affection, acceptance, and encouragement are met
Maintaining and adapting family organization and management to meet changing needs	Satisfaction with organization and management Daily schedule Role of each family member Strengths and weaknesses in organization and management Role flexibility Availability of external supports Policies for including others in family (e.g., friends, neighbors, relatives)

TABLE 1-3
Assessment of Family Developmental Tasks (Continued)

Task	Useful information
Functioning in the community	Satisfaction with community involvement Leisure activities outside home Organizations belong to, (e.g., PTA, volunteer, parents groups) Use of community resources, (e.g., day care, baby-sitting) Availability of community resources Satisfaction with available resources

SOURCE: Adapted from: Hymovich, D. P. Assessment of the chronically ill child and family. In D. P. Hymovich and M. U. Barnard (Eds.), *Family health care (Vol. 1) General perspectives*. New York: McGraw-Hill, 1979.

ahead, or behind in mastering the tasks of that stage in the life cycle. Just as we evaluate the average, early, or late development of children, we can begin doing this with their families as well.

If, as we believe, mastery of developmental tasks can be considered evidence of healthy individual and family functioning, then it is necessary for the health professional to assess the degree to which such mastery is taking place and to provide guidance in areas that need strengthening.

Otto (1963, 1973) has identified a framework for assessing family strengths. These strengths have been incorporated into each of the developmental tasks so that the reader can use them in assessing task mastery and wherever possible capitalize on those family strengths that are present. The clinician will need to consider a number of factors related to each for the family's developmental tasks. These considerations are listed in Table 1-3.

It is the health providers' role to identify those families whom they can help and those who are in need of referral. Generally, three types of families can be identified (Korsch and Aley, 1973, pp. 13–14). One group of parents are those who come primarily for a checkup and immunizations, who seem to be managing well, and appear confident in their child rearing and able to cope with problems that arise. Generally, these families do not need nor do they want help and support. A second group of families are those with major psychological problems that require intensive treatment. These families usually need to be referred for psychiatric care. A third group of families are those with mild social or emotional problems and for whom we can usually provide help, support, and reassurance. We would add to this a fourth group: those families who do not show up at all. These are the families about whom we know relatively little and who might benefit from outreach programs.

EDUCATION

Principles of Teaching and Learning A major function of the health care providers is to meet the educational needs of their clients—parents and children. To ensure that our educational endeavors are meeting the client's needs, some principles of teaching and learning should be kept in mind (Clayton, 1965; Hilgard, 1975; Redman, 1976). Learning takes place when:

1 There is genuine respect for and acceptance of the learner (parent, child) as an individual.
2 The atmosphere allows for acceptance of differing value systems.
3 The learner is allowed to explore personal feelings and attitudes.
4 Motivation to learn comes from the learner's perceived needs and desires. (Learning under intrinsic motivation is preferable to learning under extrinsic motivation.)
5 The maturational level of the learner is taken into account.
6 There is recognition of individual differences in rates and ways of learning.
7 The learner believes the content is relevant and meaningful, is related to his or her life-style, and has immediate application.
8 The learner is actively involved in determining satisfactory solutions to problems.
9 Reinforcement of the learner is a part of the teaching-learning process. (Learning under the control of reward is usually preferable to learning under the control of punishment.)

What this means in terms of everyday practice is that "giving information" does not necessarily mean the client has received it. We need to find out what is relevant to the parent and child and proceed from there. If we believe certain knowledge is important for them that does not seem relevant to them at the time, then we need to find ways to motivate their interest in these topics. If they are not motivated to see its relevance, it is unlikely the information will be retained or used.

Approaches to Parent Education A variety of approaches are available to practitioners in addition to discussions with an individual parent. Some of the child development books available for parents can be recommended and discussed with parents, either individually or in groups. Many parents are no doubt already familiar with these sources of information, and they may have many questions about the information in them. Pamphlets, such as those available from the government, drug companies, distributors of baby products, and special interest groups can be read in the home, clinic, or office. Some of these booklets are published in several languages. Sources of health education materials are available from the Health Insurance Institute in New York.

A number of mediated self-instructional materials are available for office use. These include audiotapes, audiovisual slide tape and film-loop presentations, films (usually 8 mm), videocassettes, and closed-circuit television productions.

Other approaches, such as "cluster visits" for mothers of young infants (Feldman, 1974; Gozzi, 1970), parent education classes sponsored by groups such as the American Red Cross and community centers, Dial Access (Bartlett et al., 1973), or Health Educational libraries (Collen and Soghikian, 1974), have been suggested as possible means of educating clients.

Although there has been research dealing with the effectiveness of various approaches to health education, many of the studies have been poorly designed and most of the findings are inconclusive (Richards, 1975; Veenker, 1965). It seems that for the present, practitioners need to assess their own teaching styles, the needs of their particular clients, and the resources available to them (see Table 1-4). Some parents may benefit from only one type of educational approach, while others may need a combination of approaches to meet their needs.

Basic Concepts to Cover Regardless of the educational approach or approaches used, there are certain basic concepts, in addition to routine care, that should be covered. These concepts are as follows:

1   Child development follows predictable patterns that are related to age: There are typical child behaviors and illness patterns at each stage of development; the way children see the world at each stage differs from how adults view the world. Families go through developmental stages just as children do. This information can be provided in terms of "anticipatory guidance" as to what is likely to occur in the near future and in terms of management of ongoing behaviors.
2   Although children and parents follow these general patterns of development in broad outlines, no two children or parents are alike: within each stage children grow and develop at different rates. Children have differences in temperament that have important implications for child

TABLE 1-4
Criteria for Evaluating Health Education Materials

Relevance to your objectives	Stated objectives or goals; flexibility
Author or producer	Qualifications; reputation
Content	Accuracy; impartiality; up-to-date; scope (adequate coverage); organization; suitable level: vocabulary load, conceptual density
Format	Appropriate for content; appropriate for audience
Learner	Involvement; background requirements
Technical qualities	Clarity (print, sound, picture); synchronization (sound and picture); suitable captions
Physical characteristics	Durability; repairability; ease of handling
Logistics	Space requirements; maintenance requirements
Interest	Relevant to user; aesthetically pleasing
Cost	Per unit, per user; investment: initial, long term; useful life—cost of updating; supplemental costs: repair, replacement, storage, additional equipment
Published information regarding material	Field tested; date and period of data collection; method of data collection; sampling details; measurements used

rearing. Parents also have different temperaments, as well as individual needs that must be met if they are to cope successfully with the stresses involved in raising a family.

3   Within the limitations imposed by developmental stages and individual differences, parents can influence the development of their children: Parents can influence the language and mental development of their children by providing models and stimulating experiences; influence the frequency with which different behaviors are expressed by following the basic principles of behavior modification; help children recognize, accept, and express in constructive ways feelings of aggressiveness, dependency, and sexuality; play an important role in fostering the development of self-esteem in their children; and learn to communicate more effectively with each other and their children.

4   Parents have needs that should be met just as their children have needs.

5   Families have strengths and resources for coping with the stresses and crises involved in family life. These strengths deserve recognition and should be utilized by family and professional.

Anticipatory Guidance   The aim of anticipatory guidance is to prevent the development of emotional and behavioral disturbances occurring because of disordered parent-child relationships. Anticipatory guidance involves teaching parents what to expect in terms of their child's physical, emotional, social, and cognitive development before changes occur. By reducing parental fears of dealing with the unknown and identifying behavior as stage specific, rather than abnormal or undesirable, we can help parents feel more secure in their abilities to respond to their children and to establish sound relationships. Such guidance is most helpful when it is geared to individual rather than general needs, since no single family can be assumed to follow the typical patterns. Therefore, as practitioners, we need to determine the values, orientations, and child-rearing styles of each family with which we are working.

Through anticipatory guidance, parents can be given suggestions for managing their children to achieve optimum development. They can also receive guidance in decision making and problem solving related to current situations so they can use these skills in the future. The concept of anticipatory guidance can also be applied to helping parents anticipate and plan for changes that will occur in their own and their family's development. It can also be useful in helping parents set realistic and reasonable goals for themselves as well as their children.

Since any form of abrupt or disruptive change may precipitate a crisis, family members should be adequately prepared for family developmental changes (Glasser and Glasser, 1970).

Hansen and Aradine (1974) identified areas in which parents expect to receive guidance. These areas include:

1 Child growth and development and the parent's role in fostering positive development
2 Common child-rearing issues and the rationale for proposed approaches
3 Child behavior and its management
4 Management of the sick child at home and the rationale for care
5 Balancing the needs, care, and problems of all family members
6 Needs and problems of the parents themselves
7 Family relationships associated with personal and interpersonal crises
8 Ways to effectively utilize and relate to health care providers and other community resources

To provide anticipatory guidance effectively, the intitial level of parental understanding needs to be assessed. If specific advice seems indicated, it is wise to first find out what the parents have already done. They may have already tried what you are about to suggest or they may have inadvertently done something that needs correction—such as given an improper dose of medication (Korsch and Aley, 1973).

A planned schedule of anticipatory guidance can be developed to take into account the stages of child, parent, and family development and common problems likely to occur at each stage.

Brazleton (1975a) and Hill (1960) describe their approach to the use of stage-related anticipatory guidance during well-child visits. Books, such as those by Fraiberg (1959) and Ilg and Ames (1970), contain good descriptions of typical stage-related behavior and are appropriate for many parents. Some other basic parenting skills that may be useful to teach parents on a routine basis are as follows.

Behavior modification principles can be applied in a variety of ways in helping parents manage their children's behavior. A variety of approaches have been employed in training parents. Parents have been verbally taught the basic concepts of the approach (Patterson et al., 1975) or the more specific techniques of management (Alvord, 1971; Madsen, 1965). Some parents have been directly taught particular techniques such as defining behaviors, counting and recording their frequency, and applying reinforcements (Patterson et al., 1975). A variety of individual and group training methods have been used, including lecturers, movies, programmed instruction books, discussion, modeling, and direct coaching. It should be pointed out that as they are modifying their child's behavior, parents are also changing their own behavior. Studies have consistently demonstrated that when the parents' behaviors change so that desired behaviors receive reinforcement from the parent and undesirable behaviors are ignored or punished, the child's behavior changes in desired directions (O'Dell, 1974).

Teaching parents simple interactive verbal games has been shown to increase a child's vocabulary and scores on various developmental tests. Books by Gordon (1970, 1972) are examples of these. Uses of these in health care settings are described by Gutelius et al. (1972), Jason and Kimbrough (1974), and Scarr-Salapatek and Williams (1973).

Increasing the effectiveness in the way families communicate with each other would seem to be a worthwhile and productive measure. Ability to express feelings in constructive ways and respond to the feeling tone as well as the content of what others are saying appears to enhance communication and problem solving. Although adequate conclusive studies are still lacking, such approaches as transactional analysis (Harris, 1969), parent-effectiveness training (Gordon, 1970), and similar approaches hold promise.

MAKING RECOMMENDATIONS AND PRESCRIBING TREATMENTS

The final function of a client-provider encounter is to try and introduce a positive change in the system through specific interventions. This may take the obvious form of prescribing a drug for a specific illness or, more subtly, trying to change the way a parent is responding to a child. Here, the problem for the provider becomes one of trying to limit the interventions to those areas that are reasonably supported by objective data rather than simply trying to impose one's own values and beliefs on another. This is particularly true when working with families of diverse cultural backgrounds.

As yet, no one has definitive information on how to optimally rear children. Guidelines to successful parenthood are lacking (Rossi, 1968). Information is readily available concerning the infant's nutritional, clothing, and medical needs, and general prescriptions are given that indicate a child needs loving physical contact and emotional support. But guidelines do not exist for rearing children to become the kind of competent adults that are valued by society.

In fact, the adults who do "succeed" in American society show a complex of characteristics as children that current experts in child care would evaluate as "poor" or "bad." Biographies of leading authors and artists, as well as the more rigorous research inquiries of creativity among architects or scientists, do not portray childhoods with characteristics currently endorsed by mental health and child-care authorities. Indeed, there is often a predominance of tension in childhood family relations and traumatic loss rather than loving parental support, intense channeling of energy in one area of interest rather than an all-round profile of diverse interests, and social withdrawal and preference for loner activities rather than gregarious sociability. Thus, the stress in current child-rearing advice on a high level of loving support but a low level of discipline or restriction on the behavior of the child—the "developmental" family type as Duvall calls it—is a profile consistent with the focus on mental health, sociability, and adjustment. Yet the combination of both high support and high authority on the part of parents is most strongly related to the child's sense of responsibility, leadership quality, and achievement level, as found in Bronfenbrenner's studies and that of Mussen and Distler. (Rossi, 1968, p. 36)

However, as mentioned earlier in the review of child-rearing studies, none of these approaches explain much of a child's behavior. Because of this, health care workers should avoid inflicting their own favorite child-rearing ideology on the parents and should support what they are doing as long as the child is adapting well to the approach being used. When there is an obvious "lack of fit" between a particular child and the style adopted by the parents, the health care worker can help them modify their response pattern to better fit the type of child (Chamberlin, 1974).

Health care providers may be asked for advice concerning the effects of maternal employment on family life. To help parents make a decision, we can provide them with available data while trying not to color it with our own personal opinion. Howell (1973b) suggests providing parents with information concerning the importance of (1) working conditions that are consistent with the working mother's skills and abilities and that provide adequate rewards (recognition, promotion, salary); (2) the changes in family functioning as a result of the mother's becoming employed, and the support systems available, and (3) options for child care and the possible effects of the mother's employment on the children.

Other examples of introducing change are covered in each section under management of common stage-related problems and some other less common but developmentally important problems.

Helping Families Cope with Stress and Crisis

The general concepts and principles applicable to management of families coping with developmental stresses and crises can be extended to considering the care of families facing situational crises. It is important, however, to remember that a situational crisis is likely to be superimposed on an ongoing developmental crisis.

INTRODUCTION

Illness is only one of many probable stresses on the family at a given time. Very likely some of the following stresses exist in any family much of the time: (1) interpersonal problems between family members, (2) debt, unemployment, change of jobs, (3) recent changes of dwelling place and consequent disruption, (4) problems associated with child care and discipline, and (5) concurrent illness of other family members.

Research at the Laboratory of Community Psychiatry, Harvard Medical School, provides information about the ways families and individuals cope with crises (Hirschowitz, 1974–75). Families that are coping in a healthy way invest their energies into "intelligent worry work," share their distress, are able to maintain hope, and can recognize their temporary need for dependence and interdependence and seek assistance appropriately. They are able to use their energies for problem solving and planning, and when these energies are depleted, they are able to take "time out" for rest and recreation. Maladaptive patterns of coping include the family's attempt to avoid the problem, or when it cannot be avoided by looking for someone to blame. They may blame someone or something external to the family or may select an internal scapegoat. This family scapegoat is often the youngest child or oldest daughter. Some families deal with crises by asking someone to "take over" for them, while others maintain an independence from sources of help. In some cases, the father may invest all his time and energy in work and remain away from the home. Family members may resort to drugs, alcohol, or food.

CRISIS INTERVENTION

To help families cope with the developmental and situational crises they are facing, the following guidelines for guidance are recommended (Hirschowitz, 1974–75):

1 Help families understand the predictable physiological and psychological changes that may occur.
2 Accept their temporary dependency by seeing them often and letting them gradually return to independent functioning.
3 Encourage them to confront the demands of reality while ensuring they receive adequate rest. They should be encouraged to reduce their normal work responsibilities.
4 Help them to express their emotions in ways they find acceptable.
5 Collaborate with them in using a systematic problem-oriented approach in solving their problems. Caplan (1964) refers to this as the "decision counseling method" whereby the professional first helps the

person delineate the problem and then together they explore the possible options available for solving the problem. Once the person decides what is to be done, he or she attempts to carry out the decisions that are made. The professional then helps the person assess the outcome of the intervention, and if it was not satisfactory, the problem-solving process is repeated.

6 Link family members to appropriate resources.

7 Function as a role model by communicating confidence and hope that problems can be surmounted and that grief does pass.

The child's reaction to a crisis is molded to a very considerable extent by his or her parents' response to it (Silber et al., 1958; Wolfenstein, 1965).

ILLNESS

The modern urban family, with the high emotional demands placed on it, possesses relatively weak resources with which to cope with the impact of illness (Craven and Sharp, 1972).

To recover from the crisis presented by a child's illness, parents are called upon to accomplish the following tasks: (1) to understand and manage their child's illness, (2) to assist their child in understanding and coping with the illness, and (3) to meet the needs of all family members, as well as those of the ill child, by maintaining their own health and each family member's individual integrity (Hymovich, 1976). The degree to which parents are able to accomplish these tasks can be used as a guide for measuring parental success in coping with the stress of illness.

Parents with ill children have several basic needs (Hymovich, 1976). They need (1) trust in themselves and in the health professionals assisting them, (2) information, (3) guidance and support, and (4) resources to cope with the crisis. This includes human resources, such as one's own health and physical resources, such as adequate finances. There will be variations in the degree of need for individual parents as well as differences in their ability to cope with the illness.

To understand and manage their child's illness, parents need specific information about their child's condition, including an explanation of the nature of the illness and the physiological and behavioral changes that can be anticipated during the course of the disease. Also necessary is an explanation of the cause of the illness and its prognosis. Even well-educated parents have many misconceptions about the origin, nature, and outcome of their children's illnesses (Kennell et al., 1969; King, 1962) and, therefore, need specific information. Some degree of anxiety and guilt are common reactions of all parents when their children become ill. Adequate and accurate knowledge tend to be associated with fewer feelings of self-accusation (Meadow, 1968; Wright, 1960). There is some evidence to suggest that parents who understand their child's illness are more apt to comply with the recommended medical regimen (Marston, 1970; Tagliacozzo and Kenji, 1970).

To manage the child's illness at home, parents generally need detailed explanations of the care they are expected to give, including, when appropriate, demonstrations of specific procedures they are expected to perform. They should know what changes the therapy will cause and how long it will be before changes occur. They need to know the unfavorable as well as the favorable signs and symptoms they are expected to look for. This implies imparting knowledge about the therapy, such as medications, as well as the disease process itself.

Since the need for repetition is usually great, it might be useful to give written materials to the parents so that some reference is available to them whenever they want it. These materials may describe such things as the child's illness and therapy, specific observations to be made, or instructions for procedures. They may be printed forms which are already available, or they may be handwritten communications for specific individuals.

Vulnerable Child   Prevention of the vulnerable child syndrome should be considered following a child's severe illness. The health provider should not continue to impress the parents with the seriousness of their child's illness once recovery has occurred. Before discharge, it should be emphasized that the child's recovery is, or will be, complete, that no special precautions will be necessary, and that the child will not be more vulnerable to illness than other children. It is also useful to point out that after a severe illness many parents have a natural tendency to wonder if they could have prevented it in some way and to treat the child specially. A return appointment is suggested if the parents come to recognize such tendencies in themselves or if the health provider knows of predisposing factors to such tendencies.

Parents whose child was critically ill at some point may indicate they worry about the child "for no reason." Asking them how sick their child was or whether they sensed their child's condition was critical encourages their disclosing fear the child will die prematurely (Green and Solnit, 1964). Management of children with functional heart murmers is an example of how the health care provider can unintentionally foster a vulnerable child syndrome (Bergman and Stamm, 1967).

Once the vulnerable child syndrome is recognized and a thorough examination is complete, the parents should be informed that their child is physically sound. Then they need help in understanding the symptoms related to the child's being considered special as a result of the earlier illness. If the parents are unable to accept and utilize this information, they should be referred for psychiatric treatment (Green and Solnit, 1964).

For parents who are able to recognize and accept the reasons for their exaggerated concern and the child's behavior, the mutual reinforcement of anxiety and symptoms are interrupted. Parents then become able to (1) set limits, (2) discontinue overprotecting and infantilizing the child, (3) deal better with problems of separation, (4) be more realistic about the child's complaints, (5) make adequate sleeping arrangements, and (6) stop telling others and the child that "they nearly lost him."

Chronic Illness The interpretation of a chronic disability is a repetitive and evolving process that includes attention to both words and feelings, and is directed toward the parents' eventual acceptance of the reality of the handicap. Obviously this cannot be accomplished in one sitting; it is facilitated by a series of visits. Since the visits are for the benefit of the child and parents, the parents should decide when they will return.

It is particularly important for parents of chronically ill children to learn the effects the disability may have on their child's growth and how they can foster their child's developmental capabilities. They also need to understand the normal developmental tasks of children and how their child's chronic illness affects these tasks.

Numerous pamphlets and some books are available for parents of ill children (Pless and Satterwhite, 1971). Most of these are related to chronic handicapping conditions (such as cleft lip and palate, epilepsy, rheumatic fever, cerebral palsy). These pamphlets can be used in conjunction with verbal explanations; however, since they do not represent all professional viewpoints, they may be confusing if they differ from the way in which a particular child is being managed.

Since many of the therapies for chronically ill children are time consuming, they will disrupt family routines already established, and parents will need support and guidance as they learn to alter their lifestyle. Parents need to know about resources available in the community that can assist them in managing their child's illness. These resources might include other health care personnel (such as social workers, occupational or physical therapists) or special facilities (such as schools, homemaker services, and sheltered workshops). Parents of chronically ill children often rely on a variety of special community agencies and services. In addition, they need to know what regular facilities are accessible to their children.

FIGURE 1-13   by Debra Hymovich

Other resources available to parents of ill children might be friends and neighbors or members of their extended family. Parents of chronically disabled children may have difficulty finding a baby-sitter who is able to manage their ill youngster. As a result, these parents may rarely be able to go out together. An important family resource is the health of the parents. In order to provide continued care to their ill child, parents need to maintain their own health. This is often difficult to accomplish if they are unable to find or afford assistance.

Specific ways in which parents can help the siblings of disabled children include maintaining open and honest communication with them about the condition and its meaning (Kew, 1975).

The parents will need guidance and support as they adapt to this crisis. They will also need accurate information about the condition and its management. Whenever possible, point out the abilities of the child as well as the disabilities. In this way parents may begin to look at the strengths of their child in addition to liabilities. They will need this focus as they learn to help their child cope with the condition.

CHILD AND FAMILY DEVELOPMENT

Hospitalization If a child is to be hospitalized, parents (and the child, if old enough) should be informed about the treatments and procedures the child is receiving. Communication should remain open so that parents can inform and be informed about their child's progress. Whenever feasible, parents need to be involved in providing direct care to their young children. This is one way they can cope with their anxiety and guilt feelings about the child's illness. However, it is equally important for them to receive sufficient relief from direct care in order to get some rest.

For parents to adequately prepare their child for hospitalization and the procedures that will be performed, they need to have information about what will occur. This means that a good orientation needs to be planned for them. It should include discussion with their physician and nurse, a tour of the hospital unit, preferably with their child, if possible, and adequate written information about what to anticipate.

To assist their child in understanding and coping with the illness, parents need knowledge about how children of different ages respond to

FIGURE 1-14 Parents waiting to admit their daughter to the hospital.

by Debra Hymovich

the stress of illness and hospitalization. (For a discussion of age-specific responses, see Chapters 3 through 5.)

Parents who know their child's reactions to stressful situations can use this information in deciding how far in advance preparation should begin. There are some parents who prefer not to prepare their child in order to spare unnecessary worry, and it is vital that we stress the importance of such preparation with these parents. Studies have shown that children who are prepared for hospitalization and procedures are less anxious than children who are not prepared (Johnson et al., 1975; Melamed and Siegel, 1975; Wolfer and Visintainer, 1975). It is also crucial that parents be aware of the necessity of being honest with their children.

When a child is hospitalized, arrangements need to be made for the care of siblings remaining at home. The effects of separation on the healthy children need consideration if the illness is prolonged. Parents may need help in managing their schedule to provide time to meet the needs of their spouse and of their well children. Siblings need an honest explanation of their brother's or sister's illness and what caused it. They often need help in developing explanations for their friends and neighbors. To alleviate their anxiety over what is happening to their sibling, children should be permitted to visit with each other in the hospital.

Children often believe illness and hospitalization are punishment for some misdeed. Parents may have threatened to send the child to the doctor or hospital as punishment and thus help develop this feeling. Parents should be informed of the dangers inherent in this practice and should be encouraged to refrain from such threats.

Parents need preparation for possible changes in their child's behavior. They may need considerable guidance and support as they help their child return to the preillness state. Regressive behavior such as soiling, enuresis, and thumb sucking are common following hospitalization, as are disturbances in eating and sleeping behavior. Parents have indicated that children may have difficulty going to sleep at night or they may awaken during the night from frightening dreams. After discharge, the child may cling excessively to his or her mother and become disturbed at any attempt on her part to move away. Or, the child may reject his or her mother and pay no attention to her at all.

DEATH

Hill (1965) views death as family dismemberment. Kaplan (1968) indicates that individuals must accomplish certain psychological tasks in the resolution of a crisis such as death. The family must also accomplish certain tasks as a group. Thus death, as a crisis-provoking event, affects the intrapsychic adjustment of the individual as well as intrafamilial adjustment.

Families must give permission for the grief process to proceed. There must be encouragement of mourning and expression of feelings (Goldberg, 1973). Vollman et al. (1971) and Williams et al. (1972) report their recent study using crisis intervention with bereaved families as a method of primary prevention of later medical or psychiatric disorders. They have noted that families with effective communication systems better meet the stress of a death.

TWO

Pregnancy and Fetal Development

P regnancy is part of the family's continuing life experience and can be viewed as an additional stress superimposed on the usual life stresses of that family unit. It is a time of heightened sensitivity, changing feelings, and increased susceptibility to crisis. Childbearing has a tremendous impact on the entire family, not just the pregnant woman (Horsley, 1972; Howells, 1972a).

The emphasis of this chapter is primarily on the psychosocial aspects of the pregnancy phase of family development and the application of this knowledge to clinical practice. The intent is not to play down the importance of the physiological changes and their application nor is it to swing the pendulum too far in the direction of psychosocial management. Rather, it is to stress those aspects of assessment and management not readily found in any single volume. The reader can readily find information about the physiological aspects of management in a variety of maternity and obstetric texts. A brief review of fetal development and the risks to the fetus and pregnant woman are also presented.

FETAL DEVELOPMENT

The fetal period represents the most rapid period of growth and is crucial in determining one's ultimate development. Fetal development is a truly remarkable phenomenon, as growth occurs from a single cell at the time of fertilization to a fully developed infant 9 months later. Following is a brief overview of fetal development based on the writings of Arey (1974), Moore (1977), and Watson and Lowrey (1967).

After the sperm and ovum fuse, the rapid cell divisions which follow form a hollow sphere, the blastocyst, that takes about 2 or 3 days to move down the fallopian tube and become implanted in the lining of the uterus. This implantation takes another 3 or 4 days and is completed by 6 or 7 days after fertilization.

As the outer cell mass of the blastocyst invades the lining of the uterus to form the placenta, the inner cell mass continues to multiply and form the embryo. This "embryonic disk" develops into three layers. From the outer layer (ectoderm) the skin, hair, nails, sense organs, and nervous system develop. From the middle layer (mesoderm) and associated mesenchyme develop the supporting structure of the body: bones, cartilage and muscle, the linings of the abdominal and pleural cavities, and the cardiovascular and urogenital systems. Out of the inner layer (entoderm) evolve the mouth and pharynx and the respiratory and digestive systems.

Embryonic Period (4 to 7 Weeks)

By 3 weeks of age, the brain and heart have begun to form, as have the tubes that develop into the central nervous system and the intestinal tract. At the fourth week, somites form on either side of the tubes and from these come the muscles and bones. At 4 weeks of age the embryo does not look like a baby. It has a head and tail and is only one-quarter of an inch long. Starting from a single cell the embryo has now enlarged an astonishing 50 times in size and 8000 times in weight!

In the second month the eyes and ears begin to form, limb buds begin to develop into arms and legs, and the sex organs become visible. The mouth and nose are also beginning to take shape. It is at this time that abnormalities of development may lead to the formation of cleft lip and cleft palate.

Fetal Period (8 Weeks to Birth)

By 2 months of age the baby has eyes, ears, and a nose, and the hands have fingers and the feet have toes. The head is still large in proportion to the body. The abdomen protrudes because it contains the intestines and liver that are too large for the abdominal cavity. The fetus is now slightly more than an inch long.

By the end of the second fetal month, the major elements of all the

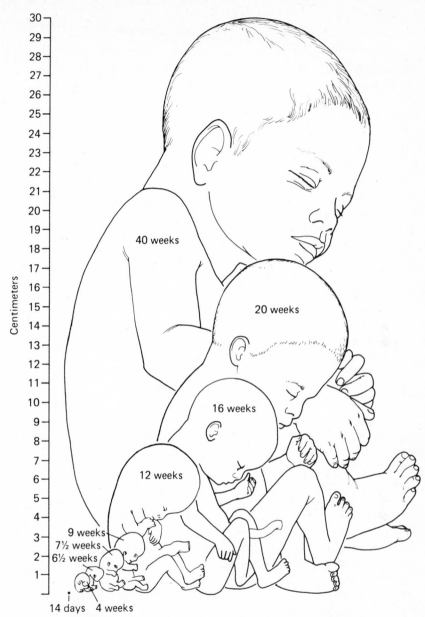

FIGURE 2-1 Fetal development, 14 days to 40 weeks. *(Adapted by D. P. Hymovich from Arey, Developmental anatomy, (7th ed.), Philadelphia: Saunders, 1965, p. 101; Fitzpatrick et al. Maternity nursing (11th ed.), Philadelphia: Lippincott, 1966, pp. 82–83; and Understanding conception and contraception, Raritan, N.J., Ortho Pharmaceutical Corp., 1968, pp. 41–45. Reprinted with permission from D. P. Hymovich, and S. R. Reed, Nursing and the childbearing family: A guide for study. Philadelphia: Saunders, 1971, p. 83.)*

organs are formed and the subsequent growth of the fetus is devoted to their further elaboration. This is one of the most critical periods of development, and disturbances during this time period may give rise to major congenital malformations.

By the third month, the developing organs begin to form specialized functions, such as forming blood in the liver, insulin in the pancreas, and urine in the kidneys. By the end of the first trimester, the fetus may make brief, jerky movements on its own.

During the fourth month, further specialization of body functions continues: hair grows, finger and toe nails form, and oil glands appear in the skin and manufacture the greasy, tenacious substance known as vernix caseosa that protects the skin from becoming macerated and waterlogged. Eyelashes also appear and eyelids open.

By the fifth month the fetus looks like a little baby in every respect. It weighs about one-half pound and is about 10 inches in length from head to toe. If delivered at this time the baby would move, its heart would beat, and there might even be feeble, irregular respiratory movement, but it would be too small and immature to survive. By the end of the fourth month one may be able to hear the baby's heart beat, and between the fourth and fifth month, the mother feels the baby's movements (quickening). By the twentieth week, the sucking reflex is present and the pattern of respiratory movement begins.

By 28 weeks (7 months), the fetus is fully developed but lacks subcutaneous tissue and looks red and wrinkled. This age period generally demarcates the zone between viability and nonviability. Infants born after this period show the following characteristics according to the length of the gestation period.

From 28 to 32 weeks, movements are meager, as muscular tone is poor and reflexes hardly present. Breathing is shallow and irregular, and the cry is either absent or very weak. Sucking and swallowing are present but there is no definite sleep-wake pattern. There may be mild avoidance reactions to bright light and sound.

From 33 to 36 weeks muscle tone increases and more reflexes become present. There are now definite periods of being awake, and a well-established hunger cry is present.

From 36 to 40 weeks muscle activity is sustained and tone is good. The Moro reflex is strong. There is active resistance to head rotation, and the baby tends to lift its head when put in the prone position. Periods of alertness are definite and of greater duration than earlier. The infant cries loudly when disturbed or hungry, and there is a good, strong sucking reflex.

Over the last 6 to 8 weeks subcutaneous fat is deposited and the baby's weight increases from an average of 1½ to 2 pounds at 6 months to an average of 7 pounds at birth.

The expected time of birth is approximately 280 days from the first day of the last menstrual period, and most infants are born within 10 to 15 days of this time.

FAMILY DEVELOPMENT

Transition to parenthood, especially with the first infant, is said to be more difficult in the United States than either marital or occupational adjustment (Rossi, 1968). Factors contributing to these difficulties include: (1) cultural pressures that lead many young women to still consider motherhood necessary for individual development; (2) the irrevocability of parenthood; (3) inadequate guidelines, preparation, and training for parenthood; (4) the abrupt transition from pregnancy to parenthood that does not allow for a gradual taking on of responsibilities; (5) the child's need for mothering is absolute, while the woman's need to mother is relative (Benedek, 1959); and (6) in many nuclear families, the mother is isolated from assistance and must assume the total responsibility for infant care taking.

FIGURE 2-2

CHILD AND FAMILY DEVELOPMENT

Women facing a second or third pregnancy usually find it easier than the first because of their previous physiological and emotional maturation; however, the fatigue and burdens associated with additional children may present other difficulties for them (Benedek, 1970b). In studying women who have had a number of pregnancies, Caplan (1959, p. 56) states that different things come to the surface with each succeeding pregnancy. A sudden increase in maturity is seen after the birth of the second baby; the woman's perception of reality is less influenced by internal fantasies, and she is better able to carry out her adult role without being too dependent or independent of others. It is not known if this goes on progressively through successive pregnancies.

Pregnancy can be viewed as a developmental phase (Duvall, 1977), as a turning point (R. Rapoport, 1965), or as a period during which there is an increased susceptibility to crisis (Caplan, 1961). This susceptibility may be related to the changing roles within the family, feelings related to sexuality, stresses related to unexpected or imposed pregnancies, and economic and/or social problems.

Motivation for Parenthood

TWO-PARENT FAMILIES

Parenthood is described as a stage in the family life cycle that represents an important step in human development (Benedek, 1959; Erikson, 1963). Individuals are motivated to become parents for a variety of healthy and unhealthy reasons (Ackerman, 1958; Jessner et al., 1970; Smart and Smart, 1976). They may decide to have children because it is the natural thing to do; as evidence of their sexual maturity and virility; as a family duty; as a religious obligation; or as a potential source of help and support for the parents. Children may also be wanted as a means of keeping a poor relationship together, avoiding loneliness, realizing unfulfilled goals, or attaining security. A couple may want children for the sake of the child itself and to help the child develop as an individual. Motivation for more than one child may include disappointment with the first child, the desire to provide a companion for the single child, love of children, or to replace a lost child.

Couples may hesitate to have children because of the pressures related to overpopulation, fear of being bad parents or of the children's effect on their marriage, restrictions imposed by children, economic cost, or because they do not enjoy children (Smart and Smart, 1976). They may also decide to postpone having children until they feel they are ready for parenthood, to advance their careers, or to avoid having unwanted children (Duvall, 1977).

When 1600 currently married women were asked why they did not want more than their desired number of children (Espenshade, 1977, p. 21), financial reasons were mentioned by 60 percent. Concern over population problems was seen predominantly among women wanting two children (the number popularly associated with zero population growth). Health concerns and general restrictions on parents were cited by those wanting only one child but declined rapidly for these wanting more than one child. The most common reason for wanting two children was companionship for a sibling.

SINGLE PARENTHOOD

Shainess (1966) indicates that out-of-wedlock pregnancy falls largely into three categories: (1) purely accidental, in which a pregnancy was neither intended nor likely to be acceptable; (2) the sociocultural milieu is such that the pregnancy is accepted casually, and not likely to result in

FIGURE 2-3

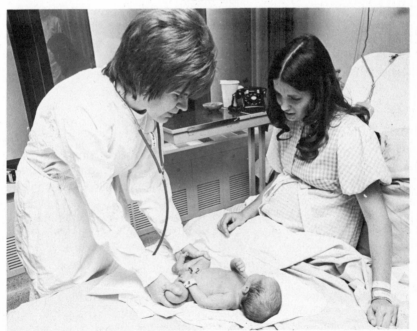

CHILD AND FAMILY DEVELOPMENT

seriously diminished social status; and (3) the pregnancy is deliberate and often repeated. The girls in this last group use illegitimacy as a retaliatory weapon against mothers whose relationships with their daughters have been destructive, resulting in defiance and competitiveness. These girls seem to feel they will never belong to anyone unless they create someone themselves.

Today, an increasing number of single women consider keeping their babies. Alternatives, such as abortion and adoption, may also be considered. The decreased stigma attached to producing and raising a child outside of marriage reflects a change in attitude held by society.

A woman considering single parenthood is faced with the same tasks as a married couple. Decisions need to be made about providing space and equipment for the new infant and supporting herself and the baby financially. If she chooses not to work, she will need to consider the types of assistance available to her (e.g., social welfare, extended family).

ADOPTIVE PARENTS

Adoptive parents are parents by choice. A couple who is unable to give birth to children may choose to adopt them. A man who marries a woman with children of her own may sometimes choose to adopt them. Although still uncommon, single persons may also adopt children, usually older children. Parents may choose to adopt, rather than have natural children, because they want children but do not want to contribute to overpopulation.

General Characteristics of Two-Parent Families at the Time of First Pregnancy

"The timing of a first pregnancy is critical to the manner in which parental responsibilities are joined to the marital relationship" (Rossi, 1968, p. 31). During the early stage of marriage, prior to the coming of children, young couples are engaged in establishing their roles with one another, their parents, relatives, and the community; obtaining and maintaining a home; finding satisfactory ways of supporting themselves; dividing responsibilities among themselves; planning for possible children; and maintaining their own motivation and morale (Duvall, 1977). The extent to which the tasks of newly married couples are accomplished depends upon the individuals involved and the length of time the couple has been married prior to the first pregnancy.

The newly married couple is faced with a variety of tasks to be worked out as they master the central developmental issue of intimacy. The extent to which they have been able to master these tasks is relevant to their adaptation to the new issue of generativity (Erikson, 1963). The couple is faced with developing patterns for resolving interpersonal conflict and making decisions. Raush et al. (1963, p. 372) suggest that ineffective coping tends to be associated with "intrapsychic conflict and the use of ego defenses such as repression and denial; overt signs of such ineffective coping will include manifest anxiety and forms of somatic behavior characteristic of intrapsychic conflict."

In some families, one or both partners may be working, while in others one or both may be in school. Marriage and parenthood are increasingly taking place before schooling of the husband, and often of the wife, has been completed (Davis, 1962; Ginsberg, 1966). Graduate students are, increasingly, men and women with full family responsibilities. Within the family many more husbands and fathers are still students, often quite dependent on the earnings of their wives. It has generally been accepted and increasingly expected that women will work following marriage. As a result, more egalitarian relations between husband and wife are being seen in these families.

Much of our lack of knowledge regarding family functioning is due to the lack of a clear definition of terms such as marital satisfaction and marital accommodation. "Marital accommodation" is a particularly useful term for discussing the health of a marriage because it implies that couples must accommodate to something less than perfect adjustment rather than resolve all their problems. Accommodation in marriage encompasses three processes: mutualization, idealization, and marriage enchantment (Benson, 1968, p. 115). Through *mutualization* the activities of each become interdependent and coordinated as they develop new habits and routines. The process of *idealization* is one in which both persons develop heightened pleasure in one another by focusing on each other's strengths and reducing awareness of weaknesses. Two processes are involved in the process of *enchantment:* first, the increase of wish or confidence that marriage is desirable, and second, the growing conviction that marriage with the current partner will be "a most enthralling state."

Developmental Tasks of the Parents-To-Be

MEETING THE BASIC PHYSICAL NEEDS OF THE FAMILY

Space Prospective parents may react to the coming of their first baby casually and do very little to provide space and equipment before it arrives. Others become involved in buying many items and making elaborate preparations by reorganizing their living space for the expected infant. In some cases it becomes necessary for the expectant couple to find new housing because the space may be too small or there may be restrictions against children in their current dwelling.

Stott and Latchford (1976) report that changing residence during pregnancy had an insignificant effect on later child morbidity for middle-class families; however, among the poorly housed, there was a 43 percent greater child morbidity at 4 to 5 years of age. This effect rose consistently with the extent to which the family was separated from their home community. For lower-class mothers who reported being upset or distressed at moving away from their own mothers, the excess child morbidity was 82 percent. The source of stress appears to be the displacement from familiar surroundings rather than making a tiring trip. Childhood morbidity included physical, neurological, and behavioral disturbances.

Finances At the time of the pregnancy, both prospective parents may be working; however, should the woman decide to stop working, earnings decrease while expenses increase (Caplan, 1961; Duvall, 1977). The cost of having a baby varies widely and is related to the family's place of residence, income, and individual values. Couples generally have to pay for medical and hospital services, baby furniture, equipment, and clothing, including maternity clothing. The cost of bearing and caring for an infant during the first year is estimated to be approximately $2300 (Duvall, 1977, p. 209).

Selecting a Method of Feeding for the Infant The decision to breast- or bottle-feed is generally based on considerations such as believed convenience, status, and cultural factors. Two investigations involving the questioning of nulliparous women in pregnancy about feeding choice reported that bottle-feeding choice was significantly correlated with mother-centered reasons, whereas those planning to breast-feed tended to give reasons concerning the welfare of the baby (Adams, 1959; Brown et al., 1960).

McKigney (1971) indicates the financial cost of breast-feeding has been overestimated in the Western world because of an unrealistic and unnecessary emphasis on the absolute need for large amounts of expensive animal protein foods in the diet of the lactating woman. Satisfactory nutrient intake can readily be met by low-cost foods, especially cereal-legume mixtures, and physiological calorie reserves, laid down in pregnancy in the form of subcutaneous fat, that are available to the lactating woman. Recent studies suggest that the energy expenditure of lactation is about one-half what it was previously believed to be (Thomson et al., 1970).

Artificial feeding with pasteurized cow's milk in 1970 cost nearly $3 per week. The cost is relatively high compared with other mixtures, refrigeration is required, the volume indicated may be too great for some children under 6 months of age, and the addition of sugar or some other highly concentrated source of energy would dilute the already marginal content of several vitamins and minerals (McKigney, 1971).

ASSISTING EACH MEMBER DEVELOP HIS OR HER INDIVIDUAL POTENTIAL

Preparation for Parenthood Men and women have less preparation for parenthood than they do for other roles (Rossi, 1968). There may be opportunities in the home as they are growing up to learn something about areas relevant to successful family life: sex, home maintenance, child care, interpersonal competence, and empathy. If the home is deficient in these areas, the children are left with no preparation for what is

FIGURE 2-4

by Debra Hymovich

CHILD AND FAMILY DEVELOPMENT

often a major segment of their adult life. Little preparation for parenthood can take place during pregnancy. That which does occur is usually confined to reading, consultation with friends and parents, discussions between husband and wife, and a minor nesting phase in which the equipment and a place for the baby are prepared in the household. The transition to parenthood is therefore abrupt, and the new parents acquire immediate, 24-hour responsibility for their infant (Rossi, 1968).

Preparation for Motherhood   The pregnant woman is preparing for a new role, whether it be that of becoming a mother for the first time or of becoming the mother of an additional child. The development of motherliness is seen as a gradual transition from being the dependent nurtured one through the increasingly active and autonomous stages to becoming the nurturing person (McFarland and Reinhardt, 1959).

Several stages are considered critical in the development of motherliness. The female child's identification with her mother is believed to be a critical first step in a woman's ability to meet her child's needs. Studies indicate a correlation between a mother's recall of the mothering she received and the solicitous care she gives her own infant, as early as the second postpartum day. For example, Frommer and O'Shea (1973) found that primiparous women who indicated either temporary or permanent separation from their mothers before 11 years of age were more vulnerable to problems in managing their infants during the baby's first year of life and had a statistically greater incidence of depression. Benedek (1949) correlated the qualities of motherliness, in its developmental phases, with cyclic hormonal fluctuations during pregnancy. Other factors determining a woman's mothering capacity prior to her infant's birth include the woman's personality potential, attitudes toward femininity, sexuality, values and philosophies, relationship with her husband, how welcome the pregnancy is, motivations for pregnancy, and the conditions of pregnancy, delivery, and the early postpartum period (Shainess, 1965).

In preparation for motherhood, the woman needs to first validate the reality of the pregnancy (Colman and Colman, 1971). If the pregnancy is unwanted, consideration will need to be given to its continuation or termination. Even when the baby is wanted, ambivalent feelings are likely to be present. These feelings may be exaggerated by the physiologic responses of nausea, vomiting, fatigue, and lack of appetite. The woman may have strange fantasies or dreams about the unknown organism growing within her. Emotional responses that occur during pregnancy are discussed later in this chapter.

Once the pregnancy has been validated, the mother-to-be becomes involved in incorporating and integrating the fetus as an integral part of her body image (Tanner, 1969). This period, usually the first trimester, is characterized by an increased self-absorption with concern about bodily and mood changes. Deutsh (1945) refers to this psychic dynamism as a transfer of interest from the outside to the inside of her body. At this stage of fetal embodiment, the fetus is not yet perceived as a separate object and is often viewed as being unreal, an "abstraction" or generalization rather than an individual.

About the time quickening occurs, the woman begins to perceive the infant as a separate individual rather than an extension or integral part of her self (Caplan, 1973; Tanner, 1969). There is now a tendency to assign a sex to the baby and to describe it with specific characteristics. Concerns about abnormalities and complications also become evident.

Sometime during the second or third trimester, the pregnant woman begins preparing for a care-taking relationship with her infant. She usually develops an increased interest in child-care activities, begins accumulating clothing and equipment, and plans for the child's future. By the end of the third trimester, most of the pregnant women interviewed by Tanner (1969) had selected a method of infant feeding and had confidence in their ability to feed successfully; had made plans for the baby's arrival at home; and had given thought to managing their baby's care. This is in contrast to 40 mothers interviewed by Adams (1963), who reported they could not recall active interest in infant care during their pregnancy. Only six (15 percent) reported having discussed care-taking activities to any extent during this period, and only eight (20 percent) indicated they had done any amount of reading on the subject. A number mentioned they were more interested in changes in themselves during their pregnancies and their babies had not seemed separate and real to them until after delivery.

Rubin (1967a, b) has presented some evidence that five categories of operations are involved in attaining the maternal role. These operations represent the taking in and taking on of a new role and letting go of a former role or status. The process consists of mimicry, role play, fantasy, introjection-projection-rejection, and grief work. Through mimicry the woman adopts the behavioral manifestations of the pregnant status by such things as wearing maternity clothes before they are actually needed or following certain cultural taboos, such as not eating particular foods. Although similar to mimicry, role play involves acting out what it would be like to be a mother. The woman might baby-sit for others, help with child care, or perhaps adopt a pet to care for. Fantasies related to what life would be like for herself and imagining what the baby will be like are also part of this process. Through the operation of introjection-projection-rejection, some action is developed within the woman herself. She then finds a role model and fits that model's behavior to that which she is experiencing. If the "fit" is a good one, it serves to reinforce the woman's beliefs; if the "fit" is a poor one, it is rejected. The end point of these four operations of taking in and taking on the maternal role is the woman's identity of herself as a mother. The final operation, grief work, is involved in the process of letting go of her former identity in some roles. For the multiparous woman, this grief work includes becoming disengaged from established ties with her other children.

The *first trimester* is characterized by nausea and vomiting, sometimes regarded as a psychogenic symptom; considerable increase of emotional lability; increased irritability; and varying degrees of depressive mood states (Baker, 1967; Kaij and Nilsson, 1972). Associated with these symptoms are a decrease in libido and often increased aggressiveness towards the father of the fetus, with a paradoxical dependency on him and other family members, especially her mother (Baker, 1967). During this time many women show ambivalence. Ambivalence may make it easier for women to withstand loss of the fetus during this time with a minimum of emotional repercussion (Baker, 1967). Tiring easily and an increased need for sleep are outstanding features of the first trimester. In fact some multiparas state that sleepiness is their first sign of pregnancy (Kaij and Nilsson, 1972). This is also a time when marital stresses may become apparent. Many women develop some minor craving or aversion and will test their husbands' affection by their willingness to provide for their cravings.

During the *second trimester* there is usually increased emotional stability and frequently an apparent increase in self-confidence and drive (Baker, 1967). Early ambivalence disappears, and the women begin to organize their households. The most common complaints at this time are heartburn and gas. From the fourth month on, abortion or miscarriage is likely to be felt as a true loss of the child and more serious emotional repercussions are possible (Baker, 1967).

The second trimester and the first part of the third trimester are relatively free from psychological symptoms and many women often feel healthy, with a sense of well-being during this period. Some women who experienced a decrease in sexual activity during the first trimester now report a better sexual relationship than before pregnancy. The majority of women, however, experience a diminished desire and less satisfaction. A fear that intercourse may harm the fetus is often reported.

During the *third trimester* there may be an intensification of psychosomatic and psychoneurotic responses but this seems infrequent. The relative absence of depression is particularly significant at this time

PREGNANCY AND FETAL DEVELOPMENT

(Shainess, 1966). In many women there seems to be an emotional blunting, which has been characterized by Deutsh (1945) as a narcissistic regression or withdrawal from external objects to the self.

As labor approaches, there tends to be an increased physical and emotional lethargy with an undercurrent of anxiety. Usually the woman begins to make increasing demands on her husband to manage the practical realities of day-to-day affairs.

During the last portion of this third trimester, mental symptoms again increase in frequency. Generally they are symptoms of psychomotor tension, restlessness, and anxiety. During the last few weeks panic attacks may appear. There are also increasing physical discomforts that cause concern, such as calf cramps; backaches; disturbed sleep; varicosities of the legs, vulva, or anus; and dyspnea and edema. Just prior to delivery these discomforts often become increasingly evident.

Many women are concerned with the imminent birth, although fear and anxiety are often denied or concealed. Often they fear the baby will be malformed or stillborn, but most of all the woman worries about herself and the possible complications, pain, or death. Primiparas tend to be more concerned about the child, multiparas about themselves (Kaij and Nilsson, 1972; Winokur and Werboff, 1956).

On the day of the baby's birth, some women have a sudden urge to

FIGURE 2-5

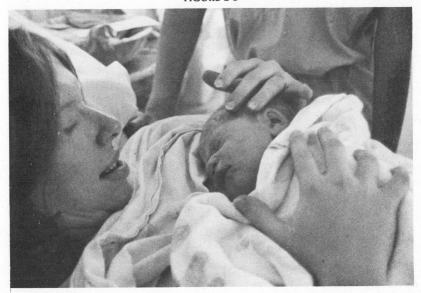

be active while many others experience a curious calm and detachment (Baker, 1967).

There appears to be a time lag between the time of the baby's birth and the development of what Levy calls "full maternal feelings." This time lag can be predicted by the pregnant woman's attitude toward her fetus. The more intense the positive relationship and the more the expectant mother endows the fetus with human characteristics, the shorter will be the time lag after the baby is born. For pregnant women who do not personify the fetus, their newborn infant is seen as a new individual, and after birth the mother will have to develop a relationship with it (Caplan, 1961).

Preparation for Fatherhood　The literature concerning fathering and preparation for fatherhood is scanty. The Colmans (1971), Chabon (1966), and Deutsh (1945) have discussed the importance of the father's involvement in pregnancy and how this involvement has been curtailed by maternity and obstetric practices in the United States. This practice is gradually changing as consumers are demanding more involvement during this period. Factors contributing to evolving concepts of the father's role include changing family structures, shifting of the cultural definition of masculinity, and increasing recognition of the emotional importance of fatherhood (Jessner et al., 1970).

FIGURE 2-6

by Susan McCabe

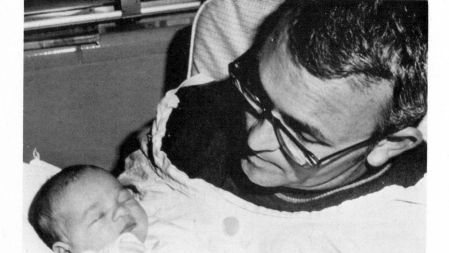

PREGNANCY AND FETAL DEVELOPMENT

The first task for the father-to-be is adaptation to marriage (Benson, 1968). Becoming a parent is a critical transition and it is even more so if it is superimposed upon marital difficulties because of incomplete accomplishment of the first task (Dyer, 1963).

According to Benedek (1970c), the sources of fatherliness come from an innate biologic bisexuality and from past experiences of biologic dependency on his mother. During his wife's pregnancy, the father relives his identification with his own parents. He also has fantasies regarding the infant, often seeing the child as an extension of himself. Jessner et al. (1970) caution against viewing fatherliness as identical to motherliness rather than complementary to it.

During the first trimester, the main task of the husband, as well as his wife, is to accept the reality of the pregnancy. During the second and third trimester the husband is said to be working through the psychological problems aroused by the pregnancy crisis (Colman and Colman, 1971).

Roehner (1976) gathered first-hand information about the feelings and needs of prospective fathers. A multiple-choice questionnaire was completed by 26 men whose wives were pregnant with either their first or subsequent children. These men indicated they felt proud (50 percent); were worried about money (42 percent) when they first learned of their wives' pregnancy; there was no change in their relationship with their wives since the pregnancy (38 percent); and their relationship was closer (50 percent). About one-half the men believed they were needed more by their wives now than prior to the wives' pregnancy. Many of the men (85 percent) felt their most important function was to help their wives deal with their physical and emotional problems, and one-half of them felt it was also important to make sure their wives remained healthy. When asked who helped them with problems and questions about becoming a father, 35 percent said they had no problems, 27 percent were helped by their wives, 23 percent by no one, and a small number indicated health personnel (12 percent) or family and friends (8 percent) were helpful.

In a study by Fein (1976), concerns expressed by husbands during pregnancy were related to labor and delivery, parenting, providing and receiving support in the weeks following birth, and possible long-term changes in their lives. Some of the men indicated they were observing other children, a few went out of their way to care for children, and some were reading about parenting and child development.

In many cultures, the father's role in childbearing is emphasized. Couvade is a widespread cultural practice of rituals, taboos, and responsibilities of the father during the childbearing period. The *couvade syn-*

drome is a psychogenic condition in which the expectant father suffers from symptoms similar to those of his pregnant or laboring wife (Trethowan, 1972). Estimates of the incidence of this syndrome range from 11 to 50 percent, depending upon the symptoms included in the definition. Trethowan (1972) indicates it probably occurs in about one in every four or five expectant fathers. The common symptoms are nausea, vomiting, alterations (usually loss) of appetite, indigestion, and toothache; abdominal swelling is rare. These symptoms usually begin towards the end of the second or early in the third month of pregnancy but may occur at any time. About the time the wife begins labor, the husband commonly suffers from sympathetic labor pains. Many fathers also experience anxiety. Trethowan reports that 40 percent of the 327 expectant fathers he studied reported they were anxious during their wives' pregnancy. Over one-half these men also complained of other symptoms, such as depression, insomnia, tension, nervousness, irritability, headaches, weakness, and stuttering. An additional 30 percent of the 186 men with physical symptoms did not admit to being anxious over their wives' pregnancy. Trethowan suggests two possible explanations for this: (1) there is really no relationship between anxiety and physical symptoms, or (2) physical symptoms are the outcome of repression and conversion of the anxiety. Further research suggests the second explanation is likely in some cases.

PROVIDING EMOTIONAL SUPPORT AND COMMUNICATING EFFECTIVELY WITH ALL FAMILY MEMBERS

The primary task for both parents at this period is to learn about and adapt to the pregnancy and to maintain a satisfactory relationship with each other, and if other children are present, with them too. Pregnancy is a crucial period for the development of the parent-child relationship and for interpersonal relationships within the family. "During pregnancy, both the intrapersonal forces in the pregnant woman and the interpersonal forces in her family are in a state of disequilibrium" (Caplan, 1959, p. 46).

The increase in size of family membership necessitates changes in the entire psychodynamic system. The number of relationships increases, and "emotional contacts and material commodities" have to be shared (Howells, 1972a). The occurrence of pregnancy and childbirth has the potential for enhancing or destroying the functioning of the family group. Since first-time parents must assume the parenting role without any prior experience in such a role, they tend to take on their roles based on

PREGNANCY AND FETAL DEVELOPMENT

FIGURE 2-7

experiences in their families of origin. If these previous experiences differ for husband and wife they can cause conflict among the parents.

Emotional Responses to Pregnancy WIFE The woman's emotional changes occurring during pregnancy can be attributed to hormonal and general metabolic changes as well as to psychogenic variations. The secretion of progesterone during pregnancy may be one of the factors related to the general introversion and passivity of the pregnant woman as well as her primary narcissism (Benedek, 1970a) There is common agreement that all women have both positive and negative attitudes toward their pregnancy and that during this time they experience an increase in anxiety or tension (Grimm, 1967). There is increasing support from research findings to indicate a pregnant woman's emotional state can influence the activity level of the fetus (Sontag, 1944) and newborn infant (Ferreira, 1960; Turner, 1956); cause spontaneous abortion

(Dunbar, 1954; Weil and Tupper, 1960); and predispose the developing fetus to anomalies (Strean and Peer, 1956).

Studies of pregnant women indicate a wide variety in the content of their fears and conflicts. The most commonly mentioned are related to death or injury of mother or child, abnormality of child, difficulty of labor, inadequacy as a mother, changed marital or family relationships, and financial problems.

There is some evidence that knowledge of a woman's attitudes toward aspects of feminine development are predictive of attitudes and reactions to childbirth. Results of Newson's interviews (1955) of 123 postpartum mothers revealed intercorrelations between feelings toward menstruation, sex, childbirth, breast-feeding, infant care, and the desirability of being a woman. "Positive" attitudes in one area were related to positive attitudes in other areas.

Studies about the relationship of personality variables assessed early in pregnancy and postpartum adjustment and attitudes toward the child are scanty, and it is difficult to draw conclusions from them (Grimm, 1967). However, personality variables measured early in pregnancy have been found to relate to the woman's emotional adjustment and the occurrences of a normal range of physiological symptoms later in pregnancy, so that it is possible to make some predictions of the course of pregnancy on the basis of these early psychological measurements. Nilsson (1972) found that 17 percent of 165 randomly selected Swedish women showed signs of mental disturbance (e.g., depression, anxiety states) during pregnancy. Most of these difficulties were of a "reactive" nature, that is, associated with unsatisfactory environmental factors (such as unmarried, unsatisfactory housing, low social class). These women had fewer histories of dysmenorrhea and sickness during pregnancy than women without disturbances.

Caplan (1961) describes a number of emotional changes that occur during pregnancy. These include:

1 *Mood swings* that appear to have no relation to external factors are common throughout pregnancy. Emotional lability, irritability, and sensitivity are increased.
2 *Introversion and passivity* begin toward the end of the first trimester and gradually increase in intensity to reach a peak around the seventh and eighth month. Women who have difficulty accepting this behavior in themselves tend to have difficulty later in their early relationships with their babies.
3 *Ego-id equilibrium* is altered somewhat towards the end of the first trimester, and this change continues into the second or third week

PREGNANCY AND FETAL DEVELOPMENT

post partum. There is a surfacing of previously unconscious needs, wishes, and fantasies. The woman becomes preoccupied with early childhood memories of old conflicts that begin to emerge into consciousness. The problems that emerge most often are related to the woman's mother or siblings or those related to sex and masturbation.

Caplan (1959) stresses several important aspects regarding this change in equilibrium. First, it is associated with relatively little anxiety, and the anxiety that is present tends to be of a free-floating nature. It may be that this anxiety accounts for many of the superstitions and fears of pregnancy. Second, the fears that occur are directly related to feelings of guilt concerning conflicts about the infant's health, although fears of her own health may also occur. She may be afraid that one of them will die during birth or that the baby will be deformed. Since not all these fears are reality based, they usually continue even when reassurance is given about the likely outcome for mother and baby. Third, as these old conflicts are reviewed during pregnancy, there is a possibility the woman may find a more satisfactory solution for them.

Various studies indicate a relationship between anxiety during pregnancy and difficulty of labor (Davids et al., 1961), the development of colic in the neonate (Lakin, 1957), and the emotionality of children (Sontag, 1944). Women who have known someone who delivered an abnormal child or someone who has had a miscarriage have statistically higher anxiety scores than women who have not known such persons (Burstein et al., 1974).

Studies of Frommer and O'Shea (1973) and by Wolkind et al. (1976) indicate there is an association between early childhood separations from parents, especially if the family situation remained disrupted, and later emotional difficulties. Although we need to be cautious against considering this a cause-and-effect relationship, such early separations can provide a sensitive index of other experiences that might lead to these difficulties.

Feelings of stress and anxiety are inevitable consequences of the rapid changes taking place during pregnancy. Despite this, however, many women experience an overwhelming sense of ecstasy at this time (Colman and Colman, 1971).

HUSBAND Caplan (1961) points out that the "upsets" of the pregnant woman are especially likely to produce upsets in her husband's relationship with her. Consequently, he is often less able to support her during this period than when she is not pregnant.

The results of an unpublished master's study by McCorkel indicated

CHILD AND FAMILY DEVELOPMENT

that for each of the 20 expectant husbands interviewed, changes occurred throughout the pregnancy (Jessner et al., 1970). Three types of reactions were delineated based on the men's primary orientations toward marriage and pregnancy. Husbands with a *romantic orientation* tended to approach their coming parenthood casually while those who were *career-oriented* regarded their changing role as a burden that interfered with professional responsibilities. The *family-oriented* husbands accepted their new responsibilities easily and looked forward to their new roles. These prospective fathers followed a pattern similar to their wives in identifying the reality of the baby. In the first stage the image of the baby was vague. With the onset of quickening and fetal movement felt by the husband, the infant became more real. The third stage of reality occurred with the changes in his wife's shape.

Maintaining Satisfactory Relationship with Spouse Relationships of husbands and wives during pregnancy take several forms. Some men work fewer hours to be home more with their wives before the birth. Some couples indicate they paid more attention to or talked more about their relationship, hopes, and feelings about the baby (Fein, 1976).

Changes in sexual desire and performance usually occur during pregnancy. The woman may either increase or decrease her sexual desire during pregnancy, and her performance may become lessened or better. Falicov's study (1973) of sexual adjustments during pregnancy revealed that during the first trimester there was a decline in frequency of coitus, sexual desire, and eroticism. Although there was some increase during the second and early part of the third trimester it was still below the prepregnant baseline. Reasons women gave for these changes included breast tenderness, fear of harming the fetus or of premature labor, vaginal numbness, pain on penetration, physical discomforts (tiredness, sleepiness, heartburn, nausea), and sex not being satisfying due to modified positions or restriction of movements.

Some men expressed jealousy and fear of losing their wives' love when sexual advances were discouraged or unenthusiastically tolerated. Some husbands experience a greater need for sexual intercourse during the second or third trimester, while others may be deterred by the woman's changing shape (Jessner et al., 1970).

Medical and nursing texts generally recommend cessation of sexual relationships somewhere between 3 and 8 weeks prior to delivery and 3 weeks to 3 months following delivery (Quirk and Hassanein, 1973). Studies by Pugh and Fernandez (1953) and Quirk and Hassanein (1973) concluded that abstinence is not a necessity for the healthy woman as

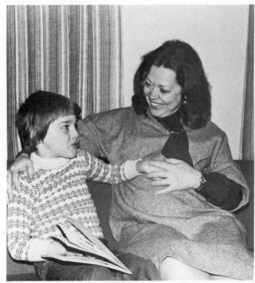

FIGURE 2-8   by Debra Hymovich

FIGURE 2-8A

by Debra Hymovich

there was no increased incidence of complications for women who abstained and those who did not.

Wife beating is known to occur during pregnancy. Van Stolk (1976) suggests this may be an indication of a dimension of child abuse; it may be the husband's attempt to terminate the pregnancy and thus avoid the impending stress of another child.

Preparing Siblings for New Baby Parents prepare their children for the anticipated baby in different ways. Some tell the young child that the new baby will be his or her baby or that the infant will be a playmate. Other parents may tell stories about the "stork" bringing a new baby, while others read and discuss one or more of the children's books about new babies. Still others may not prepare their child at all, often because they believe the child is too young. Some parents discuss the advantages and disadvantages of having a new baby and some of the feelings they may experience.

Relating to Extended Family Relationships with relatives need to be reoriented in light of the family changes taking place. Relatives may compete with each other in giving gifts and advice. Advice may consist of "old wives' tales" or may be in conflict with that of the professional. Many young couples are denied much of the emotional support they might receive from their families of origin because of separations occasioned by moving.

Howells (1972a) summarizes some of the findings about the effects of grandmothers on the pregnant women. In one study (Robertson, 1946) it was found that vomiting in pregnancy tended not to recur when the expectant woman's mother was removed from the woman. It was also noted that pregnant women talk a great deal about their mother's pregnancies and deliveries and that they claim to know all the details of their own delivery, especially if it is related to a situation in which either the mother or baby "nearly died."

MAINTAINING AND ADAPTING FAMILY ORGANIZATION AND
MANAGEMENT TO MEET CHANGING NEEDS

The multiple tasks of housekeeping and child care can be overwhelming to some mothers during pregnancy (Stolz, 1967). If the family group is large enough, older siblings may take on parenting roles in relation to the younger children.

FUNCTIONING IN THE COMMUNITY

Social activities may be curtailed or stopped to accommodate the changes occurring during pregnancy. Contact with groups that conduct expectant parents' classes is often made, and the couple or woman becomes involved in these classes.

EFFECT OF SELECTED VARIABLES ON DEVELOPMENT DURING PREGNANCY

As so thoroughly documented, there is a cluster of social and biological factors that is associated with complications of pregnancy in general, and low-birth-weight babies in particular (Ambramowicz and Kass, 1966; Birch and Gussow, 1970; Brent and Harris, 1976; Handel, 1979; Richardson and Guttmacher, 1967). These include being (reproductively speaking) very young or very old at time of conception, being unmarried, being poor, being a member of a minority group, having four or more children with short intervals between pregnancies, being small in stature, receiving no prenatal care, having a poor weight gain during pregnancy, being a heavy smoker, having a chronic urinary tract infection or other chronic illness, having a past history of previous complications of pregnancy, or being addicted to drugs or alcohol.

FIGURE 2-9

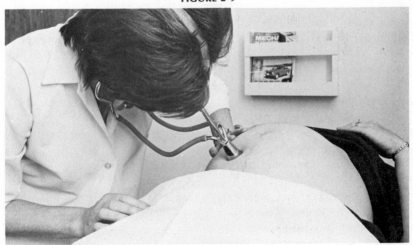

Among the factors affecting parenthood are socioeconomic status, religion, race, cultural background, and type of conjugal-role relationships (Handel, 1979). Because of the complex nature of the variables affecting development, we caution the reader to recognize that although we are artificially presenting them as separate entities, their interrelationship cannot be ignored.

Age of Parents

Women and their offspring at either end of the scale (below 17 and over 40 years) are at risk during the childbearing process (Nadelson, 1973).

ADOLESCENCE

Approximately 200,000 school-aged girls deliver babies each year, and this number is increasing by about 3000 annually (Howard, 1971). It is estimated that 1 of every 10 girls in the United States will become a mother while of high school age or younger. The majority of school-aged pregnant girls are married. About 15 percent of these girls place their babies for adoption, while the remainder choose to keep their infants. Many unmarried adolescents have chosen to have their babies even when legal abortion is an available option (Presser, 1974). Generally, the adolescent who becomes pregnant is still struggling with Erikson's developmental task of establishing her own identity while at the same time she is facing the additional crisis of generativity (creating and nurturing life) and is very apt to still be coping with the task of intimacy.

In a study of 229 urban, black, unmarried, 13- to 18-year-olds in Baltimore, 66 percent chose to deliver their baby, while 34 percent chose abortion. Of the girls choosing to deliver their infant, 80 percent were found to have either medium or high self-esteem as measured by a 10-item scale. The girls with low self-esteem were more likely to have an abortion. The girls who chose to deliver had a significantly longer relationship with their boyfriends than those who chose abortion, and over 60 percent reported their boyfriends were going to support the baby. Generally, those choosing to deliver the baby were of lower socioeconomic class and had dropped out of school prior to the pregnancy (Fischman, 1975).

In terms of diet, McGanity and colleagues' (1969) study of 800 pregnant teens found that two of every three adolescents increased food intake during pregnancy and four of five altered their eating patterns, especially with respect to decreased amount of sweets, starch, fats, and salts. Pica (in the form of ingestion of starch, clay, dirt, soil, and refrig-

PREGNANCY AND FETAL DEVELOPMENT

erator frost) was ingested by 28 percent of the prospective mothers; 75 percent ate these things because they liked them and 25 percent did so for cultural or other reasons. With the exception of calcium and iron, the main nutrient intake met or exceeded the 1964 Recommended Dietary Allowances of the National Research Council. Significant deprivation of iron, vitamins A and C, and riboflavin were found, and mean level values for hemoglobin, hematocrit, and mean corpuscular hemoglobin concentration were significantly lower in the black girls.

How much getting pregnant as a teenager adds to the risk of pregnancy and delivery by itself is unclear, as pregnancy in this age group is associated with other variables affecting outcome. The majority of teenage pregnancies, especially in the unmarried group, occur in members of the lower socioeconomic levels. Of these unmarried girls, 60 percent are nonwhite and 40 percent are white (Osofsky, 1968).

Some studies indicate an increased health risk for teenage pregnancies, including a higher incidence of toxemia, prolonged labor, prematurity, and neonatal mortality (Dickens et al., 1973; Osofsky, 1968). However, in the study of 800 pregnant teenagers by McGanity and colleagues (1969), the rates for prematurity and neonatal mortality were similar to that of regular staff patients.

OLDER MOTHERS

The risk of congenital malformations increases with maternal age. Trisomy 21 (Down's syndrome) is the most classic example. The risk for this commonest single cause of mental retardation increases from about 1 in 300 for women 35 to 40 years of age to about 1 in 100 for women over 40. Other chromosomal anomalies may also occur. Women in the 35- to 39-year age range have about a 1.7 chance in 100 of having a child with some type of fetal chromosomal abnormality, and those 40 to 45 years have a chance of about 3 in 100.

Nutritional Status

Both the long-term nutritional status of the mother prior to her pregnancy and her nutritional intake during the period of gestation will influence the intrauterine weight gain of the fetus and its subsequent weight and nutritional status (Eastman and Jackson, 1968; Thomson et al., 1970).

Although there are varied reports of infants born with specific deficiency diseases, such as beriberi, rickets, or scurvy related to maternal diet (Watson and Lowrey, 1967), the most common effect on fetal development of maternal malnutrition appears to be on birth weight. Mothers who gain less than 10 pounds during pregnancy have a significant increase in low-birth-weight babies when compared to those gaining 20 to 30 pounds (Bergner and Susser, 1970; Brent and Harris, 1976; Pitkin et al., 1972). Since poor weight gain is related to a number of other social and cultural variables, a causal relationship cannot be established, but studies on the effect of direct supplementation in Guatemala and Montreal support the notion that ensuring adequate maternal nutrition will significantly decrease the number of low-birth-weight babies that are born (Brent and Harris, 1976; Winick, 1974). For example, Perkins (1977) reports some of the results of the unpublished study conducted in Montreal by Higgins et al. from 1963 to 1971. During this time, 1636 indigent pregnant mothers attending a public clinic were given nutrition counseling that resulted in an average daily food intake of 32 grams of protein and 530 calories. They found that the mean birth weight, incidence of prematurity, and prenatal infant mortality were similar to those of private patients delivering at the same hospital and significantly lower for infants of mothers attending other public clinics who did not receive nutrition counseling. Two-thirds of the study mothers had 5 years or less of education yet gave birth to infants with the highest mean birth weights, thus demonstrating the effectiveness of nutritional counseling for educationally disadvantaged women.

Besides decreasing birth weight, there is evidence from several studies that serious malnutrition during pregnancy may result in increased rates of stillbirths and congenital malformations (Burke et al., 1949; Jeans et al., 1955). There is also reasonably good evidence that severe malnutrition during pregnancy and/or the first year of life leads to decreased brain weight and cell number (Martin, 1973; Ricciuti, 1973; Winick, 1974). However, the relationship between these findings and the functioning of the child in terms of his or her intellectual development and behavior is considerably less clear because of the association of nutritional deprivation with a variety of other social and biological insults. After a review of the available evidence Ricciuti concludes:

> Impairment of intellectual and psychological development in children as a consequence of protein-calorie malnutrition appears most likely to occur and to be rather severe and long lasting to the extent that nutritional deprivation begins in the first year, is very severe and continues for an extended period of time without nutritional remediation. On the other hand, severe early malnutrition which is subject to adequate nutritional remediation within the first 5 or 6 months of life appears relatively unlikely to reduce the intellectual functioning below normal or near normal levels.

Even in examples of the first instance, however, Ricciuti raises the possibility that remediation programs that provide enrichment of the social and learning environment, as well as calories and protein, may reverse many of the deficits thought to be the basis of permanent damage.

Maternal Health Status and Habits

INGESTION OF DRUGS AND ALCOHOL

Surveys of pregnant mothers indicate that in some groups an average of about four drugs per person are taken during the first few months of pregnancy (Brent and Harris, 1976); only a few of these drugs have been shown to have direct effects on the developing fetus but the potential hazard is great. The effect of thalidomide in producing infants with phocomelia is one of the most dramatic effects (McBride, 1961; Taussig, 1962). A number of other drugs have been implicated as well (Connely, 1964). Masculinization of the female fetus associated with administration of progesterone-containing compounds during pregnancy is another well-documented example (Wilkins et al., 1958).

Besides effects early in pregnancy, drugs administered just prior to delivery can also have a harmful effect. Neonatal thrombocytopenia from thiazide drugs and hyperbilirubinemia from long-acting sulfonamides are two examples. Reviews by Lucey (1961; McKay and Lucey, 1964) summarize much of these data. Even more frightening is when mothers inadvertently ingest toxic amounts of products that have contaminated water or food supplies, such as happened in Japan with mercury (Brent and Harris, 1976; Snyder, 1971).

The physical effects of maternal narcotic addiction, however, appear to be limited largely to the neonatal period, when withdrawal symptoms in the addicted newborn become manifest. Symptoms such as yawning and sneezing, restlessness, irritability, tremors, and occasionally convulsions occur and can result in the death of the infant if they are unrecognized and untreated (Cobrink et al., 1959).

Chronic alcoholism in mothers has been associated with congenital anomalies in newborn infants and growth disturbances (Jones et al., 1973).

SMOKING

A number of studies provide evidence that cigarette smoking by pregnant women is related to infants of lower birth weight, shorter length, and smaller head circumference. Women smoking a pack of cigarettes a day or more give birth to infants having significantly lower birth weights (average of 300 grams) than those born to nonsmokers (Brent and Harris, 1976; Butler, 1974; Davies et al., 1976; Dunn et al., 1976).

INTRAUTERINE INFECTION

Infection during the first trimester with rubella, toxoplasmosis, or cyto-megalic inclusion disease can have devastating results. The most fre-quent abnormalities of the congenital rubella syndrome are deafness, blindness, microphthalmia, congenital heart disease, microcephaly, and mental retardation (Connely, 1964; Michaels and Mellin, 1960). Micro-cephaly, microphthalmia, and hydrocephalus are the most common serious malformations in toxoplasmosis and cytomegalic inclusion dis-ease (Eichenwald, 1957; Hanshaw, 1966). The effects of other types of infections are covered in a recent review by Krugman and Gershon (1975).

CHRONIC ILLNESS

Chronic illness in the mother may increase the frequency of complica-tions of pregnancy and neonatal morbidity and mortality. Diabetes is the classic example, with increased risk of fetal and neonatal deaths from such complications as congenital malformations, the respiratory distress syndrome, and hypoglycemia. Chronic urinary tract infections also seem to increase the risk of prematurity and other complications (Abramowicz and Kass, 1966; Brent and Harris, 1976).

EXPOSURE TO RADIATION

There is substantial evidence that exposure to large doses of radiation in the first trimester of pregnancy increases the risk of developing micro-cephaly and mental retardation in the newborn period and leukemia at a later date (Brent and Harris, 1976; Miller, 1956; Murphy, 1947; Plummer, 1952; Rugh, 1958; Yamazaki et al., 1954). Such exposures have resulted from whole-body radiation associated with the atomic bomb attacks on Hiroshima and Nagasaki or from pelvic irradiation as-sociated with radium or x-ray therapy to pelvic tumors. Other studies indicate there is little risk of congenital malformation from diagnostic x-ray when exposure is kept below 5 rads (Brent and Harris, 1976). Exposure from procedures such as upper gastrointestinal (GI) series or intravenous pyelograms (IVPs) are substantially below this level and

PREGNANCY AND FETAL DEVELOPMENT

probably carry little or no risk. However, Uchida et al. (1968) have provided some evidence that even doses in this range may increase slightly the number of children born with chromosomal anomalies.

GENETIC DISORDERS

There are a number of genetic disorders that are related to congenital malformation and intrauterine growth retardation. Sensitization of an Rh-negative mother and development of erythroblastosis fetalis in infants is now seldom a problem because it can be prevented.

Socioeconomic-Cultural Variables

Poverty is frequently associated with poor health care services (Milio, 1967; Strauss, 1970; Tompkins, 1970). Cultural barriers to health care are multiple. Maternity care is based largely on white middle-class values and beliefs.

In 1971, 12.5 percent of all families in the United States had an annual income under $3000, distributed among 9.9 percent of the white population and 30.9 percent of the nonwhite population (Wallace, 1970). The expectant mother from a poverty family is usually a poor reproductive risk because of her own lifelong poor nutrition and lack of education (Perkins, 1977). These women have a high incidence of malnutrition anemia, chronic vascular disease, contracted pelves, toxemia, and other problems.

Wallace (1970) indicated a close relationship between socioeconomic status and infant mortality. She noted that in 1963 the average infant mortality rate of the low-income group in 17 states was 19 percent higher than the national average. Low birth weight was also associated with low socioeconomic status.

Rosenwaike (1971) found that the incidence of low birth weight varied inversely with the educational level of the mother. This relationship was maintained even when controlling for the mother's age, birth, order, and source and timing of antepartum care. In 1973, of those white mothers giving birth, 73.3 percent had completed 12 years or more of formal schooling while only 51.1 percent of the black mothers had completed 12 years (USDHEW, 1975, p. 4).

Racial differences are noted for birthrate, maternal and prenatal mortality, and perinatal morbidity. It is difficult to sort out how much the differences noted are related to being a member of a minority group in terms of race or because of low income and education.

In 1973, almost 75 percent of white mothers began their prenatal care during the first trimester compared with only 51.1 percent of black mothers. In addition, only 1.1 percent of white mothers received no care while 3.4 percent of black mothers received no care (USDHEW, Statistics Report, January 30, 1975). As expected there was a higher percentage of low-birth-weight infants born to mothers receiving no prenatal care (21.1 percent) compared with those receiving such care (7.2 percent).

FAMILY DISORGANIZATION AND STRESS

Various studies suggest a relationship between emotional factors and obstetrical complications (Pajntar, 1972). Some of these effects are discussed later in this chapter.

CLINICAL APPLICATIONS

Ideally, a developmentally oriented health care delivery system should begin with a program of education about child and family development for children and adolescents long before they become pregnant. This

FIGURE 2-10

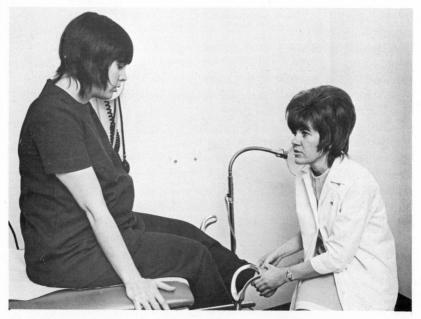

PREGNANCY AND FETAL DEVELOPMENT

would include information about human sexuality, the physiology of reproduction, child spacing, fetal development, mother-infant bonding at birth, and subsequent family and child development. Immunizing young children against rubella infection is also an important preventive measure. This could be done in association with the school systems in the geographic areas being served.

Conducting Health Visits during Pregnancy

ASSESSMENT

Baseline physical data are obtained from the woman on her first visit regardless of the trimester. Such data include (1) past medical and reproductive history, (2) date of last menstrual period, (3) average weight prior to pregnancy and current height and weight, (4) signs of pregnancy, (5) physical examination, (6) pelvic examination, and (7) blood and urine analyses.

Systematic psychological screening should take place during the first routine examination of every pregnant woman (Baker, 1967; Horsley, 1972; Howells, 1972a). Such screening should include details of the woman's developmental history and family background. A suggested assessment guide is presented in Figure 2-11. This is discussed more fully later in this chapter.

PROVIDING EDUCATION AND ESTABLISHING AND MAINTAINING SUPPORTIVE RELATIONSHIPS

Early contact with a mother having her first pregnancy is desirable for many reasons. As we have seen in the section on fetal development, during the first 3 months the fetus is most vulnerable to toxic influences, and educating mothers about the hazards to the fetus of drugs, alcohol, x-rays, smoking, and poor nutrition could prevent the formation of some birth defects and decrease the incidence of low-birth-weight babies. Such early visits can also be used to prevent psychological complications as well by:

1 Helping the parents to understand the woman's physiological, psychological, and social changes
2 Assisting each partner in learning how they can support one another and keep communication open
3 Preparing the family (physically and emotionally) for the labor and delivery experience

Basic data	Case reference

Dates of:

(a) Birth ....

(b) Marriage..

(c) Expected date of delivery ....

(d) Whether planned/unplanned?................

(e) If planned, how long trying to conceive?.....

Potential stresses

(1) Old for childbearing

(2) Unmarried*

(3) Shotgun wedding

(4) Attempted abortion or miscarriage*

(5) Relative infertility

Family history:

(f) Parents' ages, health (mental/physical)........
....

(g) Siblings' ages, health, marriage, etc...........
....
....

(h) Family history of obstetric trouble.............
....
....

(i) Death, divorce, remarriage of parents ....

(6) Any serious illness or abnormality ....

(7) Maternal or sibling obstetric complications ....

(8) Broken home in childhood

(9) Bereavement during this pregnancy*

Psychosocial supports:

(j) Husband's age, health, occupation and whether unemployed ....

(k) Husband's attitude to wife before, and during pregnancy...............................

(l) Husband's absence due to death, desertion, drafting overseas, etc...........................
....

(m) How often does she see her mother, or other close relative?

(n) Racial intolerance?

(o) Psychiatric illness in either partner?

(10) Economic insecurity

(11) No emotional support*

(12) No support*

(13) No communication* (lonely or isolated in top flat)

Subjective factors and changes perceived by the woman:

(p) Bizarre appetites, craving, irritable, altered affections, more emotional....................
....

(q) Pregnancy sickness (time and degree) ....
....

(r) Sleep and dreams ....

(s) What sex does she hope for, and what name or names has she chosen?....................

(t) What are her feelings about breast-feeding and other bodily functions? ....

(u) Any other problems?...........................

(14) Hazard of those fears which are commonly concealed unless she is given help to reveal them

FIGURE 2-11 Pregnancy assessment record. Score 1 point for each stress factor, 2 points for each marked with an asterisk (*).

0–1 = low risk

2 = high risk

3 or more = very high risk

[J. G. Howells, (Ed.) *Modern perspectives in psycho-obstetrics,* New York: Brunner/Mazel, 1972, p. 301. Used with permission.]

4 Helping parents recognize the individuality and needs of their infant and to develop skills to meet these needs

5 Helping the family move into new roles and relationships with a minimum of anxiety, conflict, and frustration

In providing guidance during pregnancy, some topics are readily approached in a specific trimester while other subjects may occur at various times throughout the pregnancy. Acton (1977) has prepared a table illustrating the approximate time a pregnant woman experiences concerns or needs specific information (see Figure 2-12). As a general rule, whenever a woman asks about a topic it should be discussed at that time as it is an indication of her readiness.

Around the end of the first trimester, introversion and passivity begin to increase gradually and to peak around the seventh and eighth months. At this time the woman has an increased need for love and affection as well as for help with household chores. This is an area where anticipatory guidance in the form of manipulating the emotional environment is very important (Caplan, 1959, p. 49). The care taker can encourage the family members (i.e., husband or mother) to provide the additional support since it is generally believed that a woman's ability to give love and affection to her child may be impaired if these needs are not met. Her husband can be helped to see that he may need to be more demonstrative during this time and that this is one way in which he can be an active partner in preparing for the baby.

It is recommended that at least two or three joint interviews be held with the husband and wife to discuss their feelings, to explain that many women experience emotional changes during pregnancy, and that these behaviors will disappear after delivery (Caplan, 1961; Horsley, 1972). Specific topics should include the sudden and unexplainable mood changes; irritability and emotional lability; and the passivity that frequently occur. The husband needs to know of these in advance, and the woman should be helped not to feel guilty.

A discussion of possible changes in sexual responses and behavior should also be discussed, since difficult marital situations may occur as a result of these changes (Caplan, 1959). Coitus promotes a feeling of closeness between partners and helps satisfy certain dependency needs of the pregnant woman, such as her increased need for nurturance (Caplan, 1973). In their study of expectant women, Quirk and Hassanein (1973) found that 66 percent of the mothers had received no information from any health professional concerning sexual responses and behavior.

Effective communication techniques to help alleviate anxiety for the

	First trimester 0–14th week	Second trimester 15–26th week	Third trimester 27–40th week
Body changes during pregnancy	▨	▨	▨
Minor discomforts			
Frequent urination	▨		▨
Heartburn			▨
Nausea	▨		
Backache		▨	▨
Dyspnea			▨
Varicose veins		▨	▨
Cramps	▨		
Constipation	▨		
Edema			▨
Vaginal discharge	▨	▨	▨
Fatigue	▨		▨
Nutrition and appropriate weight gain	▨	▨	▨
General hygiene			
Rest, relaxation, sleep	▨	▨	▨
Exercise	▨	▨	▨
Traveling	▨	▨	
Care of skin and breasts	▨	▨	▨
Douches (told *no*)	▨	▨	
Marital relations	▨	▨	▨
Smoking, use of drugs and/or alcohol	▨	▨	
Parents classes	▨	▨	▨
Discuss attitudes toward			
Pregnancy	▨		
Labor			▨
Newborn			▨
Fetal growth and development		▨	
Financial problems	▨		▨
Breathing exercises, etc.			▨
Signs of approaching labor			
Lightening			▨
False labor contractions			▨
Show			▨
Rupture of amnionic membranes			▨
Danger signals			
Vaginal bleeding		▨	▨
Abdominal pain		▨	▨
Swelling of face, hands, feet		▨	▨
Severe headache		▨	▨
Visual disturbance		▨	▨
Rupture of amnionic membranes		▨	▨
Breast or bottle feeding			▨
Labor and delivery Explanation of postpartum checks			▨
Preparation for arrival of newborn		▨	▨
Infant care		▨	▨
Family planning			▨
Immediate postpartum period			
Postpartum blues			▨
After pains			▨
Breast care			▨
Episeotomy care			▨
Circumcision care			▨
PKU test			▨
Tour of OB area			▨

FIGURE 2-12 This bar graph demonstrates the approximate times during pregnancy a woman will experience concerns or needs information in each category. From these data, a plan for teaching is made to present the information prior to her need, enabling the woman to better understand and be prepared for her experience. [*Reprinted with permission from J. P. Clausen, et al. (Eds.), Maternity Nursing Today, 2d ed., New York: McGraw-Hill, 1977, Chap. 15, by Rosie L. Acton.*]

pregnant woman include discussion, reassurance, explanation, suggestion, reeducation, and conditioning (Goodrich, 1965). Discussion means allowing opportunities for the mother-to-be to express her feelings and attitudes, not just an exchange of complaints and treatment. Providing reassurance begins with obtaining a history and performing a physical examination, followed by continued positive statements that the pregnancy is proceeding normally (if this is the case).

Since fears are not reality based, they usually continue even after reassurance with reality (that there is very little likelihood of having a deformed baby and that the number of women who die during childbirth is very small). It helps to let the woman know she will not fully believe you (Caplan, 1961, p. 83).

The point at which the possibility of difficulties (e.g., breech delivery, large baby) is communicated is a debatable issue. The amount of information given should be based on careful assessment of the individual woman's capacity to adjust to it. On the other hand, care needs to be taken not to stimulate anxiety by adopting a noncommittal attitude and giving too little or no information (Goodrich, 1965).

Maternal Nutrition   Current recommendations are that enough calories be taken to support an average weight gain of between 22 and 27 pounds (10 to 12 kilograms) (Barnes, 1978, Pitkin, et al., 1972). This will require an increased intake of calories of about 10 to 15 percent. About 30 grams per day of this extra food should be in the form of protein.

To prevent iron deficiency and megaloblastic anemias, extra iron and folic acid are also recommended. The recommended dosage for these is about 30 to 60 milligrams of ferrous sulfate per day, or equivalent, and about 0.2 to 0.4 milligrams of folate (Barnes, 1978).

Other nutritional substances required during pregnancy can generally be provided from regular dietary sources. For example, 1 quart of milk per day provides all the recommended calcium and vitamin D requirements and about one-half the protein. A more detailed discussion of diet is available in Brewer (1967).

Since almost all the caries-susceptible areas of the primary teeth are calcified after birth, the administration of fluoride to pregnant women will not affect caries formation (Kraus and Jordan, 1965).

A pregnant woman should be referred to a nutritionist or dietitian if she requires a therapeutic diet for a preexisting medical condition, a condition that develops during pregnancy, or unusual eating patterns (e.g., vegetarian) (Bradford, 1977).

During pregnancy, women need assistance and support regarding their feeding decision. An adequate lactation history and the woman's interest should be obtained. If desired, the mother-to-be should have an opportunity to meet and talk with mothers who have breast-fed successfully. Information should be provided through planned education programs, personal discussion, and use of appropriate films or books (Newton and Newton, 1972).

Mothers should be informed of the relative costs of nutrients to support lactation as compared with artificial feeding. McKigney (1971) indicates that by moderately increasing her normal diet, the woman will take in the nutrients required for lactation. The Consumer and Food Economics Division of the U.S. Department of Agriculture (1969) has developed food plans showing how a nutritionally adequate diet can be supplied at low, moderate, and liberal cost levels. The cost of an economical weekly diet for a lactating woman, based on 1970 food prices, was $7.55. Approximately one-third of that diet ($2.52) is presumed necessary to support lactation.

Guidance and Counseling   Horsley (1972) indicates that the emotional needs of expectant mothers are the subject of more disagreement than any other aspect of obstetric care. To help prevent postpartum emotional complications, the following recommendations regarding the role of professional workers during pregnancy and the postpartum period are suggested (Caplan, 1961; Gordon et al., 1965).

1   Strengthen the mother's ego by accepting her as she is, with her own characteristics and idiosyncrasies.
2   Manipulate the emotional environment to provide support for the expectant woman.
3   Provide anticipatory guidance concerning the individuality of the expected infant.

Educating the pregnant woman to realize that when the baby comes along it will be an individual in its own right, separate and different from everyone else she has dealt with in her life in the past. It is not the embodiment of her sister, or of her father, or of her mother. It is not a symbol of sex, or of a damaged sexual apparatus. It is not a cross to bear. It is none of these things. (Caplan, 1961, p. 86)

4   Provide parents with anticipatory guidance concerning the usual physical and emotional changes of pregnancy, labor, delivery, and child development. Support for the husband during pregnancy is

important but not only for his own comfort and for the sake of the marriage but also for the future father-child relationship (Caplan, 1959, p. 54). If there is a disordered relationship between husband and wife, especially around the end of pregnancy, there tends to be disturbed mother-child relationship. The husband should be told of the mood swings and emotional irritability and sensitivity in advance and the woman helped not to feel guilty (Caplan, 1959).

5 Encourage her to get adequate rest and sleep (easier said than done!). Some suggestions for this include retaining outside interests but curtailing responsibilities, not becoming overinvolved in unimportant tasks or overconcerned with keeping up appearances, and not becoming involved in nursing relatives or others during this period.

6 Suggest making friends with other couples who are experienced in child rearing.

7 Encourage her to discuss plans and worries with others—family, friends, professionals.

8 Recommend that the family not plan to move soon after the baby's arrival.

9 Provide help when a specific crisis arises.

Education for expectant parents can be provided in a variety of ways, including (1) classes sponsored by community agencies, (2) informal "bench" conferences in clinic waiting rooms, (3) multimedia presentations, (4) a one-to-one approach, and (5) mass media (i.e., booklets, pamphlets, television). There are many pamphlets and booklets published by the U.S. Department of Health, Education and Welfare, State Departments of Health, food and drug companies, and others. Education programs may be planned for various audiences such as mothers only, fathers only, both parents together, or adolescents.

Brant (1972) recommends separate classes for multigravid and primigravid women. He does not believe multigravid women need, or have the time for, an entire series of classes. The major needs of multigravidas are to express anxieties related to previous labors and become reconciled to any previous difficulties; to learn how multigravid labor differs from that of a first labor; and to learn how to cope with or avoid difficulties with the coming labor.

A variety of terms have been used to describe the psychoprophylactic techniques of preparing women for painless childbirth. These techniques are based on the Pavlovian concept for continued reflex training that enables a patient to block painful sensation by providing a counterstimulus at the appropriate time (Buxton, 1962). A variety of techniques have been successful in preparing women for natural childbirth; these techniques include hypnosis, autogenic training, the Read technique, psychoprophylactic methods, and ego reinforcement in labor (Friedman, 1972).

Friedman (1972) found a correlation between motivation and successful outcome of natural childbirth in a study of 130 women who voluntarily expressed a desire for such an experience. Women with certain gynecologic and psychosomatic disorders (i.e., severe dysmenorrhea, infertility) had a high failure rate. Of the women who were primarily motivated by "curiosity," 38 percent required anesthesia. The desire to breast-feed was considered a favorable prognostic sign because 31 percent of those who delivered successfully wanted to breast-feed as compared with only 3 percent in the unsuccessful group. Pain itself was not eliminated by training, but was made more tolerable. Of the mothers interviewed, 89 percent indicated some pain was present during labor and delivery but only 6 percent saw this as an obstacle during parturition. The women interviewed indicated the three most important factors needed to maintain "a proper mental and emotional attitude" during birth were their physicians, husbands, and their own self-confidence.

There are conflicting findings regarding the value of prenatal education in easing the transition to parenthood. Brim (1959) indicated that such preparation is not of the value desired, and booklets and leaflets given to some expectant or new parents without discussion apparently are of little or no worth (Brooks et al., 1964; Downs and Fernbach, 1973). Other researchers (Horowitz and Horowitz, 1967; Kemp, 1970) indicate that improved patient management usually results from prepared childbirth classes. Colman and Colman (1971) reported that when prenatal classes offered a chance for open-ended discussion, fears regarding pain, loss of self-control, changes in body image, and mutilation were eased. Friedman (1972) found that women who have been adequately prepared for natural childbirth had easier labors and deliveries than women without such preparation.

A recent study by Zax et al. (1975) suggests the effects of a childbirth education program patterned after the Lamaze method had relatively few beneficial effects on overall maternal attitudes (measured by MAPI, the Maternal Attitudes to Pregnancy Instrument), anxiety during labor (measured by the IPAT Anxiety Scale Questionnaire), and duration of labor. Significant differences between prepared and unprepared women were found on the subscale of the MAPI reflecting strong concern about delivery and birth, desire to actively participate in delivery, and positive interest in breast-feeding. The prepared women had significantly less

PREGNANCY AND FETAL DEVELOPMENT

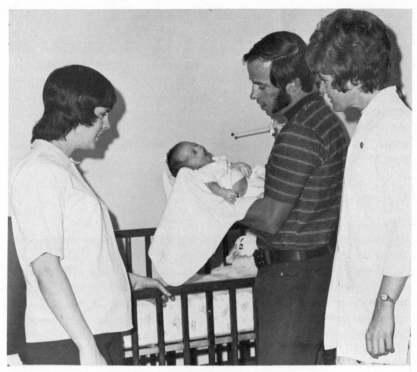

FIGURE 2-13

medication and anesthesia. The authors conclude that there are some beneficial effects of the education program that are directly related to the delivery experience. They suggest that their failure to find significant differences in anxiety scores may be a reflection of the IPAT scale's measuring a more generalized and stable trait rather than anxiety specifically related to pregnancy and concerns about delivery.

In a series of controlled experiments, Gordon and Gordon (1967) found prenatal preparation that included psychological guidance and emotional support was more effective in preventing postpartum emotional disorders than preparation involving information alone. In a nonintervention control group that received only routine information about pregnancy and child care, 46 percent of the participants had postpartum emotional disturbances lasting 4 to 6 years after delivery. When psychological guidance was included in the sessions the percentage decreased to 20 percent, and when these classes were combined with support in the home by public health nurses the number having emotional problems dropped to 9 percent. Gordon and Gordon (1967) also found that "the supported women had significantly more pregnancies than did controls, and healthier, happier children." Their marriages were better, and fewer sex problems, separations, or divorces were reported. The women were physically healthier and reported themselves to be happier than the control mothers. The supported women had learned to anticipate, investigate, and discuss their hopes and worries and "to guard against and prevent being overly stressed to the point of developing abnormal responses."

Alternatives to Routine Hospital Delivery

There is an increasing desire on the part of many pregnant couples to find alternatives to hospital deliveries that are more in keeping with their personal desires. Home deliveries, although common in some other countries, are rare in the United States. However, they are occurring more frequently, especially among the counterculture groups. Reasons given for wanting a home birth are the naturalness of the setting, as compared to the cold and dehumanizing atmosphere of many hospitals, the participation of the husband and others in the birth process, and the rising cost of hospital care. Families who wish to deliver their babies at home have been hindered in obtaining appropriate care. Resistance to change within obstetrics has continued the intimidation of those professionals who are willing to do home deliveries (Mehl, 1976).

The new birthing centers, the LaBoyer method, and home deliveries are among the options available to some. The Maternity Center Association of New York began a demonstration project in out-of-hospital deliveries for low-risk women. These women are cared for by an obstetrician–nurse-midwife team and are delivered in a homelike setting in their center's townhouse (Lubic, 1975).

As primary health care providers we need to explore the desires and options with these families and help them find the type of service they feel will best meet their needs and yet be compatible with the physical and emotional status of mother and baby. We also need to keep up with recent research findings and try to interpret them in light of the data rather than based on our biases. A recent study investigated how data were evaluated and concluded that scientists rated as high quality those research papers that agreed with their biases, regardless of whether the papers were logically consistent, coherent, or well written (Mehl, 1976).

In a recent review of home delivery research, Mehl (1976) concluded that for the matched populations studied the outcome of home deliveries was as good as for those delivering in the hospital. For certain parameters (i.e., bleeding during labor, postpartum hemorrhage, birth injuries, required neonatal resuscitation) "the home birth group fared better than their hospital counterparts."

Helping Families with High-Risk Pregnancies

IDENTIFICATION OF THE HIGH-RISK PREGNANCY

About 15 to 20 percent of all pregnancies are now being considered as "high risk," and recommendations are made that such mothers be followed by or in consultation with persons who have special training and skills in perinatal medicine (Aladjem and Brown, 1977). In some instances it may be necessary to have the baby delivered in a regional special-care facility or transferred there immediately after birth. In this latter circumstance the mother should be transferred as well to avoid separation of the family unit (Cranley, 1975).

Risk factors identified include such things as being, reproductively speaking, very young (under 17) or very old (39 or more), being unmarried or poor without an adequate social support system of family and friends, having four or more children at closely spaced intervals, having a chronic illness such as diabetes or heart disease, being addicted to drugs or alcohol or having other serious emotional problems, being at risk for genetic disorders, having a history of previous complications of pregnancy such as toxemia or premature birth, or developing complications such as bleeding or hypertension in the current pregnancy. As with all attempts at defining populations at risk, a significant proportion of these mothers will go on to have normal pregnancies and infants and some mothers in the low risk group will have complications (Lesinski, 1975), but it does provide some guidelines about when consultation is needed.

Since many of the mothers with these problems come from hard-to-reach segments of the population some type of active outreach program will be necessary to bring them into the health care system (Yankauer et al., 1953). Conn (1968) reports the successful use of trained lay home visitors to bring hard-core, inner-city women into prenatal care.

Pregnancies at Risk for Genetic Disorders It is now possible to detect infants with specific genetic disorders or the anomalies associated with advanced maternal age in the prenatal period. This has been made possible by transabdominal amniocentesis, which involves taking a sample of the amniotic fluid surrounding the fetus, culturing the fetal cells present, and doing a chromosomal and/or biochemical analysis of the cells after 3 or 4 weeks of growth (Milunsky, 1975; Riccardi and Robinson, 1975).

The amniocentesis is usually performed during the fifteenth or sixteenth week of the pregnancy and carries about a 2-percent complication risk of leaking fluid, vaginal bleeding, amnionitis, spontaneous abortion, or physical injury to the fetus (NICHDP, 1976).

Indication for prenatal detection include (Milunsky, 1975; Simpson, et al., 1976):

1 Maternal age of 35 or older
2 Previous child born with trisomy 21 or other chromosomal abnormality
3 Family history of sex-linked disorders such as hemophilia and muscular dystrophy or inherited inborn errors of metabolism such as Tay-Sachs disease
4 Previous offspring with other birth defects such as spina bifida or anencephaly

Almost every state has one or more centers that can provide counseling and prenatal detection for those who need it. All reproducing couples should be made aware that such services are available; however, they should also be allowed to decide freely and without coercion whether prenatal diagnostic information would be helpful to them in planning their family.

Sensitization of Rh-negative mothers and development of erythroblastosis in infants are now seldom a problem because of its prevention through the use of Rh-immune globulin given intramuscularly to the mother within 72 hours after delivery. However, for new mothers, determination of blood type and Rh early in the pregnancy and antibody titers later on will identify those infants at risk for erythroblastosis.

Mothers at Risk for Emotional Problems during and after Pregnancy As previously stated, routine psychological screening should be part of the care of every pregnant woman. Studies by Cohen et al. (1972) and Horsley (1972) strongly support the idea that prenatal psychological screening can be carried out effectively by persons without extensive background in psychiatry. Horsley's study (1972, pp. 310–311), confirms that it is possible to incorporate a system of psychological screening and management as an integral part of prenatal care. The study shows that an approach that freely opens up communication between expectant mothers and their professional attendants also has the long-term value of

PREGNANCY AND FETAL DEVELOPMENT

encouraging further consultation after delivery. The women who received extra support through psychological management appeared not only to enjoy easier labor, but also to have fewer behavioral problems with their infants.

Cohen et al. (1972) suggest the use of a "developmental, adaptive model" rather than one based on psychopathological concepts for prenatal screening. Areas to cover in the psychosocial assessment of the pregnant family (and considered possible relevant matters for further discussion) include the following:

1 Parental motivation for having a baby.
2 Previous separation experiences of the mother from her parents during childhood. Whether brought up by her own mother or adopted, Frommer and O'Shea (1973) indicate that childhood early separations (before 11 years) are associated with later problems in the mother-child relationship and a statistically greater incidence of depression. Baker (1967) indicates that girls who have been adopted or have had many changes of home have considerable emotional insecurity and as a result are likely to experience greater emotional reactions during pregnancy.
3 Current stresses impinging on family (other than pregnancy), such as a recent move or financial difficulties. A questionnaire containing social stress items serves to predict emotional disturbances serious enough to warrant psychiatric hospitalization (Gordon and Gordon, 1967; Larsen, 1966). Questions dealing with women's attitudes toward childbearing discriminate to a finer degree between normal women and those with mild degrees of emotional distress. Two experimental studies by Stott (1973; Stott and Latchford, 1976) indicate an association between ongoing interpersonal tensions during pregnancy, such as marital discord, insecurity, and employment and financial problems, and morbidity in their children in the form of physical illness and abnormalities, neurological dysfunction, developmental lags, and behavior disturbances. With the exception of witnessing violence, no short-term stresses were found to be associated with child morbidity.
4 How prospective parents feel about the coming child. Women who are likely to have complications during childbirth are those who during pregnancy "manifest a negative attitude to the pregnancy, show concern for the condition of the child, see their employment as disrupted, describe a greater number of contacts with women who have had complicated pregnancies and describe their mother's health as poor" (Pilowsky, 1972, p. 164). They also have a greater

number of somatic complaints, are anxious and tense, and have a negative attitude toward doctors. Thus, their pregnancies have more attributes of a crisis. The husbands of these women were found to be more outgoing and socially effective than husbands of wives with no complications.

5 Parents' knowledge and concerns about pregnancy and delivery. Asking the expectant woman about what her mother and friends have told her about pregnancy and delivery is a productive way of assessing anxiety and also provides her with an opportunity to express her feelings (Goodrich, 1965). Generally, anxiety is expressed as a specific fear (e.g., abnormal infant, death, pain, mutilation, inadequacy in caring for baby, changes in marital relationships). This same question would likely elicit similar information from prospective fathers.

6 Previous history of psychiatric disturbances.

7 Health status of couple's parents and siblings; if dead, the cause of death.

8 Maternity experience of woman's mother.

9 Developmental status of each parent, including age, degree of maturity, how each feels about self.

10 The available support persons for family whom can they rely on for help if needed.

11 Integrity of marriage, including the extent to which earlier developmental tasks have been mastered, communication patterns, and support system.

With less disturbed families the primary health care worker can often help prevent more serious problems by providing the guidance and support previously mentioned (Caplan, 1973). If the family is obviously disturbed, referral to a mental health professional is indicated.

Pregnant Adolescents The pregnant adolescent presents different management problems during all phases of her obstetric care (Jorgensen, 1972). An important role of the professional working with pregnant adolescents is to help them receive educational and social services as well as medical services. Information concerning school-aged mothers is available from the Consortium on Early Childbearing and Childrearing, Child Welfare League of America, and the National Alliance Concerned with School-Age Parents (NACSAP), in Syracuse, New York (Braen and Forbush, 1975).

Flowers (1969, p. 787) suggests five important facets of prenatal care related to the teenager: (1) nutrition, (2) education in the biology of human reproduction, (3) preparation for childbirth, (4) psychic support during pregnancy, and (5) development of good habits in preventive medicine. Prenatal adolescent clinics are developing throughout the country to provide a combination of education and medical and social service care (Howard, 1972; Jorgensen, 1972; Smith, 1971). Family planning is made available early in the postpartum period and encouragement and support are available to them as they assume the mothering role. Peer group interaction is encouraged.

There is some evidence that such antepartum intervention does affect postpartum behavior of adolescent mothers (McGanity et al., 1969; Smith et al., 1975). In 1973, Klerman and Jekel evaluated two comprehensive programs (medical, social, and educational services) for school-aged parents. They concluded that in terms of infant health, child spacing, and mother's education these programs had a positive effect for more than 1 year after delivery but by 2 years the impact was noted only in the educational area. They indicated that crisis intervention will have a short-term impact on young mothers, but more innovative and flexible programs are needed for more sustained impact.

The adolescent who is pregnant will need considerable guidance in looking at her alternatives before deciding whether to keep or terminate the pregnancy. Once a decision has been made, she will then need the support of the health professional as well as her family as she faces an abortion or continues the pregnancy.

THREE

Infancy

The first year of life is a period of rapid change in many parameters of a child's development. From a completely dependent newborn, the child emerges with the ability to move about with ease and communicate needs and feelings to others. This is also a period of rapid change for the family, particularly when the new infant is the firstborn child. The many needs of young infants require a reorganization of family roles and a reexamination of family values.

DEVELOPMENTAL TASKS OF THE INFANT DURING THE FIRST YEAR OF LIFE

DEVELOPING AND MAINTAINING HEALTHY GROWTH
AND NUTRITION PATTERNS

This is one of the major developmental tasks of infants because of their very rapid growth during this period.

Early Growth Patterns From an average birth weight of approximately 7½ pounds (3.4 kilograms) and an average length of 20 inches (51 centimeters), the infant gains at a rate greater than during any other time of postnatal life. From birth to 6 months, weight gain is about 1 ounce

(28 grams) per day, or approximately 2 pounds (1 kilogram) per month. From 6 to 12 months, this rate of weight gain drops to approximately ½ ounce (14 grams) per day, or about 1 pound (½ kilogram) per month. This means that the child is approximately doubling birth weight by 5 months of age, and tripling it by 1 year. A recent report indicated this rapid growth has become even more accelerated, with doubling by 4 months (Neumann and Alpaugh, 1976). (See growth charts in Appendix A.)

Height increases are also very dramatic, with an increase of about 1 inch (2.5 centimeters) per month for the first 6 months and about ½ inch (1.2 centimeters) per month for the second 6 months (Faulkner, 1957b, 1962; Simmons, 1944). (See Appendix A.)

Another striking area of growth is the brain. From an average head circumference at birth of 13¾ inches (35 centimeters), there is an increase of approximately ½ inch (1.2 centimeters) per month during the first 4 months of life, for a total growth of 2 inches (5 centimeters). Over the next 8 months, 2 more inches are added. From age 1 to 2 years there is only an addition of 1 more inch (Eichorn and Bayley, 1962; Faulkner, 1962; Nellhaus, 1968). Fontanelle size varies quite widely over the initial months (Popich and Smith, 1972).

Subcutaneous fat begins to be laid down in the fetus at about 34 weeks of gestational age and increases in rate of deposition from then through the time of birth to reach a peak at about 9 months of age, when many babies normally look quite pudgy. After 9 months the gain in subcutaneous fat falls to zero and skin-fold thickness decreases abruptly until age 2½ years and more slowly to 5½ years of age. At this age the actual thickness of subcutaneous tissue is on the average about one-half that at 9 months, and most children look rather skinny (Garn and Haskell, 1960; Maresh, 1966; Stuart and Sobel, 1946).

Deciduous tooth eruption is extremely variable, with the most active time being between 9 and 18 months. In Faulkner's study (1957) of 200 subjects, 20 percent had their first tooth eruption between 3 and 6 months, 60 percent between 6 and 10 months, and 20 percent between 10 months and 1 year. Only three children did not have a first tooth by 1 year of age, and in all three children these erupted before age 18 months. All the children in this sample had a complete set of deciduous teeth by 3 years of age.

Nutritional Needs   To meet these large growth increases, the calorie requirements are approximately 50 to 55 calories per pound (110 per kilogram) at birth, of which about 2½ grams of protein per pound of body weight (3 to 4 grams per kilogram) is recommended. Vitamins A, C,

CHILD AND FAMILY DEVELOPMENT

and D also must be provided, as well as iron for hemoglobin formation and fluoride if tooth decay is to be minimized (Watson and Lowrey, 1967).

Although there is a fad in this country to start the feeding of solid foods at a much earlier time, careful studies on nutrition indicate there is no advantage in providing calories, other than that through milk, for some time. In 1958, the American Academy of Pediatrics Committee on Nutrition reviewed existing research and reported there were no data to suggest any benefit from adding solid foods before 2½ to 3 months of age. In a more recent statement, Foman and his colleagues (1969) suggest the addition of solid foods is not necessary before 6 months of age.

Eating Behavior In general, the rapid growth during the first year is associated with good appetite and few feeding problems. However, in their temperament study, Thomas et al. (1968) found some babies who, as part of a general pattern of negative reactions to new situations,

FIGURE 3-1

by Susan McCabe

would initially spit out all new foods. If the mother persisted in offering the foods, these infants would gradually adapt and would eventually take them. In contrast, other babies would readily accept any new food at the first try.

Reactions to weaning from the bottle or breast to a cup also vary considerably. In the retrospective data obtained in interviewing mothers of 5-year-olds, Sears et al. (1957) report that about one-third of the children had evidence of some emotional upset at weaning. Only 5 of the 356 children were said to have a severe reaction in which they cried for extended periods and refused to drink from a cup. While there was some relation of upset to the abruptness of the method used there were still marked individual differences regardless of methods.

FIGURE 3-2

by Susan McCabe

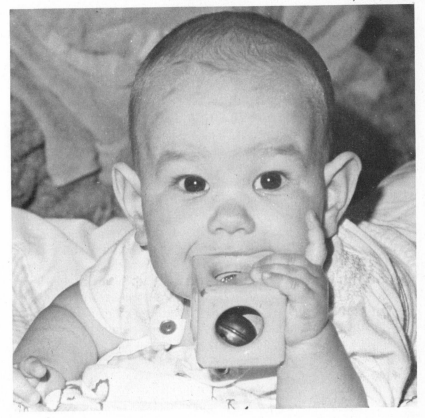

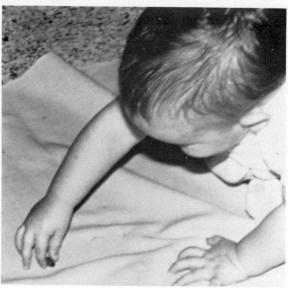

FIGURE 3-3   by John McCabe

LEARNING TO MANAGE ONE'S BODY SATISFACTORILY

Knowledge about the development of motor abilities in young children is largely based on the early studies of Bayley (1935), Gesell and colleagues (1940), McGraw (1943), and Shirley (1933), with some recent additions by Neligan and Prudham (1969).

In general, muscular development proceeds from head to toe (cephalocaudally) and from trunk to extremities (proximodistally). During the first 4 months, most of the development centers around the head, with the onset of smiling, following objects with the eyes, and maintaining steady control of the head in different positions. From 4 to 8 months, development is most marked in the musculature of the trunk and proximal part of the extremities. The infants learn to roll over, sit without support, and grasp things in their hands. From 8 to 12 months, development progresses to the legs, arms, feet, and fingers. Creeping, standing, walking, transferring objects from hand to hand, putting things into the mouth, and the ability to pick up small objects with a pincer grasp of thumb and index finger are the most prominent accomplishments.

Milestones for sitting and walking are reported by Neligan and Prudham (1969). These milestones (see Table 3-1) are based on mother reports to health visitors for over 3000 children born in Newcastle, England, between 1960 and 1962.

TABLE 3-1

Age of Accomplishment of Sitting and Walking Milestones

Milestones	Age accomplished, months		
	3%	50%	97%
Sitting, unsupported (at least 1 minute)	4.6	6.4	9.3
Walking, unsupported (10 steps or more)	9.7	12.8	18.4

SOURCE: Table based on data from Neligan, G. and Prudham, D. *Developmental medicine and child neurology*, 1969, pp. 413–423.

Sleeping The onset of sleeping through the night also follows a predictable pattern. In one study of 95 infants (Beal, 1969), the median age for obtaining an 8-hour interval between night-feedings was 5 weeks. Again there was considerable variation, with 12 of the infants already having eliminated one night-feeding at the time of discharge from the hospital, and three others who did not give up night-feedings until 8 to 15 months of age. All but three had achieved an 8-hour span by 4 months of age. The median age for achieving a 12-hour span between feedings was about 3 months. In another study by Moore and Ucko (1957), 70 percent of the infants ceased waking in the night by 3 months of age. This phenomenon appears related to maturation of the central nervous system and is also related to changing patterns in the EEG (Parmelee et al., 1964). In spite of popular beliefs, age of sleeping through the night is not related to the type or amount of food intake. There are at least three controlled studies indicating that the time of introducing solid foods is not related to age of onset of sleeping through the night (Beal, 1969; Deisher and Goers, 1954; Grunwaldt et al., 1960).

LEARNING TO UNDERSTAND AND RELATE TO THE PHYSICAL WORLD

Piaget identifies six stages of cognitive development during the first 2 years of life and calls this the sensorimotor period of development because the infant solves simple problems by trial and error through physical manipulations (Ginsberg and Opper, 1969; Piaget, 1952). These stages are summarized as follows:

Stage 1 (birth to 1 month): During this stage the infant's innate reflex responses, such as sucking, are organized into functioning patterns.

Stage 2 (1 to 4 months; primary circular reactions): Infants' actions lead to chance events that have positive value, and they gradually learn how to make the event happen again and again. An example would be sucking on a finger that reaches the mouth by chance. Infants gradually learn to manipulate their bodies to make this happen again.

Stage 3 (4 to 10 months; secondary circular reactions): Infants now learn to make events happen with objects separate from their own bodies in the external environment. An example is making a crib mobile move with body movements.

Stage 4 (10 to 12 months; coordination of secondary schemata): The infant can originate new approaches to problem solving rather than simply repeating old ones learned by trial and error. The baby becomes goal-oriented and can generalize solutions to new situations.

Stage 5 (12 to 18 months; tertiary circular reactions): Infants become curious about objects as objects and interested in novelty for its own sake. They may discover something by chance but then make interesting innovations in using or exploring it.

Stage 6 (18 months to 2 years; beginning thought): This is the transition period, when the infant begins to use mental symbols and words to refer to absent objects.

The major milestone of this period is the development of object permanence. Until about 7 months of age, infants act as though objects that are removed from view no longer exist. For example, if one covers a toy that the child has been interested in with a handkerchief while the

FIGURE 3-4

by John McCabe

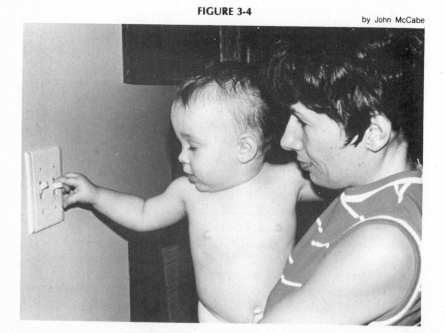

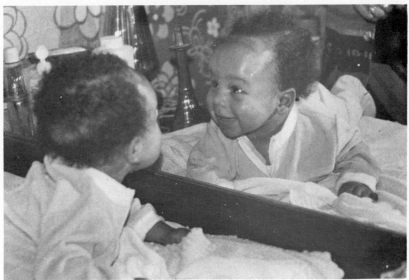

FIGURE 3-5   by Elizabeth Tong

infant is looking, he or she will not search for it under the handkerchief. It is only at about 8 to 10 months of age that the infant will search for the missing toy, indicating knowledge that it is there even though it is out of sight (Harris, 1975).

DEVELOPING SELF-AWARENESS AND A SATISFYING SENSE OF SELF

The major achievement in this area during the first year is that children begin to separate themselves from the environment and become aware that their actions can influence what goes on around them. Body exploration is prominent, as is manipulation of objects (Gesell et al., 1974).

As part of this development, infants first learn to trust others in their environment to meet their needs (Erikson, 1963). Gradually, they begin to develop some trust in themselves to communicate these needs to others. As they learn to manage their bodies effectively, these infants are laying down the foundations for increasing self-awareness and self-esteem.

LEARNING TO RELATE TO OTHERS

Crying and smiling are two types of infant behavior that have considerable significance for the development of early social relationships.

Crying   In a study of 80 infants, Brazelton (1961) found that the crying time of infants follows a predictable pattern. Starting with a median of about 1¾ hours per 24 hours at 2 weeks of age, crying time increases to a peak of 2¾ hours per day at about age 6 weeks and then gradually decreases to less than an hour per day by 3 months of age. There were marked individual variations, with a group of "heavy fussers" who cried about 4 hours per day at 6 to 8 weeks, and a group of "light fussers" who were already down to less than 1 hour of fussing per day during the same time period. As they grew older, most babies concentrated their crying time into "fussy periods," with the majority occurring from 6 to 11 P.M. Emde and colleagues (1976) have some additional longitudinal data on crying during the first year for 14 infants.

Most mothers report that after a month or so they can distinguish different types of crying. Some types indicate hunger or discomfort, others a need for social attention in the form of holding and cuddling, and still others the irritable crying of the fussy period.

Smiling   Detailed observations by Wolff (1963) on the development of smiling during the first 3 months of life of eight infants indicate that facial configurations suggestive of smiling were noted within the first 24 hours of birth. Such spontaneous smiling was usually seen during periods of light sleep and drowsiness. It was also found that such smiles could be produced in response to various auditory stimuli such as bells, whistles, and a human voice. By the third week of life, the smile became more social, responding consistently to the human voice during a time when the infants were awake and alert. By 4 weeks, some of the infants began to make definite eye-to-eye contact and smile in response to a human face. The nodding head was an especially effective stimulus.

In a larger sample, Soderling (1959) reported that 70 percent of the infants developed a social smile between 3 and 5 weeks. None were thought to have this before 2 weeks of age, and all responded to social stimulation with a smile by 6 weeks of age.

Social Discrimination and Attachment   Several stages of socialization can be identified in the first year of life. These stages are related to discrimination between social and nonsocial objects as well as differential attachments to various individuals in the environment.

DISCRIMINATION BETWEEN SOCIAL AND NONSOCIAL OBJECTS   The first stage is the development of the ability to distinguish between social and nonsocial objects. Infant responses to an observer's face and voice are compared to responses to nonsocial auditory and visual stimuli. In a study by

Yarrow (1967), 65 percent of the infants were responding differentially to these stimuli by 1 month of age and by 5 months almost all were responding differentially.

ATTACHMENT TO THE MOTHER   The infant's ability to distinguish mother from other caretakers and the emotional upset shown in response to being approached by a stranger or the mother's leaving the room have all been taken as signs that the infant has become "attached" to the mother. This tendency of the young to seek and maintain close contact with one or more members of the same species has been observed to occur almost universally among animals as well as humans and has obvious survival value for the vulnerable infant. It is a major milestone of infant development during the first year of life.

Initial evidence of attachment takes the form of a difference in the approach behavior the infant shows toward the mother in comparison to that of a stranger. The infant responds to the mother with more smiling, vocalizing, following longer with the eyes, more generalized motor ac-

FIGURE 3-6

by John McCabe

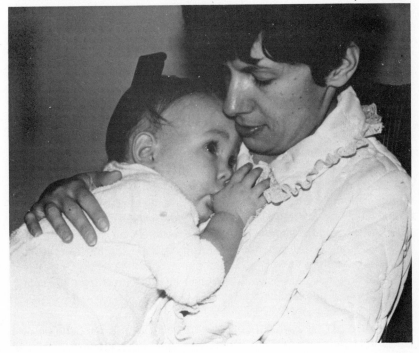

tivity, and quieting sooner when picked up. In Yarrow's sample (1967), this type of discrimination was noted in 21 percent of the infants by 1 month of age, 40 percent by 3 months, 71 percent by 5 months, and 96 percent by 8 months.

As the infant grows older, further evidence of attachment is shown by signs of distress, such as crying, when the mother leaves the area or when a strange person approaches. Fear reactions to strangers become prominent between 5 and 10 months of age (Tennes and Lampl, 1964). Schaffer and Emerson (1964b) found no evidence of these fear reactions under 6 months of age in their sample, but 42 percent were showing some distress by 8 months of age, 85 percent by 10 months of age, and 97 percent by 13 months. The intensity was highest around 10 months of age. In this same study, separation protest was noted in three infants 6 months of age or younger (5 percent), and was present in 57 percent of the sample by 8 months, 83 percent by 10 months, and nearly 97 percent showed this behavior by 13 months.

Emde et al. (1976) found that stranger distress and separation distress follow a different timetable and seem to represent different facets of development. They feel that stranger distress is related to the onset of fearfulness to strange situations in general rather than related to attachment. In their study, stranger distress peaked at 9 months and leveled off for the rest of the first year. Separation distress was more erratic, becoming prominent only toward the end of the first year and continuing to increase in intensity on into the second year.

In a study of the natural history of separation protest in 22 firstborn children, Kennell and Bergen (1966) found the onset in the second half of the first year as reported by others and an increase in frequency and intensity of reactions up until about 18 months of age.

In looking at variables that might be associated with intensity of attachment, Schaffer and Emerson (1964a) indicated there were no significant relationships between sex, birth order of child, type of father occupation, specific child-rearing practices related to feeding and toilet training, or the number of times a mother was away from the child during the week. There was a trend for children taken care of by few care takers to show more intense separation reactions than those with many, but these differences did not reach significance for the sample size (N = 36). Mothers who responded quickly to their child's cries and initiated more interactions with them had infants who reacted to separation with more intensity.

ATTACHMENT TO PERSONS OTHER THAN THE MOTHER In the Schaffer and Emerson study (1964a), 75 percent of infants also showed evidence of

FIGURE 3-7   by Susan McCabe

attachment to the father by 18 months of age, and others became attached to siblings and grandparents as well.

REACTIONS TO PERMANENT SEPARATIONS   By studying infants placed into adoption from foster homes at varying ages, Yarrow (1967) was able to gauge the amount of upset related to a permanent change in caretakers. Infants under 3 months of age did not show any clear-cut reaction. By 3 months of age about 10 percent showed considerable crying and feeding disturbances and 40 percent showed a mild reaction. By 4 months these figures were 20 and 60 percent, and by 6 months 58 and 91 percent. All infants placed after 8 months of age showed considerable upset in reaction to the change. As might be expected, the more marked the change in physical environment and care-taking style of the mother, the greater the upset.

Early Sexuality   Although there is considerable writing about the importance of early sexual behavior for later development, empirical data are difficult to find. Reports by Galenson and Raphe (1974), Kleeman (1965, 1966, 1975) and Spitz (1962; Spitz and Wolf, 1959) indicate that handling of the genitalia is frequently observed in infants during the last half of the first year and appears to be part of a general pattern of body

TABLE 3-2

Summary of Typical Stage-Related Characteristics During First Year of Life

Time period	Growth, nutrition, and health	Body control	Relate to world	Sense of self and relate to others	Family tasks
		Infant tasks			
Post partum (in hospital)	Typical newborn behaviors: hiccups, straining with bowel movements, spitting up, noisy breathing, crying, rashes				Parent-child bonding, mother in "taking-in" phase with need for rest and support, adapting to new roles and space, sibling reactions, postpartum blues
	Individual differences: activity, irritability, sociability, threshold, soothability				
Early weeks at home	Rapid growth, skin rashes, digestive upsets	Sucking reflex, maintains muscle tone when held	Organization of innate reflexes	Crying increases	Coping with fatigue and providing mutual support, increasing knowledge and skills in child rearing, home making and vocation, becoming sensitive to infant communications, reestablishing sexual relations
1 to 4 months		Holds head up, follows with eyes, smiles	Primary circular reactions	Smiles, crying decreases, sleeps through night, coos, babbles	

TABLE 3-2 (Continued)

Summary of Typical Stage-Related Characteristics During First Year of Life

Time period	Infant tasks				Family tasks
	Growth, nutrition, and health	Body control	Relate to world	Sense of self and relate to others	
4 to 8 months	Slowing of growth, teeth eruption, respiratory infections	Rolls over, sits up, reaches and grasps, hand to mouth	Secondary circular reactions, object permanence	Early attachment, imitates sounds, babbles	Agreement on child-care procedures and discipline, relating to community
8 months to onset of walking	Slowing of growth, decrease in appetite, increase in subcutaneous fat, respiratory infections	Crawls, stands, walks, pincer grasp, normal variations in foot and leg configurations	Object permanence, curiosity, coordination of secondary schemata, tertiary circular reactions	Separation anxiety, stranger fear, temper outbursts, body exploration, jargon, words	

exploration that is going on at that time. This "genital play" is sometimes accompanied by erections in boys and signs of pleasure such as smiling and rhythmic movement in both sexes, but generally is not persistently pursued or performed with enough intensity to be called "masturbation." However, Kinsey (1953; Kinsey et al., 1948) reported data on nine male and seven female infants under 1 year of age who were observed to rhythmically manipulate their genitalia to the point of an orgasm that was very similar in characteristics to that seen in adults, except for the lack of ejaculation in the males. Whiting and Child (1953) also report that in some cultures rubbing the genitalia of babies is used as a method for calming an upset child. Of interest is the observation of Spitz (1945) and Provence and Lipton (1962) that infants cared for in institutions handle their genitalia considerably less than home-reared infants.

Communication Skills In general, the following patterns have been described (McCarthy, 1946): (1) By 6 weeks of age most infants are making vowellike vocalizations. (2) By 3 to 4 months these have developed into repetitions of vowel and consonant sounds called babbling: ma ma, ba ba, da da. Both these productions are frequently spontaneous and occur when the infant is left alone in the crib. Deaf infants vocalize and babble as much as hearing infants during this time period, so this phenomenon appears to be motor in origin. (3) By 5 or 6 months of age, these sounds become associated with heard sounds as the infant repeats sound combinations from the environment. (4) Differences in pitch and inflection come into being around 9 or 10 months of age. It sounds as though the infant is talking, but what comes out is unintelligible (jargon). Also at this age the infant mimics sounds heard from others that may sound like true words but which are not yet associated with actual objects. (5) At around 1 year of age, words that are clearly associated with external objects make their appearance.

One of the best overviews of normal speech development is that by Morely (1957), based on data from the Newcastle upon Tyne study sample of 1000 children. In a detailed report of a subsample of this group (*N* = 114) the average age for use of first words was 12 months, with a range of 6 to 30 months; 7 percent were said to talk before 8 months of age and 2 percent did not attempt to use words until after 2 years. Once they started, the late-talking children progressed rapidly and were using adequate speech at 3½ years of age. All children in the sample were of normal intelligence, and no child was later found to have developmental aphasia or severe delay in the development of speech after 4 years of age.

In a study of children by Neligan and Prudham (1969), about 3 percent of their sample were using three or four words for objects or people by about 9 months of age, 50 percent by age 12 months, and 97 percent by 20 months (girls) and 22 months (boys).

See Table 3-2 for a summary of typical stage-related characteristics during the first year of life.

FAMILY DEVELOPMENTAL TASKS

The arrival of each addition to the family necessitates reorganization in order to meet new needs that arise. With the birth or adoption of an infant, roles need to be reassigned and family values reevaluated. Family developmental tasks are primarily related to establishing a stable family unit, reconciling conflicting tasks of each family member, and providing mutual support for each individual's developmental needs (Duvall, 1977).

During the infancy period, particularly with the firstborn infant, parents are faced with the task of reconciling conflicting conceptions of their roles and the role of their infant. Each parent is faced with working out his or her role as an individual person, spouse, and parent. Their expectations of themselves, of each other, and of their child need to be clarified. At the same time the new parents are faced with accepting and adjusting to the strains and pressures of parenthood (Duvall, 1977).

First-time parenthood is a new developmental phase, during which the marital relationship is strained until a new equilibrium can be established. Several studies indicate that parenthood is a critical experience and that marital satisfaction decreases following the birth of the first baby (Dyer, 1963; Feldman and Rogoff, 1968; LeMasters, 1957). In fact, Rossi (1968) believes that transition to parenthood is more difficult in American society than either marital or occupational adjustment.

Of the 46 couples interviewed by LeMasters (1957) 5 years after the birth of their first child, 83 percent indicated the transition experience had been one of severe or extreme crisis, and 53 percent of 32 couples interviewed 2 years after delivery by Dyer (1963) described the transition as a crisis event. Hobbs' study (1965) of 53 randomly chosen couples in Greensboro, North Carolina, indicated that, at 10 weeks post partum, mothers experienced more crisis responses than fathers, but these were generally mild, with only 13 percent of the mothers reporting even moderate crisis responses. Reiss (1971) suggests that perhaps these differences occur because the realization and consequences of strain are not recognized until later or that it is easier to recognize the crisis intellectually once one is out of danger.

MEETING THE BASIC PHYSICAL NEEDS OF THE FAMILY

The extent to which the family adapts its housing arrangements to accommodate the young infant depends in some measure on the family's standard of living (Duvall, 1977). As the standard of living improves, accommodations are made to provide the infant with a space of its own. Families are more likely to move when they have infants and small children than at other stages in the life cycle (Hill, 1970; U.S. Bureau of Census, 1969).

As the infant begins to creep, crawl, and walk, adaptations need to be made to protect the child from injury and to protect breakable items from damage by the child.

The family is faced with the burden of meeting the financial costs of the expanding family. Costs for the new baby include providing furnishings, layette, and food; paying the antepartum and hospital bills (or meeting the insurance costs); and baby-sitter expenses. In addition, parents may still be paying for furniture and other household equipment, a car, and/or a house. The first baby may arrive while one or both parents may still be preparing for a vocation. The mother, previously employed, may leave work for a time or may return to work, often necessitating paid child-care arrangements. The father may be unemployed or may take on an extra part-time job to assist in meeting the financial burdens. Families may meet their financial expenses in a variety of ways, including borrowing money, spending savings, receiving gifts from grandparents, or making do with what they have.

ASSISTING EACH MEMBER DEVELOP HIS OR HER INDIVIDUAL POTENTIAL

During the infancy period, parents and children are adjusting to their new roles of mother, father, and sibling. The primary parental task is to learn to care for the infant with competence and assurance (Duvall, 1977) while reconciling their conflicting tasks of spouse and parent.

Tasks of the Mother Shainess (1965) indicates that a woman's mothering capacity is determined long before her first infant is born. It is determined by the woman's personality potential, attitudes toward femininity, values and philosophies, relationship with her husband, how welcome the pregnancy is and the motivations for it, and the conditions of pregnancy, delivery, and the early postpartum period.

The new mother is caught in the conflict of wanting to be dependent upon others to make decisions for her and the baby and at the same time feeling she is expected to make independent decisions regarding the baby. For the teenage mother, this is an especially difficult conflict because the teenager is also experiencing the dependence-independence conflict between adolescence and adulthood.

TAKING ON THE ROLE OF MOTHER   Mothering, a function of the mother role, is a learned behavior (Rubin, 1961), while motherliness is an emotional feeling that develops as the mother has increasing contact with her child. Benedek (1970a, p. 165) describes motherliness as "a quality resulting from the psychological organization of the individual." The mother's feelings are reflections, not only of her interactions with the infant but also of her relationships with her husband and/or other children, as well as her own personality. It is postulated that motherliness originates early in pregnancy.

Rubin (1967a,b) describes three phases of maternal-role development occurring during the puerperium: taking in, taking hold, and letting go. The taking-in phase generally lasts from 2 to 3 days. During this time the mother's primary concern is with her own needs for food and sleep. She is often quite talkative during this period and relives the details of her labor and delivery experience.

The taking hold begins around the third day post partum and lasts approximately 10 days. At this time, mothering tasks become very important and take priority over other tasks; the new mother becomes increasingly independent and autonomous in caring for her infant. The practical aspects of mothering include the basic tasks of feeding, holding, clothing, and protecting the baby from harm and overstimulation (Steele and Pollock, 1968). If the mother is unable to master the task of caring for her infant with competence and assurance, she is apt to feel inadequate and a failure and that the baby is rejecting her. Her inner drive for excellence makes her especially vulnerable at this time to frustrations and failure, and she tends to become hypercritical and intolerant of herself. If she feels secure in her ability to care for the infant, she is then able to help her husband and other children in meeting their needs.

The last phase is a letting go of one's former identity in some roles that are incompatible with the maternal role. This has been equated with Lindemann's concept of grief work, whereby the individual reviews in memory her previous attachments and events associated with former roles. For most women this stage lasts until about 3 to 4 weeks after the infant's birth.

MAINTAINING SENSE OF SELF   Maintaining a sense of personal worth and autonomy is an important task during these early months of parenthood. The new mother is striving to continue some aspects of her own personal development. She wants to retain some satisfying contacts with personal interests and stimuli. Following the baby's birth, the mother is no longer free to do things on the spur of the moment, as provisions need to be made for the care of the baby. This can be a problem for both the primipara and the mother whose children are older and more independent (Ross Laboratories, 1959).

Among the areas of concern to new mothers are factors related to the emotional and physical self (Russell, 1974). They worry about their personal appearance, loss of figure, and being tired. Many of the mothers express feelings of being "edgy" or emotionally upset. The new mother has to learn to gear her activity to a period of decreased physical vigor during the period of involution and lactation. This pressure is compounded by the loss of sleep as she is awakened by the baby during the night.

Once the mother is home with her new infant, she begins to come to grips with the strenuous responsibility of caring for the newborn. The daydreams she may have had during pregnancy are usually shattered as she tries to work out a schedule and adjust to the baby's crying and getting up at night. The strain of 24-hour care leads to chronic fatigue and often to frayed nerves. She may feel guilty because she considers the baby to be a lot of work.

The baby has many needs for which it is dependent upon the mother while she still has personal needs of her own. Consequently, although she loves the baby, she may also at times resent the intrusion on her privacy or plans.

For many new mothers, a conflict arises as they try to determine how to divide their time to meet the demands of the new baby and still have time to be with their husbands. Some mothers may resolve the conflict by becoming so involved with their infants that little time is spent with their husbands.

POST PARTUM The first 24 hours after delivery represent a period of restoration; the woman is generally drowsy and physically and mentally relaxed. The next 3 or 4 days are characterized by extreme emotional lability (Kane et al., 1968; Nilsson, 1970; Yalom et al., 1968). Many women later describe these days as a "dreamlike" state, and to the observer they appear slightly euphoric.

The "third day blues" or "maternity blues," generally described as depressive states, are experienced by about 70 to 80 percent of the women. The blues are characterized by crying, slight euphoria, irritability, and emotional lability. Kaij and Nilsson (1972) suggest these symptoms may either be physiologically based rather than psychological in origin or they may have the psychological function of "protecting the mother from everyday activities during the important period when the mother-child imprinting takes place" (p. 371).

There is a small group of women who, even during the first postpartum week, may be showing indications of more serious troubles. These subtle signs, often difficult to distinguish from the blues, include psychomotor retardation, lack of interest in the child, and lack of concern about the practical and emotional problems they will encounter after returning home. These women are to be distinguished from those, especially primiparas, who are unaware of the difficulties ahead, are anxious to get home with their infants, and may insist on being discharged early even against medical advice (Kaij and Nilsson, 1972).

During the second half of the first postpartum month many of the neurasthenic symptoms experienced in the first trimester reappear. Many women tire easily, need more sleep than usual, feel irritable, and complain of a number of psychosomatic symptoms (Kaij and Nilsson, 1972). The women's decrease in sexual desire that occurred during pregnancy may persist during this time, and sometimes decreases even more.

CARING FOR THE INFANT WITH COMPETENCE AND ASSURANCE   Adams (1963) studied the concerns of 40 married primigravidas between 17 and 36

FIGURE 3-8   by Elizabeth Tong

years of age regarding their ability to provide physical care and comfort to their newborn babies. Interviews were conducted at 2 days, 1 week, and 1 month post partum. Twenty mothers had infants of normal birth weight and 20 had infants who were premature by birth weight. On the whole, these women had little information about infant care. About 50 percent had attended prenatal or hospital classes, but only six stated they had discussed infant care, and eight indicated they had done much reading regarding infant care. Mothers of premature infants used nurses in helping to care for their newborns at home, while mothers of full-term infants tended to rely on family and friends. At the end of 1 week, 65 percent of the mothers of preemies compared with 10 percent of the full-term group saw their husbands as most helpful; however, at the end of the first month both groups saw their husbands as most helpful.

Feeding was the area of greatest concern to both groups of mothers during the baby's first month. Crying was of lowest anticipated concern at 2 days but concerned about one-third of the mothers after leaving the hospital. Bathing and caring for the navel was of concern through the first week. The greatest number of questions about care-taking activities occurred after they had cared for their infants for 1 week and the fewest after 1 month. The two groups of mothers had similar concerns. Feeding questions were most often (higher for normal weight) related to amount and frequency of feeding. Mothers of preemies were more concerned with how to feed. The major question regarding bathing was how to hold the infant and that regarding crying was why babies cried. Other less frequent concerns were related to taking the baby outdoors, elimination, hiccups, rashes, weight, and sleep.

Mothers frequently mentioned varying degrees of apprehension of the new fathers. The most frequently mentioned concern was the husband's timidity in holding the baby.

Mothers who had experience caring for small infants before the births of their own infants had less anticipatory concerns about bathing, crying, and care of the navel and/or circumcision. Mothers who cared for their infants in the hospital had more questions at 2 days regarding bathing, feeding, and crying; at the end of the first week of care they had only one-third as many questions about these areas as those who did not care for their infants in the hospital. Mothers who attended classes indicated less concern with bathing (50 percent versus 80 percent not attending), crying (50 percent versus 80 percent) and care of navel and/or circumcision (50 percent versus 80 percent). Class attendance made little or no difference with regard to feeding and "other" concerns.

GUIDING THE NUTRITIONAL INTAKE OF THE INFANT   Although the decision to breast- or bottle-feed is generally made prior to the infant's birth, the baby's feeding behavior and nutritional intake is regarded by the mother as an indication of her mothering competence. In a study of 26 mother-infant pairs (4 breast-feeding, 22 bottle-feeding), Ainsworth and Bell (1969) identified nine maternal patterns of interaction pertinent to feedings. Four of these patterns were designated as "feeding on demand," four as "feeding according to schedule," and one as "arbitrary." The flexible-demand feeding schedule was used consistently by mothers who were found to be most sensitive to their babies. These mothers also responded promptly to their infants' crying, delighted in their behavior, tended to see things from their babies' perspective, and to give their babies considerable physical contact outside routine care. Mothers who used a rigid or arbitrary feeding schedule tended to have distorted perceptions of their babies, took little or no delight in the babies' behavior, generally underestimated or used teasing and tormenting behaviors in their social interactions, and generally restricted contact with the babies to routine care.

Niles Newton (1971) indicates that differences between nursing and nonnursing mothers are related to a variety of factors. One factor is the type of breast-feeding practiced: (1) *unrestricted* (no rules restricting amount or frequency of sucking), or, as is common in this country, (2) *token breast-feeding* (severe limitation of sucking by social customs). Another important factor is the mother's initial feeding experience with her baby. In our culture the initiation of bottle-feeding is likely to be the least stressful while the initiation of token breast-feeding may leave the mother feeling inadequate and in pain.

The mother's personality and her general adjustment to life situations may vary with her choice of infant feeding. Cornell's study (1969) of 60 mothers indicated significantly less neuroticism manifested by mothers who were breast-feeding their babies. Adams (1959) found significantly greater dependency in pregnant women who planned to bottle- rather than breast-feed. She also found more disturbed behavior on eight items of the Blackey test.

Maternal interests and behavior are related to lactation to some extent, but the relationship is selective and does not seem to affect all care-taking behavior. Study results are inconclusive concerning the correlation of breast- or bottle-feeding with differences in maternal behavior. In one study, Newton et al. (1971) found that 71 percent of breast-feeding mothers stated they sometimes or often slept or rested in bed with the baby as compared with 26 percent of bottle-feeding mothers.

The lactating mother Physiologically, lactation is maintained by the se-

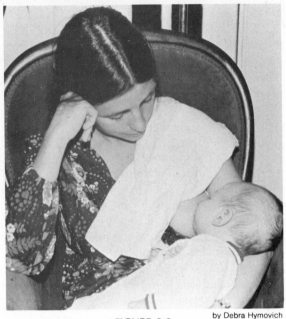

FIGURE 3-9 by Debra Hymovich

cretion of prolactin from the anterior pituitary gland as a result of sucking stimulation, and the ejection reflex, which causes oxytocin to be released from the posterior pituitary gland when the nipple is stimulated. Most mothers experience some discomfort when the baby begins to nurse; however, as milk secretion increases and the ejection reflex permits quick release of milk, discomfort usually disappears. The hormonal changes accompanying lactation inhibit ovulation. Nonlactating women on the average ovulate (as measured by basal body temperature) 73.5 days after delivery. The length of time before ovulation begins in the lactating woman varies, depending upon the duration and completeness of the breast-feeding. Once weaning is begun, ovulation and menstruation rapidly follow (Newton, 1971). The amenorrhea of continuing lactation conserves maternal iron stores, although the production of breast milk draws on the mother's stores of other nutrients, particularly calories (Pan American Health Organization, 1970).

Breast disorders arising during lactation generally result from poor functioning of the ejection reflex because it is subject to inhibition by emotional influences (i.e., pain, fear, embarrassment, uncertainty). Breast engorgement, often associated with nipple pain, and due to retention of milk in the breast, perhaps secondary to vascular congestion and edema, results in the breasts feeling full, hot, and painful. Mastitis, usually due to staphylococci, is characterized by either generalized or localized swollen, hot, and painful breasts. In some instances, mastitis may progress to a localized abscess. Galactoceles (minor obstructions of the mammary duct) are common and result in localized areas of tenderness (Newton, 1971).

Reviews of the literature by Caldwell (1964) and Davis and Ruiz (1965) indicate that the relationship between breast-feeding and later infant behavior appears to be ambiguous. Both desirable and undesirable correlates of breast-feeding have been reported, and in some studies no evidence of association was found. A study by Kennell and Bergen (1966) showed that about the time their baby was 3 months old, American mothers who were breast-feeding were likely to feel oppressed and this feeling often led to abrupt and impulsive weaning. Heinstein (1963) studied 94 adults who had been either breast-fed (token or unrestricted) or bottle-fed in the late 1920s. He concluded that girls who had warm mothers did much better with breast- rather than formula-feeding, while girls with cold mothers showed less disturbance if they had been formula-fed rather than breast-fed. Similar correlations were not found in boys, whose overall breast-feeding was less.

Tasks of the Father TAKING ON THE ROLE OF FATHER According to Benedek (1970c), the sources of fatherliness come from an innate biologic bisexuality and from past experiences of biologic dependency on the mother. During his wife's pregnancy, the father relives his identification with his own parents. The father also has fantasies regarding the infant, often seeing the child as an extension of himself.

An important task of the father during this period is to adjust to his new role as a father. This task includes reconciling conflicting conceptions of his role as husband, father, and person; adapting to the new pressures and routines of fatherhood; and learning to care for the baby. Russell (1974) found that 272 first-time fathers described fatherhood as "bothersome." This was interpreted to mean a slight or moderate crisis. He also noted that fathers of new infants tended to be bothered most by interruptions in sleep and rest, suggestions from in-laws about the baby, increased money problems, changes in plans, and the additional work required by the baby.

Fathers are also involved in learning the basic essentials of child care (Duvall, 1977) to enable them to feel comfortable with their infants and to provide some assistance to their wives. By mastering this task the father should feel increasingly comfortable in his interactions with his infant. Fein's study (1976) of 30 men who attended childbirth prepara-

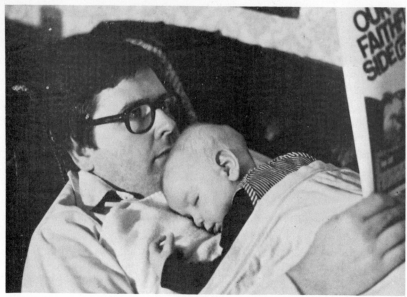

FIGURE 3-10
by Jean Miller

tion classes with their wives lends some support to this notion. The data suggest that men who were able to develop a role that met their needs as well as those of their wives and infants adjusted better to parenthood than men who were unsure of the role they wanted in relation to their babies.

We are only now beginning to look more closely at the father's role in infant and child development. Early writings of Bowlby (1951) and Freud stressed the mother-child relationship as being the most important in the early years of development. The father's role was seen as one of providing economic and emotional support to the mother. This widespread belief in the primary importance of mother-infant relationships is also shared by social-learning theorists (Ainsworth, 1969; Bijou and Baer, 1965; Maccoby and Masters, 1970) and by cognitive developmentalists. Kohlberg (1966; Kohlberg and Zigler, 1967), for example, states the child's tie to the mother is deep and that a relationship with the father is formed sometime between 4 and 8 years of age. Recent studies by Lamb (1976a, 1977) and others (Cohen and Campos, 1974; Kotelchuck, 1976; Willemsen et al., 1974) indicate that infants are clearly attached to their fathers as well as their mothers from 7 months onward. Differential reactions are noted in stress-free and stressful situations. When both parents are present in stress-free situations infants show no preference for one parent over the other, while in stressful situations they tend to seek comfort from their mothers (Lamb and Lamb, 1976).

Greenberg and Morris (1974) reported that the birth of an infant had a profound impact on the father. The fathers reported positive attitudes toward their newborn infants and an awareness of the personality and individuality of the infant.

Lamb (1977) suggests that babies have different kinds of experiences in their relationships with each parent. His studies indicate that fathers hold their infants most often to play while mothers hold them most often to engage in care-taking functions. Fathers tend to engage in vigorous, physically stimulating games or in unpredictable and unusual types of play while mothers more often choose conventional games such as pat-a-cake or games involving toys. Rendina and Dickersheid (1976) also found that fathers were more involved in social activities, especially play, with their firstborn infants, rather than in care-taking activities.

PROVIDING EMOTIONAL SUPPORT AND COMMUNICATING EFFECTIVELY WITH ALL FAMILY MEMBERS

Accepting the Infant's Individuality   In order to provide emotional support for their infant, parents need to accept the baby as he or she is, rather than as the idealized infant they anticipated. Many parents indicate that their baby becomes a "person" to them usually between 4 to 9 weeks after birth and that the infant seems to recognize them between 2 and 7 weeks of age (Robson, 1967).

Becoming Attached to the Infant   MATERNAL ATTACHMENT   Maternal attachment is an extremely complex phenomenon. Rubin (1961) refers to it as a mother's ability to recognize her infant as an individual, to determine her relationship to the baby, and to commit herself to the child's growth and development. According to Robson and Moss (1970, p. 977) maternal attachment is "the extent to which a mother feels that her infant occupies an essential position in her life. Components of this phenomenon are: feelings of warmth or love, a sense of possession, devotion, protectiveness and concern for the infant's well-being, positive anticipation of prolonged contact, and a need for and pleasure in continuing transactions."

Full maternal feelings may or may not occur when the mother first sees her newborn infant. In fact, they may not occur before the third week of life and even then may be intermittent and brief. Until full maternal feelings are experienced, the mother may wonder about her maternal capacity and even about the wisdom of having a child (Robson and Moss,

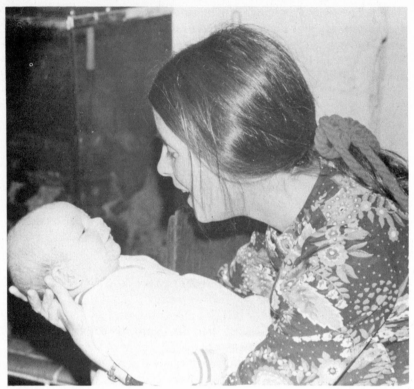

FIGURE 3-11   by Debra Hymovich

1970). Mothers may feel guilty if they expect an immediate warmth toward their infants and then find this is not immediately present.

Klaus and Kennell (1970) indicate that mothers demonstrate an "orderly progression of behavior" in becoming attached to their infants and that attachment is fairly well developed by birth. Continuous development of this behavior is partially dependent on the state and temperament of the infant. The mother's first tactile contact with her infant is exploratory, and is usually made with the fingertips and later with the palm of her hand (Rubin, 1963). Robson (1967) suggests that positive maternal feelings are generally fostered by eye-to-eye contact and by the infant's social smile.

Close emotional contact between mother and infant during the first days of life may facilitate maternal behavior (Klaus and Kennell, 1976). Kennell and associates (1974) studied primiparous mothers who gave birth to full-term infants and who were planning to bottle-feed their babies. The 14 mothers in the control group had routine contact with their newborn infants, while the mothers in the experimental (extended-contact) group were allowed an additional 16 hours of contact with their infants, including 1 hour with their naked babies within 3 hours of birth. Their findings indicated that at 1 month, mothers in the extended-contact group picked up and soothed their babies more often when they cried, tended to stay at home with their babies, and spent more time fondling and en face with their infants. Significant differences between the two groups of mothers were also found when their babies were 1 year of age. Of the mothers who returned to work or school, the mothers with extended contact missed their babies, soothed their crying infants more, and were more likely to kiss their babies. Mean scores of the infants on the Bayley test were 98 for infants of extended-contact mothers and 93 for control infants ($p > 0.05$). These data suggest evidence of an important attachment period shortly after birth.

Attachment is interactional in nature, affected by the continual interplay of qualities in both mother and child. Moss (1967) believes that mother-infant social interaction is based on a reciprocal, learned stimulus-response relationship. Not only is the infant dependent upon the mother, but there is also a dependence of the mother on her infant for reinforcement. Although the mother-infant relationship is initiated by the mother, she searches for some response from her infant. Levy's study (1959) of mother-neonate interaction strongly suggested that the infants' arousal levels at the time they are brought to their mothers for feeding determined not only their feeding activity but also their mothers' responses to them. According to Robson and Moss (1970), the release of human maternal feelings appears to depend largely on the infant's capacity to exhibit behaviors characteristic of adult forms of social communication. The condition of the infant will therefore affect the quality and quantity of maternal behavior (Brody, 1956; Moss, 1967). As a social stimulus, the mother provides sensory stimulation (auditory, visual, tactile) to her infant through cuddling, talking, and playing, as well as by simply being present (Yarrow, 1961, p. 485).

Brazelton (1975b), in his analysis of mother-infant interactions, has described the process of reciprocity, in which the mother and infant become synchronous with each other in cycles of attention and non-attention. He believes that mother-infant interaction is not a simple stimulus-response model but that a variety of maternal behavior clusters are involved in stimulating the infant. The rhythmicity between primary care giver and infant is an essential ingredient in their developing relationship.

Variables influencing the maternal attachment process include the

CHILD AND FAMILY DEVELOPMENT

presence of a care taker, the "fit" between mother (care taker) and infant, and the sex of the infant. From studies of institutional environments, where development of attachment is absent or delayed, Yarrow (1961) has concluded that "a stable caretaker who provides individualized attention is essential" for development of the attachment relationship. However, group care itself does not necessarily result in absent or delayed attachment (Ainsworth, 1967; Caldwell et al., 1970; Schaffer and Emerson, 1964a,b; Spiro, 1954). It appears that in these situations, although cared for by multiple care takers, the child has a distinctive relationship with one person. A contingent relationship involving a high degree of maternal responsiveness is one factor affecting attachment (Ainsworth and Bell, 1970; Schaffer and Emerson, 1964a). A number of studies provide support for the notion that attachment is facilitated or hindered by the amount and variety of social stimulation provided by the care taker (Bell, 1970; Caldwell, et al., 1970; Casler, 1961; Schaffer and Emerson, 1964a).

Yarrow (1963) indicates that the "fit" between mother and infant is an important variable in the development of attachment, that is, the extent to which the two are similar in temperament, activity level, and modality preferences. One consequence of lack of fit is that the mother may give the baby less social stimulation and less nurturance than a mother who has a good fit.

In the process of becoming attached to her infant, the mother is engaged in a definable physical claiming process, as well as a psychological identification of the infant whereby infants are identified with values perceived as "good" by their mothers. These processes have been seen as basic to the mother-infant unit (Ainsworth, 1964; Bowlby, 1951; Brody, 1961; Coleman and Provence, 1957; Ritvo and Solnit, 1958; Robertson, 1962; Winnicott, 1960). Claiming and identification are frequently associated with positive values in mothers, fathers, and significant relationship figures.

> Disclaiming and malidentification are the processes through which the newly born infants can be, and are, identified with negative, toxic, dangerous qualities which mothers experience in themselves, the fathers of their infants, and other significant relationship figures. Those mothers whose self-esteem is minimal or absent; who experience themselves as damaged, defective and dangerous beings do not appear to believe they can produce healthy, able safe babies. They show signs of experiencing their infants as they experience themselves, as damaged, defective dangerous forces and beings. Toxic identification sometimes begins before or during pregnancy as well as at post-partum. (Morris, 1968, p. 27)

Disclaiming and malidentification processes are said to be associated with destructive physical, emotional, and intellectual learning experiences, as well as with a combination of these expressed in social learning and behaviors (Malone, 1963; Morris and Gould, 1963; Taylor, 1968). Malidentifications are more apt to occur in new mothers who have never felt pleasing to their own mothers or who have an unsatisfactory relationship with their husbands. They are also more likely to occur when a significant person is ill, threatened by death, or dies, or when the family is susceptible to financial and other social stresses (Morris, 1968).

Caplan (1961, p. 103) defines a healthy mother-child relationship as:

> ...one in which the mother reacts to the child *primarily* on the basis of her perception of the child's needs as a person in his own right, respect for those needs, and her attempts to satisfy them to the best of her ability, in line with the accepted practices of her culture and her society. There are four elements, (a) perception, (b) respect, (c) satisfaction of the child's needs, and (d) the child being seen as a person in his own right.

The healthy relationship involves reciprocal gratification of both mother and child. The mother satisfies her needs to be motherly, protecting, comforting, and nurturing when she interacts with her infant. She is gratified by satisfying her baby's needs.

Caplan's definition of a healthy mother-child relationship implies a psychological separation of the child from the mother. Psychological separation of the mother and baby may not occur at the time of the physical separation brought about by cutting the umbilical cord. The symbiotic relationship, in which the mother relates to the child symbiotically as though it were a part of herself, may continue for a period of time. In our culture, the gradual change from a symbiotic to diatrophic (one structure supporting another) relationship usually begins about 3 months after birth and is reasonably complete by the baby's first birthday (Caplan, 1961, p. 108).

There is increasing evidence to support the notion that the amount of time a parent spends with the child is not a useful index of the child's attachment to either parent (Fein and Clarke-Stewart, 1973; Pederson and Robson, 1969; Schaffer and Emerson, 1964b). Clark-Stewart's findings (1973) indicated that the amount of time the mother actually played with, stimulated, or provided affectionate contact accounted for only about 5 percent of the infant's waking day.

Leiderman (1975) identifies two principal factors that affect the mother-infant relationship and its development. The temporal determinants include the time of initiation and the continuity and quality of the mother's contact with her newborn infant. Structural determinants refer to the sex and birth order of the infant and possibly to a variety of socioeconomic variables.

Brazelton (1975b) describes mothers' reciprocal behaviors with their infants as being "smoother, more low keyed, more cyclic" than the behaviors of fathers. Mothers use behaviors such as vocalization, smiling, looking and patting, and attempts to "contain" the babies through smiles, and so on. They are sensitive to the competing physiological demands of their babies and do not appear in such a hurry for the babies to smile, reach, or vocalize.

PATERNAL ATTACHMENT   We strongly believe that paternal-infant attachment and relationships are important and worthy of our attention and reinforcement. The fact that this section is shorter than the previous one in no way indicates its lack of importance, but rather the state of current research. Only within the past few years has much been written about the development of attachment between fathers and infants, and researchers are just beginning to look at the triadic relationship of mother, father, and infant. It is generally believed that the father's support of the mother can enhance interactions for all three family members.

Greenberg and Morris (1974) refer to the father's absorption, preoccupation, and interest in his infant as "engrossment." In this study of 30 first-time fathers' feelings about their newborn infants, the researchers found that within the first 3 days of his infant's birth, the father develops a feeling of preoccupation, absorption, and interest in his baby. The newborn's face, activity, and eye movements are significant to the father, and he often perceives these activities as the infant's response to him. No highly significant differences in engrossment were noted in fathers who were present at the infant's birth and those who were not, although the fathers who saw the birth generally commented that "when you see your child born, you know it's yours."

Lamb (1976a) found evidence of qualitative differences in the nature of the infant's interaction with mother and father. Fathers were more likely to hold the babies to play, while mothers more often held them to perform care-taking functions. He indicated that babies responded more positively to physical contact with their fathers.

Brazelton (1975b) indicates that most, though certainly not all, fathers seem to have a more "playful, jazzing-up approach" to their infants. Their timing is rhythmic, with an even quality, but their behaviors have a more "incisive" and "heightening" quality than those of

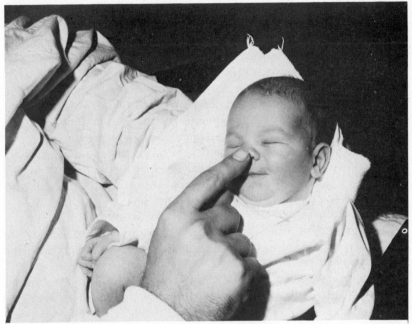

FIGURE 3-12 *(Reprinted with permission from Hymovich, D. P. and Barnard, M. U. Family health care. New York: McGraw-Hill, 1973, p. 216.)*

mothers. By 2 or 3 weeks infants respond differentially to their fathers, with higher, deeper, and somewhat more jagged cycles than with their mothers. In addition they are more wide-eyed, playful, and bright-eyed.

Parke (1975) has studied mother-father-infant triadic relationships. In both middle-class and lower-class families, the father took a more active and dominant role than did the mother, in that he touched, vocalized, and held the baby more than his wife did. The mother, however, smiled at the baby more often than the father. Parke's studies have not revealed any behavioral differences between mothers and fathers when each is interacting alone with their infant. Parke believes there are parallels between maternal and paternal behavior, although we do not yet have data to support this belief. He concludes from his studies that the father is much more involved in and responsive toward his infant than our culture has acknowledged.

Learning Cues of Infant Communication   Learning the cues of infant communication is a prerequisite to satisfactory parent-infant interaction.

During this stage, parents are learning to anticipate and recognize their baby's needs (Friedman and Friedman, 1977; Spaulding, 1969).

Empathy is a necessary ingredient in a mother's effective communication with her infant. According to Lidz (1976, p. 128), "A proper empathy permits a consistency in responding to the infant's changing needs and ways which permits a type of nonverbal communication to become established between mother and child that eases the first year of life and can help greatly to keep his discomforts and tensions minimal."

As mentioned earlier, a high degree of maternal responsiveness to her infant's signals affects the infant's ability to become attached to its mother. It is suggested that the mother's sensitivity to her infant's signals and ability to individualize her behavior facilitates the infant's ability to differentiate itself from the external environment.

Ainsworth and Bell (1970) indicated from their study of 23 middle-class mother-infant pairs, that the mother's sensitivity to her baby's signals was significant in the infant's development of attachment. This sensitivity included her noticing the cries, interpreting them accurately, and responding to them promptly and appropriately. The extent of the father's empathy and its effect on the infant have not been studied.

Maintaining Satisfactory Relationship with Spouse   To maintain a satisfactory relationship with one another, the new parents need to reestablish ways of being a couple (Duvall, 1977). If the couple has not successfully resolved the tasks occurring during the establishment and pregnancy phases of family life, they will carry over these problems into this new stage of development. Caplan (1961) indicates that sometimes a husband and wife are so clearly attached to each other that they regard the presence of children as an interference. They see the children as being in the way of their completely satisfying each other's needs.

The new parents must reestablish their sexual relationships with each other following the infant's birth. Falicov (1973) found that 19 primiparas indicated their sexual performance greatly increased after pregnancy, ultimately surpassing the prepregnant level. However, in a study by LeMasters (1957), the men reported less sexual responsiveness from their wives. In the early puerperium there was anxiety regarding the resumption of relations. Fatigue and physical discomforts (perineum and breasts) reduced both the desire and the frequency of sexual activity.

If the obstetrician has suggested the couple not become sexually active for the weeks following delivery, this can place considerable strain on their relationship. This is often a time when the wife may need reaffirmation of her femininity and desirability and the husband may need such fulfillment. Clark and Affonso (1976) suggest that many couples do not follow such advice and therefore may feel guilty and worry about the consequences.

There is some evidence that breast-feeding behavior and attitudes may be allied to sexual behavior and attitudes toward the opposite sex. Masters and Johnson (1966) noted that nursing mothers, as a group, were interested in as rapid a return to active intercourse with their husbands as possible. In their study, Sears and colleagues (1957) found that mothers who breast-fed were significantly more tolerant of sexual matters such as masturbation and social play in their children.

The father may react to the child's seemingly displacing him in his wife's life with resentment without recognizing the cause (e.g., the arrival of a younger sibling when he was a child). The hostility caused by feelings of rejection will make it difficult to respond to his wife with

FIGURE 3-13   by Debra Hymovich

affection. Dyer (1963) reported that 62 percent of the husbands he interviewed felt they were being neglected by their wives 6 months after the baby was born. Gilman and Knox (1976) found that 91 percent of white, middle-class fathers who went out alone with their wives after the birth of the baby reported better than average marriages, while only 78 percent of those with restricted social lives reported happy marriages.

Supporting Siblings of the New Infant   If there is a second child in the family, a new relationship may develop between the father and the older child. The father frequently assumes a more active role in providing physical care. He may also expand his role in the social life of the child (Clark and Affonso, 1976). Men vary greatly in their ability and willingness to take part in the care of the infant.

Adjusting to the Strains of Parenthood   Gordon and Gordon (1967) attributed postpartum emotional distress to a variety of causes. Moving to new communities brings with it the concomitant need to depend upon professionals and new acquaintances rather than on family and old friends. After the birth of the baby, most women are confined to home and "must yield much personal freedom, economic reward, social prestige and friends." Young husbands must also reorient their thinking as they assume their new obligations as fathers. It takes time and preparation to develop skill in helping their wives in their new roles. They find wives turning to them for both practical and moral support in caring for the infant as well as for extra affection, interest, and morale boosting. In fact, the Gordons report that studies have shown the birth of a first child can precipitate extreme anxiety and even acute psychotic breaks in fathers. Their studies have shown that a father who feels insecure over his own masculine image and worries about his role as a model for a son is more likely to be upset after the birth of male children, while the mother is more prone to emotional problems when the infant is a daughter.

Gordon and Gordon (1967) identify three categories of stresses that impinge upon young parents. The first are the *sensitizers*. These are extremely upsetting experiences, especially from childhood, such as parental divorce, serious personal illness, and separation from loved ones. Mothers who had a greater number of stresses in their background were more likely to have emotional difficulties following childbirth than mothers with fewer stresses. Of the women whose disturbance was serious enough to require psychiatric intervention, three-quarters reported seven or more such stresses.

The second category of stresses includes the *pressurizers*, that is, the continuous or repeated stresses of living that are particularly numerous for socially mobile couples. Examples of pressurizers include no relatives available to help with baby care, husband frequently away from home, or illness in the wife. Pressurizers are particularly significant in maintaining an emotional disorder once it develops. The Gordons found that women with many current conflicts and no help or guidance developed emotional disorders lasting 6 months or more. This was true even for women without previous sensitization. On the other hand, many sensitized women who received adequate support from husbands, families, or professionals overcame their difficulties within 6 weeks of delivery.

In Larsen's study (1966) of military wives, she also found that women with the advantages of a good income, practical help and support, previous child-care experience, and few obstetrical complications adjusted best to maternity. The well-adjusted women felt favorably toward motherhood, placed a high value on babies, and were in agreement with their husbands' attitudes.

The third source of stress is the *precipitators.* These are described as the "final shock or series of shocks" leading to emotional breakdown. Emotional collapse may be precipitated by events as the birth itself, moving to a new home, the husband's loss of a job, or unexpected illness or death in the family during the prenatal period.

Emotional lability is a common occurrence for new mothers during the early postpartum period (Baker, 1967). A few days following delivery, many women find they have an unexpected degree of depression, usually referred to as the "4-day blues." Although the blues syndrome occurs following home and hospital deliveries, it appears to be more common following a hospital confinement (Cone, 1972). No significant relationship was noted between the incidence of depression and maternal age, parity, or method of delivery (Cone, 1972). Hamilton (1962) suggests the onset of postpartum reactions occurs on the third day, while Shainess (1966) suggests that subtle mood changes are likely to be observable by the second day.

A study by Liakos and colleagues (1972) provided evidence that occurrence of the 4-day blues is more common when there is no maternal figure living at home or when the infant is unwanted by the mother or by both parents. Cone's study of 193 new mothers indicated that of the 44 percent who became depressed during the early puerperium, those who were breast-feeding became depressed only on the fourth and fifth postpartum days while those who were bottle-feeding were affected any time from the third through the eighth day.

Facilitating Infant Development Bromwich (1976) suggests the occurrence of a six-stage progression of maternal behaviors deemed favorable to infant development that occur when a mother interacts with her infant. These behaviors were developed as part of the UCLA Infant Studies Project, the aim of which was to enhance the quality of maternal-infant interaction. These stages of maternal behavior were used for assessment of the dyad and as a guide for intervention to enhance the cognitive and affective development of the child. The levels are as follows (Bromwich, 1976, pp. 440–441). The mother

1 Enjoys being with her infant
2 Is a sensitive observer of her infant, reads the baby's behavioral cues accurately, and is responsive to them
3 Engages in a quality and quantity of interaction with her infant that is mutually satisfying and that provides opportunity for the development of attachment and the beginning of a system of communication
4 Demonstrates an awareness of materials, activities, and experiences suitable for her infant's current stage of development
5 Initiates new play activities and experiences based on the same principles as activities and experiences suggested to or modeled for her
6 Independently generates a wide range of developmentally appropriate activities and experiences, interesting to the infant, in familiar and in new situations and at new levels of the child's development

MAINTAINING AND ADAPTING FAMILY ORGANIZATION AND MANAGEMENT TO MEET CHANGING NEEDS

As the new parents learn to accept and adjust to new strains and pressures, they become involved in establishing and maintaining new and healthful family routines. As the new father learns to conform to the new routines, he begins to adapt his eating, sleeping, and resting habits to the patterns established by the baby and mother.

The new mother gradually learns to readjust her time schedule to allow for the necessities of child care, as well as for some recreational activities for herself. She also learns to adapt family routines to meet the changing needs of the growing infant and to assure sufficient rest, relaxation, and sleep for each member.

Levinger (1964), in a study of 60 families in Cleveland, found that parent role specialization increased following the arrival of children. For a time the wife may be the expressive leader with the children more than the husband. But with each other, equality in expressiveness remains.

Fein (1976) found that, following the birth of their first infant, new fathers who adjusted to the changes in their lives developed either a breadwinner or nontraditional role. Those who established the bread-winner role ($N = 10$) set up distinct divisions of labor with their wives that seemed to be satisfactory for both of them. Wives of these men seemed to enjoy being full-time mothers. The nine men in the nontradi-tional role were deeply involved in their babies' care, and almost all their wives wanted to combine mothering with work or school. The 11 men who were having a relatively more difficult time adjusting to their new family life seemed unsure of which role they wanted to adopt; their wives, too, seemed relatively unsure of the role they wished for them-selves.

Supervision of the children for the working mother becomes an im-portant consideration.

FUNCTIONING IN THE COMMUNITY

The parents' position in society changes once they have a child. They begin to establish new sets of relationships with couples who have chil-dren of the same age. Mothers often compare their children's devel-opment and share advice with each other (Lidz, 1976).

EFFECT OF SELECTED VARIABLES ON INFANT AND FAMILY DEVELOPMENT

SEX

The literature on the effect of sex is quite variable, but in general there appear to be few, if any, consistent sex differences in child development and behavior during the first year of life (Maccoby, 1966). Those differ-ences that do exist are important because parents, especially fathers, were found to view and label their infants differently on the basis of the child's gender (Rubin et al., 1974).

Several studies have indicated differences in maternal perceptions depending upon the sex of their infants. For example, 1-day-old girls were reported to be significantly softer, smaller, finer featured, and more inattentive than 1-day-old boys, although there were no significant differ-ences in their heights, weights, or Apgar scores.

The sex of the infant may affect attachment. Small-sample studies suggest that infant girls are more precocious in such attachment-related behaviors as reaction to strangers (Robson et al., 1969); female infants seem more sensitive to tactile stimulation (Bell and Costello, 1964), and their early social behavior (e.g., smiling) is more likely to elicit a re-sponse from the mother than is the case for boys (Lewis, 1972).

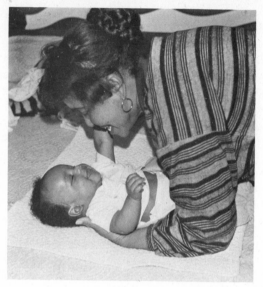

FIGURE 3-14 by Elizabeth Tong

It has been found that mothers pick up their crying 3- to 12-week-old female infants more often than their crying male infants. They also stimulate and arouse the girls more often, imitate vocalizations of female infants more often (Moss, 1967), and smile and talk more often to 2-day-old female infants (Thoman et al., 1972). Will and colleagues' data (1976) indicate that mothers behave differently toward a 6-month-old infant based on their perceptions of the infant's sex, and it appears that mothers are not aware of their differential treatment.

ADOLESCENT PARENTS

One of the factors influencing the development of mothering is the woman's developmental level. According to Erikson (1963), the young adult is psychologically ready for and has a commitment to mutual intimacy. If she has reached the stage of acquiring intimacy and solidarity while avoiding a sense of isolation, she will be able to accept, provide for, and relate to another individual—in this case her infant.

Child-rearing practices and attitudes of adolescent mothers have not been systematically studied, and much of our knowledge is indirect and anecdotal. One of the problems faced by adolescents is having to drop out of school once the baby is born because they do not have child-care arrangements that enable them to continue attending school. In a study by Smith and colleagues (1975), more single mothers (57 percent) were found to be actively engaged in completing their formal education and vocational training than married teenagers (17 percent).

In their study of 134 adolescents approximately 8 months following delivery, Smith et al. (1975) found that the maternal grandmother was the major infant care taker (42 percent), followed by the adolescent herself (36 percent). A few used baby-sitters, siblings, or other relatives for care taking. Of the single girls interviewed, 46 percent used their own mothers to care for the infant compared with 31 percent of the married teenagers.

Young mothers tend to view infant stimulation as likely to spoil the child (Williams, 1974). At the same time it is believed that these teenagers are good candidates for training in child rearing because they enjoy playing with their children and they have a great deal of energy.

It has been suggested that the self-concept of adolescent mothers may not be especially well established because of their stage of development. However, a recent study by Fischman (1975) indicated that 80 percent of urban, black, unmarried 13- to 18-year-olds who chose to deliver their infants had either medium or high self-esteem as measured by a 10-item scale.

Adolescent mothers living at home with their own mothers were likely to have greater difficulty accepting their parental responsibility than those living away from home because of the tendency for the grandmother to take over the infant's care. This may increase the insecurity generally present in most young mothers with their first babies. The adolescent is often in conflict over her love of the baby and desire to care for it while at the same time wanting to be with her peers (Smith et al., 1975).

Breast-feeding is rare in school-aged mothers (Williams, 1974). One reason is that it tends to be associated with being poor, and buying bottles, formulas, and so on, for the baby is an indication that one can afford to purchase things for the infant. Other possible reasons are that breast-feeding is considered physically repulsive to many teenagers, there is a lack of privacy if one is living in an extended family, and breast-feeding is thought to be impossible (an all-or-none proposition) if the mother is at work or in school all day.

TEMPERAMENT

As noted previously, there is considerable range of normal variation in the dates of attainment of specific milestones and also in the temperament characteristics of young children, thus making some easier to rear than others.

Although Thomas et al., (1968) found that the behavioral character-istics of infants were not stable enough for predictive purposes until about 3 months of age, Brazelton (1961, 1973), Korner (1973, 1974), Soule (1974), and others have noted differences in newborn responsivity that may affect the initial pattern of mother-infant interaction. Newborn infants were found to vary in such behaviors as frequency and duration of crying, soothability, self-comforting behavior, "state" alterability, stimulus threshold, "state" clarity, and the like.

By 3 months of age many of these initial variations and such tran-sient conditions as "colic" have disappeared or been muted, but there still remains a number of infants (about 10 percent) with the "difficult child" cluster of temperament characteristics: irregularity in biological functions; intense, negative reactions to new situations; slowness in adapting over time; and a predominantly negative mood (Thomas et al., 1968). A new mother whose baby displays these patterns is very likely to think she is doing something radically wrong and needs continuing reassurance from the health provider that both she and the baby are normal (Brazelton, 1961).

HEALTH STATUS

Intrauterine Infection   The impact on many areas of development of intrauterine infections is brought out in the study by Chess and colleagues (1971). In this study, evaluations were made of the function-ing of 243 children being followed in a birth defect clinic in New York City after a rubella epidemic. About one-third of the children had visual, cardiac, and neurological defects, and over two-thirds had some evidence of hearing loss. In almost 50 percent, two or more of these defects were present.

One-half of the children had some evidence of either a psychiatric disorder or mental deficiency, or both; 7 percent had symptoms of infantile autism. Not all these disorders were irreversible, however; 15 percent of the children were diagnosed as having reactive behavior disorders that developed because external circumstances and environ-mental handling were inappropriate for that particular type of child. Only about 3 percent were diagnosed as having "cerebral dysfunction," which for the purpose of this study was defined as children in whom there coexists independent evidence of both involvement of the central nervous system and behavioral symptoms generally associated with brain damage (hypo- or hyperactivity, attention abnormalities, and impulse control disorders).

Nutrition It appears that both the quantity and quality of intake are important. For example, heavier women who gained more weight than lighter women had heavier babies and lower rates of prematurity (Eastman and Jackson, 1968; Singer et al., 1968), and Fomon et al. (1969) found that the higher the caloric value of an infant's formula the greater the weight gain between 8 and 42 days of age.

Low Birth Weight The overall incidence for the United States and England of infants born weighing under 2500 grams is around 7 percent (Drillien, 1964; Harper, 1962; Werner et al., 1971). These low-birth-weight infants include those of normal gestational age who come from small mothers or multiple births; full-term, small infants from a single pregnancy and from normal-sized mothers whose births are associated with placental insufficiency (such as prenatal hypertension, toxemia, infected placenta); and the "true premature" of less than 37-weeks gestation. In one study of 140 consecutive low-birth-weight babies, 44 percent were in the first group, 21 percent in the second, and only 35 percent were true prematures (Werner et al., 1971). These differences are important because the incidence of later developmental problems varies according to type. The highest incidence of delays and deviations occurs in the true premature and the lowest in the small infants from the normal pregnancies of small mothers.

Another important outcome variable is the birth weight by itself. The incidence of developmental delays and deviations is much higher in the very small premature infant under 1500 grams. Fortunately, this group makes up only about 10 to 15 percent of the total low-birth-weight group (Drillien, 1964; Harper et al., 1975).

Teberg and colleagues (1977) report a study of 176 infants born between 1965 and 1970 who weighed less than 1500 grams at birth. No significant developmental and neurological differences were found when infants weighing 1000 to 1500 grams were compared with those weighing less than 1000 grams. Of the entire group, 67 percent were found to be developmentally and neurologically normal.

It is also clear that small prematures do not occur at random in the general population (Abramowicz and Kass, 1966; Birch and Gussow, 1970; Yankauer et al., 1953). The incidence of prematurity is increased for (1) mothers who lose weight or gain less than 10 pounds during their pregnancy, (2) very young mothers, (3) those who are not married at the time of conception, and (4) mothers of low socioeconomic status. From this it is obvious that low birth weight is associated with a wide variety of other environmental factors that may affect the development of the child as much as or more than the event of premature birth by itself. Since many of the follow-up studies have not taken these factors into account it is difficult to know how big a role they play in developmental outcomes.

Studies that have taken account of environmental factors have generally found there is an interactive effect. Infants from favorable socioeconomic environments and with a mildly reduced birth weight are usually indistinguishable from full-term infants, while the premature weighing under 1500 grams from a poor socioeconomic environment has the highest incidence of physical and developmental problems. These combined effects occur for all parameters of development, including physical growth and cognitive and social development.

Perhaps the best longitudinal study in this regard is the *The Children of Kauai* (Werner et al., 1971). In this study, the outcome of 2703 consecutive pregnancies is reported over a period of 10 years. These pregnancies resulted in 1963 live-born children, of which 140 (7.2 percent) had a birth weight under 2500 grams. Outcome measures included growth, health status, and intellectual and social development. These were evaluated in terms of a perinatal stress score of 0 to 3, with the 3 indicating a birth weight of under 1800 grams, plus or minus other complications. Environmental measures included estimates of the intellectual and socioeconomic status of the mother, family stability, and the amount of intellectual stimulation and emotional support being provided to the child in the home.

At the 2-year follow-up the degree of perinatal stress was related to all aspects of child development, with the deficits increasing proportionately to the amount of perinatal stress. The environmental measures were also correlated with these outcomes, and the two were additive. For example, the authors found:

> The effect of a deprived home environment was especially pronounced for children with moderate and severe perinatal stress. The difference in mean Cattel IQ's (scores) around age 2 between children with severe perinatal stress growing-up in a favorable environment and those with severe stress growing up in a predominantly unfavorable environment amounted to 16–34 IQ points depending upon the environmental variable. It was especially dramatic for the socioeconomic status and the family stability ratings. In contrast the differences in mean Cattel IQ's between children with severe perinatal stress and those without any perinatal complications, growing-up in an adequate early environment, though significant, amounted to only 6 to 7 IQ points. (Werner et al., 1971, p. 55)

The importance of environmental influence was even more dramatic at the 10-year follow-up. Only with the small group experiencing severe perinatal stress was there still a significant relationship between stress and outcome. For the much larger group of low-birth-weight babies weighing between 1500 and 2500 grams at birth there were hardly any differences in the outcome measures.

This study is important not only in showing the effects on development of the interaction between perinatal stress and environmental factors and the long-term deficits associated with severe perinatal stress, but also in placing these small numbers of children in proper perspective by comparing them with the much larger numbers of children in the general population with similar or worse deficits that appear largely environmental in origin. For example, the authors of the study report the following:

> The educational stimulation received in the home was the best criterion to differentiate between children with and without achievement problems, IQ's below 85, language and perceptual problems. Of the children of Kauai whose homes were rated "high" or "very high" in educational stimulation (on the basis of opportunities provided for enlarging the child's vocabulary, availability of books, intellectual leisure-time activities, and encouragement of discipline and work habits), only 14 per cent (9 children) had achievement problems in school. In contrast to this 62 per cent (276) of the children in whose homes few or none of these opportunities were available had difficulties with the basic school subjects in school. Only 21 of 378 children who had poor grades or were in special classes came from the group with severe perinatal complications. (Werner et al., 1971, p. 69)

Therefore, in following low-birth-weight babies, one can expect a higher incidence of below-average measures in physical, intellectual, and social and emotional growth, but at least some of these deficits will be related to the environmental correlations of low birth weight rather than to low birth weight and perinatal stresses by themselves.

Leifer and colleagues (1972) demonstrated significant differences in attachment between mothers of full-term infants and two groups of mothers of preterm infants at 1 month of age. Mothers separated the first 3 to 12 hours (except visual contact) from their preterm infants did not behave differently from mothers of preterm infants permitted early (2 to 3 days after birth) tactile contact. But, those with prolonged separation (3 to 12 weeks) did have more divorces (5 versus 0) and relinquished more babies for adoption (2 versus 0).

Central Nervous System Dysfunction CEREBRAL PALSY Studies of the early motor and speech development of children with spastic hemiplegia and cerebral palsy show average delays of 6 to 15 months in attainment of both milestones (Denhoff and Holden, 1951; Hood and Perlstein, 1956). Similar delays are seen in children with mental retardation. But in that disorder, motor development generally shows the least lag while the area of slowest progress is the acquisition of language.

MENTAL DEFICIENCY   Because of the relative ease of identifying these children soon after birth, the development of children with Down's syndrome provides an opportunity to study the effects of severe mental deficiency. The longitudinal study by Carr (1975) that follows a group of 45 of these children to age 4 and contrasts their development with a normal control group is a rich source of such data. The following descriptions from this study are of the development of home-reared infants. Infants reared in institutions were even more retarded in their development.

Developing and maintaining healthy growth and nutrition patterns   On the average, the babies with Down's syndrome were described as excessively sleepy, less alert, less eager for food, and having a weaker sucking reflex when compared with normal infants. Fewer of the mothers were success-ful in breast-feeding, and many of the babies had to be put on a regular schedule because they were so undemanding and would sleep long pe-riods of time unless awakened. Nothing is reported in this study about the growth patterns of the children.

Learning to control one's body satisfactorily   The mean age of walking for the home-reared children with Down's syndrome was 28.8 months, compared with 14.4 months for the control group. By 3 years of age 80 percent of the children were walking.

Only 22 percent of these children were using a pincer grasp of thumb and forefinger by 15 months of age. By 3 years of age, 82 percent were doing this. The average age of passing this item on the Bayley test is about 9 months.

In terms of self-care, the children with Down's syndrome were considerably delayed in acquiring the ability to feed themselves. At 15 months of age only 34 percent of the children were feeding themselves with their fingers and only 16 percent were using a spoon. In the normal control group the percentages for these skills were 95 and 57 percent, respectively. In another study, Share and Veale (1974) reported lags of 10 to 24 months for these areas.

Learning to understand and relate to the physical world   The intelligence quotient (as measured by the Bayley Test of Infant Development) of home-reared infants averaged about 80 at 2 months of age and dropped fairly sharply to 60 at 10 months of age. There was then a more gradual decline to an average level of 40 by age 2. The control group maintained an average level of 100 during this same time period. For infants not raised in the home the fall was somewhat steeper, with an average score of around 25 at 10 months and a gradual fall to about 20 at 2 years. Only 4 percent of the children scored over 80 at 10 months of age. The pattern of development also seemed different, with long plateaus of no increase in abilities interspersed with short periods of rapid gains.

Learning to relate to others   Crying patterns did not differ significantly from the control group. Smiling was assessed at only two points in time. None of the children could produce a social smile at 6 weeks, and all of them could at 6 months.

Language development was delayed, with only 14 percent of the children with Down's syndrome saying two words by age 2. Physical expression of anger (temper tantrums) was common in both groups but significantly more common in the controls. Of the children with Down's syndrome, 44 percent were said to have never had a tantrum by age 15 months, whereas this was true for only 15 percent of the controls. At 15 months, control children were more active and getting into things, but this seemed to be largely related to their more advanced motor development.

Sensory Deficits BLINDNESS Fraiberg (1970) has studied the effect of blindness on infant development. Smiling in response to the mother's voice was noted at 3 to 4 weeks of age, though several repetitions were needed as a stimulus. As the child grew older, the most reliable stimulus was some kind of gross tactile or kinesthetic stimulus such as bouncing, jiggling, tickling, or nuzzling. Overall, she noted that blind children do not smile automatically in a greeting and do not smile as frequently as sighted babies. The smile itself appears somewhat muted when compared to that of others. At 6 to 13 months, most of the babies reacted to being held by a stranger with crying, screaming, and physical resistance.

Fraiberg (1975) also noted delays of 6 to 7 months in crawling and walking of children. The sighted child can walk independently about 3 months after walking with hands held. The blind child may not do so until 8 to 9 months later. The median age of creeping was 13 months and of walking across the room 19 months. Some of these developmental lags could be markedly decreased by training the parents to provide additional help and encouragement.

DEAFNESS The initial vocalizations of deaf children (crying, cooing, babbling) are apparently indistinguishable in tone and quality from those of hearing children. After about 6 months, the frequency of spontaneous vocalizations decreases and sounds lack the inflections so characteristic of the "jargon" used by the hearing child (Lenneberg et al., 1965).

In a study by Schlesinger and Meadow (1972), 40 deaf children were contrasted with 20 hearing children. For the majority of deaf children the lag in language development averaged about 16 months. In contrast, studies of a few children learning to communicate with sign language or a combination of oral and sign language indicate their ability to communicate (with signs) is close to that of hearing children (Schlesinger and Meadow, 1972).

Severe Emotional Disturbances AUTISTIC AND PSYCHOTIC CHILDREN In a retrospective study of the early developmental characteristics of brain-damaged, autistic, and schizophrenic children, no behaviors were found to be unique to any diagnostic group, though all three clinical groups had more symptoms than the normal control group (DeMyer et al., 1973).

There was some tendency for the autistic and psychotic children to be more withdrawn and poorly communicative in speech than either the brain-damaged or normal controls, but there was considerable overlap. When compared to the control group, the children in the clinical groups were more often described as showing less interest in their environment as a whole, but having a tendency to stare in a preoccupied way at close objects. They also had slower-than-average speech and motor development. These developmental deviations are similar to those described in children experiencing social deprivation and are probably nonspecific reactions to a variety of insults.

Other studies show that the first year of development in children who later develop childhood schizophrenia is often quite normal, while children with infantile autism often show abnormalities soon after birth (Bender, 1942, 1947; Creak, 1961; Kanner, 1943). Many of these latter children have feeding problems, and one of the first signs of disturbance is their failure to make postural adaptations in anticipation of being picked up as do normal children. The most striking deficits, however, are in social development.

Autistic children seem happiest when left alone. They do not seek attention and in general act as though people around them do not exist. They manipulate parts of a person like they would objects but do not make eye contact or relate to the person as a person. There is little or no evidence of separation anxiety or fear of strangers. Motor and speech development are often retarded, but this is uneven with some aspects near normal.

FAMILY SIZE AND STRUCTURE

Single Parenthood   Children of single parents are apt to be exposed to multiple care takers at an early age, as most parents must work to care for themselves and their children (Williams, 1974). For example, many adolescent mothers live with their parents and their infants receive supplemental care from member(s) of the extended family, especially the grandmother. For the single parent, some strains may be more difficult if there is no one with whom to share the burdens of baby care.

Working Mothers   In this country, over one-third of all mothers work. The age of the child is a major factor in determining the percentage of mothers working and the proportion of time worked. This is true for both black and white mothers, although a higher proportion of black mothers work in all child age categories.

In March 1974, 30 percent of all married women from intact families with children under 3 years of age were working. Of mothers with children under 6 years, 33 percent were employed, and 51 percent with children between 6 and 17 years were working. Two-thirds of these women were employed full time. For single mothers, 45 percent with children under 3 years were employed (86 percent full time), while 54 percent with children under 6 years and 67 percent with school-aged children were working (80 percent full time) (Bronfenbrenner, 1976).

Yarrow et al. (1962) studied 50 working and 50 nonworking middle-class mothers in Washington, D.C. These two groups did not differ in their definition of the accepted female role in marriage or in their preference for their present way of carrying out their roles. The mothers in both groups who were satisfied with their present roles did equally well in their mother roles, but of those mothers who were dissatisfied, those who remained at home did a poorer job as mothers than those who went to work. The working, college-educated mother planned more time with her family on weekends than did the high school–educated mother. The high school–educated mother increased her control over her children and gave them more responsibility for doing things around the house. Yarrow's work indicates that working or not working is not the key to how a mother carried out her mother role, but that her satisfaction with what she was doing and her educational level were more important factors.

SOCIOECONOMIC AND CULTURAL INFLUENCES

Reports regarding social class differences indicate minimal difference in the affective elements of mother-child interaction (Bayley and Schaefer,

1960; Tulkin and Kagan, 1972) and larger differences in verbal interaction and cognitive stimulation (Levine et al., 1967; Tulkin and Kagan, 1972). In fact, Moss and colleagues (1969) found that "less well-educated mothers provided more physical stimulation for their infants than better educated mothers." There are data to support the notion that lower-class mothers do not believe they can do much to influence their children's development (Minuchin et al., 1967; Tulkin and Kagan, 1972).

In 1972, Tulkin and Kagan studied the interaction of 30 middle-class and 26 working-class white mothers with their 10-month-old infants. They found that in the working-class homes there was more "extraneous noise" and crowding, the children had more interaction with adults other than their mothers, and spent more time in front of television sets than did the middle-class babies. In addition, the working-class infants had somewhat fewer environmental objects with which to play (pots, magazines, and so on) and spent less time with "no barriers." Middle-class mothers entertained their infants and gave them things to play with more often than did the working-class mothers. They also responded more frequently and quickly to their infants' spontaneous fretting.

The relationship between breast-feeding and social class is very complex, and study results depend upon the location and period of history when the data were collected. In America, it appears that breast-feeding is generally linked with high social status (Newton, 1971), although this, too, tends to be associated with location. For example, Meyer (1968) reported 50 percent of the babies born in Oregon, 49 percent in Utah, and 86 percent in Rhode Island were totally bottle-fed.

A longitudinal study of black and white infants from birth to 1 year (Kasius et al., 1957) demonstrated that the black babies weighed slightly less than their white counterparts except at age 3 months. The white infants were slightly longer at birth, but by 3 months there was no difference in length, and by 1 year the black children, especially the girls, were slightly longer.

Social Deprivation Delays in development of children being reared in institutions providing only custodial care have been reported (Dennis, 1941; Provence and Lipton, 1962; Spitz, 1945). The effects of deprivation are brought out in a detailed study by Provence and Lipton (1962) of infants being reared in an institutional setting providing minimal social stimulation. The babies and children were well cared for physically, but were fed with propped bottles, rarely talked to or played with on a one-to-one basis, and seldom allowed to play out of their cribs.

Comparisons were made between the development of these children ($N = 75$) and a group of family-reared infants ($N = 75$). The differences noted were as follows:

DEVELOPING AND MAINTAINING HEALTHY GROWTH AND NUTRITION PATTERNS Nothing is said about this task in the Provence study, but others have noted poor weight gain and some "failure to thrive" in infants reared under conditions of social deprivation (Coleman and Provence, 1957).

LEARNING TO CONTROL ONE'S BODY SATISFACTORILY In the first 3 or 4 weeks of life there were no detectable differences in the motor development of the two groups of infants. The first easily observable difference occurred in the second month of life in regard to the way the infants reacted to being held. The institutionalized infants did not make postural adjustments, were not cuddly, and felt rather more like sawdust dolls.

The ability to stabilize the head when pulled from a prone to a sitting position was delayed beyond that of the home-reared infants. In the lower extremities less kicking action was noted, and the infants did not put their feet down voluntarily to support a fraction of their weight when held in a standing position. Prone behavior such as rolling over and creeping was near normal, but sitting, standing, and walking were all delayed. Specific figures for these delays are not given, but by 10 months of age the mean developmental quotient for the institutionalized infants was 85 compared to 106 for those reared in homes.

The ability to perform the pincer grasp was present at about the normal time, but the infants did not make use of it in the same way as home-reared infants. Considerably less manipulation and spontaneous play with test materials during developmental testing were noted from 8 months on.

The only type of motor activity that was increased in the institutionalized infants was rocking. The onset of this was noted at around 4 to 5 months and peaked about 8 months of age. This first appeared as head rolling in the prone position and then progressed to rocking back and forth on all fours. In spite of these delays and deviations, motor development was the least impaired of all the major areas.

LEARNING TO UNDERSTAND AND RELATE TO THE PHYSICAL WORLD By 4 or 5 months of age differences were noted between the two groups in the way they responded to test materials and toys. The institutionalized infants explored and manipulated objects less, and later on they did particularly poorly on test items that required use of two or more objects simultaneously. There was no evidence that the infants had developed the concept of "object permanence" by the end of the first year, as they would not seek out covered-up toys or objects. There was no evidence of the infants becoming attached to a particular toy, and in general their patterns of play were repetitive and poorly elaborated.

DEVELOPING SELF-AWARENESS AND A SATISFYING SENSE OF SELF The main thing noted in this area was considerably less exploration and manipulation of all body parts as compared to the home-reared infants.

LEARNING TO RELATE TO OTHERS *Crying and smiling* Smiling in response to social stimulation occurred at about the normal time, but the amount of crying appeared markedly reduced.

Communication skills Of all areas of development, the most striking effects were on speech development. By 2 months of age, a decrease in both frequency and quality of vocalization was noted. As mentioned previously, crying was rare, nonspecific, and poorly differentiated. The failure to develop a system of communicative vocal signals was dramatic. It was noted that the repertoire of sounds that the average baby uses for communication with people was available, but minimally used. There were no specific, recognizable words by 1 year of age, and the emotional expressiveness of sounds was markedly constricted. Understanding of language was also retarded, but less than language production.

Social discrimination and attachment One of the earliest differences noted was the tendency for institutionalized infants to look intensely at people or objects for long periods of time. This became apparent at about 3 to 4 months of age and persisted throughout the first year. In spite of this apparent concentration, the infants were delayed in distinguishing between persons and things, and made little effort to initiate or pursue a social contact. There was a blandness of emotional expression and a passiveness toward being examined at an age when most home-reared infants would actively push away the examiner's hand. Imitating adult behavior was delayed, as was evidence of attachment in the form of separation upset and stranger anxiety. Perhaps the most striking lack was the ability to use an adult in any way for either play, pleasure, or relief of distress.

Sexuality In comparison to home-reared infants, a decrease in both sucking and genital play was noted. Other than rocking, the infants seemed unable to use their own bodies for pleasure or relief of distress.

Comparison of Patterns for Mental Deficiency and Social Deprivation The pattern of developmental lag in socially deprived infants is quite different than that for those with Down's syndrome. In the latter, significant differences are noted by 6 weeks and the gap widens considerably by 6 months of age, with some leveling off after that. In contrast, the lag in the development of socially deprived infants gradually develops over time. The differences are not too marked at 6 months of age but become increasingly so by 1 year and are still widening by 18 months.

CHILD-REARING STYLE AND SPECIFIC TRAINING PROCEDURES

Ainsworth and Bell (1970) present data to suggest that the amount of infant crying in the latter half of the first year and the quality of the mother-child attachment are related to the degree of sensitivity the mother shows in perceiving and responding promptly and appropriately to her infant's signals and communication. Just what role individual differences in infant temperament play in this is not clear because the differences found in the infant's attachment behavior are assumed by these authors to be the result of the mother's handling pattern.

Much of the data on early intervention programs were discussed in Chapter 1. Specific approaches used in medical settings are discussed under "Prevention and Management of Developmental Delays" later in this chapter.

MASS MEDIA

Definite differences were noted in the characteristics of parents who were highly influenced by communication sources (interpersonal, mass media, organized education) than those who were not. The "high seekers" of information tended to be women with smaller families and younger firstborns, and they stressed values less than beliefs about infancy, heredity, and learning. They were influenced by their previous experiences with children and responded to the dependent behavior of their own children. The "low seekers" were mothers with larger families and older firstborns (Stolz, 1967).

CLINICAL APPLICATIONS

Health care providers need to be available to the family during the early period following delivery to assess and, when appropriate, intervene in fostering parent-infant bonding. These early visits in the hospital can be used to acquaint parents with the characteristics of their newly born baby, help them learn to perform the necessary care-taking tasks, and support them in their own development.

For the normal baby as well as for the baby with problems, contact should be maintained with the new family during the first few weeks at home as this is frequently a difficult period of adjustment for many. Such contacts might include telephone calls and visits by community health nurses. Gordon and Gordon (1967) found that for parents who also attended antenatal classes, postpartum support and assistance in the home provided by public health nurses were far more effective than the classes alone. Only 9 percent of women who were guided informally outside antenatal classes by obstetricians and nurses developed postpartum emotional difficulties in comparison to women without this additional guidance.

Parke (1975, p. 63) believes "that the care of infants (should be)

FIGURE 3-15

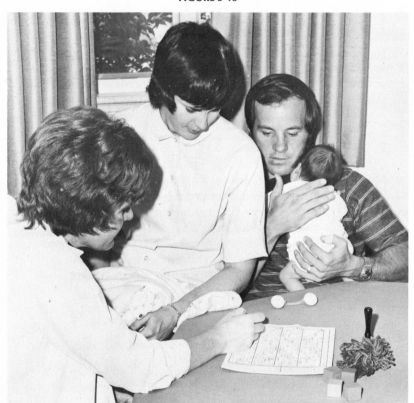

acknowledged as natural and appropriate male behavior." To do this we can encourage open visiting policies for maternity units and father visits for well-child and sick-child care. To facilitate such vists, clinic and office appointments will need to be scheduled at times when it is possible for the father to attend, and fathers will need support from health professionals, as well as their wives, as they undertake such care.

See Table 3-3 for a summary of selected discussion topics and health care activities during the first year of life.

The Healthy Infant

IMMEDIATE POSTPARTUM PERIOD

During the postpartum period (taking-in phase), the mother usually needs an opportunity to review her labor and delivery experience to understand what has happened before she is ready to move on to assuming her role of mother. At this point she needs someone who can listen nonjudgmentally and who can clarify any misconceptions she may have.

Parent-Infant Bonding Parent-infant bonding can be facilitated in the immediate postpartum period (fourth stage of labor) by giving the new parents an opportunity to become acquainted with their infant. The new

FIGURE 3-16

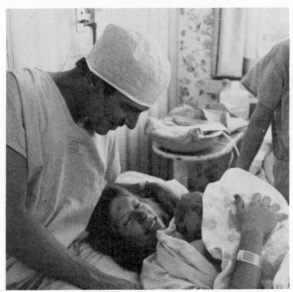

TABLE 3-3

Summary of Discussion Topics and Health Care Activities During the First Year of Life (Family Development)

Time period	Physical needs	Individual potential	Emotional support and communication	Organization and management	Function in community	Home visits
Postpartum (in hospital)	Child-care equipment and clothing	Parents' questions and concerns about child-rearing	Postpartum blues, sibling preparation	Establishment of new routines and roles		Answering mother's questions and concerns, management of crying, food preparation and hygiene
Early weeks (at home)	Household arrangements for safety and convenience	Child spacing	Father participation and support	Dealing with stress and strains of change	Awareness of and utilization of community resources	Demonstration of cognitive stimulation activities Emotional support

TABLE 3-3 (Continued)

Summary of Discussion Topics and Health Care Activities During the First Year of Life (Family Development)

Time period	Physical needs	Individual potential	Emotional support and communication	Organization and management	Function in community	Home visits
1 to 4 months	Provision of nutritious foods	Mother-role satisfaction and maternal employment				
4 to 8 months	Budgeting	Time away from child	Maintenance of husband-wife relationship			Environmental safety
			Relationship with grandparents		Participation in community activities	
8 months to onset of walking	Environmental safety	Maintenance of outside interests				Emotional support

mother should be able to hold and cuddle her baby right away. Klaus and Kennell (1976) suggest waiting until the woman expresses her desire for the infant before placing it on her chest. If she is planning to breast-feed, feeding can be encouraged at this time. If the father is present, he too should be involved in the acquaintance process. If the mother and baby are healthy, the new family should have an opportunity to be together for a period of time shortly after delivery. The infant is generally in a quiet, alert state, and there is opportunity for reciprocal parent-infant interaction to take place.

Rooming-in for mother and infant, unlimited father visiting with his wife and infant, and sibling visits are means of fostering family unity during the lying-in period. Frequent contacts between health providers and the family provide opportunities for assessment and guidance.

Understanding Infant Characteristics When ready, the parents can be helped to learn about the individuality of their new infant in a number of ways. During the first few days, performing a complete physical assessment of the infant in the parents' presence can be used to point out the baby's individual characteristics, to answer questions about their infant, and to provide some anticipatory guidance concerning changes they may expect in the next few weeks. The Neonatal Behavioral Assessment Scale (Brazelton, 1973) can be used to help parents learn the behaviors and strengths of their own infant. As Brazelton (1976, p. 135) so aptly puts it: "We need to 'uncover and expose' the infant's strengths to parents, to demonstrate the infant's behavior on which they can rely and to support young parents in their own individualized endeavor to reach out for, attach to and enjoy their new infants." The scale consists of six categories that measure 27 behavioral responses of the infant. These categories are habituation, orientation, motor maturity, variation (in behaviors), self-quieting abilities, and social behaviors.

Suggestions based on findings using this scale need to be made with caution because there are as yet no data that speak to the predictability of the findings as the infant matures. As with any tool of this nature, single observations may not be indicative of the baby's behavior over time and several assessments may give a more accurate picture of the infant. Recognizing these limitations, it is still a valuable tool to use with parents. When we are assessing the infant in the parents' presence, it enables us to act as role models in handling the infant, as well as to help the parents identify their child's strengths and behavioral characteristics. In addition, it provides us with an opportunity to discuss the parents' perceptions of their infant and to suggest ways of adapting approaches to the child's individual needs and responsiveness. For example, infants

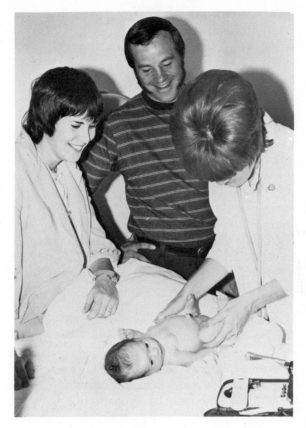

FIGURE 3-17

with low sensory thresholds and high irritability need to be protected from overstimulation while those with low responsiveness may need considerably more sensory input than average if a satisfactory pattern of parent-child interaction is to be established (Korner, 1973, 1974; Soule, 1974; Tronick and Brazelton, 1975).

Common Stage-Related Behaviors   There are a number of normal newborn behaviors that often cause worry or concern in new parents unless they are aware of the normality of such behaviors. To educate parents about these, the following areas should be discussed before the mother's discharge and a handout with information, such as the following can be provided.

1 *Sneezing.* Most babies sneeze repeatedly and this does not mean they are catching cold.

2 *Noisy breathing.* Some babies make a rattling sound when they breathe. This is usually related to mucus in the back of the nose and gradually disappears when the baby is 5 or 6 months of age.

3 *Hiccups and spitting up after feeding.* Babies frequently have hiccups after eating, and some also bring up small amounts of milk. This tends to disappear when the baby begins to sit up and is not harmful in any way.

4 *Getting red in the face and straining with bowel movements.* Most babies look like they are having a hard time passing a stool, but as long as the stool is soft most of the time and the baby does not actually cry when having a bowel movement, nothing need be done. Avoid use of laxatives or suppositories.

5 *Swollen breasts and vaginal bleeding.* Both male and female babies frequently have swelling of tissues in the breast areas, and female babies often have some bloody discharge from the vagina during the first week or so after birth. These are related to stimulation of the tissue by the mother's hormones during the pregnancy and gradually disappear without treatment.

6 *Crying and sleeping through the night.* Most babies have irritable periods when they cry more than one would think they should, usually during the late afternoon or early evening. If the baby is eating all right and otherwise seems well, the crying does not mean anything serious is wrong. Crying reaches a peak when the baby is around 4 to 6 weeks of age and then occurs less often. Most babies are sleeping through the night by 3 months of age.

7 *Skin rashes.* Most babies develop temporary skin rashes on the cheeks and in the diaper areas. These are generally irritations from wetness and rubbing and respond to protective ointments such as petroleum jelly, A&D Ointment, or the like. Leaving off rubber or plastic pants at night is useful in helping to clear up diaper rashes.

8 *Mother "blue" spells.* Many mothers feel weepy and blue for a few days after coming home with a new baby.

If any of these symptoms persist or are worrying, contact with the health care providers is recommended for help in deciding if anything needs to be done.

Infant Feeding   Whether the mother chooses to breast- or bottle-feed her baby, she will need support and guidance as she learns this new task. The advantages of demand feeding, how to recognize the infant's hunger and satiety, and the variation in amount taken at each feeding are important points to cover with all mothers. Mothers who are bottle-feeding also need information concerning formula preparation and the amount of formula the baby may take at each feeding. Advice should take into account the cost of such feeding as there is a wide variation in cost of foods that meet the recommended daily allowances (Lamm et al., 1977). In the early months the types of formula or food source for lactation contribute the largest amount to the cost of feeding. The cost of Beikost (foods other than milk and formula) becomes important in determining cost of infant feeding once solid foods are begun. There is a wide range in the cost of food fed to the infant during the first year. The least expensive formula is one made from evaporated milk.

The Lactating Mother Following birth, provision of sufficient sucking stimulation to produce adequate secretion of milk is necessary. This can be accomplished by initiating breast-feeding within an hour after birth or as soon as possible thereafter; encouraging demand feeding; and avoiding prelacteal, supplementary, or complementary bottles while lactation is being established.

The breast-feeding mother needs guidance in relation to the following areas: (1) positioning self and infant; (2) helping the infant latch onto the breast and removing the infant from the breast; (3) length of nursing time; (4) managing engorged and painful breasts; (5) using supplementary or complementary feedings; and (6) diet required for lactation. It is suggested that the easiest place to breast-feed a baby at night is in bed lying next to the mother. This enables the mother to sleep while the baby sucks (Newton, 1976).

To manage nipple pain and breast engorgement, adequate function of the ejection reflex needs to be encouraged. Methods for encouraging this include letting the baby nurse first on the unaffected or less affected breast, permitting adequate time for nursing, reducing distractions for mother while she is nursing, and assisting milk ejection with intranasal oxytocin spray (Newton, 1971). Avoiding the use of soap and using a bland, hydrous lanolin are likely to be helpful for sore nipples.

Treatment of mastitis includes bed rest, antibiotics, analgesics, and ice bags. The Newtons (1972) indicate the desirability of keeping the breast empty and suggest that allowing the baby to continue to nurse may be the best way to do this. If mastitis progresses into a localized abscess, incision and drainage are necessary. Routinely weaning the baby should not be necessary, although the temporary removal of milk by hand pump may be advisable. Minor mammary duct obstructions may be treated by manual expression or sucking adequate to empty the breast. Aspiration or excision may be required if a larger cyst develops.

Inhibition of the milk ejection reflex can be prevented by providing

privacy and freedom from embarrassment during feeding, peaceful surroundings, and limitation of visitors (hospital or home); and continued
emotional support from health personnel and from a woman who has
successfully breast-fed (Newton and Newton, 1972). Lactation failure is
largely due to psychological factors. In a study of 956 women who
breast-fed their firstborn infants, Ladas (1972) found a very high correlation between information and/or support and outcome of breast-feeding.
One of the best sources of help for parents is the LaLeche League, with
branches throughout the world.

By moderately increasing her normal diet, the woman takes in the
nutrients required for lactation (McKigney, 1971). The Consumer and
Food Economics Division of the U.S. Department of Agriculture (1969)
has developed food plans showing how a nutritionally adequate diet can
be supplied at low, moderate, and liberal cost levels. Approximately
one-third of the weekly diet for a lactating woman is presumed necessary
to support lactation.

Breast-fed babies will need fluoride supplementation because this is
not transmitted through breast milk (Backer Dirks, et al., 1974; Ericsson,
1969; Ericsson, et al., 1972). This is usually given in the form of vitamin
drops with added sodium fluoride. Health providers should also be
aware of what drugs can be transmitted through breast milk so they can
give guidance about this. Several good reviews are available on this
subject (Drugs in Breast Milk, 1974; Vorherr, 1974).

The hormonal changes accompanying lactation inhibit ovulation.
Nonlactating women on the average ovulate (as measured by basal body
temperature) 73.5 days after delivery. The length of time before ovulation begins in the lactating woman varies depending upon the duration
and completeness of the breast-feeding. Once weaning is begun, ovulation, menstruation, and the likelihood of pregnancy follow rapidly
(Newton, 1971). The amenorrhea of continuing lactation conserves maternal iron stores, although the production of breast milk draws on the
mother's stores of other nutrients, especially calories (Pan American
Health Organization, 1970).

Jelliffe and Jelliffe (1971) summarize the recent studies regarding the
effects of oral contraceptive preparations on lactation. There is evidence
that earlier types of contraceptive pills, especially those containing high
doses of estrogen and administered shortly after delivery, interfere with
lactation. More recent studies suggest that low-dosage progestagen compounds do not interfere with lactation when administered orally or by
injection.

Preparation and Support of Siblings Siblings need preparation for the
arrival of the new baby and should be encouraged to discuss the feelings

FIGURE 3-18

of jealousy and competitiveness they may feel. Warrick (1971) has suggested that taking a picture of the new baby home to the siblings may be helpful. Having the siblings see the new baby in the hospital is also useful.

Questions that can be asked regarding siblings' reaction are as follows (Clark and Affonso, 1976, p. 70).

> Most children get their noses a little out of joint when they have to share their mother with a new baby. How do you anticipate it will be in your home?
>
> What will you do if your child strikes the baby?
>
> What will you do if your child demands the baby's bottle (or your breast)?
>
> What would you tell a mother who asked you what you would do about an older child who has begun to wet the bed again?
>
> What will you do if your child shows anger toward you when you arrive home with the new baby?

THE EARLY WEEKS AT HOME

Contact should be maintained with the new family during the first few weeks at home as this is frequently a difficult period of adjustment for many. Such contacts might include telephone calls and visits by community health nurses.

The Developing Parent-Infant Relationship Morris (1968) indicates that within the early weeks of infant life, "mother-infant unity" is satisfactory if the mother finds pleasure in her infant and taking care of it; understands her baby's affective states and can provide comfort; and can read cues for new experiences and sense the baby's fatigue level.

Several observations by the health provider give clues to the quality of the mother's relationship with her infant (Miller, 1968). When you say, "My what a nice baby," the majority of mothers look at their infant and hold it a little closer. About 5 to 10 percent do not, and this may indicate that a problem exists. Other observations include how the mother guards her infant when placed on the examining table and how she comforts her irritable or crying baby. The mother's appearance (i.e., sad or depressed) is another clue that potential problems may be present.

The signs of poor maternal adaptation listed by Morris (1968) are useful guidelines in assessing the mother's development during these early weeks (see Table 3-4). If the mother appears to be having difficulty taking on her new role, an assessment of possible current stresses is necessary in order to determine appropriate intervention. Specific areas to consider are her support system, financial difficulties, unemployment of husband, and serious illness or death in the family.

Broussard's Neonatal Perception Inventory (Broussard and Hartner, 1971) is a short instrument designed to determine a mother's perception of her infant by comparing it with perceptions of the "average" infant. The areas explored are the crying, feeding, spitting up, sleeping, bowel movements, and settling down behaviors of the infant. Broussard has found the mother's perception of her infant at 1 month of age to be associated with the child's emotional development at 4½ years of age and at 10 or 11 years (Broussard, 1975). It was found that for mothers who did not rate their infants as better than average, the children were at risk for later developmental problems. The mother's rating of her infant can be used to determine the mother's baseline perceptions and priorities for intervention and, when indicated, early preventive measures can be taken to foster healthy mother-baby interactions (Erickson, 1976).

SELECTED TOPICS FOR DISCUSSION

The general approach to conducting well-child visits include providing emotional support, screening, education, and intervention. These are discussed in Chapter 1. Some specific areas of education to be covered at different time periods during the first year are as follows:

First Few Weeks *Crying* In the newborn period and again at the 2- to 4-weeks visit, the natural history of crying is discussed with the mother

TABLE 3-4

Signs Mothers Give When Not Adapting to Their Infants

1. See their infants as ugly or unattractive.
2. Perceive the odor of their infants as revolting.
3. Disgusted by drooling of infants.
4. Disgusted by sucking sounds of infants.
5. Upset by vomiting, but seem fascinated by it.
6. Revolted by any of infant's body fluids which touch them or which they touch.
7. Annoyed at having to clean up infant's stools.
8. Preoccupied by odor, consistency, and number of stools.
9. Let infant's head dangle, without support or concern.
10. Hold infants away from their own bodies.
11. Pick up infant without warning it by a touch or by speech.
12. Juggle and play with infant, roughly, after feeding even though it often vomits at this behavior.
13. Think infant's natural motor activity is unnatural.
14. Worry about infant's relaxation following feeding.
15. Avoid eye contact with infants, or stare fixedly into their eyes.
16. Do not coo or talk with their infant.
17. Think that their infants do not love them.
18. Consider that their infants expose them as unlovable, unloving parents.
19. Think of their infants as judging them and their efforts as an adult would.
20. Perceive their infant's natural dependent needs as dangerous.
21. Fears of infant's death appear at mild diarrhea or minor cold.
22. Convinced that their infant has some defect, in spite of repeated physical examinations which prove negative.
23. This feared defect tends to migrate from body system to disease, and back again.
24. Conceal the defect site, or disease feared. If asked what they fear they disclaim knowing. They will reply to the reverse question of, "What do you hope it is *now?*"
25. Major maternal fears are often connected with diseases perceived as "eating" diseases: leukemia, or one of the other malignancies; diabetes; cystic fibrosis.
26. Constantly demand reassurance that no defect or disease exists, cannot believe relieving facts when they are given.
27. Demand that feared defect be found and relieved.
28. Cannot find in their infants any physical or psychological attribute which they value in themselves (probably the most diagnostic of these signs and readily elicited).
29. Cannot discriminate between infant signs signaling hunger or fatigue, need for soothing or stimulating speech, comforting body contact, or for eye contact.
30. Develop inappropriate responses to infant needs:
    They over- or underfeed
    Over- or underhold
    They tickle or bounce the baby when it is fatigued.
    Talk too much, too little, and at the wrong time.
    Force eye contact, or refuse it.
    Leave infant in room alone.
    Leave infant in noisy room and ignore it.
31. Develop paradoxical attitudes and behaviors; example: Bitterly insist that infant cannot be pleased, no matter what is done, but continue to demand more and better methods for pleasing it.

SOURCE: From: Morris, Marian G. Maternal claiming—identification process: Their meaning for mother-infant mental health. In Ann Clark, Margaret Bunell, and Emilie Henning, (Eds.), *Parent-child relationships: Role of the nurse.* Rutgers Univ., The State University of New Jersey, New Brunswick, N.J., 1968, pp. 34–35.

so she will not be surprised when the frequency and the intensity of the crying increases during the first 6 weeks of life and concentrates into certain "fussy" periods.

Mother as a person   At the early visits of the infant, the mother's physical and emotional status should also be evaluated. The mother's energy to cope with the demands of child rearing can be assessed by her appearance and responses to questions concerning amount of sleep she is getting, the amount and kinds of food she is eating, and her health (i.e., any pain or acute or chronic illnesses). If you are practicing in a setting where mother and baby care are practiced concurrently, the mother's weight and hemoglobin can also be evaluated (Bishop, 1976).

Other   Introduction of solid foods, use of car seat belts (American Academy of Pediatrics, 1974), the reason for immunizations, the importance of sensory stimulation (talking, patting, and rocking the infant), and how other family members are reacting to the baby are topics to be discussed.

3-months Visit   *Health and safety*   The hazards of rolling off surfaces when the child begins to turn over in the next few weeks is discussed.

FIGURE 3-19

by Susan McCabe

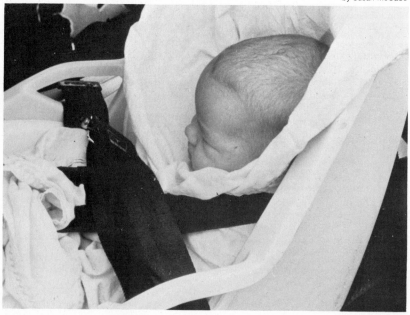

Growth and nutrition   Some discussion of infant feeding is important at this stage. The infant's need for iron-containing food and the addition of solid foods in general may become of interest at this point if the mother is concerned about her infant's nutritional status.

Anderson (1977, p. 38) suggests that infants who are fed solid foods before they have "outgrown their primitive reflexes and/or postural responses are at a decided disadvantage when attempting to communicate to their mothers their attitudes regarding the feeding experience." He suggests that the introduction of solids should begin when infants are able to sit without support and have good head and neck control so they can more readily communicate their willingness or unwillingness to accept the food. Although there is wide variation, these criteria are usually met by 4 to 6 months of age.

Cognitive development   Ascertaining whether the parents feel it is appropriate to "talk" to a baby and encouraging them to do so, as well as providing other types of tactile, visual, and auditory stimulation, is important. Many parents do this naturally, but some do not. This can usually be ascertained through office observation and having the parents

FIGURE 3-20

by Elizabeth Tong

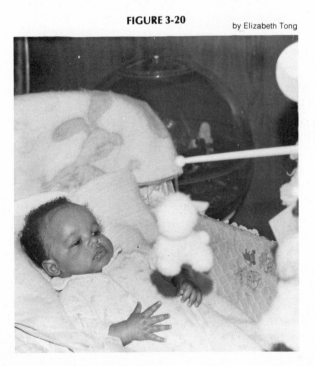

describe a "typical day" with the baby in the home. Gordon (1970) has described simple games and activities that parents can participate in with young children. Overstimulation can also be a hazard, and a good guideline to use is that any activity should be pursued only as long as it is enjoyable for both parent and child.

Individual differences   Getting across the idea of individual differences can be done in a number of ways. Inquiring about how the infant responds to a number of different care-taking situations will help the provider ascertain the temperament traits of the baby, and these can be discussed with the parent. Some physicians have the mother fill out the questionnaire about temperament developed by Carey (1970) and discuss the results with her at the next well-child visit. Books appropriate for parents about individual differences have been written by Brazelton (1969) and Chess et al. (1965).

Family functioning   This is the time for a discussion of the older siblings' response to the new infant. Evidence of how the children are adapting to the new baby may be elicited through questions such as "Can you leave the two children alone in a room?" "What do you do when your child hits the baby?" "How much extra attention is your child demanding from you?" The mother may need help to see that the older child may feel left out and to determine whether she can find 15 to 20 minutes a day to spend exclusively with the older child.

6-months Visit   *Nutrition*   Teeth are generally beginning to make their appearance, and it is a good time to discuss the relation between ingestion of sugar and dental caries and the role of fluoride in the prevention of tooth decay.

Social development   Most infants are now showing by their behavior that they can distinguish between mother and other persons, and this is a good time to introduce the concepts of "attachment" and the related negative reactions to strangers and protest over separation from the mother that are soon to come. This will relieve many parental guilt feelings about having "spoiled" their baby and will help them understand why their formerly placid baby gets so upset during the physical examination.

Sexuality   Most babies have found their genitals, and a discussion of early sexuality is appropriate.

Mother as a person   There are times during the postpartum and infancy periods when the mother's needs seem to take precedence over those of her baby or because of personality difficulties she becomes anxious in caring for the infant. At such times it is more beneficial to foster her security than to admonish her or warn her of the consequences of her behavior (Lidz, 1976). These approaches most likely will cause the mother to feel guilty and perhaps distrust her care takers and possibly not return for further visits. Suggesting methods of recreation can be helpful in relieving the mother's guilt about requesting this. She needs some time away from the child in order to pursue her own interests but may need help in realizing this is appropriate (Miller, 1968).

10-months Visit   *Growth and nutrition*   The slowing growth pattern can be discussed, with its accompaniment of a decrease in appetite and increase in food finickiness, though most babies at this age are still eating well. Many battles over the spoon can be headed off by reassuring the parents about the normal growth pattern of the child and the importance of self-feeding for the development of autonomy. Giving a few suggestions about how to cope with the mess that results may also be appreciated.

Many babies normally look fat and pudgy at this age as this is a time when much subcutaneous fat is laid down. We do not recommend any dietary attempts to deal with this unless the infant was also fat during the first 6 months of life or there is a strong family pattern of obesity. In this latter situation some attempt to cut down the total calorie intake is probably indicated. Inquiry about pica is also a useful screening question for the possibility of lead ingestion.

Hammar (1975) has outlined a prevention program for infants in families in which one or both parents are obese. Breast-feeding alone is recommended for the first 6 months. After this time infants at or above the 97th percentile of weight should receive iron-fortified, lower-caloric proprietary formulas (16 calories per ounce) and solid foods carefully chosen to exclude those with high calories, such as wet, packed cereals, eggs, mixed dinners, and desserts. Snack foods like potato chips and soda pop, which are high in calories and low in nutrients, should also be avoided. Substitution of skim milk or half-skim milk is not recommended because they lack some of the essential fatty acids necessary for growth.

Confining the child to a playpen for long periods encourages sedentary activity and should be avoided. The whole family can be encouraged to keep up an active exercise program.

The effects of these recommendations have not been adequately tested, however. Using a somewhat different approach, Pisacano et al.

(1978) describe a successful preventive program in a private practice setting. They did make use of skim milk after 3 months of age.

Social development   Usually, stranger-fear and separation-protest are well developed at this age, but there are wide variations in individual differences. If present, it is again worth noting how the parents are reacting to this and relieve guilt feelings about "spoiling" or attempts to suppress this behavior with punishment.

Curiosity and getting into things   By 10 months of age, many children are crawling and some are even walking, and this is a good time to discuss the importance of exploration and manipulation in the intellectual development of the child, as well as the hazards present in terms of falls,

FIGURE 3-21

by Susan McCabe

poking into electric fixtures, and ingesting poisonous substances. While some restrictions on mobility with gates, for example, are useful to the parents' peace of mind, there is some evidence that keeping a child in a playpen for long periods inhibits cognitive development (White and Watts, 1973).

Some attempts at baby-proofing the house will avoid many hassles, but some parents have successfully taught the child to stay out of parent possessions by being willing to consistently distract or remove the child whenever he or she begins getting into forbidden territory. The parents should have a bottle of Syrup of Ipecac USP on hand, have some idea of when and how to use it, and the number of the nearest poison control center if there is one in the area.

Discipline and limit setting   The into-everything stage is a good time to bring up the subject of discipline in general. A surprising number of parents expect a child of this age to respond to verbal commands given from across the room. Heading off such unrealistic expectations can do much to decrease frustration for both parent and child.

1-year Visit   A review of previous topics such as relation of growth patterns to appetites, safety precautions, cognitive stimulation, and discipline is in order. It is also worth exploring the parents' ideas about toilet training at this time so that they have some knowledge of what constitutes toilet-training readiness and some idea when the average boy and girl are likely to be trained.

The High-Risk Infant

GENERAL PRINCIPLES

Before we can be of assistance to parents who have given birth to a premature or abnormal baby, we need to examine our own reactions and feelings toward such events. New mothers (and, probably, fathers) are searching for cues of acceptance or rejection of the baby (and, most likely, themselves) and are therefore very sensitive to our behaviors.

There is probably no completely satisfactory way to tell parents their child has a problem. However, it is important to be honest and frank with them as well as tactful and compassionate. Honesty regarding the likely prognosis is important—recognizing, of course, that it is often difficult to draw the line between hope and despair.

During the initial stage of shock and disbelief, parents can absorb only a limited amount of information regarding their child's condition. Information should be communicated very clearly and repeated many times (Drotar et al., 1975). Mutual parental support may be fostered by seeing both parents together rather than seeing each one separately.

Thain and colleagues (1977) identify several stages in the process of communication between physicians and parents of a disabled child. The first stage occurs at the delivery table. The mother (and father, if present) should be shown the baby, and any obvious defects should be briefly discussed. The second stage occurs on the first day following a thorough examination of the infant. At this time a discussion of the child's problems should take place with both parents. Once the diagnosis is confirmed (stage III), an in-depth discussion of the treatment should be set up with both parents. Plans for treating the immediate or acute problems, as well as long-term goals for therapy, should be discussed. Fourth, the child's development should be followed and communicated to the parents, along with suggestions for fostering development. Counseling (stage V) requires many visits and repetitious explanations over a long period of time.

Some parents have benefited from meeting with other parents whose child has had a similar problem, and such a visit may be arranged early in the postpartum period.

The mother who has an abnormal child should express her grief and regret rather than deny it. Most women will experience some feeling of loss and will mourn the child they had hoped for (Baker, 1967). As part of the grief response, these parents may become angry toward the medical and nursing staff. They will need help in talking about and dealing with their early feelings about the child, as well as assurance that their negative and angry feelings are acceptable (Prugh, 1953; Will, 1975). Obviously, we cannot give such assurance without first accepting it ourselves.

Loneliness and anxieties have been reported by many parents following the birth of their infant. "Mothers often had intense concerns about their infant's appearance, and fantasies that their children had died" (Drotar et al., 1975).

Baker (1967) believes that because of the emotional lability during the first few days after childbirth, most women will feel strong maternal feelings toward the child, however deformed. It is suggested that early or immediate contact between parents, particularly the mother, and infant be permitted to foster bonding because an increased incidence of mothering disorders have been found to occur following a long period of mother-infant separation (Klaus and Kennell, 1970).

No single approach to mothers will be appropriate, however. For example, 2 of 15 mothers invited to enter the nursery refused because of their infants' poor prognoses and they did not wish to become attached to their babies. It is not known at this time whether it is better for a mother to grieve over a "baby" that exists in her fantasy or over one with which she has had some interaction and to which she has developed some real attachment.

Benfield and colleagues (1976) studied the feelings and responses of 101 mother-father pairs whose critically ill newborns survived following referral to a regional center. The majority of these parents experienced anticipatory grief reactions: (1) sadness, (2) anger, (3) loss of appetite, (4) guilt, (5) difficulty sleeping, (6) preoccupation, and (7) irritability. Significantly more mothers than fathers reported the first four of these feelings. Anticipatory grief did not appear to be associated with the severity of the infant's illness. Other responses included wanting to be left alone, disbelief, depression, crying, praying for the baby, and thinking the baby might die.

Fathers reported alteration in their daily activities following the infant's referral. Generally, they visited the babies and their wives, worked 8 hours, and left their other children with friends and relatives. Of special concern was the high cost of medical care and the potential for financial disaster. Most mothers visited their babies immediately following discharge, regardless of their obstetricians' advice. There has been an attempt in some areas to transport the mother to a large medical center prior to delivery in order to improve care for the high-risk mother and infant.

EARLY MANAGEMENT

Low Birth Weight   The period following the birth of a preterm infant is likely to be an especially difficult one for the new parents. They are constantly aware of the potential dangers for their baby. The infant's tiny size and the strange equipment often surrounding the baby are frightening. Information regarding the infant's condition may be minimal or inconsistent because of the infant's precarious state. The mother's contact with her infant may be limited by hospital policy (hopefully, we can soon eliminate such practices) or because the infant has been transported to a regional center for specialized care.

Leiderman (1975) reported that a mother's separation for 3 weeks from her premature infant in the immediate postpartum period may lead to decreased feelings of competency and decreased maternal attachment. These feelings and behaviors sometimes continued for as long as 1 month following the mother's reunion with her infant; however, they were no longer present 12 months after the separation.

Additional stresses also impinge upon the new father as a result of the premature birth. Besides getting his wife safely to the hospital, he may have to make child-care arrangements for their other children and arrange to be away from work. He is at the same time concerned about his wife and their new baby. If the baby is transported he may find himself visiting the infant in one hospital, his wife in another, and his other children at home or with friends or relatives.

In their studies of parents of premature infants, Caplan et al. (1965) studied the coping processes used by mothers following the birth of their premature infants. Factors found to be predictive of a favorable outcome in terms of the mother's relationship with her infant 6 to 10 weeks after discharge from the hospital were: (1) a moderate to high degree and expression of anxiety concerning the infant and the mother's caretaking competence; (2) active seeking of information about the baby; (3) strong maternal feelings toward the infant even when unable to see or hold the baby; (4) support of her husband and a mutuality in their relationship; and (5) previous experience with a premature infant.

Kaplan and Mason (1960) also identified four psychological tasks facing mothers of premature babies and found an association between the mother's ability to master these tasks and a favorable outcome regarding the mother-infant relationship. Although these tasks were identified specifically in relation to the mother, it is probable that they also apply to the father. These tasks are to:

1 Prepare for the possible loss of the child whose life is in jeopardy.
2 Face and acknowledge maternal failure to deliver a full-term baby.
3 As the baby improves, the parent's response must become one of hope and anticipation.
4 Come to understand how a premature infant differs from a normal baby in terms of its special needs and growth patterns. To this last task should be added the need to understand how this prematurely born infant has needs similar to those of a full-term infant.

Fanaroff, and colleagues (1972) and Caplan et al. (1965) suggest that the maternal visiting pattern is a useful technique for predicting later maternal behavior. They also recommend that in addition to the infant's weight and progress, maternal competence and attachment should be criteria for discharging the infant from the nursery.

Infant with Congenital Anomalies Difficulties encountered by parents with malformed children include complexities of ongoing physical care, uncertain developmental prognosis, parental concern regarding doing the right thing, and repeated hospitalization (Drotar et al., 1975).

Most of the literature dealing with responses to the birth of infants with physical or mental abnormalities is related to the reactions of mothers. One exception is the hypothetical model of Drotar and his colleagues (1975) used to describe parents' adaptation to the infant with a congenital malformation. Parents are believed to progress through five stages: (1) shock; (2) denial; (3) sadness, anger, and anxiety; (4) adaptation as evidenced by an increased ability to care for the infant and increased satisfaction with the baby; and (5) reorganization, where the parents evidence greater satisfaction with the baby and can identify their infant's strengths. An important point made by the authors is that when the time durations for each phase are asynchronous, the parents are likely to experience a temporary emotional separation.

Their study suggests that maintenance of satisfactory relationships between the parents is often a crucial aspect of positive adaptation. The crisis of a baby's birth has the potential for bringing the parents closer together through mutual support and communication or for estranging the parents from one another. The ongoing demands imposed by the baby's care increased the isolation between parents, especially if they did not share responsibilities for the child's care. Parents who had a different time duration of reactions to the birth were temporarily emotionally separated from one another—they usually did not share their differing feelings with one another.

Mercer (1975) analyzed the responses of five mothers who gave birth to infants with visible defects at four time phases: the first 8 days, second week through 1 month, 2 months, and 3 months. The foremost task demonstrated by the mothers was that of identifying social acceptance and support for their babies and themselves. This occurred through evaluating others' reactions to the babies (especially important were their husbands' responses), appraisals of self (more often disparaging), and responses of support from others. Cognitive behaviors noted by these mothers were related to their knowledge, beliefs, wishes, and plans for their infants. Mothers were oriented toward planning for the future. Plans for self were more evident during the first 2 weeks, and around the third week this focus shifted to planning for their babies. Little planning for other members of the family was noted during the first 3 months. Other activities included reviewing the past and sorting out facts around the birth. The emotional behaviors were the subjective feelings and observable affects on the mothers. These behaviors were observed less frequently than the social and cognitive behaviors and included shock, anger, fear, guilt, hope, withdrawal, and depression.

D'Arcy (1969) found mothers were helped to cope with having children with Down's syndrome by (1) the support they received from their husbands and other relatives; (2) being able to discuss their problems with other mothers of such children; (3) seeing children more handicapped than their own; and (4) by their religious beliefs.

Parents of babies with cleft lips and palates are distressed by the appearance of their infants and even after surgery feel uncomfortable exposing the children to others (Tisza and Gumpertz, 1962). Of major concern is infant feeding, and considerable support and guidance is needed as they become experienced in feeding the baby. It is believed babies with cleft palates vocalize less and in a more monotonous manner than babies without this deformity. Speech development is delayed, although receptive language is not. The possibility of hearing impairment necessitates repeated hearing tests. Parents often fear their child's intellectual functioning may be impaired. The findings of Tisza and Gumpertz indicate the majority of children with cleft lips and palates but without multiple congenital anomalies (which may include mental retardation) follow the characteristic pattern of their families, ranging in intelligence from dull-normal to superior.

One type of infant that needs special management is the one born with genitalia that are not completely male or female. A large clitoris with no scrotum or testes, a small rudimentary penis, an empty scrotum, or gonadal masses in the labia of an otherwise normal-looking female, all raise the question of the child's genetic sex. Rearing studies have shown that parents behave differently toward boys and girls from an early age. When sustained, these differences are of utmost importance in shaping the child's gender identity. For this reason it is very important that an unequivocal sex assignment be made for the child before leaving the hospital and that corrective surgery of the external genitalia be performed as soon as it is feasible, to reinforce the parents' perception of their child as a boy or a girl. Sex assignment is generally based on whether a satisfactorily functioning penis can be constructed regardless of genetic sex. Consultation with someone experienced in the management of these problems is recommended (Money et al., 1955a,b; Money and Ehrhardt, 1972).

Infant Death Evidence of mourning in mothers whose babies die includes sadness, loss of appetite, increased irritability, inability to sleep, preoccupation with the lost infant, and inability to return to normal activities (Kennell et al., 1970). Wolff (1972) followed for 3 years 40 women who delivered stillborn infants or whose infants died in the early neonatal period. One-half of the women became pregnant again, while the remainder either returned to (or began) work or school or intensified their household family routines. None of the women developed significant psychiatric difficulties. A large number (actual number not reported) indicated they did not want another baby, and one-half of these resorted to sterilization. Wolff reported that although hospital procedures, placement of patient, and staff attitudes played a role in the woman's comfort or discomfort, they did not appear to affect the eventual resolution of the loss. None of the women in this study had an opportunity to hold or cuddle their infants, and their cathexis therefore was not to a real object but to a fantasized one.

For the woman who loses her infant at birth, or shortly thereafter, some degree of depression is inevitable and essential for her future emotional health. She should not be urged to forget the child or to have another to replace it (Baker, 1967). It may be kinder to remove the woman from the maternity ward in such an instance.

Kennell et al. (1970) recommend three meetings with parents following the death of their newborn infant in which the hospital staff communicates accurately and honestly with the parents. At the time of the baby's death, it is important to give the parents some idea of the feelings they are likely to experience and the length of time they will last (intensity begins to decline in 1 to 6 weeks and is minimal by 6 months). Indicate it is mutually beneficial if the parents talk with each other about their feelings. Go over the same thing with the parents a day or two later. The parents are interviewed again 3 to 4 months after the death, to "inquire about their activities and mood as an indication of how they are working through their grief" (p. 348), to review autopsy findings, and answer any questions. Although the grief reaction is a normal process, it may become abnormal when it is denied or delayed (Lindemann, 1944; Parkes, 1967); consequently, parents should receive support in talking about their feelings.

In a retrospective study, Cullberg (1972) interviewed 56 Swedish women whose infants died shortly after birth. The interviews were 1 to 2 years post partum. Nine women denied any reaction, while the remainder reported reactions of grief and apathy and feelings of emptiness and inadequacy. These reactions developed within hours to a few days after the initial shock reaction. Most women returned to their usual work during the second or third month, and 1 to 2 years later (the time of the interview) most of them seemed to have regained their mental stability. Grief reactions accompanying the death of premature infants tended to be shorter than those following the death of a malformed infant.

Regardless of the age of the children, the death of their newborn sibling will affect them in some way. The children's concept of death and their parents' response to the loss play a role in how they are affected. Of particular importance is the parents' attitude toward sharing the loss with their other children.

Open, honest parent-child communication should be encouraged. Explaining death to children is a difficult task; however, the infant's death and the parents' feelings of sadness need to be shared with the children. The children will be aware that something has happened. Their fantasies can be very frightening.

Young children think in concrete terms; therefore, terms such as "died" and "buried" should be used with them rather than equating death with sleep, for the child may then fear going to sleep (Gartley and Bernasconi, 1967). It is particularly important to help the child realize that he or she is not the cause of the death.

Management of Common Problems

"DIFFICULT" BABIES

One of the most important tasks of the primary health care worker is to help parents adapt their child-rearing pattern to the needs of their particular child rather than blindly follow some theory advocated by experts. The wide range of individual differences in temperament was discussed earlier, and one of the common problems encountered is the mother who reacts with an overstimulating response pattern to a baby with the "difficult" constellation of temperament characteristics.

This situation often presents itself to the health provider in the following manner: The mother of a baby between 2 weeks and 2 months of age calls and describes her baby as crying continuously. A careful physical examination reveals an irritable but otherwise normal infant. Asking the mother to describe a typical day with the infant usually reveals all or most of the following. When the baby cries the mother tries to feed it and may be feeding the infant every hour or two, day and night. The infant takes an ounce or two of formula and continues to fuss. The mother responds by walking, rocking, patting, and/or bouncing the baby. Sometimes the baby quiets temporarily only to start fussing again if put down. At other times the continued stimulation results in increased crying, which spurs the mother on to more rocking, jiggling, and so on. As the baby cries vigorously he or she may swallow considerable air, resulting in the passage of flatus which in turn leads to concern about "colic" and the prescription of drugs or even enemas by the physician. This crying and handling pattern frequently continues into the night, with little rest for anyone. The history generally reveals that somebody is almost continuously doing something to the infant (Chamberlin, 1967).

Although this type of pattern can evolve with any mother having a baby with a "difficult" temperament or "colic," certain mothers seem especially vulnerable. New mothers with little experience, mothers who are isolated or receiving little support from other family members, and mothers who have had difficulty getting pregnant, repeated miscarriages, or a previous stillborn child seem to be especially at risk. The health provider can provide support to the mother by reassuring her that both she and the baby are all right and that she will be provided with help in managing her infant. Taking time to understand the factors in the mother's background and current life situation that may be aggravating the situation is helpful. It is also important to provide clear guidelines of how she can cut down the amount of stimulation. We usually discuss this in terms of a "vicious circle," with an infant of this temperament pattern becoming more, rather than less, irritable and fussy with frequent handling. Specific instructions are given not to feed the infant any more often than every 3 to 5 hours. When the infant fusses the mother can pick it up, check to see if everything is all right, and try and soothe it. If the child keeps fussing the mother is instructed to put the infant down and not pick it up again for 15 minutes by the clock. This procedure is repeated as often as necessary until the infant falls asleep. Usually, when the amount of stimulation is cut down, the infant becomes less irritable, the mother less nervous, and the vicious circle is interrupted. Providing frequent telephone contact with the mother during this time is also helpful. On rare occasions, when the mother seems unable to respond to these suggestions, the baby is admitted to the hospital for a day or two and the vicious circle is interrupted in this manner. It is important to recognize the infant's contribution to the pattern and reassure the mother that many mothers have trouble with these types of babies. Books on individual differences that may be helpful to mothers with "difficult" babies are those by Brazelton (1969) and Chess et al. (1965).

QUIET ADAPTABLE BABIES

At the other end of the spectrum is the quiet, adaptable baby who makes few demands on the environment. The mother, particularly if she is busy or preoccupied, may interpret this quietness as an indication that all the infant needs are being met and she may develop a response pattern of "too little" contact. A description of a "typical day" may reveal that the mother props the bottle with feedings and interacts very little with the baby between feedings, other than for routine physical care. The baby sleeps a great deal and is not very responsive. These babies often present as not gaining weight properly. We have encountered this pattern in families where the mother is overwhelmed with the demands of many small children and trying to cope with a poverty-level income. We have also seen this pattern develop with mothers having a postpartum depression or other emotional difficulties that keep them preoccupied with their own problems. It is important to recognize the infant's contribution to the pattern. A less-placid baby would react to such underfeeding and low contact with vigorous protests, forcing people in the environment to respond in some fashion. Management depends upon the underlying cause. Busy mothers whose lack of contact is through misunderstanding of their baby's quietness will often respond to simple education about the need of infants to be held and stimulated. Mothers under stress from severe emotional or family problems will need to have these resolved before much can be done about the interaction pattern. (See also "Failure to Thrive" later in this chapter.)

SLEEP PROBLEMS DURING THE LAST HALF OF THE FIRST YEAR

A common problem is the infant who was sleeping through but now awakens and cries in the middle of night. This may be precipitated by a cold or ear infection, but the pattern continues after the illness is over. Carey (1974) showed that some of these infants have a generally low threshold for stimuli of all kinds. Usually this phenomenon is temporary unless the parents respond to it in a way that perpetuates the problem. If the parent develops a pattern of going immediately at the first cry and either feeding the infant, getting him or her out of the crib and holding for long periods, or taking the child into their bed, the problem generally persists.

Waiting 5 or 10 minutes before going in will often allow the infant to fall back to sleep of his or her own accord. If this does not happen, the parent can help the infant resettle but should not take him or her out of the crib or provide feedings. If the infant does not settle and seems upset, sitting in front of the open door outside the room and reading or doing something that does not involve direct interaction with the infant will often provide enough reassurance so he or she can return to sleep. This type of problem can usually be resolved in several nights if the parents can be convinced that letting the infant cry it out for a couple of nights is not psychologically harmful. In this regard parents who have had a traumatic upbringing themselves or mental illness in the family are often particularly reluctant to hold back an immediate response. Exploring their feelings about this with them will often reduce their anxiety about the infant to a more manageable level.

HEAD BANGING, HEAD ROLLING, AND BODY ROCKING

In various reports from private practices (Traisman et al., 1966) and community studies (DeLissovoy, 1962) the prevalence of this kind of activity is around 5 to 15 percent. Generally, there is a higher incidence with boys (20 percent) than girls (7 percent). Onset is usually around the latter half of the first year (averaging about 8 months) and generally ends spontaneously at around age 3 or 4 years, although sometimes they continue much later than this. These phenomena occur mostly at bedtime or at naptime before the child is asleep, but some children have been noted to engage in this kind of activity while they are actually sleeping. In one study of 135 children (Kravitz, 1960), 50 percent rocked or banged less than 15 minutes, and about 25 percent continued this for an hour or more before falling asleep. DeLissovoy (1962) observed a number of children in their homes and provides some good descriptions of the different forms of behavior.

The etiology of this activity is unknown. In the past there was some attempt to connect this with either mental retardation or severe emotional disturbance, since a number of children with these disorders were observed to engage in repeated rhythmic activities in institutions. Another theory was that this results from overrestriction of activities, which appears to be based on observations in animals (Lourie, 1949). In a large majority of children, however, no such etiology has been found, and it seems for some youngsters to be a normal tension-release phenomenon similar to sucking fingers. For instance, in the report by Kravitz, the mother-child relationships of 135 head bangers were studied and rated good in 68 percent of the families, fair in 15 percent, and poor in 17 percent.

There is some evidence to suggest that these children have a higher-than-average need for other kinds of rhythmic activity, since many have been reported to be especially interested in music and dance, and head rocking can sometimes be stopped by putting a metronome or loud, ticking alarm clock next to the bedside (DeLissovoy, 1962).

Mothers become concerned about this habit because they think that the child may injure his or her head, are upset by the noise, or are afraid this may indicate some kind of emotional disturbance or mental deficiency. There have been no reports of serious head damage caused by this type of activity. In one study (Kravitz, 1960), electroencephalographs were performed on a group of head bangers and all were found to be normal. Also, as we have seen, the large majority of these children are neither retarded nor emotionally disturbed.

If screening has indicated that no severe child or family pathology exists and that the child has not been confined extensively in some way, simple reassurance is often all that is necessary. If the noise itself is a nuisance, the bed can be put on cushioned blocks or padding can be put along the walls. The use of a metronome or loud, ticking alarm clock has already been mentioned and is reported to stop the habit in some children, although this has not been verified in any systematic way. Others suggest providing rhythmic outlets for the child, such as dancing, use of a hobby horse, swaying seesaws, and so on. One author recommended putting these children in a hammock.

THUMB AND FINGER SUCKING

In a selected sample of 70 babies followed through the first year of life, 61 manifested appreciable amounts of extra sucking of fist or finger that were not associated with feeding (Brazelton, 1956). The intensity of such activity increased from birth rapidly up to a peak at about 6 or 7 months of age. By 9 months of age, 45 babies had spontaneously ceased this extra sucking except when tired, hungry, or unhappy, and by 1 year of age, 57 (93 percent) of the babies had spontaneously given up this activity. By age 2, only two were still spending appreciable amounts of time in this area and were considered "problem suckers." There were marked individual differences, with more intense, active babies doing more sucking than the placid, easygoing ones. It was concluded that extranutritional sucking is common in healthy and contented babies when it is not prevented and will disappear spontaneously in the large majority of babies by 1 or 2 years of age.

However, reports by others indicate that sucking is still common in older preschool children. In a cross-sectional study of nursery school children, approximately 40 percent of 2-, 3-, and 4-year-old children were reported to suck their thumbs (Honzik and McKee, 1962). A higher percentage of girls (50 percent) were thumb-suckers than boys (30 percent). In a longitudinal study of 248 children reported by these same authors there was a steady decline from about 30 percent at age 2 to about 10 percent by age 6 and approximately 0 percent by age 12.

In another study of 2650 infants and children in a private, middle-class, suburban practice, about 45 percent of the total group had sucked their thumbs at some time (Traisman et al., 1966); 75 percent started sucking during the first 3 months and the remainder during the next 3 months. The average age at which thumb-sucking stopped was 3.8 years. In a few children it persisted up to 12 to 15 years of age. Of the total group, 5 percent were thought to have behavioral or psychological problems, but there were no differences between suckers and nonsuckers. There were no differences in incidence between boys or girls or between breast-fed babies and those not breast-fed. Those who sucked their fingers or thumbs also sucked longer during feedings.

Forceful attempts to stop the practice have generally been traumatic and unsuccessful (Klackenberg, 1949). For the large majority of children simple reassurance by the parents is all that is necessary. For children still sucking after age 5 an attempt at behavior modification appears worthwhile. The relationship between thumb-sucking and malocclusion is discussed in Chapter 4.

Some have suggested early substitution of a pacifier since children who use them seldom suck their fingers and generally give them up earlier (Rittelmeyer, 1955). However, there is some evidence to suggest that the use of a pacifier increases the incidence of dental caries (Kohler and Holst, 1973).

BREATH-HOLDING SPELLS

This is an interesting phenomenon that assumes clinical importance because of the anxiety it causes parents and the fact that it is sometimes misdiagnosed as a seizure disorder. Mild breath-holding spells are quite common. In one report of 697 children attending an army clinic, about 6 percent had breath-holding spells, with the majority being quite mild (Linder, 1968). Mild attacks are usually precipitated by an emotionally disturbing event, and there is a sudden cessation of respiration at or soon after the onset of crying. The breath holding is very brief and may or may not be associated with cyanosis.

The usual sequence of a severe attack is that it is precipitated by frustration, pain, or fright, following which the child cries vigorously for about 15 seconds and then stops breathing in the phase of complete expiration for 30 or 40 seconds. He or she becomes cyanotic and semi-comatose and assumes an opisthotonos position. On occasion this may be accompanied by clonic convulsive movements. According to Livingston (1970), attacks of this severity rarely occur before 6 months of age. The average age of onset is about 12 months, and an initial attack after 4 years is unlikely. Frequency varies considerably. Of the 242 patients reported by Livingston, about 40 percent of the attacks were

TABLE 3-5

Features Which Help to Differentiate Severe Breathholding Spells from Epilepsy

Feature	Severe breathholding spells	Epilepsy
Precipitating factor	Always present	Usually not apparent in young children
Crying	Almost always present before onset of convulsion	Not usually present
Cyanosis	Always occurs before loss of consciousness	When present, occasionally occurs at onset of seizure, but usually after attack has been in progress (prolonged seizure)
Opisthotonos	Usually present	Rarely occurs
EEG	Almost always normal	Usually abnormal, but may be normal

SOURCE: Reproduced with permission from Livingston, S. *Journal of the American Medical Association,* 1970, *212,* 2232. Copyright 1970, American Medical Association.

occurring once a day or more. The frequency of occurrence was generally low at first then increased gradually and peaked at around 2 or 3 years of age. Most spells had spontaneously disappeared by 5 years of age. These episodes can usually be differentiated from seizures by a careful history, as shown in Table 3-5. The etiology of these episodes is unknown. There is often a family history of similar spells, suggesting a genetic predisposition. Frequently they are associated with behavior problems and decrease in frequency when the problems of parent-child interaction are lessened.

Long-term follow-up shows that almost all disappear by 5 years. Only three children (0.8 percent) in a group of 384 developed epilepsy, and there was no clinical evidence of cerebral damage in any other child in spite of frequent episodes. Intervention by health care providers usually consists of reassurance to the parents of the nonseriousness of the problem and providing assistance with any rearing problems they may be having with the child. Drugs are of no value and should not be used.

DEVELOPMENTAL LAGS

The main question is whether a developmental delay is caused by a potentially handicapping condition whose effects can be minimized by early referral to someone who is skilled in working with children having this problem, or whether it is simply a developmental variation that needs only the passage of time to be resolved. This is often a difficult question. As noted in many of the sections on specific areas of development, there is a considerable range of normal variation for every milestone, and some overlap may be expected in the age of milestone attainment of normal children and those who later turn out to have specific problems such as cerebral palsy, mental retardation, and the like. One of the reasons for this overlap is that development does not always progress at an even rate, but rather in fits and starts. Children in a plateau period may be behind their peers at a given point in time but catch up rapidly in the next spurt of progress.

For example, Table 3-6, based on data from Neligan and Prudham (1969), shows that later attainment of a single milestone increases only slightly the chances of finding a child with a low IQ. Delays in both milestones substantially increase the risk, but even here there were many notable exceptions, especially for girls. While there is no simple way to determine which children to refer for further evaluation, answers to the following questions should be of help.

FIGURE 3-22

by Elizabeth Tong

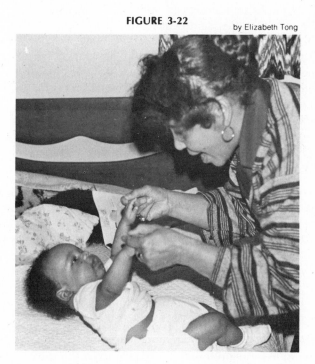

TABLE 3-6

Relationship between Age of Onset of Walking and Talking and IQ at Age 5

Milestone	Mean IQ at age 5	
	Male	Female
Early walkers (before 10 months)	113 (N = 98)	116 (N = 96)
Late walkers (after 10 months)	104 (N = 93)	115 (N = 85)
Early talkers (sentences before 17 months)	109 (N = 38)	117 (N = 56)
Late talkers (sentences after 17 months)	100 (N = 53)	108 (N = 50)
Both walking and talking late (boys after 36 months; girls after 35 months)	90.5 (N = 75)	101.2 (N = 13)

SOURCE: Table based on data from Neligan, G. & Prudham, D. *Developmental medicine and child neurology*, 1969, *11*, 423–431.

Does the child see? Following with the eyes is well developed by the end of the second month, and simple observation plus identification of the red reflex should answer this question.

Does the child hear? Observing or having the mother observe whether the infant startles with noise is a gross screen. By 6 months of age, many babies can localize sound by turning toward it, and hearing can be screened using simple office tests (Bordly, 1959; Ewing and Ewing, 1944). During the last half of the first year, the character of the hearing child's vocalizations change, showing variations in tone and pitch and then imitation of sounds produced by the parents. Consistent absence of these phenomena are indications for referral for a more formal hearing evaluation. The presence of any of the following predisposing conditions would also raise one's index of suspicion: family history of deafness, hyperbilirubinemia, congenital rubella, and/or use of streptomycin or other ototoxic drugs at birth.

Is there evidence of neuromotor dysfunction? This generally shows up as poor coordination and/or balance in large and small motor activities and would be an indication for a neurologic examination. A history of low birth weight, bleeding, or toxemia during pregnancy or neonatal asphyxia would also increase one's level of suspicion. Muscle tone and reflexes can be ascertained with a physical examination. Watching how the child reaches for and manipulates objects can help pick up gross degrees of ataxia or tremor.

Is there evidence of delay in more than one area of development? Many normal children may be lagging behind in one or occasionally two areas, but lags in more than one area raise the possibility of mental deficiency and further evaluation is indicated.

Are the head size and shape normal? A head circumference under the 3d percentile is suspicious of microcephaly unless it is proportional to the rest of the child's measurements. The standards of Nellhaus (1968) are useful in this respect.

How does the child relate to people? Does the child respond to familiar persons with smiles, an increase or decrease in activity, and/or vocalizations? Does the child show evidence of attachment? Can he or she use adults for assistance and pleasure? Lack of eye contact and other "attachment" behaviors in the infant over 6 months of age raise the possibility of "autism," and further evaluation is indicated.

Is there any evidence of an understimulating environment? Is there little adult-child interaction? Does the mother regularly prop the bottle when feeding? How much mother-child contact is there between feedings? Is there poor weight gain and growth as well as retarded function? Are verbal and social areas of development less advanced than the motor and manipulative? All these suggest the possibility of low stimulation.

Is there evidence of neglect and/or abuse? Unexplained bruises or burns, repeated accidents, ulcerous diaper rash from infrequent changes, and/or a failure to gain weight that is greater in degree than failure to gain height all suggest the possibility of neglect or abuse and are indications for a social service evaluation of the home.

Was the child premature? A birth weight of 2500 grams and/or a gestation period of less than 37 weeks is the conventional definition of a premature infant used in most centers. Prematurity by itself does not appear to either retard or accelerate developmental sequences. However, the developmental status of a premature infant must always be appraised in terms of an age corrected for the degree of prematurity rather than simple chronological age determined from the date of birth. Without doing this, an erroneous diagnosis of mental retardation might be made. Knobloch and Pasamanick (1974) present a method for making this correction based on how well the observed days of prematurity (number of days between date of birth and expected date of confinement) agree with calculated days of prematurity (empirically determined from a table relating days of prematurity to birth weight; see Table 3-7). If the observed

TABLE 3-7

Days of Prematurity Calculated for Given Birth Weights
(Derived from Baltimore Study of Premature Infants)

Birth weight, pounds, ounces	Calculated days of prematurity
5–8	22
5–0	32
4–8	43
4–0	53
3–8	64
3–0	74
2–8	85
2–0	95
1–8	106

SOURCE: Reproduced with permission from Knoblock, H. and Pasamanick, B. (Eds.) *Developmental diagnosis*, Hagerstown, Md.: Harper & Row Publishers, 1974, p. 256.

days are within 3 weeks of the calculated days, the number of observed days are added to the date of birth, and that is the date used to determine chronological age. If the observed days are greater than the calculated days by more than 3 weeks, 3 weeks is added to the calculated figure, and that number of days is added to the date of birth. If the observed days are less than 3 weeks from the calculated days, 3 weeks is subtracted from the calculated days, and that amount is added to the calculated number of days taken from the table.

Prevention and Management of Developmental Delays There have been a number of approaches to the prevention of development disorders in high-risk infants. Summaries of the literature are discussed in Chapter 1.

In terms of practical applications in medical settings, Gutelius et al. (1972) and Brooks (1971) describe a program with inner-city adolescent mothers in which a public health nurse makes visits to the homes to help foster constructive types of parent-child interaction. Gordon (1970) has written a book describing simple verbal interaction games that can be used with parents to teach them how to stimulate the intellectual and language development of their child.

Scarr-Salapatek and Williams (1973) describe a program with premature infants that starts in the nursery with hospital staff and continues in the home with the mother. Cornell and Gottfried (1976) review the results of a number of intervention programs involving premature babies.

Children coming from homes with little stimulation and who already show lags in social and language development can be helped with a program such as that described by Jason and Kimborough (1974). Some infant specialists feel that it is not the specific training procedures used that are important but that these projects help the mother respond more sensitively to her child and increase her enjoyment in caring for him or her (Bromwich, 1977).

Children raised in chaotic environments where there is little hope of working directly with the mother apparently do better if they can be cared for during most of the day in a day-care setting with specially trained paraprofessionals who work with no more than two infants at a time (Pavenstedt, 1973).

Infants with mild lags in some areas of development, without evidence of any of the previously mentioned factors, can generally be followed with repeated measures until the nature of the lags becomes clear. Many turn out to be simply normal variations in development.

Helping Families Cope with Stress and Crisis

DISTURBED PARENT-CHILD RELATIONSHIPS

Hartman (1968) identifies the general characteristics of disturbed mothering behavior as: (1) inaccurate evaluation of the infant's responses, (2) inconsistent and stereotyped interactions, (3) shifts between emotional involvement and withdrawal, (4) interaction with infant only for necessities (i.e., feeding, bathing, changing diapers), (5) limited play (usually tactile), (6) tension when carrying out care activities, and (7) either gross unconcern or overinvolvement with the infant's health. Two basic patterns of mothering were noted in disturbed women: (1) the *distant* mothering pattern, which is said to be a reflection of viewing the external world as depriving and nonsatisfying, and (2) the *involved* pattern, reflecting the woman's feeling of helplessness and lack of effectiveness in a disappointing and powerful world.

When one suspects problems in the mother-child relationship, a thorough assessment of the family's life history, including past and current life events, pregnancy, and the perinatal period, should be carried out. Events regarded as significant in the life history of families experiencing disorders of maternal attachment are listed in Table 3-8.

With all these types of problems, care must be taken not to confuse

TABLE 3-8
Significant Life Events that May Explain Disorders in Maternal Attachment

Past events	1. Early prenatal life deprivations
	2. Loss of parent figures early in the life of the parent
	3. Illness during parent's childhood
	4. Death or illness in prior children
Pregnancy events	1. Protracted emotional or physical illness
	2. Death or major illness of key family figures
Perinatal events	1. Complications of parturition
	2. Acute illness in mother or infant
	3. Prematurity
	4. Congenital defects
	5. Diseases
	6. Iatrogenic or institutional disruptions
Current events	1. Marital status
	2. Mental illness
	3. Medical illness
	4. Alcoholism, drugs
	5. Financial crises

SOURCE: From: *Maternal attachment and mothering disorders: A round table,* sponsored by Johnson and Johnson Baby Products Co., Oct. 18 & 19, 1974, Copyright 1975, p. 11.

deliberate abuse with skin lesions caused by folk medicine practices in some cultures (Sandler and Haynes, 1978).

Child Abuse and Neglect Severely disturbed parent-child relationships may result in physical abuse or neglect of the child. In one study it was estimated that 10 percent of the injuries of children seen in a hospital emergency room were due to child abuse (Holter and Friedman, 1968). Usually, the injury presented in the form of contusions and abrasions, a fracture or dislocation of an extremity, a blunt head injury, or a burn. Simple lacerations and ingestions were seldom found to be related to abuse. Sometimes, x-rays revealed multiple areas of bone injuries in different stages of healing. Often the history of how the injury occurred was vague or contradictory. Frequently there was also evidence of neglect, with poor weight gain and inadequate personal cleanliness (Helfer and Kempe, 1968).

Kempe, Helfer, and their associates (1972) have done much to help us understand the mix of past and present events that lead up to the abusing incident. The profile drawn of the abusing parent is one who has received physical abuse in his or her own upbringing, is currently isolated in the community, with inability to trust or use others in times of need, and who is experiencing, or has recently experienced, some kind of life crisis that has overtaxed his or her precarious coping capacity. The parent's expectations for the child are often unrealistic in terms of what the child is expected to accomplish, particularly in terms of responding to the parent's own need to be mothered. Finally, the child is often special in some way, either in reminding the abusing parent of some disliked person or presenting special problems in management, such as having the temperament characteristics of a difficult child, being slow in development, or having a birth defect.

MANAGEMENT   If the type and circumstances of the injury are suspect and there is evidence of any of the previously mentioned background factors, it is important to admit the child to the hospital for protection while an adequate evaluation is carried out.

Kempe and Helfer (1972) estimated that only about 10 to 20 percent of the parents of abused children are psychotic or psychopathic, requiring highly specialized psychiatric treatment and/or permanent removal of the child from the home. The majority, though often severely deprived, can be helped enough through a relationship with a warm and responsive person to provide a safe home for their child. This will only take place over a period of time, however, and close supervision is necessary. The approach recommended is based on trying to understand the background factors and to help the parent deal with the precipitating crisis by focusing on his or her needs as well as those of the child. The immediate decision of whether it is safe to send the child back to the home while a helping relationship is being established is not an easy one and usually requires the input of a social worker or other person who has had considerable experience in this area. Laws in many states now require that any case of suspected abuse be reported to a protective agency for further evaluation and follow-up.

Placing the child in a day-care center for part of the day, having a trained parent aide or public health nurse make frequent visits to the home, and enlisting the support of other formerly abusing parents in such organizations as Parents Anonymous have been helpful in preventing the reoccurrence of injury to the child (Kempe and Helfer, 1972).

Failure to Thrive   Sometimes, the presenting problem is simply one of poor weight gain rather than abuse. Many of these families have the same characteristics of isolation, suspicion, and role reversal as families involved in actual physical abuse. With others, the mother may be in the depths of a postpartum depression and unable to meet the needs of her child (Coleman and Provence, 1957; Elmer and Gregg, 1967). Occasionally, an overburdened mother with many small children gets into problems because she tries to save time by propping the bottle and has little or no contact with her baby other than over diaper changes. Management depends upon the nature of the underlying problem.

POSTPARTUM EMOTIONAL ILLNESS

Minor psychiatric illnesses, such as neuroses, nonpsychotic depressions, and asthenic reactions, are common during the postpartum year, with an incidence of about one in four women; the psychoses are rare. Pathological reactions differ from the "natural" course of emotional responses in terms of their intensity, duration, subjective misery and impairment of functioning, and number of symptoms (Kaij and Nilsson, 1972).

Neurotic reactions are much more frequent than psychotic illness. Although they are often regarded as minor they can be handicapping when severe (Baker, 1967). Anxiety states and reactive depressions are among the common neurotic illnesses. The onset of anxiety states is usually accompanied by somatic complaints, such as tension, tremors, palpitations, or muscular pains. The mother tends to be overanxious about, and oversolicitious with, her infant; however, her patience is short-lived.

Reactive depressions, common the first few postpartum weeks, are generally associated with emotional lability, tearfulness, irritability, aggressiveness, fatigue, insomnia, and complaints of being miserable (Baker, 1967; Kaij and Nilsson, 1972). Postpartum fears are common, especially if the woman feels abandoned by her husband. The characteristic fear of infanticide is usually combined with a fear of insanity. Sexual difficulties, including decreased libido and incapacity for orgasm, may become prolonged or chronic. These reactions are often precipitated by the increased stress from the demands of motherhood, and prognosis is largely determined by the nature of the outside stresses impinging upon the woman. Many believe the 4-day blues is a short-lived reactive depression.

Kaij and Nilsson (1972) report no association between parapartum neurosis and prepregnancy somatic illness or somatic complications of pregnancy and parturition; however, a preexisting neurosis was found to be one of the most powerful predictors of postpartum mental health. Women who had a poor or unsatisfactory relationship with their mothers during childhood and those who had early object losses generally had poorer sexual adaptation before marriage, a negative attitude to the pregnancy, and more postpartum neurosis. A number of subjective gynecological symptoms (such as genital pains, feeling of laxity in abdominal wall and perineum, temporary decrease of lochia) were associated with a high number of postpartum symptoms. Sign of delayed postpartum genital involution was found to be significantly related to both prepregnancy and postpartum neurosis.

The incidence of puerperal psychiatric reactions is estimated to be between 2 and 8 percent of female admissions to mental hospitals (Herzog and Detre, 1976). About one-half of these reactions occur within the first 2 weeks post partum and two-thirds within the first 4 weeks. An additional 25 percent occur between 4 weeks to 6 months post partum and about 15 percent occur during pregnancy. Most reactions occur in women between 22 and 28 years of age, and rarely before 20 or over 40 years (Protheroe, 1969). From 10 to 15 percent of the mothers with psychotic reactions are single.

Psychotic symptoms generally begin between the third and sixth day post partum and peak during the first month (Kaij and Nilsson, 1972). Most investigators suggest that postpartum psychosis results from a combination of at least two and often three of the following stresses: (1) genetic-constitutional, (2) social-environmental, and (3) physiologic-endocrine (Herzog and Detre, 1976).

The most conspicuous feature is a clouding of consciousness that ranges from slight disorientation to violent delirium. It may present as general anxiety, apprehension, or perplexity. Hallucinations, delusions, and infanticidal impulses may also be present. The woman "often exhibits an extreme dependency with a demanding attitude toward her near relatives" (Kaij and Nilsson, 1972, p. 365). Unless an earlier psychiatric history is available it is difficult during the acute stage to make a formal diagnosis of the condition. Generally, women who present with a postpartum psychosis show the same signs as persons with an acute nonpuerperal psychosis (Herzog and Detre, 1976).

Baker (1967, p. 45) indicates that "it is often easier to describe a patient's condition in terms of the symptoms, the previous personality, and current stress, rather than give a brief but unhelpful diagnosis." He stresses the difficulty in drawing the line between the neurotic symptoms and a person's normal reactions under stress.

Management   Family physicians or other health care providers are in an excellent position to assess family resources in coping with postpartum stresses if they have provided care for any length of time. They are more likely to know the family members' (often extended as well as nuclear) usual responses to stress than the person providing just the obstetrical care. If psychiatric illness is suspected the woman should be referred for psychiatric treatment.

Because of rapid changes that can occur in the mother's mental state, she should be assessed at frequent intervals. It is wise to warn the client and her relatives that considerable fluctuations are possible and that the woman is under increased stress from the new demands of motherhood. Such a reaction may also be precipitated by the loss of a child or a miscarriage, especially late in pregnancy (Baker, 1967).

The entire family should be involved in treatment of puerperal psychiatric illness, with maintenance of the mother-baby relationship as a primary concern.

Admitting the baby to the hospital along with the mother is often beneficial. Baker (1967) points out that the stress of such an illness may serve to unite the family, or, if mishandled, may lead to disorganization.

HOSPITALIZED INFANTS

Because of studies such as that by Provence and Lipton (1962), most institutions caring for infants in this country now make a special effort to provide extra contact and stimulation. This has been shown to be important in premature nurseries as well as in foundling homes. Scarr-Salapatek and Williams (1973) combined early stimulation programs in the premature nursery with a home program following discharge from the hospital and demonstrated consistent developmental gains for this group when compared with infants who received only routine care.

It is difficult to assess the specific emotional impact of hospitalization on very young infants. We do not know how small infants perceive or remember pain. The greatest impact of hospitalization is probably separation—separation of the infant from the mother and the mother's separation from her baby. It has been suggested (Klaus and Kennell, 1976) that separation during early infancy may interfere with normal "bonding" of the mother to her baby and that this may be associated with later disturbances in parent-child relationships.

The effects of hospitalization on 76 infants under 1 year of age were studied by Schaeffer and Callender (1959), and reactions to short-term hospitalization fell into two distinct syndromes related to the age of the child. For infants under 7 months of age, there was very little evidence of upset. Crying was relatively infrequent, and the infants responded to attention by members of the staff almost as well as to that given by the mother. Feeding generally went without difficulty, and motor activity was thought to be normal. The only striking difference between home

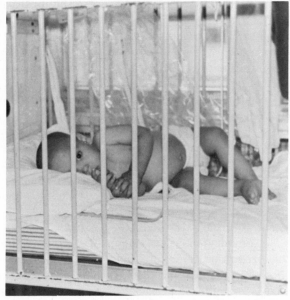

FIGURE 3-23   by Debra Hymovich

and hospital noted by these mothers was a decrease of vocalizations in the hospital.

On the other hand, the group of infants 7 months of age and older showed striking reactions. They were acutely upset at the separation from mother and cried inconsolably. Motor activity alternated between periods of subdued withdrawal and episodes of violent struggling and restlessness. The infants reacted to approaches by strangers with either fear or negativism and were often seen despondently clinging to the mother when she came to visit. Some children reacted with periods of rocking and thumb-sucking, though these were rather infrequent in the sample as a whole. Food refusals were common. All these symptoms became less intense toward the end of the hospital stay.

A differential response was also noted after the infants went home. Those under 7 months of age went through a brief period of a day or two of excessive preoccupation with their new (home) environment, with long periods of intense staring at their surroundings, and with little or no response to attempts by the mother to interact with them. A number also awakened and cried at night for several days. The mean length of such reactions was about 3 days. The older group reacted mainly by over-dependence on the mother with crying, clinging, and demands to be held. These infants also had sleep disturbances. The mean duration of these kinds of upset was about 15 days.

Nine infants showed no upset reaction at all. Four of these were under 2 months of age. The one child over 7 months with no reaction was only hospitalized 4 days.

Quinton and Rutter's data (1976) indicate that single hospital admissions lasting 1 week or less, regardless of the age at which they occur, are not associated with chronic emotional or behavioral disturbances. There was some indication, although not statistically significant, that repeated hospital admissions were associated with disturbances in children from disadvantaged families as measured by teacher ratings. About 8 percent of the children with psychiatric disorders had experienced multiple hospitalizations before 5 years of age, compared with 2.9 percent of psychiatrically normal children.

Management Recommendations based on these observations are that elective hospitalization be carried out before 7 months of age, if possible. Should hospitalization be necessary, it is highly recommended that parents, especially mothers, be permitted maximum active involvement in the care of their infants to prevent potential disturbed relationships later. It would seem that during the early infancy period maternal-infant (and probably paternal-infant) bonds are developing, and separation is likely to be more difficult for the mother than the infant; however, once the infant becomes aware of the mother as an important love object, separation becomes equally difficult for the baby.

Parents with older children at home may need guidance in looking at the impact of their separation on these older children as well as on the infant. Decisions will need to be made concerning the relative advantages and disadvantages of the mother's rooming-in with her sick infant. Her needs for peace of mind, support, rest, and sleep should also be considered.

The expected reactions of infants to hospitalization and separation should be explained, as well as the possible responses following discharge. Knowing that short-term hospitalizations can cause temporary disturbances and may be followed by increased fretfulness, night waking, and changes in bowel functioning and eating behavior can help minimize parental concerns.

SUDDEN INFANT DEATH SYNDROME (SIDS)

One of the most distressing things that can happen to any family is to come into a room and find their baby dead in bed. It is estimated that such an event occurs in 2 or 3 of 1000 live births in the United States (NFSID Pamphlet). In this syndrome, an apparently healthy infant, or one with a slight cold, usually between the ages of 3 weeks and 7 months, is put to bed and found dead some time later. Autopsy reveals either nothing or a minor inflammatory reaction of the respiratory tract. Besides grief, parental reactions frequently involve feelings that they are somehow to blame for this dreadful occurrence. Nakushian (1976) found that fathers tend to withdraw and become engrossed in their work or hobby while mothers tend to remain in the memory-filled house. Physical reactions to their grief, such as insomnia, anorexia, nightmares, and somatic complaints, are common.

Management   The primary health care worker can be of considerable help to these families during this difficult period. The experience of one nurse who visited 130 of these families the week after the death of their infant has led to the following recommendations (Pomeroy, 1969): (1) An autopsy should be performed as soon as possible and a telephone report given to the parents by the doctor who performed it; (2) after a verbal explanation the parents should be given a fact sheet about SIDS (available from the National Foundation for Sudden Infant Death); (3) a follow-up visit to the family should be made by a person who is knowledgeable about the subject; and (4) the family can be put in contact with other families in the same area who have gone through the same experience and who can provide appropriate emotional support. This latter recommendation can be put into effect by referring the family to the local chapter of the National Foundation for Sudden Infant Death if one is available in the area.

Nakushian (1976) advises that parents should be visited as soon after the infant's death as possible because she found that the parents with the earliest visits made the quickest and best adjustments. She also recommends that the home visitor help the family work through their feelings by the following: (1) Ask them about the infant's status a week or so before death and gradually lead up to time of death. These questions will elicit information concerning guilt feelings and blame. (2) Encourage the parents to communicate with each other and to share their grief. (3) Talk with other children in the family and encourage the parents to talk with them.

FOUR

Toddler and Preschool Years

This chapter covers development during the stages commonly referred to as the toddler and preschool periods. The toddler period generally includes 1- to 3-year-olds, while the preschool years extend from age 3 until approximately 6 years of age. The majority of parents of these children are in their early adult years. The first section presents developmental tasks of the youngsters, while the second section identifies parental and family developmental tasks. The third section deals with the effect of selected variables that influence development during this period. In the fourth section, common, and some of the less common, developmental problems encountered in early childhood are discussed and ways in which knowledge of normal and problematic development can be applied by the clinician in the clinical setting are examined.

INDIVIDUAL DEVELOPMENT: DEVELOPMENTAL TASKS

Developing and Maintaining Healthy Growth and Nutrition Patterns

GROWTH PATTERNS

By the end of the second year, the child's birth weight has usually quadrupled (Vaughn and McKay, 1975). From age 2 through 5 years weight gain continues at a slow and steady pace of about 4 to 5 pounds

(2 kilograms) a year. Height gains are about 3 to 4 inches (8 to 10 centimeters) per year from ages 1 to 3 and about 3 inches (8 centimeters) per year for ages 3 through 5 (Faulkner, 1962; Simmons, 1944). Tables for predicting adult height from early measurements have been developed by Bayer and Bayley (1959). The thickness of subcutaneous fat generally declines during this time, and many preschoolers look rather skinny (Faulkner, 1962; Garn and Haskell, 1960; Maresh, 1966; Stuart and Sobel, 1946). (See Appendix A for growth charts.)

NUTRITIONAL REQUIREMENTS

Caloric needs average around 1200 to 1500 per day for the preschool child (Harper, 1962). As the growth rate subsides, protein requirements are based on the size of the tissue mass rather than on the rate of growth, and for the early preschool child are estimated at about 1.2 to 1.4 grams per kilogram per day (Fomon, 1974). If one uses serum albumin as an indicator of adequacy, protein deficiency is relatively rare in this country. In the Ten-State Nutrition Survey (Garn and Clark, 1975) only 2.5 percent of 633 children under 6 years had values less than 3.0 grams per 100 milliliters. In the preschool nutrition survey of 678 children between 12 and 36 months of age, only one child had a level this low (Owen et al., 1974). However, protein calorie malnutrition remains an extremely important problem in less developed countries (Jelliffe and Stanfield, 1978). Because of the slowed growth rate, vitamins and iron supplements are seldom needed past age 2. Fluoride administration in some form continues to be important in caries prevention. Specific requirements for vitamins and minerals can be found elsewhere (Fomon, 1974).

Eating Behavior   Given a slowing of the growth rate, it is not surprising that lack of appetite and refusals to eat certain types of food are common characteristics of these youngsters. According to MacFarlane and colleagues (1962) these behaviors peak around 4 years of age, though in Chamberlin's study (1974) these complaints were more common for 2-year-olds. In one study, vegetables such as spinach, carrots, green beans, and peas headed the list of foods most frequently refused (Eppright and Fox, 1969). The effect of mealtime atmosphere in relation to appetite and food intake is brought out nicely in an observation by Widdowson (1951) who found low food intake and poor growth in a group of institutionalized children related to the fact that mealtimes were used to publicly chastise and punish children who had broken institution rules.

Learning To Manage One's Body Satisfactorily

LARGE MUSCLE DEVELOPMENT

Motor development can be followed in young children in terms of their increasing ability to engage in a variety of activities requiring coordination of large muscle groups. Table 4-1 summarizes some of the milestones used in various developmental tests (Bayley, 1969; Frankenburg, 1975; Ireton and Thwing, 1972).

SMALL MUSCLE DEVELOPMENT

Small muscle development and coordination can be followed in terms of the development of writing and drawing skills, management of eating utensils, dressing and undressing, learning of domestic skills such as sewing and/or use of tools, and the playing of musical instruments. Table 4-2 presents a rough summary of when the majority of children achieve various fine motor skills (Ames and Ilg, 1951; Gesell, et al., 1940).

INDEPENDENCE IN SELF-CARE

During these years, children are faced with two of Erikson's developmental tasks. Toddlers are learning to accomplish activities in a self-

TABLE 4-1
Summary of Age of Accomplishing Selected Milestones Used In Various Developmental Tests

Age of child	Activity
18 months	Walks unassisted
2 years	Runs forward in open space
	Picks up object without falling down
3 years	Rides tricycle
	Jumps in place, jumps from bottom stair step
	Walks up and down stairs holding on to rail
	Throws small ball forward, kicks large ball forward
	Climbs small ladder, such as on a slide
4 years	Walks downstairs using alternate feet
	Catches large ball
	Hops on one foot
	Can do somersault, walks on toes
5 years	Skips
	Walks balance beam without aid

FIGURE 4-1   by Debra Hymovich

FIGURE 4-2   by Elizabeth Tong

FIGURE 4-3   by Debra Hymovich

willed and independent manner (autonomy). Once these children can trust themselves to function autonomously they are then ready to develop skill in planning and carrying out activities (initiative). Their increasing large and small muscle development enables these youngsters to become relatively self-sufficient in such tasks as eating, dressing, washing, and toileting. According to the milestones of tests developed by Frankenburg (1975), Gesell et al. (1940), and Ireton and Thwing (1972), the following profile emerges.

Eating   In terms of self-feeding, 18-month-olds can feed themselves with a spoon but there may be considerable spilling. Between 2 and 3 years spilling becomes considerably less and children can successfully pour liquid out of a small pitcher. There is frequent getting up from the table. Between 3 and 4 years children can use a fork successfully and pour easily from a pitcher. Between 4 and 5 years, they can spread and cut with a knife, clear their own place at the table, and wipe up spills.

Dressing and Undressing   Two-year-olds can help undress and dress themselves by taking off socks, pulling up or down pants, and the like.

TABLE 4-2
Summary of Small Muscle Development

Age	Figure copying	Drawing behavior with crayon and paper	Other
18 months		Scribbles off paper	
2 years	Copies vertical line	Scribbles, stays on paper	Builds tower of four cubes Eats with spoon, little spilling Turns pages one at a time
3 years	Copies a circle	Makes unrecognizable doodle and names it	Uses hammer to pound nails Uses fork Builds tower of eight cubes Unbuttons buttons
4 years	Copies a cross	Crude, but recognizable drawing	Buttons buttons Makes small cut with scissors on line
5 years	Copies a triangle and square	Simple, clearly recognizable drawing Draws a person with three parts	Able to cut long line with scissors Spreads and cuts with knife
6 years	Copies a diamond	Draws a person with six parts	Ties shoes

By 3 years, children can undress pretty well, including unbuttoning buttons, but they mix up front and back when trying to dress. By 4½ years, the majority of children dress and undress themselves with little assistance except with such items as back buttons or tying shoes. The ability to tie shoes comes around 5½ or 6 years.

Washing and Toothbrushing In terms of personal hygiene most children are washing their hands by 2½ years, brushing their teeth and washing their face by 3½, and taking a bath with minimal supervision by about 5 years.

Toileting Sometime around the second year, the child's source of pleasure shifts from the mouth to the anal region (Freud). The child's task at this stage is to learn to regulate the two mutually conflicting activities of holding on (retention) and letting go (elimination). There are fairly marked sex differences in toileting behaviors, with girls being about 6 months ahead of boys. For the largely middle-class sample of Ireton and Thwing (1972), about two-thirds of the girls had achieved bladder and bowel control by 26 to 29 months of age, whereas it was not until about age 3 that two-thirds of the boys had reached this state of development. By 4 years the majority of both sexes were going to the toilet by themselves and managing clothes without difficulty, and by 5 years they could manage all aspects competently, including wiping themselves.

Roberts and Schoellkopf (1951) give a cross-sectional view of a large sample of middle-class, 2½-year-old children. In terms of stool frequency, 89 percent of the children were having at least one bowel movement a day, with a small subgroup (10 percent) reporting two to three movements per day. About 4 percent had a bowel movement every other day and less than 1 percent about once every 3 to 4 days. Another 8 percent were irregular enough so that they did not fit into any of these categories. Their mothers considered 20 percent to have some problems with constipation, and about 12 percent received either enemas or laxa-

FIGURE 4-4

by Elizabeth Tong

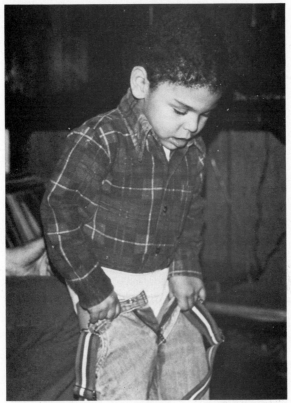

FIGURE 4-5   by Elizabeth Tong

tives for this. About 25 percent of the boys and 10 percent of the girls were still thought to require frequent parental reminders about going to the bathroom to prevent accidents. About 16 percent of the boys and 8 percent of the girls were seen as problems in that they refused to have their bowel movements in the appropriate place at least once or twice a week. Urinary frequency was also noted. About 10 percent of the sample were said to void about every hour or more, with the majority (80 percent) voiding about every 2 or 3 hours.

In another sample of 100 middle-class children followed longitudinally, 43 percent of those at or near their second birthday were described as very or somewhat resistant to sitting on the potty, but this had dropped to 2 percent by age 3 (Chamberlin, 1974). Of the 2-year-olds, 71 percent were said to have a bowel movement at least occasionally in

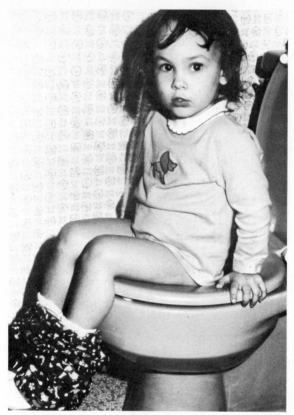

FIGURE 4-6   by Susan McCabe

their pants. This decreased to 17 percent at age 3 and 1 percent by age 4. Of the 4-year-olds, 7 percent were still wetting themselves during the day with some regularity; 26 percent were doing so at night. Except for bedwetting, which only gradually disappears, the large majority of children usually become toilet trained sometime between 2 and 3 years of age.

Learning to Understand and Relate to the Physical World

HOW THE YOUNG CHILD SEES THE WORLD

During the early part of this period, toddlers are still learning about the world through their senses (Piaget's sensorimotor stage of development).

FIGURE 4-7   by Susan McCabe

Much of their understanding comes through looking, touching, listening, and manipulating objects, others, and themselves. Around 2 years, as language development increases, the child enters the preoperational stage of development. During this stage, the child has some ability to represent things mentally and can begin to solve problems by mental trial and error as well as by physical means. The most striking characteristic of this period is the egocentric nature of the child's thinking and his or her inability to attend to more than one aspect of a given situation at a time. This latter aspect is dramatically brought out in the conservation experiments of Piaget in which children are shown equal volumes of colored water. One of these is then poured into a tall, thin container and the other into a short, fat one. The child of this stage invariably identifies the long, thin vessel as containing more fluid because it looks "bigger" than the short, fat one. It is not until 7 or 8 years that the child realizes that the volume is the same even though the shape has changed (Piaget, 1951, 1952).

This limited perception shows up in other ways as well. Preschool children cannot see things from the point of view of others and think that all people think and feel the same way they are thinking and feeling at any given point of time. Because of this they do not feel it necessary to communicate thoughts verbally. When playing with other children the young child may seem to be communicating, but when one actually listens to the conversation, the child is mostly talking to him or herself with a "collective monologue." In fact, the ability to understand other people and communicate one's thoughts verbally is not fully functioning until about 7 years of age.

This inability to understand that one's own view is subjective causes children to believe they are the center of the world and leads to a whole group of animistic and magical conceptions. Children of this age see themselves as the cause of many disparate events. If there is a death, divorce, or illness in the household, they think they are to blame. Thoughts and events are seen as equivalent with inability to understand that dreams are mental representations rather than something that has actually happened.

Living qualities are attributed to inanimate objects, so that if the child trips over a chair he or she is likely to say that the chair did it on purpose, or if asked why clouds move replies they are following him or her and so on.

There is an inability to distinguish fantasy from reality. Preschool children tend to believe literally what they see on television, hear in stories, or are told by their parents. An example of this literal interpretation is one study in which 3-, 4-, and 5-year-old children were shown a dog with a cat's mask on its face (Taylor and Howell, 1973). Almost all the 3-year-olds thought the animal was a cat, and not until 5 years did the majority recognize it as a dog with a mask.

Time Concepts   Bradley (1947) divided the understanding of time into three aspects. The first is the concept of the continual flow of time, as with growing up and getting older, and so on. The second is broad divisions of time such as past, present, and future (yesterday, today, and tomorrow), and finally the more finite divisions of time, such as seconds, minutes, hours; morning, afternoon, night; days, weeks, months, and years.

Ames (1946) used observations of nursery school children, from ages 18 to 48 months, to estimate the development of time concepts in the young child. The 18-month-old children had little sense of time other than the immediate present; by 2 years there was some differentiation of the present, with the child being able to respond to "wait a minute" or "soon" in answer to requests. There was also some understanding of simple time sequences, such as "you can play after snack time," but no understanding of "tomorrow."

By 3 years, time sense is more advanced. Children know roughly when they will go to bed, what they will do tomorrow, and that winter and Christmas happen every so often. Of the 3-year-olds, one-half could tell how old they were. There is still not much understanding of terms referring to the past, such as "yesterday," and little appreciation of duration, such as an hour.

At 4 years, children have a reasonably clear idea of the events of the day and how they relate to each other, can tell you whether it is morning or afternoon, and have some appreciation of the cycle of seasons, such as last summer and next summer. They can usually tell when their next birthday will occur. The idea of an hour's duration is still very sketchy.

At 5 years, children are beginning to understand finer divisions of time, can name the days of the week, and can tell you what day it is. They also know what time bedtime and breakfast are, but cannot tell the actual time by reading a clock. It is likely that children who recognize numbers can read the time on a digital clock.

Gothberg (1949) studied the time concepts of retarded children and found that not until children had achieved a mental age of 6 years could they understand different parts of the day such as night and morning and not until a mental age between 7 and 8 years could the child grasp the comparative duration of minutes, hours, and days. Of his sample, 50 percent could tell time at a mental age of 7 years but this did not reach 100 percent until a mental age of 11 years.

EARLY MORAL DEVELOPMENT

In terms of moral development the children of this stage tend to judge themselves or others as "good" or "bad" on the basis of the effects of a given action without taking into account the intent of the person involved. Thus, the child who trips accidentally and breaks two glasses is "morally" worse then the child who smashes one glass deliberately in a fit of anger. Rules are seen as unchangeable and inviolable, and fear of punishment is the main reason given for obeying rules (Kohlberg, 1963; Piaget, 1948). The child's superego (Freud) begins to develop at this stage, and many of the values, beliefs, and rules of the parents become internalized.

CONCEPTIONS OF THE BODY

Children under 5 years have little understanding of the working of the body. For example, in one study it was found that although children usually know by the age of 7 years that the heart is an important part of the body, they still explain what it does in terms of describing how it beats, or by vague statements that we need it in order to live (Gellert,

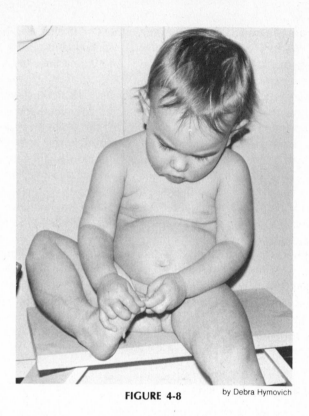

FIGURE 4-8   by Debra Hymovich

1962). Older children increasingly associate heart function with breathing, usually in a confused manner. It was not until age 13 that most children could explain what the heart does in terms of its pumping blood around the body.

Only one child below the age of 7 years reported the lungs were related to breathing, and many gave responses indicating they thought the lungs had something to do with chewing. Only by age 9 or 10 could the majority associate the activity of lungs with breathing.

DEATH AND DYING

Children in the preoperational stage of cognitive development do not see death as a permanent condition and may equate it with sleep. Their egocentric outlook also makes it likely that they will hold themselves responsible for a death in the family. This can be of particular intensity when a sibling dies because the surviving child may have already "wished" the child dead many times as the result of past squabbles (Childers and Wimmer, 1971; Koocher, 1973; Melear, 1973; Nagy, 1948).

CAUSATION OF DISEASE

Children often view illness in terms of punishment for some kind of misbehavior.

Developing Self-Awareness and a Satisfying Sense of Self

From a psychosocial perspective, the components of a satisfying sense of self at this stage consist of learning to view oneself as an autonomous person without feelings of shame and doubt (toddler period), followed by a developing sense of initiative while overcoming feelings of guilt (preschool period) (Erikson, 1963). Thus, as children develop and practice new physical and cognitive skills, they come to feel good about themselves or to have doubts about their functioning.

FIGURE 4-9   by Susan McCabe

CHILD AND FAMILY DEVELOPMENT

SELF-CONCEPT

The progression of ideas about the self can be pieced together from a number of different observations. Gesell et al. (1974) outlines the following sequences. By 9 months, children begin to respond to their names. At 2 years, children call themselves by name and use pronouns such as you, me, and I. By 30 months, gender identification is relatively well established, and children can recognize and articulate their needs and wants. By 4 years, boasting is rather common but some statements of self-criticism also make their appearance. At 6 years, value judgments about one's own behavior are commonplace.

Ames (1952) provides more detail, with descriptions of behavior indicating self-awareness and self-evaluation in nursery school children. She notes that not infrequently 3-year-olds make comments about their own ability: "I can go by myself" or "I can do that by myself." They call the teacher's attention to their own products or powers and may boast

FIGURE 4-10   by Debra Hymovich

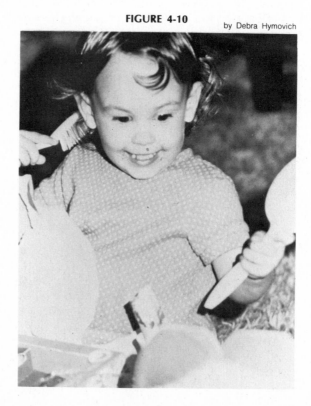

about them. They also were observed to do this with peers. By 3½ years there is less showing off and more concern about liking and being liked: "I like you—do you like me?" At age 4 boasting is again prominent and some negative criticism also makes its appearance: i.e., "I can't do this very good."

This overview has been confirmed and expanded on by others looking at specific aspects. In their studies of the rearing of children with ambiguous genitalia, Money et al. (1955a,b) clearly demonstrate the early development of gender identity and the hazards involved in trying to change this after 18 months of age.

Studies of the development of racial awareness show that for both black and white children such awareness appears about age 3, increases "rapidly over the next few years and is more or less firmly established by the time children enter grade school" (Proshansky, 1966). Indirect evidence that negative evaluations of self can be present as early as age 3 is provided in studies (Clark and Clark, 1947; Goodman, 1952; Morland, 1962; Stevenson and Stewart, 1958) which show that in a dominant white culture, black children already show a greater desire to play with

FIGURE 4-11

by Debra Hymovich

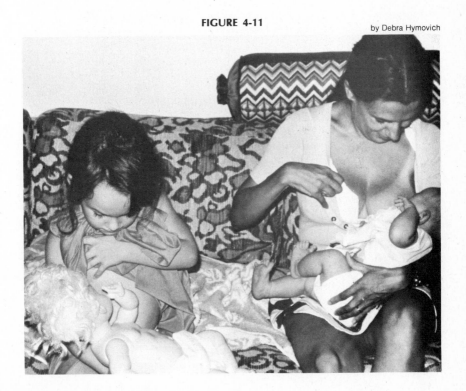

white children by this age than vice versa and are more likely to play with white dolls than black by nursery school age.

White and Watts (1973) provide information about self-concept formation from a different perspective. Through staff and teacher observations and developmental testing they identified a number of 6-year-old children who appeared to be particularly competent ("able to cope in a superior fashion with anything they met, day in and day out"). They observed these children in detail and compared them with a group of less competent children and tried to identify how these two groups differed. In terms of self-concept the competent children were more frequently noted to praise themselves and show pride in their accomplishments. This characteristic distinguished more competent from less competent children down to age 3.

All these studies indicate that by age 3, children have some firmly established ideas about who they are and are beginning to form attitudes about their own self-worth.

GENDER IDENTITY AND BEHAVIOR

Money and Ehrhardt (1972) outline the sequences involved with normal gender identity. (1) Sex chromosomes determine which gonads will

FIGURE 4-12

by Debra Hymovich

become ovaries and testes. (2) The gonad secretes hormones that lead to differentiation of the internal and external reproductive anatomy and also, apparently, to the establishment of pathways in the brain and peripheral nerves that will influence later sexual behavior. (3) The external physical differences serve as a stimulus to the parents and other significant adults to respond to the child with rearing behavior that reinforces and shapes his or her sex-role behavior and gender identity. The central nervous system "programming" from prenatal hormones also leads to behavioral traits that are interpreted as masculine or feminine, as the case may be, which reinforces the parenting. (4) The hor-

FIGURE 4-13

by Elizabeth Tong

CHILD AND FAMILY DEVELOPMENT

FIGURE 4-14   by Debra Hymovich

monal changes at adolescence confirm the gender identity and prepare the person for reproduction and parenthood. The capacity of "falling in love" that develops at this time eventually assures attachment to a member of the opposite sex for a long enough period to make pregnancy a likely outcome (unless active methods are taken to prevent this), and the mother-child "attachment" phenomenon that occurs at birth generally ensures parental affection and continuity of care of the child.

The growing child ordinarily responds to two sets of gender stimuli. He or she tends to identify with and model the behavior of the parent of the same sex and reciprocates in a complimentary manner with the parent of the opposite sex. Thus, the child is not only learning what to do that is labeled as "masculine" or "feminine" by the culture involved, but also what not to do in terms of the role behavior of the opposite sex. This learning also encompasses what to expect from and how to respond to members of the opposite sex.

Cross-cultural studies show that there can be enormous differences in the content of what is defined as "masculine" and "feminine" behavior and that gender confusion does not arise as long as there is clear differentiation of the separate reproductive and erotic roles of the sexes (Mead, 1955; Money and Ehrhardt, 1972).

> Provided that a child grows up to know that sex differences are primarily defined by the reproductive capacity of the sex organs and to have a positive feeling of pride in his or her own genitalia and their ultimate reproductive use, then it does not much matter whether various child care, domestic, and vocational activities are or are not interchangeable between mother and father. It does not matter if mother is a bus driver and daddy a cook. It does not even matter if the father (by adoption) is a female to male transsexual provided his hormonal and surgical masculinization has given him the outward appearance and voice of a man and provided he relates to the child's mother as her lover and husband irrespective of how they actually perform coitally. (Money and Ehrhardt, 1972, p. 14)

Apparently, what does lead to difficulty is a confusion in roles, such as when a transvestite father dresses in women's clothing or the parent of either sex dislikes his or her own sexual role enough to convey a negative impression of the erotic and reproductive role of the penis or vagina. The effect on gender identity and role performance of being brought up by a lesbian mother is unknown.

There is considerable evidence that biologic factors do influence sex-role behavior: observers of nursery school children have repeatedly noted boys to be more active and aggressive than girls (Hattwick, 1937; Jersild and Markey, 1935). Studies of animal behavior show many species where male behavior is significantly more active and aggressive than female behavior (Hart, 1974). Infants exposed to androgens in utero and raised as females from birth have a greater tendency to show some "tomboy" characteristics than those not exposed to androgens in utero (Money and Ehrhardt, 1972).

However, studies of children with discrepancies between sex of assignment and rearing, and such biologic variables as chromosomal sex, gonadal sex, hormonal sex, external genital morphology, or internal reproductive structures, indicate that sex of assignment and rearing is the strongest predictor of later gender-role behavior and orientation (Money et al., 1955a,b). That is, children adopt the gender characteristics of the way they are reared regardless of whether this coincides with genetic sex or these other biological variables. Although the sample is small ($N = 11$), these studies indicate that attempts to change the gender identification of a child after 18 months or 2 years of age is frequently unsatisfactory and carries with it considerable emotional risk.

Learning to Relate to Others

During the toddler and preschool years, children are learning the foundations for social relations with others.

COMMUNICATION SKILLS

Words and Sequences   One of the best overviews of normal speech development is that reported by Morely (1957) from the 1000-family Newcastle upon Tyne longitudinal study. The speech development of every tenth child was investigated in detail ($N = 114$). Development during the first 3 years was based on reports by health visitors who saw the children in their homes at regular intervals. Later speech development was assessed by examination of the children by a speech pathologist as well as by history. All the children in this group were thought to have normal intelligence, and no child was found to have developmental aphasia or severe delays in the development of speech beyond 4 years of age.

The average for use of first words was 12 months, with a range of 6 to 30 months. Of the children, 7 percent were said to talk before 8 months of age and 2 percent did not attempt to use words until after 2 years. Two children who did not use words before age 2 progressed rapidly thereafter and were using adequate speech at 3½ years of age. By 2 years of age, 89 percent were using at least simple word sentences and all but one child had achieved this level by age 3. The average age that word sequences were used was 18 months, with a range of 10 to 44 months. The average time from onset of intelligible words to use of word sequences was around 6 months of age, but in some the time interval was longer (10 to 24 months).

Intelligibility of Speech   Two-thirds of the children were easily intelligible from the onset of speech, but one-third passed through a period when their speech was hard to understand. For the sample as a whole, 69 percent were intelligible to strangers by 2 years of age and 84 percent by age 3. Four children were still unintelligible on entry to school at age 5. It was found that some children who had achieved normal speech would relapse into patterns of defective articulation at times of excitement or emotional stress, or when self-conscious. There were marked individual differences in the patterns of development, with some children proceed-

FIGURE 4-15   by Elizabeth Tong

ing at a steady rate and others with starts and stops and periods of regression.

Templin (1957) reports a detailed study of speech development in a sample of 480 children of a mixed socioeconomic background from 3 to 8 years of age. Ability to articulate words correctly increases with age until adult levels are reached by about 8 years. The overall accuracy of articulation of speech sounds by 3-year-olds is approximately 50 percent that of 8-year-olds. In general, boys were about a year behind girls and children from lower socioeconomic levels were a year behind children from families of upper socioeconomic levels. The ability to pronounce vowels and diphthongs was generally ahead of the ability to pronounce consonants, with z, wh, th, and j being the consonants most frequently misarticulated. The mean number of words in sentences increased from about four at age 3 to eight words at age 8. Correct grammar usage was already apparent in most 3-year-olds.

ATTACHMENT

As noted in Chapter 3, infants begin showing distress with separation from the mother toward the end of the first year of life.

In their study of the natural history of separation protest in 22 firstborn children, Kennell and Bergen (1966) report that these reactions increase in frequency and intensity until a peak at about 18 months of age. After the age of 1½ years, most of the children appear less overwhelmed but continue to react vigorously up to 2½ years of age. Toward the end of the third year, all these children were able to accept separation under ordinary circumstances, and by 34 months of age, all but one child entered nursery school without difficulty. Most of these children reacted to separation by crying and clinging and, in some instances, with anger in the form of screaming and temper tantrums. A few reacted by becoming more subdued and quiet. Reacting to the mother's return was often one of ignoring her initially for a short period of time. The majority of the mothers felt that the crying and clinging was "spoiled" behavior, and some reacted with annoyance or punishment.

PEER AND ADULT INTERACTIONS IN GROUP SETTINGS

Observations of the behavior of children in nursery school settings form the bulk of the data here, though home observations are becoming increasingly more prominent (Ames, 1952; Hattwick and Sanders, 1938).

In group settings, 18- and 21-month-old children largely play by themselves, ignoring others or treating them as objects (i.e., pushing them out of the way, grabbing a toy from them). There is some interaction with the teachers, but this is mostly in time of distress or need. Two-year-olds begin to notice others in that their play becomes more parallel (playing near but not with another child). They cannot share, and aggressiveness is somewhat more personal, with deliberate attempts to take away toys from others. A frequent activity is obtaining and hoarding possessions. "Mine" is a favorite word. There is more interaction than formerly with the teacher, and the child engages in play with adults.

By 2½ years there is definitely more relating to other children as persons, but the chief form is quarreling over toys. There is much physical aggression directed toward others but the child may not fight back when attacked. Children of this age seldom solve their own problems and either seek help from the teacher or one gives in and withdraws. Some rudiments of cooperative play are seen, but groupings are temporary and activities change rapidly. Interactions with the teacher still predominate over interactions with peers.

By 3 years, child-child interactions equal or exceed that with the teacher and social skills are more advanced. Children show some idea of taking turns and making polite requests of others. Play is more often in groups of two than in larger groups. There is less physical aggressiveness, but verbally excluding behavior becomes more common: i.e., "you can't come in here," "go away."

TODDLER AND PRESCHOOL YEARS

By 3½ years, cooperative play becomes more organized. Most children engage in lively, imaginative play, with groups of three or more, which involves considerable cooperation and give and take. Children of this age often solve their own squabbles by taking turns, finding substitute toys, and so on. Children are seen as individual persons with special individual characteristics, and the concept of friendship is now very important: "I like you, do you like me?" Excluding others from play is still frequent but often of only a temporary nature, and a child who is excluded in one game is likely to be included in the next.

At age 4, peer interaction dominates and cooperative play activities are often sustained for 15- to 20-minute periods or longer. There is little interaction with the teachers, but the children can verbalize friendly feelings toward them and often do so. They will now express friendly feelings toward peers as well, but excluding comments and derogatory remarks are still strong. Jealousy is also frequent and expressed verbally.

Descriptive play patterns at different ages are also discussed in the proceedings of a recent conference on the role of play in child development (Curry and Armand, 1971; Sutton-Smith, 1976).

SEXUALITY

Curiosity The study of Hattendorf (1932) is still one of the best sources of data. Over 3000 home interviews in a Minneapolis suburban school district were conducted with mothers of children between the ages of 2 and 14 years. About 40 percent of these children were in the preschool age period. The main preschool concerns were (1) where babies come from, (2) physical differences between the sexes, and (3) the names and functioning of organs involved in reproduction and elimination. Only 15 percent of the 2-year-olds were said to have asked questions. This increased to 45 percent for 3-year-olds, 50 percent for 4-year-olds, and 70 percent for those aged 5 years. There were no significant sex differences in types of questions asked.

Gesell et al. (1974) state that 2½-year-olds begin to inquire about mothers' breasts; 3-year-olds comment about differences in genitalia and postures in urination and ask where babies come from. By 4 years, the child shows some interest in how babies get out of the "stomach," and 5-year-olds are beginning to be curious about how the baby gets in there as well.

Taking a different approach, Conn (1940, 1947, 1948) used a doll-play interview technique to ascertain the sexual knowledge and understanding of over 200 children referred to a child guidance clinic. Of these children, 25 were under 6 years of age. About 50 percent of the 4- to 6-year-olds knew about genital differences between boys and girls but

CHILD AND FAMILY DEVELOPMENT

there was still considerable confusion among 4- and 5-year-olds about where babies come from: most thought that God produced the babies and that they could be bought at a store or obtained at a hospital. It was not until 7 or 8 years that these children began to grasp the concept that the baby grows inside the mother and not until 10 or 11 years that some awareness of intercourse and the father's role in reproduction became evident.

Nakedness In a middle-class sample of 100, about 5 percent of the 3-year-olds were said to indicate some discomfort about being seen in the nude (Chamberlin, 1974). This percentage increased to 20 percent at age 4 years and 33 percent at age 5. In a study by MacFarlane et al. (1962), reactions which ranged from panic to being ill at ease when seen undressed peaked in the preschool age period. Of the girls, 25 percent displayed moderate to severe discomfort from ages 3½ through age 5, and 20 percent of the boys had similar reactions.

Masturbation Masturbation to the point of orgasm becomes more common in 3-, 4-, and 5-year-old children. MacFarlane et al. (1962) define vigorous stimulation of the genitalia once a week or more as a "problem" and indicate that on the average 10 percent of the boys and 6 percent of the girls did this during the preschool years, with a peak of 16 percent at age 4 for boys. However, in the Kinsey et al. data (1948), only 2 percent of the women interviewed recalled masturbating to the point of orgasm by 5 years. However, Kinsey estimates that in an uninhibited society one-half or more of all children would reach climax through masturbation by age 3 or 4.

In one study (Chamberlin, 1974), the statement "rubs or plays with sex organs" was said to be very descriptive for 6 percent of male 2-year-olds and somewhat descriptive for 60 percent. These percentages remained relatively consistent through age 5. For girls, the figures are 4 and 42 percent, respectively, at age 2 and fluctuate around this level for the next 3 years. In a sample of 5-year-olds (Sears et al., 1957), 59 percent of the mothers reported their children had masturbated at some time or another.

Sex Play Exposing and manipulating the genitals of one another is reported as common in the preschool age period (Gesell et al., 1974). Sears et al. report 54 percent of their sample of 5-year-olds as having engaged in some sex play with other children. In Chamberlin's study (1974), mothers indicated that this happened in about 4 percent of the 3-year-olds, 9 percent of the 4-year-olds, and only 15 percent of the

5-year-olds. Using recall data, 8 percent of the women in Kinsey's study recalled sex play with boys by age 5 and 1 percent indicated they had actually had coitus; 2.6 percent of males recalled having coitus by age 5. In cultures more open about sexuality it is not unusual to see coitus between preschool children (Mead, 1955), and this has also been observed in communal living situations in the United States (Eiduson et al., 1973; Johnston and Deisher, 1973).

See Table 4-3 for a summary of typical stage-related characteristics of the child and family.

FAMILY DEVELOPMENT: DEVELOPMENTAL TASKS

Meeting the Basic Physical Needs of the Family

One of the difficulties faced by parents at this stage is that of providing indoor and outdoor space, as well as privacy, to meet the differing needs of the various family members (preschooler, parents, and perhaps a new infant or grandparents). Providing for the safety of the child, especially during the early years of this period, is a major concern.

Financially, this can be an unpredictable period for young parents. Among the possible difficulties are unexpected costs of illnesses or accidents. In addition, there may be expenses for nursery schools and baby-sitters. Duvall (1977) reports that the majority of working mothers of preschoolers are doing so because their income is a necessity.

> The high cost of medical care, continuing insurance, installment buying, debts and mortgages complicate even well-planned family economics and are disastrous to those less carefully organized. In recent years, a growing awareness of the financial hazards facing young families has led to the development of such cushioning resources as group hospitalization and medical service plans, well-baby clinics, cooperative nurseries, child guidance clinics, mental hygiene services, family service facilities, parent education agencies, adult and child recreational programs, and special facilities for the care and education of all types of exceptional children. That such helpful resources are not yet generally available—or even known to the rank and file of families who need them is all too true in most communities. (Duvall, 1977, p. 263)

Assisting Each Member Develop His or Her Individual Potential

Two of the parental tasks during this stage are helping their child develop a positive self-concept and handling the child's aggression (Duvall, 1977). Accomplishing these tasks can be especially difficult for families belonging to minority races or ethnic groups.

TABLE 4-3

Summary of Typical Stage-Related Characteristics of Child and Family
(Ages 1 through 5)

Age of child	Growth, nutrition and health	Body control	Relate to world	Self-awareness	Communication	Peer relationship	Adult relationship	Sexuality	Family tasks
1–2 years	Slowing growth rate and decreased appetite; foot and leg "problems"	Runs, builds tower with blocks	Sensory motor, curiosity, points to named pictures	Says own name, recognizes self in mirror	Words, transient stutter	Solitary or parallel play, aggression or withdrawal	Separation problems, frequent adult contacts, stubborn, temper, whine	Handles genitals	Adaptation of family routines to small children
2–3 years	Frequent coughs and colds; high fevers	Toilet trained, eats with spoon, climbs small ladder	Symbolic thought, egocentric, animistic	Gender identity, awareness of differences in skin color	Short sentences, uses pronouns, transient stutter	Little sharing, some interactive play	Frequent help-seeking from adults	Curious about sex differences	Socialization of children

TABLE 4-3 (Continued)
Summary of Typical Stage-Related Characteristics of Child and Family
(Ages 1 through 5)

Age of child	Growth, nutrition and health	Body control	Relate to world	Self-awareness	Communication	Peer relationship	Adult relationship	Sexuality	Family tasks
3–4 years	Looks skinny	Dresses self, copies a circle, rides tricycle	Egocentric, understands "tomorrow," counts to five	Pride in accomplishments, self-evaluation, verbalizes feelings	Understandable speech, uses plurals	Cooperative play, definite friendship	Separates easily, less adult dependency	Interested in where babies come from	Meeting increasing vocational demands, coping with frequent childhood illness
									Maintenance of husband-wife relationship
4–5 years		Draws recognizable person, buttons buttons, cuts with scissors, skips, walks on balance board	Egocentric, distinguishes reality from fantasy, knows colors	Evaluates self	Articulates most beginning sounds, understands prepositions, communicates well with others	Sustained dramatic play	Mostly peer interaction in group settings, can use adults for help	Sex play with other children	Maintenance of individual interests
									Participation in community activities

Emmerich (1969) asked parents of preschoolers what parental goals they saw as important in interpersonal relationships and childhood socialization. Parents ranked a list of positive goals in the following order: (1) trustingness, (2) obedience, (3) friendliness, (4) assertiveness, and (5) independence. In order of importance the parents did not want their children to develop the following characteristics: (1) avoidance, (2) aggression, (3) submissiveness, (4) overfriendliness, and (5) dependency.

White and Watts (1973) have tentatively identified characteristics of mother-child interaction that may be predictive of children with a high degree of competence. Youngsters between 12 and 33 months of age were observed in their homes with their mothers. Specific techniques used by the mothers included teaching, facilitating, routine talking, observing, and restricting. Mothers of the more competent children tended to use teaching and facilitative techniques more than did mothers of the less competent children. When the competent child was interacting with mother, the "average" mother encouraged about twice as many activities as she discouraged, initiated about one-third of the child's activities, and was twice as successful in controlling the child as not. Although parents of both groups of children used playpens and highchairs infrequently, the more competent children spent more time in highchairs, while the less competent spent significantly more time in the playpens. Generally it was found that mothers spend little time interacting with their young children. During 65 to 75 percent of the researchers' observation times, the mother and child were either in different rooms, or, if in the same room, they were not looking at each other. For the remaining time, some interaction was taking place but much of it was not classified as intellectually stimulating.

PARENTAL DEVELOPMENT

Most parents of young children are still in Erikson's stage of generativity versus stagnation, in which they are primarily concerned with guiding the next generation (Erikson, 1963). However the concept of generativity is broader than this and includes productivity and creativity. Not only are the parents busy with socializing their children, but many are also involved in establishing their vocations and creative interests. The parents are still coping with the developmental tasks mentioned in Chapter 3. As their child continues to develop, so do the parents. During the child's phase of developing autonomy, the parents are faced with learning to accept these developmental changes and hence some loss of control while maintaining necessary limits. As the child enters Erikson's stage of initiative, the parents enter their next phase of learning to separate from their child by allowing increasing independence while modeling the necessary standards (Friedman and Friedman, 1977). The parents are also continuing to develop as individuals (with their strengths and limitations) and as a married couple (Duvall, 1977).

The demands of child care, homemaking, and work often leave parents little time for self-development or development as a couple. Couples who are successful in continuing their development "encourage these individual and joint tastes, interests, and friendships that strengthen their confidence in themselves and in each other" (Duvall, 1977, p. 261).

Providing Emotional Support and Communicating Effectively with All Family Members

SPOUSE RELATIONSHIPS

A summary of studies related to families of preschoolers found that during this stage, husbands and wives tend to have fewer arguments with each other, feel less resentful or misunderstood, and less often refuse to talk because they are angry with each other than at any other time since they were married (Duvall, 1977, p. 260). On the other hand, they tend to get away from home less often, laugh less often, work together less often on a stimulating project, or calmly discuss something with each other less often than formerly. Terman et al. (1938) found that lack of expression of affection was a major indicator of unhappiness for both husbands and wives. As indicated earlier, one of the difficulties during this period is finding time, privacy, and energy for close relationships with one another. Feldman and Rogoff (1977) found that having a second child decreased marital happiness and satisfaction more than did having the first child.

PARENT-CHILD RELATIONSHIPS

Changes in parent-child relationships occur throughout the early childhood period. Conditions contributing to these changes include: (1) changes in the child from dependency to autonomy, (2) changes in parental attitudes about the amount of care and attention the child needs, (3) parents' concept of a "good" child, (4) the child's preference for outsiders (i.e., teacher if attends nursery school), and (5) the child's developing preference for one parent (Hurlock, 1975, p. 108). Once

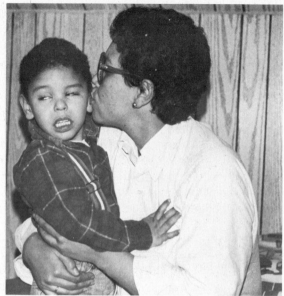

FIGURE 4-16   by Elizabeth Tong

FIGURE 4-17

by Elizabeth Tong

children begin to differentiate parents, they begin directing some concerns and interests to one parent and some to the other. They also become increasingly adroit at playing one parent against the other!

The father plays a more active role in the life of his preschooler than he did during the child's infancy (Weiner and Elkind, 1972). As the child's interaction with, and affection for, the father increases, the relationship with the mother becomes more diluted. Fagot (1974) observed 12 toddlers (18 to 24 months) interacting at home with their mothers and fathers. She found that both parents praised girls more, criticized boys more, and joined in play with boys more often than with girls. However, boys were also left to play alone more often than were girls.

In lower-class families, there was found to be less conversation among family members and less encouragement for the child to talk than in middle- or upper-class families (Deutsch, 1965).

SIBLING RELATIONSHIPS

Firstborn youngsters often experience the birth of a sibling, while later-born children have to come to grips with relating to older siblings. The younger child's relationship with older siblings usually alternates between companionship and rivalry. At times, the child may respect and enjoy being with them or turn to them for help and protection. On the other hand, the youngster also comes to resent their prerogatives and to compete with them for parental attention and approval, often seen in the form of tattling. Stone and Church (1973) suggest that sibling rivalry may be peculiar to small, nuclear families, indicating that in large, extended families or in communal societies such rivalry may not develop or may take very different forms. Through the teaching and modeling of siblings, the younger children may become quite advanced in verbal and other learning skills.

Legg et al. (1974) interviewed 18 families concerning their children's preparation for and reaction to the birth of a sibling. These parents rarely attempted any preparation for the child under 2 years of age. For the older children, some parents used children's books and neighborhood babies to help explain the coming baby. Most mothers felt that having the older child visit in the hospital was a positive experience for the child. When the fathers had been especially active in caring for the older sibling while the mother was hospitalized, the stress of the birth was considerably diminished.

Following birth, most of the regression was for the bottle or pacifier and interference with toilet training. Negative feelings of the older child were almost always expressed directly toward the mother. There was

FIGURE 4-18

FIGURE 4-19

often no direct aggression against the infant until the baby was old enough to interfere with possessions or play. The situations that seemed to increase the child's difficulty in adapting to a new sibling were moving to a new house, placing the infant's crib in the preschooler's room, or continuous, full-day care for a considerable time prior to the infant's birth.

White (1975) indicates that differences in sibling relationships exist depending upon the age differential between the children. Siblings around 2 or 2½ years of age are predominately home- and mother-oriented, while children around 4 years are becoming more peer-oriented and have other interests than just the attention of the mother. When the next older child is at least 3 years older than the baby, family relationships tend to be more pleasant than when the age difference is less than 3 years. The closer in age the two siblings are, the more likely is the older one to behave in a hostile manner toward the younger child.

Adapting Family Organization and Management to Changing Needs

Success in achieving more mature roles in the family depends not only on what needs to be done, but also on how decisions are made, how roles are assigned, and how each family member feels about his or her responsibilities (Duvall, 1977). As the child gets older, he or she gradually takes on more responsibility (dressing, toileting, washing) for self-care although still with help and supervision. Preschoolers become increasingly interested in what is going on in the household and want to "help" with many of the activities. These children will identify with the same-sex parent and try to imitate their activities.

An exploratory study by Smith et al. (1969) indicated that in two-parent families, fathers of preschoolers are more involved in household responsibilities, particularly child care, than at any other time in the family life cycle. At the same time, they spend significantly more time out of the home than do men with older children.

For families living near extended family members, the services rendered by middle-class grandparents peak during the preschool years (Adams, 1964).

Functioning in the Community

The potential danger during this stage is that the family becomes preoccupied with itself and has limited contact with events in the community (Duvall, 1977). The mother may be home all day or rushing between work and home, while the father is busy with his work and often outside meetings connected with it, and his many roles within the family itself.

As the children begin to expand their horizons (i.e., nursery school, kindergarten, religious school) the parents are brought into some of these activities. They may become involved in parents' meetings or community projects affecting their youngsters. Family excursions utilizing community resources such as parks, zoos, and playgrounds expand contacts with the broader community.

Contacts with health care facilities are maintained as the child is brought for periodic health maintenance visits as well as for the various illnesses and accidents that tend to occur.

EFFECT OF SELECTED VARIABLES DURING THE TODDLER AND PRESCHOOL YEARS

Sex

In the preschool age period, girls generally score higher on intelligence tests than boys, and are more advanced in language development and in

FIGURE 4-20

by Debra Hymovich

FIGURE 4-21   by John McCabe

the learning of self-care skills, such as toileting. In peer play, boys are more aggressive and more active, although the latter finding is less constant than the former (Maccoby, 1966).

Temperament

The main effects of variations in temperament characteristics on child development are in terms of problems encountered when adults in the child's environment misinterpret their meaning and react to them in a way that leads to negative patterns of interaction.

The temperament characteristics of the "difficult child" continue to present problems to many parents during this period because they intensify some of the typical stage-related problems such as negativism and temper outbursts. In the Thomas et al. longitudinal study (1969), 10 of the 14 children with this temperament constellation developed behavior problems of sufficient intensity during this period to require some outside assistance in management. These often develop in the form of "vicious circles" when the parents' response pattern increases rather than decreases the behavior in question. More will be said about this under "Management of Common Stage-Related Problems."

The "slow to warm up" cluster of withdrawal reactions to new situations, slow adaptability, mild intensity, and predominantly negative mood, may also present problems to parents and teachers. A child with this group of characteristics is slow to participate in new activities, and may initially stand on the sidelines rather than actively engage in a nursery school or day-care program. The teacher and/or parents may interpret this as a sign of anxiety or an emotional problem. They may withdraw the child from school or become impatient and try to pressure the child into participation. Either response is likely to aggravate the child's tendency to withdraw.

The child with a high activity level and short attention span gets into trouble if expected to remain still and attentive for long periods of time. Unless parents, teachers, and clinicians are aware that this pattern can be a normal temperament characteristic, the child may be mislabeled "brain damaged" and treated accordingly.

Children with a strong characteristic of persistence may have trouble shifting from one activity to another. If not given warning ahead of time they may react to the change with a full-fledged temper tantrum which, if not understood, can lead to a vicious circle of negative reactions between adults and children.

Health Status

CENTRAL NERVOUS SYSTEM DYSFUNCTION

Mental Deficiency   The longitudinal study of children with Down's syndrome by Carr (1975) provides one of the best detailed views of the effect of moderate to severe mental deficiency on development. The early development of these children is described in Chapter 3. Observations during the preschool age period are as follows.

LEARNING TO CONTROL ONE'S BODY SATISFACTORILY   All motor milestones are delayed. Not until age 4 were more than 90 percent of the children walking alone and picking up small objects with a pincer grasp. At 4 years of age, 69 percent of the children with Down's syndrome were feeding themselves, but none of them could dress themselves completely and only 10 percent were going to the toilet alone. The percentages for the normal control group used in this study were 93, 34, and 63 percent, respectively.

LEARNING TO UNDERSTAND AND RELATE TO THE PHYSICAL WORLD   As measured on standard tests, the intellectual quotient remains on the average at around 40 or 50, with a mental age of slightly less than one-half the chronological age.

LEARNING TO RELATE TO OTHERS   A little over one-half the children could say at least two words by age 3, and about 23 percent were using words to make their wants known to their parents. Only 5 percent were making use of two-word phrases at that time. By age 4, these percentages had increased to 77, 41, and 21 percent, respectively.

At 15 months of age the control children were creating more problems about getting into things, but by 4 years the children with Down's syndrome were clearly more of a problem in this regard. At 4 years, about 87 percent were said to be getting into household areas that they should not, whereas only 24 percent of the control children were described in this way. The controls, on the other hand, were more likely to be getting into trouble in more sophisticated ways, such as with play using water or dirt.

Over one-half the mothers in each group thought their children were easy to manage, and about 10 percent of each group were thought to present enough difficulties in management to be considered "problems." When the mothers were asked what sort of things upset their children there were some interesting differences. The greatest single cause of upset for children with Down's syndrome was noise, which upset 38 percent of the sample and only 2 percent of the controls. Control children were much more often upset by frustration and disapproval. In terms of needing lots of attention, about one-quarter of each group were said to need "much cuddling." At 4 years of age, more of the control children (27 percent) were waking 2 or more times a week during the night than the retarded children (18 percent).

In terms of aggressive behavior with peers, the retarded children were somewhat less aggressive and less likely to get into quarrels, and their mothers were more likely to step in when they did. None of these differences were very great, however. The majority of both groups hit back when attacked.

DEAFNESS

Learning to Control One's Body Satisfactorily Most studies show deaf children behind their hearing peers on learning self-care skills such as dressing and toilet training. Children of hearing parents are usually farther behind in these areas than children whose parents are deaf. As might be expected, hearing parents of deaf children are more protective than parents of normal-hearing children, and this is thought to account for the difference (Meadow, 1975).

Learning to Understand and Relate to the Physical World Results of psychological testing show that if the tests administered are those that do not require a high level of language comprehension, either for administration or for response (such as the performance section of the WISC), deaf children usually score within the normal range although mean scores may be somewhat lower than those of hearing children. In terms of concepts, deaf children learn them in about the same sequence and in the same manner as do hearing children, but at a later age (Furth, 1966).

Learning to Relate to Others The development of oral language in the hard-of-hearing child is considerably retarded when compared with that of a normal-hearing child. It is unusual for the deaf child of 4 or 5 years to know as many as 200 words without special training, whereas the child with normal hearing has command of an average of 2000 words (Hodgson, 1953). Comparison of the written language of deaf and hearing children indicated that material written by deaf students had a less complex vocabulary and sentence structure and generally resembled that of younger, hearing children (Clark School for the Deaf, 1940).

The communication deficits also affect peer interactions, with hearing children being more social and interacting more with each other than deaf children. Communication is largely limited to the here and now, so that play patterns tend to be less complex and organized (Heider, 1948). Most studies show a higher incidence of adjustment problems in deaf children, but the incidence of serious mental illness does not seem to be increased.

SEVERE EMOTIONAL DISTURBANCE

Infantile Autism and Childhood Schizophrenia The most striking defects in these children are in their social development. Children with both types of disorder have somewhat similar developmental patterns. The main difference is that disturbances in childhood schizophrenia are often preceded by 1 or 2 years of normal development, while signs of autism appear soon after birth. Both show impaired relationships with others, with a preference for being alone, lack of eye contact, and inability to form close relationships. Speech is not used to communicate but rather to recite nursery rhymes, prayers, list of objects, and other memorized phenomena. Personal pronouns are repeated as heard with no change to suit the altered situation.

Other characteristics of psychotic children are fears of noise and movement, and their great sensitivity for, and resistance to, any environmental changes. Development in other areas may be retarded, but this is uneven, with some areas of functioning approaching normal (Bender, 1942; Creak, 1961; Kanner, 1943).

Grandparents Living with Family

The presence of aging grandparents can have considerable impact on the preschooler. If the grandparent is active and energetic this provides the child with an additional source of affection, companionship, and stimulation. On the other hand, the presence of an ailing grandparent may curtail a child's self-expression. The parents' feelings and reactions to the grandparents may be reflected in their behavior toward their children (Weiner and Elkind, 1972).

Stress and Crisis

SOCIAL DEPRIVATION

The lags in speech, motor, adaptive, and personal-social development of infants in institutions has already been described in Chapter 3. Most of the infants in this study were placed into family environments between 1 and 2 years of age. A follow-up study of 14 of these children after 1 to 5 years with families revealed dramatic gains, along with some evidence of residual impairment (Provence and Lipton, 1962). The use of language for asking questions and expressing ideas and fantasies and verbalizing feelings came very slowly and was not as well developed as that of a normal, family-reared child. A lessened capacity for the enjoyment and elaboration of play and an impairment of imagination were also evident.

It was also noted that the previously institutionalized child rarely turned to familiar adults either for help in problem solving or comfort and reassurance even after several years in a family environment. They also showed a superficial, indiscriminate, friendly response to strangers.

The ability to control expression of feelings and delay immediate need gratifications appeared impaired. Some impairment of thinking, such as difficulty in generalizing from one situation to another, lack of persistence in problem solving, and excessive concreteness of thought, were also noted.

CHAOTIC AND ABUSIVE FAMILY ENVIRONMENTS

Pavenstedt (1967) and her colleagues give a detailed description of how children 2½ to 6 years of age from grossly disorganized home environments functioned in a small, group nursery school setting. The families from which these children came were characterized by alcoholism, promiscuity, abuse and neglect, chronic unemployment, mental illness, and criminal behavior which could often be traced back several generations. At first glance these children seemed alert, responsive, and well coordinated; however, when examined more closely, there were many obvious delays and deviations in their development. Similar types of defects in development are reported in follow-up studies of children subjected to physical abuse (Elmer and Gregg, 1967; Martin et al., 1974). Pavenstedt's findings are as follows:

Developing and Maintaining Healthy Growth and Nutrition Patterns
Nothing is mentioned about the children's growth characteristics, but their eating behavior was described as "greedy" and "stuffing food in their mouths." The children also showed concern that their food would be taken away and resentment if others seemed to be getting more than they were.

Learning to Control One's Body Satisfactorily In some ways the children seemed advanced in motor skills and coordination. Along with this, however, was a lack of self-protective mechanisms so that they were continually injuring themselves through their lack of impulse control. Motor activity was frequently used as a discharge of tension and in literally "running away" from frustrating situations. They were much less accomplished than their age mates in areas such as dressing themselves and going to the toilet.

Learning to Understand and Relate to the Physical World There was a marked contrast between the children's extraordinary alertness and sensitivity to aspects of the environment that might have some kind of danger associated with it, such as a sudden noise or change in location of an adult, and their lack of attention to other aspects, such as the toys and materials that usually excite the interest of children in this age group. There was little manipulation or playing with objects or expressions of curiosity about what something was or how it worked. Although they responded to the reading of stories in an attention-getting way, they did not appear to listen to or understand what was being said. They had little knowledge of the names and usages of everyday things. There was an apparent lack of the concept of "object permanence" because the children would not go after a toy that fell off the table or was behind something.

Although many children of this age have trouble distinguishing reality from fantasy, this difficulty was extreme in these children. They reacted to pictures in books as real events, showing fear of or wanting to pick up the animals shown. One child expressed fear when seeing an animal cracker. They also did not have the capacity to generalize from one situation to another, even though the action involved was very similar.

Developing Self-Awareness and a Satisfying Sense of Self   There were many evidences of a negative self-concept in these children. They made deprecating remarks about themselves, referred to themselves in the third person ("her want this"), and they disliked looking at themselves in the mirror or in photographs. There was a profound lack of confidence in their ability to do even simple tasks ("You do it, me can't") and a lack of pride in their accomplishments. They did not respond to praise and seemed to have no drive toward mastery or completion of any kind of activity. They displayed a "pseudoautonomy," with some ability to assume responsibilities at a more mature level than their age mates, such as looking after younger siblings and taking care of themselves for long periods without adult supervision.

Learning to Relate to Others   There was no evidence of attachment to specific adults. The children approached adults with a superficial friendliness that did not differ for people with whom they had been in contact for long periods and complete strangers. There was much seeking of the teacher's attention but an inability to use the teacher appropriately for instrumental help or emotional support. When disturbed, the children did not turn to adults for comfort and acted as though they expected to be punished and scolded for any show of emotion. There was no specific stranger or separation anxiety. Many of the children did not say good-bye to their mothers on school entry.

Relationships with peers were characterized by fear, distrust, and the need for immediate gratification. There was hardly any spontaneous conversation between the children and little interaction other than impulsive grabbing of another's toys. Sociodramatic play was conspicuous by its absence.

Communication skills were immature and constricted. Vocabularies were small. Poor grammar and difficulties in pronunciation often made the children difficult to understand. There was more reliance on nonverbal types of communication, such as gestures, plaintive looks, or whining and nagging.

Expression of feelings was very constricted. There was no display of exuberance, enthusiasm, or spontaneity. The children were rarely noted to cry when hurt. Many of the children could not express anger directly to the teacher or to another child. When feelings were expressed, they were more likely to take the form of hysterical shrieks.

COMPARISON BETWEEN CHILDREN RAISED IN ENVIRONMENTS OF SOCIAL DEPRIVATION AND SOCIAL CHAOS

In comparing children raised in chaotic environments with those raised in the quiet but unstimulating environments of institutions there are some interesting similarities and differences. Difficulties in forming close relationships, poor communication skills, and difficulties with problem solving and generalizing solutions were common to both groups of children. The orientation to danger and hyperalertness to any change in the environment, the tendency to respond to frustration with diffuse motor activity, and "pseudoautonomy" were more often found in children raised in chaotic environments. The striking tendency of the children from chaotic environments to devalute themselves and their constant expectations of punishment were characteristics not mentioned in the description of the institutionalized children.

CHRONIC ILLNESS AND DISABILITY

The effects of chronic conditions on young children and their families depend to some degree on the nature of the problem and the extent of involvement. In general, these long-term disabilities interfere with the usual socialization processes during these early years. Children with mobility, sensory, and/or communication deficits can be hindered in (1) developing autonomy and increasing independence from their parents, (2) exploring their physical environment, (3) developing an appropriate sexual identity and satisfying sense of self, and (4) establishing social relationships with peers (see for example, Battle, 1974; Freeman, 1967; Gralewicz, 1973; Waechter, 1975). Specific examples of the effects of some of these long-term problems on the child's developmental tasks are covered above under "Health Status."

During these early years, the children begin to realize they are "different" from others, and they may find themselves being surpassed by normal, younger siblings. This is often a difficult time for parents and children alike. Because young children are not yet future oriented, they find it difficult to understand how the pain and discomfort of some therapeutic programs can be helpful to them in the future.

Inadequate community resources may now become a reality for parents as they seek day-care and/or nursery school experiences for their disabled children. The extent to which parents are able to foster independence and continued growth in their children will depend not only on the nature of the child's condition but also on the parents' responses to it. It is not uncommon to see parents reinforcing dependency behaviors in their handicapped children (Battle, 1974). Sibling rivalry may become pronounced during this period, as parents are likely to spend more time with their disabled youngster and to apply differing standards of behavior for their normal and handicapped children.

SEPARATION AND DIVORCE

The recent in-depth study by Wallerstein and Kelly (1976) provides some insights into the effects of divorce on preschool children. Wallerstein and Kelly interviewed 34 preschool children from 27 families with no previous history of psychiatric or psychological contact. Four to six interviews were conducted with each family member over a period of 6 weeks. The nine youngest children (2½ to 3¼ years) all responded to the divorce with observable behavioral changes, including regression, increased aggression, fearfulness, acute separation anxieties, sleep problems, fretfulness, and neediness. The symptoms were temporary when either the parent or a competent substitute care taker was able to meet the children's needs.

In the middle preschool group of 11 children (3¾ to 4¾ years), only about half of them reacted to the disruption with regression. Many of them became irritable, whining, and tearful. Both aggressive behavior and fear of aggression were seen. These children "seemed painfully bewildered by the loss of one parent" and tried to understand their relationships with both parents. Fantasy and self-blame were also responses of this group. McDermott (1968) also found fantasy and depression to be common in this age group.

The 14 children in the oldest preschool group (5 to 6 years) responded to the separation with heightened anxiety and aggression.

These children seemed to have a reasonable understanding of the changes taking place, and the researchers did not feel their developmental progress or their self-confidence was hindered by the divorce.

At a follow-up interview 1 year after the divorce, 44 percent ($N = 15$) of the children were found to be in "significantly deteriorated psychological condition." Substantial changes in parent-child relationships were noted at this time, with a decrease in the quality of the mother-child relationship in nearly half the families. This changed relationship was strongly associated with the deterioration in the child's condition. Father-child relationships tended to improve over the year but did not prevent the child's deterioration.

CLINICAL APPLICATIONS

Selected Topics for Discussion

General principles for using well-child visits to promote the optimal development of the family and child are presented in Chapter 1. Following are selected topics for discussion during well-child visits for this stage of development. These topics are summarized in Table 4-4.

TODDLER (1 TO 3 YEARS)

Toilet-Training Readiness Although in this culture many children, particularly boys, are not ready for toilet training much before 18 to 24 months of age, parents begin to think about this much sooner. It is helpful for them to know that only about 50 percent of boys and 75 percent of girls are toilet trained with any consistency by age 2 (Brazelton, 1962; Chamberlin, 1974). If the child has a regular elimination pattern and is cooperative, "training" can commence at any time with a good chance of success, but if he or she is irregular it is generally better to wait until some "readiness" is shown in the form of wanting to be changed or wanting to sit on the potty. Pressure in the form of frequent "potting" or scolding for accidents generally backfires and prolongs the whole process rather than shortens it. Brazelton (1962) describes a very gradual child-oriented approach to counseling parents in this area. Azrin and Foxx (1974) recommend another approach based on behavior modification principles. One of the authors (DPH) has found their book to be especially useful in helping parents determine their child's readiness for toilet training. Generally, if the child is ready, the approach is successful;

FIGURE 4-22   by Susan McCabe

if the child is not ready, the parents have concrete evidence of this and are willing to wait a few months.

The Stubborn, Temper, Whine Syndrome   Warning parents about the coming of the "terrible twos," with frequent stubbornness, temper outbursts, and whining types of behavior should occur before 18 months since these behaviors often peak considerably before the child's second birthday.

Parents need to know that this is an important milestone in the child's development of autonomy and ability to control the environment. Rather than arbitrarily attempting to squelch it, the parents can be aided in coping by encouraging them to ignore behavior that does not encroach on the rights of others or endanger the child's safety and to use distraction and temporary isolation (putting in a nonstimulating area or specific part of the house for short periods of time) for behavior that

TABLE 4-4
Summary of Selected Delivery of Care Topics and Activities Related to Child (Ages 1 through 5 Years) and Family Development

Age of child	Growth, nutrition, and health	Body control	Relate to world	Self-awareness	Relate to others	Family development
		Development of toddler and preschooler				
1–2 years	Relation of slowing growth rate to feeding "problems;" pica and poisoning; natural history and management of coughs, colds, and fever	Accidents, toilet training readiness	Importance of looking at picture books, labeling items	Need for praise and encouragement, gender identification, development of autonomy	Separation anxiety, managing "terrible twos," behavior modification, discipline, limit setting	Problems obtaining basic necessities of food, clothing, housing, and health care; family roles in child care; child spacing; husband-wife relationship; sibling relationships; relationships with grandparents; family support system

Time away from children, maintenance of individual interests, mother-role satisfaction, coping with life changes and stress |
| 2–3 years | Normal variations in position of feet and legs; sugar and dental caries, brushing teeth | Accidents; dressing and undressing; toilet training | Cognitive stimulation, preschool child's egocentric way of looking at things, educational television | Need for praise and encouragement | Sharing behavior, sexual curiosity, bedtime and sleep problems, sibling relationships | Utilizing community resources

Finding adequate day-care or nursery school facilities |

TABLE 4-4 (Continued)

Summary of Selected Delivery of Care Topics and Activities Related to Child (Ages 1 through 5 Years) and Family Development

Age of child	Development of toddler and preschooler					Family development
	Growth, nutrition, and health	Body control	Relate to world	Self-awareness	Relate to others	
3–4 years	As above, visiting dentist	Management of high activity level	Tests of vision and hearing, inability to separate fantasy from reality	Development of initiative	Night waking, TV viewing, management of fears and fantasies	
4–5 years	As above, booster immunizations, tine test	Helping child develop motor skills, bedwetting	School readiness	Gender identification	Back-talk and sass, sexual curiosity, sibling relationships	

cannot be ignored. Attempts to force immediate compliance because of anxiety about being "soft on discipline" often precipitate repeated conflicts that are frustrating to all and accomplish little. Since discipline is a major concern of parents during these early years, more is said about the subject later.

Relation of Appetite and Eating Behavior to Growth Rates The rapid fall in the rate of growth after the first 6 months of life and thinning body configuration of the child after age 1 sooner or later is accompanied by a decrease in appetite and an increase in parental anxiety about food intake. Prolonged battles over clean plates and tasting a little bit of everything can be headed off through anticipatory guidance.

Stage-Related Medical Conditions The frequency of coughs and colds generally peaks during the 2- to 4-year-old age period (Bayer and Snyder, 1950; Dingle et al., 1964; Fry, 1961). Many parents develop concerns about this and may focus on the child's large-looking tonsils as the cause of these problems rather than on the relative immaturity of the child's developing immune system. Warning the parents ahead of time that the child will have frequent colds and coughs during this age period may head off pressures for the health worker to "do something." An interesting discussion on handling parental pressure about tonsillectomy can be found in an article by Furham (1959).

The flat-footed, bowlegged look of the toddler also causes much parental concern. The large majority of these "problems" are self-correcting and do not need night splints or special shoes (Holt et al., 1954; Sherman, 1960).

Guidance about the prevention of accidents and ingestions was discussed in Chapter 3. This material needs repeating in these visits as well, since 1 to 4 years is the peak age of accidents and ingestions of all kinds.

Sibling Relationships Various suggestions for minimizing a toddler's jealousy toward a new baby have been proposed. If old enough (around 2½ years), the child should be told in advance so the new baby does not come as a total surprise. The toddler can be given some share in preparation for the newcomer. Once the new baby arrives, the parents need to remember the toddler's continuing need for attention and affection; in fact, this need may temporarily increase.

Helping the child prepare for the arrival of a new baby involves including the child in the preparations and talking about the baby before it arrives. Preparatory discussion can include such things as where the

FIGURE 4-23   by Susan McCabe

baby will sleep, any concerns about the child's toys being given to the baby, and descriptions of how the child can serve as mother's helper (Weiner and Elkind, 1972). If changes need to be made in the older child's daily routine (i.e., sending to nursery school) or sleeping arrangements (new bed, different room), these should be done well in advance of the new arrival to give the child an opportunity to adjust to these changes.

Regressive behavior following the infant's birth is usually short-lived, especially if the parents are flexible enough to accept it temporarily. Parents should be informed that this behavior is likely to occur and that it will not last long. Asking the parent if it is safe to leave two children alone in the same room is one way of determining the extent of the toddler's reactions to the new baby.

Weiner and Elkind (1972) suggest mediating sibling rivalries for privilege and status by establishing age-appropriate responsibilities and prerogatives rather than trying to seek peace by following some common denominator regardless of age. The prerogatives of the older child need to be protected, and at the same time, the younger child needs to feel as loved as the older child even though not granted all the privileges.

THIRD YEAR

Not Sharing Educating parents that most children do not start to share and play cooperatively with other children until age 3 or 4 will help them develop realistic expectations for their child.

Fears and Fantasies Some of the concerns parents of children of this age bring to the clinician are about the development of fears and fantasies. Three-year-olds have a hard time distinguishing fantasy from reality and tend to believe literally what they see on television, hear in stories, or are told by their parents. Parents who in anger or jest tell children of this age they are going to send them away are often surprised at the degree of upset this produces in the child. Fears of the dark, monsters under the bed, and the like are also all common at this age (Chamberlin, 1978, p. 170).

One rather dramatic example of the child's developing imagination and fantasy life is that of the imaginary companion. These phenomena are described in detail by Ames and Learned (1946), who estimate an incidence of 20 percent in preschool children. The age range is around 2 through 5 years with a peak incidence at 3½ years. The average duration is around 6 months. Forms differ for different children and range from having an imaginary animal or person as a friend to actually impersonating these, such as by crawling around on all fours, barking, and eating food from a dish.

Although the literature suggests that imaginary companions may be the result of some kind of social deprivation, there is considerable evidence that it occurs in many normal boys and girls and is a part of a "gradient" of imaginative behavior for this age period. To support this idea is that these phenomena occur at the same time that active role playing and dramatic play is developing in nursery school. Since this is a self-limiting type of behavior, patient tolerance seems a reasonable response unless the routines become disruptive to family life.

FOURTH YEAR
This is another difficult age for many parents. The back-talk and sass ("shut up," "you dummy," and so on) of the 4-year-old comes as a shock to some parents, as does the exaggerated interest in toileting and toilet words. Playing with genitalia, voiding in public, or taking down a neighbor child's pants to compare native endowments are other typical behaviors at this stage that upset many parents. Some preparation of parents ahead of time for this type of behavior and inquiring about its occurrence during the 4-year-old visit may head off a number of parent-child battles (Chamberlin, 1978, p. 170).

Sexuality   The studies of Money and Ehrhardt (1972) indicate that gender identity is established early and that confusion about this does not occur if the child has a clear understanding of the physical differences between the sexes and their reproductive roles. In terms of child rearing they advise:

> . . . simply seeing the nudity of his own age mates without seeing the changes of pubescence and the appearance of adulthood may not be enough. There are indeed some inventive young children who come up with the idea that just as breasts and pubic hair grow later also may a penis grow out of a girl or drop off from a boy. Children who hold such theories are likely to be the ones whose sense of gender identity is insecure. . . .
>
> The ideal is for the children to be reared to know also the reproductive roles of the sex organs and to be able to look forward to their proper use of their own when the time is right. (p. 14)

Just how these recommendations are to be translated into anticipatory guidance is not so clear, but it is worth inquiring whether a 4-year-old is aware of the differences in genitalia and whether 5-year-olds have any ideas about where babies come from and how they get there. There are now a number of books on the market that deal with these facts on a level appropriate for the preschool child and which can be recommended to parents who are having difficulty with this area (Arnstein, 1967; Gruen-berg, 1970; Levine and Seligman, 1962).

FIFTH YEAR

School Readiness For 5-year-olds, the main question is often one of school readiness. Since most schools require children to have a physical examination before school entry, the primary health care worker is in an excellent position to examine "school readiness." How can this be done? About the only criterion for most school systems is chronological age. An arbitrary cutoff date is used, such as a child must be 5 years old by December 31, to get into kindergarten. The rationale for this is that younger children, on the whole, achieve at a lower level than older children, as measured by standard tests (Miller and Norris, 1967). These differences last for several years, but by the third grade are no longer significant.

While these age levels serve as useful guidelines for the average child, they are too inflexible to take into account individual differences. For example, girls, on the average, are more advanced developmentally than boys, but this is never taken into account. Also, some intellectually and socially mature children have already taught themselves to read before age 5 and it seems unnecessary to hold them back.

Even given a child in the administratively acceptable age range, there are still wide differences in developmental maturity, and some children would probably benefit from an extra year of maturation before school entry. In one study of kindergarten children by members of the Gesell Institute it was estimated that over 30 percent of the children were developmentally immature for the grade they were in (Ilg et al., 1965).

How does one predict which children are developmentally ready and which are not? The child with at least average intellect, understand-able speech, some degree of independence in terms of self-care and ability to separate from the mother, enough fine motor coordination to copy a square or circle and draw a recognizable figure of a person, the ability to attend to simple tasks for 15 to 20 minutes, and the ability to play cooperatively with peers will seldom have any difficulty with school entry. The problem is what to advise parents about the child who is behind in one or more of these areas.

Various "readiness" tests have been devised that generally rely on some kind of assessment of language skills and visual motor coordina-tion in terms of copying figures or drawing a person (Rogolsky, 1968–69). One community mental health project developed a doll-play interview in which the child's readiness was ascertained by his or her ability to separate from the mother, accompany a stranger, and carry out a sequence of constructive play with a family of dolls (Lindemann et al., 1967). The Gesell Institute determines readiness on the basis of developmental age as determined by their standard evaluation (Ilg et al., 1965).

The accuracy of these predictions has been determined by relating them to achievement tests in the first and second grade or to ratings of behavior and performance made by the child's teacher. Correlations between readiness scores and later achievement tests generally lie in the $r = .40$ to $r = .70$ range which, while useful for identifying groups of children who are likely to need some extra help, are not accurate enough to predict the fate of an individual child (deHirsch et al., 1966; Keogh and Smith, 1970). In a longitudinal study following children from age 2 through first grade we were continually impressed with the number of children having problems in nursery school who did not have difficulty in kindergarten and first grade, and vice versa (Chamberlin, 1976). In fact, almost everybody who has reported results of their predictions have found it easier to predict which children will do well than which children will have trouble (Keogh and Smith, 1970; Rogolsky, 1968–69). In one study (Brenner and Samelson, 1959), kindergarten children were classified as low, average, or high on the basis of the Metropolitan Readiness Test. Follow-up a year later showed one-third of the low-readiness group were reading above average at the end of first grade.

Even deHirsch, who developed a sophisticated approach with a variety of tests and a multiple regression formula based on one large sample of children found that predictability was considerably less accurate when she applied the same equations to a new, more heterogeneous group of children. She now recommends standardization of the tests in the individual school where it will be used (deHirsch et al., 1966).

There are a number of reasons it is difficult to predict who will have difficulty in school. One of these is that development does not always proceed at an even rate but often progresses in fits and starts. Children in a plateau period will be behind their peers at any one point in time but often catch up rapidly during their next spurt of growth. Another reason is that the way a child functions is at least partially situational. A child's difficulty may proceed from a "lack of fit" between the child and the current environment rather than from a deficit entirely within the child. These observations led one participant of a workshop devoted to the early recognition of children with learning problems to conclude: "It seems to me that our greatest hope for the identification of potential learning problems is to abandon the belief that they are inherent, stable traits of the individual. Instead we should focus on identifying the likelihood of producing certain kinds of developmental changes, given a variety of specified environmental conditions" (Keogh, 1969, p. 345).

What, then, does one do with the child who does not seem ready for kindergarten or first grade on the basis of some kind of assessment? The Gesell-trained people generally feel that delaying school entry for a year will allow many of these children to mature spontaneously to a more appropriate developmental age (Ilg et al., 1965). There are not to our knowledge, however, any studies in which the effects of delayed entry on later achievement and adjustment were contrasted with a control group of children of similar developmental ages who were allowed school entry.

If there is uncertainty about how a particular child might do, a trial period of a month or so might be helpful. This is particularly important for the "slow to warm up" child who has an initial negative reaction to new situations in general but who will, if not pressured, gradually adapt over a period of time (Thomas et al., 1968). The child's sex should also be taken into account. At any given age boys are generally less developmentally mature than girls, and a borderline boy is thus more likely to benefit from an extra year of maturation than a borderline girl. However, any child with evidence of a generalized delay in development should receive full evaluation from a professional psychologist before school entry.

While recommendations for delayed school entry may be appropriate for the middle-class child who appears developmentally immature, it has not been a successful procedure for children from backgrounds of chronic poverty with little or no cognitive stimulation. Without special help the deficits in these children tend to persist. Summer "Head Start" programs have proved to be "too little, too late," and earlier intervention programs have been recommended to try and prevent the lack of "school readiness" that these children demonstrate at age 5. In fact, some people are now recommending such programs from birth, particularly with premature infants (Scarr-Salapatek and Williams, 1973). However, even the gains produced by these programs tend to wash out after the child enters the school system unless stimulation is continued in the classroom (Schaefer, 1972).

There is also a problem for the developmentally mature 4-year-old child who is teaching himself or herself to read but whose age falls below the administrative cutoff rate. Many school systems rigidly adhere to these rules regardless of the circumstances. One way to bypass this rigidity is to send the child to a private kindergarten. Almost all school systems will accept a child in first grade who has successfully completed

by Debra Hymovich

FIGURE 4-24 Determining school readiness is an important consideration during the fifth year.

kindergarten. Unfortunately, such a solution is only available to the relatively affluent. Once in the system, there is fortunately now a greater tendency to individualize instruction so that both the fast and slow learners can proceed at a pace that is appropriate for where they are.

Of additional interest is one report describing the emotional effects of school entry on both parents and child (Klein, 1963). In this study, a group of parents met at weekly intervals starting a week before school entry and continuing for 5 or 6 weeks into the school term. In these meetings they reported that many of their children showed evidence of both regression (clinging more, wetting the bed, and increasing thumb-sucking) and a greater maturity (more independence in dressing, playing away from home, and helping with household chores). The parents also noted changes in themselves. Just before school entry there was considerable anxiety about how their children would do, because school entry was seen as a test of their child-rearing competence. After entry many parents experienced some feelings of loss and ambivalence toward the teacher who was now becoming such an important part of their child's life. Most parents and children had worked through these feelings by the end of the 6-week time period.

Management of Common Stage-Related Problems

BEHAVIORAL PROBLEMS

Behavioral problems are very common in preschool children, with negativism, temper tantrums, whining, sibling rivalry, poor eating habits, shyness, and oversensitiveness being mentioned most frequently in various surveys (Chamberlin, 1974; Drillien, 1964; Hornberger et al., 1960; Willoughby and Haggerty, 1964). The main task of the health provider is to determine if these types of complaints are typical stage-related problems that require simple reassurance and a few suggestions for handling or are of a more pervasive nature that will require detailed investigation and possibly consultation with one or more specialists.

In general, if the behavioral problem is a typical stage-related behavior, of recent origin, isolated to a single area such as eating or sleeping, or related to a recent event such as a move or birth of a sibling, some parental education, reassurance, and a few specific suggestions are usually all that is necessary for successful management. Some examples of these typical problems are as follows:

Discipline and Limit Setting There are at least six definitions of discipline in the dictionary. In talking to parents it is clear that to some the word means guidance and teaching and to others it means chastisement and punishment. These differences in interpretation often lead to quite different child-rearing styles, with some parents adopting an authoritarian style, emphasizing obedience to parental directions and physical punishment for noncompliance, while others rely more on reasoning and finding mutually acceptable alternatives for behavior that encroaches on the rights of others or endangers the child's safety (Chamberlin, 1978, p. 169). As noted in Chapter 1, these different approaches produce surprisingly few differences in the behavior of the children exposed to them, at least in the early years. Therefore, rather than advocating any one approach for all children, the health care provider can help the parent identify how the child in question is reacting to the approach being used. When there is an obvious "lack of fit" between a particular child and the style adopted by the parent, the health care worker can help them modify their response pattern to better fit the type of child (Chamberlin, 1974, 1977). (See also discussion of vicious circles.) In addition, the health care provider can help the parents work out a consistent approach to discipline, with some general guidelines such as follows.

The aim of effective discipline of a preschooler is to foster the child's self-control and social judgment without inhibiting initiative and self-confidence or causing excessive rebelliousness or compliance (Weiner and Elkind, 1972). All children need limits on behavior that encroaches on the rights of others or endangers the child's safety. After these, definitions of "good" and "bad" behavior become a matter of personal and cultural values. Discipline should be consistent in that the parents agree upon what standards of good and bad behavior they want to enforce. Absence of any consistency makes it difficult for the child to form an adequate sense of socially acceptable behavior and to develop an internal locus of control. The health care provider can help the parents adopt standards of conduct that are realistic in terms of the child's stage of development.

Parent-child conflicts can be minimized by removing some of the more obvious breakable household items that would attract a small child and by providing play areas with toys where the youngster is free to go. Taking advantage of the child's distractibility and short attention span is another way of controlling the child's behavior without frequent head-on battles of will. When limits need to be set they should be firm and definite. Because of the toddler's cognitive development, it is generally best to give simple, short commands with brief, rather than lengthy, explanations.

Parents serve as the models with whom the youngster identifies. At first, the toddler imitates what the parent is doing, and later, as the identification process develops, the child tries to be like one of the parents by taking on their role. This identification process with the adults facilitates the preschooler's internalizing their codes of conduct.

A positive approach to discipline through "reinforcing" positive aspects of behavior with praise and attention while ignoring as much negative behavior as possible has been found to be useful (Hawkins et al., 1966; Patterson, 1975). Approaches to teaching behavior modification to parents are summarized in Chapter 1.

EATING PROBLEMS

Not eating enough or not eating the right kinds of foods are common complaints of parents of children 2 through 8 years of age. For example, in one preschool survey (Chamberlin, 1974), about one-third of the parents of 4-year-olds thought their child ate too little, and over half felt their child did not eat the right kinds of food.

In most instances these concerns are related to a lack of understanding of the decrease in growth rate during this time with its accompanying decrease in appetite. Having the parents describe a typical meal scene often reveals a family drama that rivals the best of Broadway productions. While the parents perform a song and dance routine interspersed with threats, the child sits with unswallowed food, in his or her mouth or responds to attempts at force feeding by vomiting.

Management consists of reassuring the parents about the child's current height and weight, educating the parents about the growth patterns of young children, and reducing the emotions around mealtime by instructing them to put what is being served to the family in front of the child and removing it in 15 or 20 minutes without comment about what is or is not eaten. This, along with some restrictions about what is eaten between meals, will generally restore the relationship between nutritional needs and appetite that should regulate the amount that is eaten.

If the feeding problem is part of a general "vicious circle pattern" of overcoercion or overconcern about the child's health, it will be necessary to obtain more historical information and proceed as outlined under "Vicious Circle Parent-Child Relationships" later in this chapter.

Pica The ingestion of nonedible substances is a common finding in preschool children, with its highest incidence of 30 to 40 percent in the 18-month-old to 2-year-old age group (Barltrop, 1966). It is more common in children of poor black families, where its frequency appears related at least in part to cultural traditions of eating clay and starches among the women in this group (Cooper, 1957; Lourie et al., 1963). Prevalence falls off to 5 or 10 percent in children of white, middle-class suburban families. The main clinical significance of pica is its association with lead poisoning and parasitic infections such as *Toxocara canis*.

Besides cultural tradition, the main etiologic factor of pica that has been considered is dietary deficiency, particularly iron deficiency. Animal studies indicate dirt eating is a way of curing nutritional deficiency for a number of animals, and a report from South Africa (Lanzowski, 1959) indicated pica was associated with iron deficiency and was promptly cured by the administration of iron. However, in a double-blind control study by Gutelius et al. (1962), there was no difference in improvement of pica between a group of children receiving injections of iron and those receiving a saline placebo. In both groups, there was a decline in incidence of pica and improvement of iron levels. In the same study it was found that pica was associated with poor diet and poor eating habits in general, and with a higher incidence of iron deficiency anemia and lower ascorbic acid levels in the blood. There was also evidence of greater family instability and poorer supervision of the children's activities.

These multiple associations make it unlikely that most cases of pica will be cured by the administration of iron alone, but, if present, it should obviously be treated for its own sake. Educating mothers about the dangers of lead intoxication and parasitic infection from pica and encouraging them to exercise closer supervision of their children can substantially reduce its incidence (Burdé and Reames, 1973).

BEDTIME AND SLEEP PROBLEMS

Resistance to going to bed, night awakening, and bad dreams are frequent parental complaints about the sleep habits of preschoolers. In the previously mentioned longitudinal study (Chamberlin, 1974), 70 percent of the 2-year-old children were said to be at least somewhat resistant to bedtime and 56 percent were still so described at their fourth birthday. Night awakening remained relatively constant over this time period, with about one-half the children described awakening in the middle of the night with some regularity at ages 2, 3, and 4. Roberts and Schoellkopf (1951) give a cross-section of the sleeping behavior of 783 suburban children at 2½ years of age. At this age the average child was sleeping about 13 hours a day, including a 1- to 2-hour nap, usually after lunch.

FIGURE 4-25

by Debra Hymovich

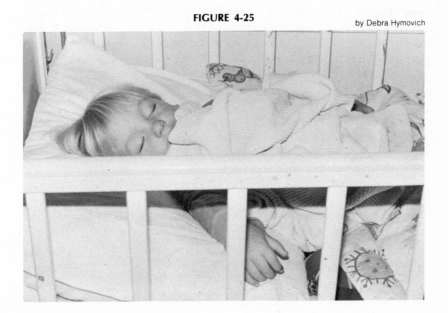

Only 27 percent of the children were sleeping in their own rooms, with 44 percent sharing a room with sibling or other adult and 29 percent sharing the parents' bedroom. Of these children, 90 percent had a definite bedtime routine that they liked to follow, and for one-third this routine was quite elaborate and ritualistic. Three-quarters of the children took a comfort object to bed with them and one-half engaged in such presleep activities as thumb-sucking, hair twisting, or rocking. Of the children, 21 percent were reported to have one or more of the following problems: resistance to going to bed (12 percent), bad dreams or night terrors (9 percent), and getting into the parents' bed (5 percent). Another 22 percent woke up, talked in their sleep, or cried briefly during the night but these were of brief duration and not considered a problem by the parents.

Not wanting to go to bed generally peaks between 1 and 2 years of age. The child cries when left alone in the crib or climbs out and comes seeking the parents. This behavior is related both to the separation anxiety common at this age and increasing attempts by the child to control his or her environment. Occasionally, long naps late in the afternoon or overstimulating, roughhouse play before bedtime may be the cause of the problem. It may also be related to a disturbance in the parent-child relationship or to tension in the home.

In general, letting children get up, spending long periods of time comforting them, staying in their room, or getting angry and spanking or scolding are all equally ineffective. Getting the child settled with a brief story, letting him or her keep a favorite doll or blanket, and using a night light are helpful but often are not sufficient to solve the problem. A parent sitting in the hallway in front of the open door in sight of the child, but not playing with or talking to the child other than to say "no, it's bedtime," when he or she tries to get out of the crib, is often a more effective means of controlling this problem. Once children find out they will not be allowed to get out of bed or entice the parent in the room for more stories or play, they will settle down and go to sleep.

Sleeping in the Parents' Bed   Having children sleep in separate rooms and beds is a relatively recent phenomenon characteristic of Western society. In many other cultures it is common for families to sleep together. There are a growing number of people in this country (including parents) who question the desirability of separate sleeping arrangements (Newton, 1976; Ratner, 1976; Thevenin, 1976). Thevenin (1976) found that the majority of 47 La Leche parents she questioned allowed their children to sleep with them. She found that with each additional child, parents tended to become more relaxed in their restrictions on shared sleeping

FIGURE 4-26   by Debra Hymovich

arrangements, and the length of time the child shared the family bed increased.

In general, this is a question of cultural and individual values and should not be a concern of the health care provider one way or the other, except when it is found to be part of a general pattern of overprotectiveness (Chamberlin, 1967· Green and Solnit, 1964; Levy, 1943) or is seen by the parents as creating a problem. The basic issue seems to be one of family togetherness versus privacy, particularly concerning sexual activity. As far as we know few data are available to support either position.

Some parents, who are concerned about their child getting into their or a sibling's bed, may consider it a problem because they have been socialized to see it as such. It would be wise to explore the basis of their concern and to let them know that little is known of the effects on children of shared sleeping arrangements and that it may not be as uncommon a practice in this country as we have been led to believe. Should the parents want to change this behavior in their children, then suggestions can be offered as discussed in the next section.

Night Waking   Waking in the middle of the night and crying or coming into the parents' bed is somewhat more difficult to deal with than resistance to bedtime. Often this pattern begins after a move or an illness. Responses, such as allowing the child to sleep in the parents' bed, playing with or feeding the child, or spanking and scolding, generally only prolong the problem. Returning the child to bed with simple reassurance or sitting outside the open bedroom door until he or she settles down is usually more effective.

Nightmares become increasingly common as the child grows older. Since most 3- and 4-year-old children cannot readily distinguish between fantasy and reality, many are frightened by fairy tales and television violence and may have bad dreams following such experiences. Avoidance of scary movies, simple reassurance, and again sitting in front of the door to the child's bedroom are generally all that is needed. Rarely, such dreams are part of a more general emotional disturbance which needs more extensive evaluation.

FEARS AND PHOBIAS

The health professional's job is to differentiate normal, developmental stage-related fears from those arising from tension in the home or internalized conflicts (phobias) within the child. Some screening questions about the child's general developmental status and what is going on at home will usually identify the child or family with more serious problems. If the fear is intense, out of all proportion to the potential danger involved, interferes with the child's activity (will not go outdoors, and so on), and does not respond to simple reassurance, a psychiatric consultation is generally indicated.

If the child's temperament pattern is such that the initial reaction to new situations is one of withdrawal, repeated exposure and reassurance, without pressure, will help him or her to adapt.

TOILET-TRAINING PROBLEMS

Resistance to Sitting on the Toilet   One of the major causes of this resistance is the lack of appreciation on the parents' part as to when their child is ready to be trained. This is discussed earlier under "Selected Topics for Discussion."

If the child is "ready" but resists sitting on the toilet, prolonged battles can be avoided by allowing him or her to get up and then try again later after a meal. If resistance is consistent over days or weeks, dropping the whole idea for several weeks or a month or two usually turns out to be better strategy than applying pressure and punishment. Behavior modification approaches have been reported to be successful with both normal and retarded children (Azrin and Foxx, 1974; Bijou, 1968). Here a system of reward is worked out for time spent sitting on the toilet and for producing the desired results. Once the pattern is established, rewards are given for every other success and then gradually withdrawn.

If resistance to toilet training is part of a more generalized "vicious circle" of pressure and resistance, management should proceed along the lines discussed under "Vicious Circle Parent-Child Relationship Problems" later in this chapter.

Encopresis   One of the most extensive studies of encopresis is that reported by Bellman (1966). In a survey of 8683 first-grade children in Stockholm, 137 (1.6 percent) were reported as still defecating into their clothes with a frequency of at least once a month. The sex ratio was about 3 to 1 in favor of males. Only four of these children had associated medical problems (operated myelomeningocele, operated anal membrane, ulcerative colitis, and subacute enterocolitis). There were no instances of congenital megacolon, and in only about 8 percent of the children was the encopresis associated with prolonged obstipation. A detailed random sample of 75 of the boys was compared with a control group of 77 matched for age, sex, and place of residence. About one-half the symptom group had never been bowel trained. The other half had adequate bowel control for at least 1 year before becoming encopretic. In about two-thirds of this later group the onset of the encopresis was associated with some life event (starting school, birth of a sibling, period of separation from the parents, or marital difficulties). Comparison of the primary and secondary cases on a number of other variables did not reveal any significant differences so they were lumped together for comparison with the boys not having encopresis.

In general, the symptomatic boys were more inhibited and passive and had more nervous symptoms than the controls and were more dependent on their mothers. They also had more difficulty making friends. There was no difference in measures of intelligence. By history there was a higher incidence of coercive attempts at toilet training by the mothers and a punitive response to accidents by the symptomatic group when compared to the control group. There was also a higher incidence of encopresis in the families of children who had this symptom (parents and siblings). The mothers of the symptomatic group were on the whole more anxious, and there was a higher incidence of mental illness in the parents (11 versus 2, $p < .05$). There were, however, no significant differences in the number of broken homes, alcoholic parents, or working mothers. Although there were the above-mentioned significant differences between the symptomatic and control groups, none was large enough by itself to be a very good predictor of who would or would not develop this kind of symptom. All one can say is that given a child with this complaint the primary care worker needs to assess the child's general developmental status and the social environment as well as the function of the bowel.

Management for children without associated constipation depends upon the degree of pathology found in the child and/or family and may vary from simple reassurance to long-term psychotherapy. A follow-up of this sample 2 years later revealed that about one-half the children had stopped defecating in their pants without any specific intervention.

The management of children in which the symptom is associated with chronic obstipation is of a somewhat different order. The major diagnostic task is to separate the rare case of Hirschsprung's disease (congenital megacolon) from the much more common functional types of constipation (Richmond et al., 1954). Onset of symptoms in the first year of life, the absence of stool in the rectum, and the lack of the physiologic urge to defecate are more characteristic of Hirschsprung's disease, but the response to the Davidson regimen of phosphate enemas and large amounts of mineral oil administered orally is a more reliable way to identify those children who will need further diagnostic studies. This approach has also been found useful in the management of children with functional constipation and soiling (Davidson et al., 1963).

Enuresis Bed-wetting is quite common in preschool children. In one survey of a group of middle-class children, 26 percent of the 4-year-old children were still wetting the bed with some frequency, and about 15 percent of 5-year-olds were still having this problem (Chamberlin, 1974). A higher incidence is usually reported for families of lower socioeconomic status. If there is no evidence of a large atonic bladder, with overflow incontinence, urinary tract infection, sacral nerve disorder, or other "disorders of arousal" such as sleepwalking, talking, and night terrors (Anders and Weinstein, 1972), simple reassurance is generally the procedure of choice. For those needing to "do something," exercises to enlarge bladder capacity have been successful in some instances and do not have undesirable side effects (Starfield and Mellitis, 1968). Tofranil has been of value, particularly in children with associated sleep disorders (Anders and Weinstein, 1972) but is not recommended for children under 6 because bed-wetting is still a common phenomenon at this age and there is the rare but serious side effect of agranulocytosis with use of this drug. Conditioning devices have also been used successfully for older children and can be tried if the child is in agreement (Behrle et al., 1956). Since enuresis is increased in children under stress it is important to evaluate the child's general development and social environment as well as the bladder.

VICIOUS CIRCLE PARENT-CHILD RELATIONSHIPS

If the child presents with multiple areas of difficulty or a single area that has not responded to previous advice and reassurance, or the behavior is causing the family considerable stress, more information will be needed to clarify what is going on. We have found it necessary to set aside about an hour of uninterrupted time for these sessions.

To gather the information needed we have found the semistructured interview developed by Rose and his associates to be very useful. This interview is described in an article by Harrington (1965). In brief, it covers the types of behavior leading to conflict or concern, the events, if any, related to their onset, the course of the symptoms over time, and what the parents think may be causing them. Basic family information is then gathered and includes the ages, educational and occupational backgrounds, and health status of the parents and other family members. After this orienting information is obtained, a developmental history is taken to identify possible central nervous system components, the early temperament pattern of the child, the parents' general way of reacting to the child's behavior in the past, and other important family events that may be related to the present difficulty. When the history is almost back up to the present, we inquire briefly into the parents' own upbringing. Sometimes this information is useful in identifying similar conflicts around eating, toilet training, and so forth, in the parents' past. Exploring their feelings about being pressured to eat, and so on, helps them to better understand why the child is responding the way he or she is. At other times, knowledge of some of the stresses experienced by the parents in their own growing-up period allows us to be more understanding and tolerant of their current behavior with the child.

After exploring this aspect of the past we return to the present and get a detailed description of the child's current behavior and how the parents are responding to it. Finally, we explore other current stresses with which the family is coping, the role of the father, and the marital relationship.

At the end of this time the picture is usually clear enough for the parents and health worker to decide on one of several courses of action.

1   If it is clear that the parents have a serious marital problem, psychiatric disturbance, or are attempting to cope with a number of difficult problems, referral to a mental health professional is generally indicated.
2   If the child shows markedly deviant behavior, slow motor or speech development, or localizing neurologic symptoms or signs, further evaluation by an appropriate specialist is indicated.

3   If the family is coping pretty well in general and the problems appear to arise from a lack of fit between a particular type of child and the response pattern adopted by the parents, a trial of brief intervention is undertaken. The majority of middle-class families we have dealt with fall into this third group.

After a little experience, one can recognize several recurring patterns. These have been described in detail elsewhere and are briefly summarized here (Chamberlin, 1967, 1974):

1   The aggressive-resistant child and a parental response pattern characterized by scolding, yelling, and spanking. Sometimes this pattern has evolved out of a pattern of response developed by parents to cope with the "difficult child" temperament pattern recognizable soon after birth. At other times things have gone well until the parents react in a punitive way to the "into everything" and negativism of the toddler, or the "back-talk and sass" of the 4-year-old.
2   Dependent-manipulating, protective-permissive patterns. This pattern often presents as a medical problem with repeated parental concerns about minor deviations in health. Having the mother describe a typical day often reveals pressures around food intake, difficulty with day and night separations, low peer contact, difficulty in setting reasonable limits, and a tendency to do things for the child that he or she could do alone. A "slow to warm up" temperament pattern may be involved. Frequently the parent has a history of contact with serious disease in the past or has had complicating events around the pregnancy of this child, such as repeated prior miscarriages, difficulty getting pregnant, or the like. If health providers do not recognize the pattern underlying the presenting complaints, they may be pressured into performing a long series of tests to rule out various rare diseases.

There are a number of approaches to interrupting these types of vicious circles that have been reported as successful (Augenbraun et al., 1967; Chamberlin, 1967; Friedman and Hansen, 1968; Thomas et al., 1968; Wahler et al., 1965). Our basic intervention strategy for these types of vicious circles is outlined in Tables 4-5 and 4-6.

Our experience has been that if these problems are going to respond to the approach outlined, they generally do so in 1 to 3 months. We make it clear to the parents at the outset that they must be willing to persist in the changes outlined for at least this long. Generally, one or two sessions with the parents are all that are necessary, along with a few follow-up telephone calls. If there is no response within this time period, reevaluation and, if necessary, referral to another source of help are indicated.

If the child is having difficulty in nursery school as well as at home, coordinating the intervention strategy with the teacher can be of additional help (Allen et al., 1964; Brown and Elliott, 1965).

Occasionally, we have found methylphenidate to be of use in the management of children with an unusually high activity level and short attention span (Eisenberg, 1972). However, the recent report of growth retardation in some older children taking this drug indicates its use should be closely supervised (Safer et al., 1972).

OTHER STAGE-RELATED PROBLEMS

Stuttering   The natural history of this phenomenon is nicely brought out in the Newcastle upon Tyne study in which a representative sample of 800 children was followed from birth through age 16 (Miller et al., 1974). Of these children, 43 had some episodes of dysrhythmic speech; in 16,

TABLE 4-5
Basic Ingredients of Brief Intervention for Interrupting Punishment-Resistance Vicious Circles

I   Decrease negative contact
   A   Decrease conflict areas by ignoring noncrucial behaviors
     Example: Resistance to eating or toilet training, temper tantrums, habits
   B   Decrease spanking and scolding by use of temporary isolation and distraction to deal with behaviors that encroach on the rights of others or endanger the child's safety
II   Increase positive contact
   A   General: Spend 15 to 20 minutes daily with child doing something both enjoy—looking at books, playing a game, taking a walk, and so on
   B   Specific: Make special effort to recognize and praise behaviors that are incompatible with those behaviors you hope to decrease or eliminate
     Example: If trying to eliminate stubbornness, praise all evidence of cooperative behavior
III   Increase support for mother
   A   Encourage father's participation and support
   B   Encourage mother to get out of the house regularly to get relief from child rearing
   C   Praise change efforts
IV   Set up definite time period for change efforts, and reevaluate at end of this time (usually 3 or 4 months); maintain contact in between
V   Expect the mother to test: "I've tried everything, nothing works"

SOURCE: Reproduced from *Pediatr. Clin. North Am.*, 1974, *21* (1), 43 with permission of W. B. Saunders Co.

TABLE 4-6

Basic Ingredients of Brief Intervention of Interrupting Protective-Permissive Dependent-Manipulating Vicious Circles

I	Respectful confrontations: After reasonable medical workup to exclude common causes of presenting complaints, stand firm on diagnosis of health and shift focus to parent-child relationship
II	Decrease mother-child contact
	A Have child sleep in own room and bed
	B If appropriate age, consider nursery school
	C Have child feed and dress self
	D Encourage peer contact
	E Encourage mother to leave with sitter periodically
III	Shift focus of contact: Have mother recognize and praise independent behavior
IV	Encourage mother to set reasonable limits: Pick area causing most distress and concentrate on this: i.e., not sleeping at night, persistent whining and fussing (if mother finds she can set limits in one area, she is generally able to do this in others as well)
V	Increase support for mother
	A Encourage father's participation
	B Praise mother's efforts at change
VI	Set up definite time period for change: Reevaluate at end of this time, maintain contact in between
VII	Expect mother to test: Bringing up new concerns about child's health and putting on pressure to do more tests

SOURCE: Reproduced from *Pediatr. Clin. North Am.*, 1974, *21* (1), 43 with permission of W. B. Saunders Co.

this occurred between 2 and 4 years and lasted less than 6 months without any speech treatment. In another 18, the periods of nonfluency lasted from 6 months to 6 years but then remitted. Of the total group, nine (21 percent) still had trouble with stuttering at age 15. In this sample, stuttering was found to be more frequent in children with lower intelligence and in those living in families with multiple social problems.

In general, the initial management of preschool children who stutter is (1) screening the environment for situations that may be causing tension in the child and alleviating this when possible, (2) reassuring the parents that many children of this age have periods of nonfluency and it is important for the parents to avoid making it worse by attempting to correct the child or by showing anxiety about his or her speech.

In general, the parents should allow the child ample time to speak, maintain normal eye contact as the child is speaking, and avoid suggesting the child modify his or her speech in any way. They can also encourage the child's speaking in situations where tensions are minimal and during periods of greater fluency. Indicating disapproval or putting pressure on the child to change usually increases the tension, which in turn increases the tendency to stutter (Counihan, 1964; Johnson and Leutenegger, 1955).

Children whose stuttering lasts longer than 6 months or who are beginning to show emotional distress at their difficulty in communication should be referred to a person skilled in working with children having this kind of problem.

Defective Articulation   As discussed earlier, the majority of children have speech intelligible to strangers by age 3, but it is often not until age 7 or 8 that many normal children reach an adult level of pronunciation. Parents can help the speech development of their child by serving as an appropriate model with frequent one-to-one contact in terms of reading stories, labeling objects around the house, and encouraging conversation. It is generally not recommended to correct the child's speech in life situations when the child tries to express needs and wants but to set aside some daily time for playing word and listening games (Wyatt, 1965). If the child is not making definite progress by 3½ or is not easily understood by strangers by age 4, a referral to a speech therapist should be made. Hearing, of course, should be tested as soon as the child is old enough to cooperate, and if there is any question of a hearing loss referral to a specialist for further evaluation is indicated.

Dental Problems   Dental caries are widespread in preschool children. From various surveys it is estimated that without adequate fluoride ingestion about 10 to 15 percent of 1-year-olds, 25 to 30 percent of 2-year-olds, and 50 to 60 percent of 3-year-olds will have dental caries (Hennan et al., 1969).

There is a consensus among investigators that the ingestion of sugar-containing foods, particularly between meals, increases the amount of tooth decay (Makinen, 1972; Weiss and Trithart, 1960; Zita et al., 1959). Some investigators have tried to implicate bottle-fed milk by itself as a cause of caries as well (Robinson and Naylor, 1963), but direct experimental work and surveys relating the amount of milk intake with caries formation do not confirm this. In fact, these reports give some evidence that the ingestion of milk actually provides the teeth with some protection against tooth decay (Jenkins and Ferguson, 1966). Giving milk with added sugar or a sugared pacifier at bedtime, however, can lead to extensive decay of the anterior maxillary teeth (Kroll and Stone, 1967; Robinson and Naylor, 1963).

The use of fluoride in drinking water is a well-documented approach to reducing the amount of dental caries by 50 to 60 percent

(Dunning, 1965; Scherp, 1971). Where the water supply is not fluoridated (about 50 percent of the population still drink unfluoridated water) it can be given in the form of drops or tablets (O'Meara, 1968). The amount needed depends on the fluoride concentration in the water supply.

MALOCCLUSION   The role of thumb-sucking in producing malocclusion is still not clear. In a study of 2650 infants and children in a private, middle-class suburban practice, about 45 percent of the total group had sucked their thumbs (Traisman et al., 1966). The average age of which thumb-sucking stopped was 3.8 years. Of the thumb-suckers, 9.7 percent developed malocclusion compared to 6.1 percent of non-thumb-suckers. While this difference is statistically significant because of the large sample size, it is of questionable clinical importance since the large majority of thumb-suckers do not develop serious problems.

Longitudinal studies of the effect of sucking on the dental arch generally show some protrusion during the habit but a tendency toward spontaneous correction as soon as it stopped (Sillman, 1942).

Whatever the cause, the longitudinal study reported by Moorrees (1959) indicates the difficulty of trying to predict final dental status from early evidence of crowding and overbite. In general, correlations from the preschool period to age 18 were quite low ($r = .30$ to $.40$) and there were a number of instances of marked spontaneous improvements. However, in some children, the defects persisted. The author concluded that only by following individual children over a period of time can one arrive at a reasonably accurate idea of whether some active intervention is needed. Collaboration with a developmentally oriented orthodontist such as described by Moorrees et al. (1962) is the preferred approach.

Management of Other Problems with Developmental Implications

GENDER IDENTITY PROBLEMS

Retrospective histories of the early childhood of adult males who have sexual identity problems and are seeking surgical sex change indicate that signs of role confusion were present from an early age (Green, 1974; Green et al., 1972). A verbalized wish to be a girl, a persistent desire to dress in girl's clothes, feminine mannerisms, a strong preference for girl's toys and activities, and preference for girl playmates were evident in many of the men by 4 or 5 years of age. Because of this, early assessment and intervention has been advised for young children displaying this kind of behavior.

Since some cross-sexed behavior is relatively common in preschool children, and no longitudinal prospective studies are available to assess the outcomes of children showing various degrees of this, it is not always clear what, if any, intervention should take place. For example, in Chamberlin's (1974) longitudinal study of about 200 normal, middle-class, suburban preschool children, mothers were asked how descriptive (very, somewhat, not at all) the following statement was of their children: "Doesn't act very masculine (if boy) or feminine (if girl)." About 5 percent of the mothers of 2-year-olds said this statement described their children at least somewhat, and 1 percent said it was very descriptive of their children. A similar percentage said this when their children were age 3. At 4 years, the percentages were 8 and 1 percent, respectively, and for 5-year-olds they were 6 and 1 percent, respectively.

At ages 3 and 4, mothers of girls were more concerned about sex-role behavior than mothers of boys (9 to 1 percent; 10 to 6 percent). At age 5, the concerns were equally distributed (6 to 6 percent) between mothers of boys and girls. Whether or not any of these children had serious gender identity problems was not ascertained, but it is highly unlikely that all did.

If there is concern about the gender identity of a child, more information needs to be gathered. Besides assessing the general adjustment of the child and family, it is important to assess the child's specific knowledge of the anatomical and reproductive differences between the sexes, the parents' response to feminine and masculine types of behavior, the amount of mother and father to child contact and interaction, the parents' acceptance of their own sexuality and reproductive roles, and what kind of role models they present to the child.

For boys, if the families are functioning reasonably well and the "feminine" behavior is not of long standing or all-pervasive, the intervention can take the form of actively discouraging blatantly inappropriate sex-role behavior and positively reinforcing that which is appropriate, with an emphasis on the latter (Bates et al., 1975; Green, 1974; Green et al., 1972). Increasing father-child contact and exposure to an interaction with adequate male-role models is also helpful. Reassessment after a 3- to 6-month trial period should clarify whether psychiatric referral is indicated. For those boys whose behavior is long standing and pervasive, direct referral to a person skilled in working with these problems is indicated without a trial of modification. A similar approach can be used with girls, although there is much greater tolerance for "tomboy" type behavior in this culture and therefore less risk of their being rejected by peers and adults.

Treatment reports indicate some success in modifying sex-role behavior and gender identity, though most of these involve small numbers and only short-term follow-ups (Bates et al., 1975; Green, 1974).

HYPERACTIVITY

Most parents of 2-year-olds describe their child as "restless, often running about or jumping up and down, hardly ever sits still," and in 4-year-olds, a high activity and noise level is common (Chamberlin, 1974). In both age groups, such behavior frequently leads to parent-child conflicts and causes parental concern, but it is a normal stage-related behavior.

"Hyperactivity" is not easily defined, since claims that a child is hyperactive often reflect the tolerance level of the annoyed person. Some children, however, are clearly more active and have shorter attention spans than average, and they create management problems for many people encountering them.[1]

Present evidence suggests that this syndrome of behavior arises from a variety of different etiologies. In some children, it appears related to an emotional disorder or is associated with evidence of central nervous system dysfunction (Birch, 1964; Rutter et al., 1970). In others, a genetic inheritance is suggested (Morrison and Stewart, 1974), and in some children it appears to be simply an exaggeration of a normal temperament trait (Thomas et al., 1968).

This type of behavior becomes most troublesome in rigid settings where the most frequent response by adults is to try and suppress it with scolding and punishment. Not requiring the youngster to sit still for long periods of time and/or finding a person who is better able to cope with a wiggly child is sometimes of help. Some successes have been reported with the use of behavior modification (Ayllon et al., 1975). If efforts to modify the environment are not successful and the child's behavior is disrupting the home or classroom, methylphenidate therapy can be tried (Eisenberg, 1972; Millichap and Fowler, 1967). This should be under the guidance of a physician experienced in these matters, however, since the medication often has to be continued for long periods of time and undesirable side effects such as growth suppression have been described (Safer et al., 1972). For further discussion of the hyperactivity syndrome in school-aged children, see Chapter 5.

[1] Reproduced from the Merck Manual, 13th ed., Copyright under the Universal Copyright Convention 1977 by Merck & Co., Inc., Rahway, New Jersey, U.S.A.

TODDLER AND PRESCHOOL YEARS

Helping Families Cope with Stress and Crisis

ILLNESS

An active imagination, egocentric thinking, and inability to readily differentiate between reality and fantasy are characteristic of young children.
As a result, they are apt to have unrealistic fears concerning their illness
and its therapy. Illness and hospitalization are usually interpreted as
punishment for some misdeed or for their bad thoughts. This, in turn,
leads to feelings of guilt about their behavior or thoughts. The preschoolers' increasing self-awareness and limited knowledge of body
functioning heighten their fear of threats to body integrity. Parents need
to understand these fears in order to support their children. For example,
it would be better to tell their child his or her tonsils are going to be
"fixed" rather than "taken out."

There is evidence to suggest that parents who understand their
child's illness are more apt to comply with the recommended medical
regime (Marston, 1970; Tagliacozzo and Kenji, 1970). The amount of
knowledge parents have about their child's illness has been shown to be
related to their feelings of guilt (Meadow, 1968; Wright, 1960). Adequate and accurate knowledge tends to be associated with fewer feelings
of self-accusation. If the parents are to manage the child's illness at
home, they need an explanation of the care they are expected to give.
This should include information and, when appropriate, demonstrations
of specific procedures they are expected to perform. Parents should
know what changes the therapy will cause and how long it will be before
these changes occur. The unfavorable as well as the favorable signs and
symptoms they are expected to look for should also be explained.
Knowledge needs to be imparted about the therapy, such as medications, as well as the disease process itself. Parents will need similar assistance if their child is to be cared for in the hospital. They need to be
informed about the treatments and procedures which their child is
receiving.

HOSPITALIZATION

The young child is especially vulnerable to the effects of hospitalization.
Studies by Vernon and Schulman (1964; Vernon et al., 1966) indicated
the incidence of psychological upset during hospitalization was greatest
in children between 6 months and 4 years as opposed to that found in
young infants under 6 months and in 4- to 9-year-old children. They also

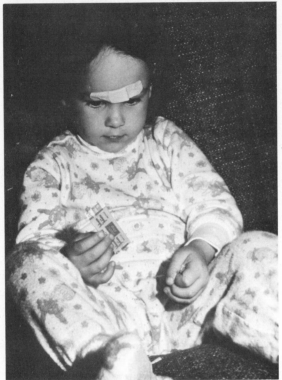

FIGURE 4-27   by Susan McCabe

found that as a result of hospitalization some of the preschoolers benefited as evidenced by more mature behaviors.

Children between about 18 months and 5 years of age are prone to numerous fears, and are struggling with the developmental crises of autonomy (toddler) and initiative (preschooler). They are more aware of the experience of separation, the strangeness of the hospital environment, and the threat of the many painful and intrusive procedures than are infants. Their sense of reality is tenuous, and magical thinking is prevalent. Beginning self-confidence is undermined as there is little in their environment, including their own bodies, over which they can have some control. "No" is ignored, and new-found skills of feeding and toileting are often not supported in the hospital setting. Fears relating to body integrity predominate, and their immature cognitive development makes meaningful explanations difficult.

TODDLER AND PRESCHOOL YEARS

The most powerful effect of hospitalization is separation from home and parents, especially the mother. Robertson (1958) describes three phases of response indicative of separation anxiety in young children. During the first phase of *protest,* the child reacts by violent crying, screaming, and clinging to mother as she tries to leave. If the mother does leave, after a period of time the child enters the second phase of *despair* and becomes quieter, withdrawn, and apathetic. The behavior regresses, and comfort may be sought by clinging to a favorite object or thumb-sucking. Unresponsiveness to nurses is common. When the child's mother comes, the child becomes angry and distressed, may first ignore her, and later cling to her and protest again when she leaves. For some children whose hospital stay is prolonged, they eventually pass from despair to *denial.* They regain interest in their surroundings, respond superficially to nurses and others, and begin to smile again. For some children symptoms of emotional disturbance related to hospitalization may not appear until the child returns home (Millar, 1970).

Elective surgery should preferably not be scheduled for children between 3 and 5 years (Korsch, 1975). When hospitalization and/or surgery is necessary, shortening the stay as much as possible and maximal visiting should be encouraged (Millar, 1970).

Because of the young child's response to separation, parents are encouraged to stay with their small children when they must be hospitalized. Providing parents with specific guidelines for caring for their child lessens their anxiety and facilitates the youngster's recovery (Roy, 1967). Providing the mother with information about her child's condition has been shown to reduce the stress of both the mothers and the children (Skipper and Leonard, 1968). Rooming-in can be especially beneficial for the young child. Consideration of the needs of other children in the family is also important. For a variety of reasons, the mother may be unable to remain with the child; however, it may be that another family member to whom the child is attached could remain in the hospital.

Branstetter (1969) believes lack of mothering care rather than separation from mother accounts for the young child's behavioral responses when hospitalized. She provided substitute mothering for a group of 14- to 36-month-old children whose mothers could not remain with them. These children readily accepted the attention and care of the mother-substitute and began to show attachment behavior toward her. Their behavior was similar to the behavior of a group of children whose mothers were able to be present.

Familiar routines and objects add to the child's sense of security when hospitalized. Parents can aid their child's adjustment by bringing familiar toys and security objects from home. They may also be able to

FIGURE 4-28   by Elizabeth Tong

continue some of their usual routines if they are rooming-in or staying for long periods. Parents can also familiarize the nursing personnel with the particular routines, needs, and likes and dislikes of their child. A good history, taken by the nurse, should elicit this information.

The child's behavioral responses to separation are extremely difficult for parents to understand. It is important to prepare parents for their child's possible responses toward them and to let them know they are still needed by their child even though they are ignored. Some parents try to avoid the child's protest by deception. It is vital that parents be encouraged to be honest with their child if the child is to continue to trust them. It is equally important for parents to realize that their presence makes it possible for the child to express feelings that might otherwise be kept to himself or herself.

Korsch (1975) recommends that whenever possible the mother should be present during treatment procedures to prevent unnecessary psychologic disturbances and convince the toddler that someone is on his or her side in this strange place. Children should be allowed to have some of their belongings with them, and parents should be encouraged to bring these along.

Preparation of parent and child for hospitalization is essential. Parents need this preparation not only for themselves but also to help their youngsters anticipate what is going to happen. Children under 3 years of age need preparation for surgery hours ahead of time, while those between 3 and 5 years should be prepared days ahead of time (Korsch, 1975). Prugh and colleagues (1953), and Jessner et al. (1952) have shown that anxieties, night terrors, and behavior problems after hospitalizations, as well as the actual adjustment to the experience, can be significantly altered by proper preparation and inpatient handling.

There are a number of children's books that may be somewhat useful in preparing children for hospitalization and surgery. Unfortunately, these books are written for the "average" child admitted to a "fictitious" hospital and they do not adequately deal with the procedures and policies of the particular hospital the child will encounter. Nor do these books adequately deal with the problem of separation. Although there is no research comparing children prepared with these general materials with children prepared with materials specific to a given setting, it is likely that the concrete, egocentric thinking of early childhood precludes generalization to different situations.

Hospitals should have their own specific booklet to give parents. The booklet should include information about the hospital, suggestions for preparing children, and guidelines to support the visiting parents. When the child is hospitalized, the nurses will be able to supplement what the parents have been able to tell him or her and clarify any misconceptions.

These books can be used as a jumping-off point for discussion of a forthcoming hospitalization. They can be used to help clarify and prepare a child for unfamiliar situations and equipment. They can also be used to stimulate questions and expression of feelings about the child's body, illness or defect, and treatments. Rereading such books following hospitalization can help a child to review, discuss, and integrate the hospital stay into his or her life experiences (Altshuler, 1974). There are books written for children with specific types of illness, for specific institutions, or for specific age groups. The pamphlet, *Books that Help Children Deal with a Hospital Experience,* is recommended as a reference for health personnel in finding available books. Altschuler (1974) recommends several criteria to consider when evaluating a book:

1 Does it meet the special needs for an individual child?
2 Does it present a realistic picture of the hospital experience?
3 Is the book a well-told story with illustrations of a high artistic quality that will be appealing to children?

Once home, the child needs to "discharge his accumulated affect, to desensitize his trauma" (Millar, 1970). This is seen in the complaining, fussy, demanding behavior as well as in fears that mother will abandon him or her again. The second need "is to be filled up with the kind of closeness he once had with his mother." The child clings to mother, becoming upset when she tries to leave. Regressive behavior such as soiling, enuresis, and thumb-sucking are common following hospitalization, as are disturbances in eating and sleeping behavior. Parents have indicated that children may have difficulty going to sleep at night or they may awaken during the night from frightening dreams. The parents need to know such posthospital behaviors are common. They can be encouraged to indulge the child for a period of time (about 10 days) before worrying about helping the child grow up again. The mother can, after a period of time, begin to leave for brief periods (½ hour) and gradually increase the time. Separation anxiety is mastered by experiences of successful separation; thus, she is desensitizing the child to separation by helping him or her master small doses of separation again.

DEATH

The primary health care provider may be in a strategic position to help parents help their young children cope with a death in the family. Parents should be helped to understand the meaning of death to these youngsters. Important points for them to understand include the following (Hardgrove and Warrick, 1974; Nagera, 1970; Watts, 1971). (1) To the toddler, death is often equated with separation, and in the case of the death of a parent separation anxiety is common. (2) Separation anxiety and feelings of guilt for bad thoughts and deeds are common among preschool youngsters. (3) Young children generally see death as reversible and may continue to expect the dead person to return. (4) Young children are generally able to sustain feelings of sadness for only brief periods of time. (5) When death occurs, children under 5 years react to the changes in their parents and may sense withdrawal and fear their loss of love (Lewis, 1971; Lewis and Lewis, 1973).

Parents can be encouraged to be honest with their youngsters about the death; to use concrete terms like death, died, and buried; to help their children see the permanence of the death; and to keep communication open so the child can ask questions as they arise. The children can be helped to see that they are not responsible for the death and that thoughts cannot cause someone to die, nor can they bring the dead person back to life. Parental physical closeness with the child should also be encouraged. Doll play and story telling are often useful in helping the child master this difficult situation. Children of this age derive comfort from ritual, and many believe they should be allowed to participate in the rituals, including the funeral, surrounding the death (Hardgrove and Warrick, 1974; Watts, 1971). The parents will also need support for themselves as they grieve the death of a loved one and help their children to mourn.

FIVE

Middle Childhood

**by Sandra Dale,
Philip R. Nader,
and Debra P. Hymovich**

The period of middle childhood extends from school entry to puberty. During this stage children establish themselves as individuals in an environment outside the family. Responsibility for self increases as the child relates to individuals and groups in the community and responds to the demands made by them.

INDIVIDUAL DEVELOPMENT

DEVELOPING AND MAINTAINING HEALTHY GROWTH AND NUTRITION PATTERNS

The elementary school years are characterized by a relatively slow physical growth rate with a decreasing velocity in both height and weight gains. Growth is steady, with average yearly gains of 7 pounds (3 to 3.5 kilograms) in weight and 2.5 inches (6 centimeters) in height (Vaughn and McKay, 1975). Most research indicates that males are taller and heavier than females during this growth period. However, with the onset of the earlier pubescent growth spurt of females, the 10-year-old female is generally heavier and taller than her male peer (Garn, 1966). (See Appendix A for growth charts.)

Body-build becomes stockier, the posture becomes more erect, and there is a loss of the lordotic and knock-kneed appearance characteristic of the toddler and preschool child. Fat diminishes and its distribution shifts, causing the school age child to appear thinner than the preschool child or adolescent. Fat distribution in girls gives them softer contours than males (Lowrey, 1973).

Skeletal growth with its corresponding changes in proportion is apparent in the expansion and width of the chest and its relatively flat appearance, with ribs sloping and shoulders dropping. Thus, rounded shoulders are typical of the school age child. A spurt in vertical growth of the face occurs in relation to the increasing respiratory needs of the growing body. Frontal sinuses are at the level of the orbital roof by 6 to 7 years. The occipital frontal circumference increases from 51 centimeters to approximately 53 to 54 centimeters, with the brain reaching adult size at puberty (Lowrey, 1973).

Dentition is in an active, changing state, with most deciduous or primary teeth being shed or replaced by permanent teeth during this period. Generally, the first molars are the first permanent teeth to erupt. As they do not replace a primary or deciduous tooth, they are frequently

FIGURE 5-1

by Debra Hymovich

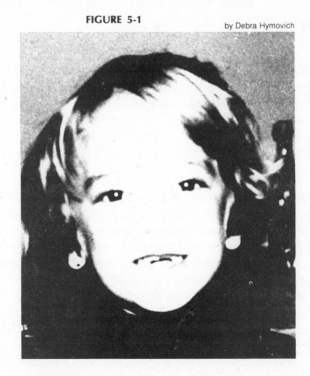

FIGURE 5-2   by Debra Hymovich

not recognized as permanent teeth. The transition period from primary to permanent dentition is hazardous, and the teeth are highly susceptible to environmental changes. The site and order of eruption are of more importance than the timing of eruption. Malocclusion usually occurs because of rapid closing of a space due to a discrepancy in the sequence of eruption (Lowrey, 1973). The desired and normal sequence is shown in Table 5-1.

Nutrition   With the decrease in velocity of growth during the school age period, caloric requirements per unit of body weight also decrease. Nutritional requirements remain greater than caloric requirements. Due to the amount of muscular activity and requirements for building and repairing tissues, adequate protein intake should contain sufficient amounts of all the known essential amino acids to meet the maintenance needs, besides providing an extra amount for protein deposition compatible with normal growth. It is recommended that 10 percent of the child's total caloric intake be protein, with 25 to 50 percent derived from animal sources or other sources of high quality (Kraus and Hunscher, 1972). Two to three cups of milk daily will cover many of the mineral

TABLE 5-1
Normal Sequence of Eruption of Permanent Teeth*

Mandible		Maxilla	
1	First molar	2	First molar
3	Central incisor	5	Central incisor
4	Lateral incisor	6	Lateral incisor
7	Cuspid	8	First bicuspid
9	First bicuspid	10	Second bicuspid
11	Second bicuspid	12	Cuspid
13	Second molar	14	Second molar

*The numbers indicate the usual sequence of eruption.
SOURCE: From Lowrey, G. H. *Growth and Development of Children* (6th ed.). Copyright 1973 by Year Book Medical Publishers, Inc., Chicago, p. 369. Used by permission.

and vitamin requirements. In addition, two or more servings of vegetables, fruits, breads, and cereals are desirable. The recommended daily allowance of iron is 12 to 15 milligrams.

Eating Behavior The school age child brings past nutrition and eating habits from the home environment into middle childhood. If these habits are not optimal, this period is at risk for the formation of poor nutritional patterns. Children are easily influenced by environment, peers, and television viewing. Increased snacking and empty calories can be major problems. School breakfast and lunch programs can be of great assistance in encouraging good eating practices, as well as in providing the necessary nutrients essential for learning, perception, and attention. It should be noted that while supplemental programs have demonstrated their worth in growth achievements, their value in improving attention span and school performance are still questionable (Paige et al., 1976). Of great concern in the United States is the problem of obesity, especially among school children (Neumann, 1977). As a rule, overeating, accompanied by little exercise, is the chief cause of obesity. If obesity is prevalent among family members, the eating habits of the entire family may require reorganization. Unless the child is grossly obese, vigorous reducing is not advised. Being mildly overweight at about 10 to 11 years of age is often observed to be a spurt in body weight prior to a rapid gain in height and is generally only of short duration.

The Ten-State Nutrition Survey (USDHEW, 1972) identified another

FIGURE 5-3   by Elizabeth Tong

FIGURE 5-4   by Debra Hymovich

problem caused by inadequate eating behaviors—that of hemoglobin and iron deficiency. The highest percentage of low hemoglobin values was found in black children. While concentration of essential nutrients was basically the same in the diets of lower- and middle-income families, the amount of available food was related to family income. The average dietary intake of iron per 1000 kilocalories was essentially the same regardless of economic status. Thus, the greater proportion of iron and hemoglobin deficiency noted among lower socioeconomic groups speaks to a lower quantity of food intake, not necessarily a lower quality of food intake.

LEARNING TO CONTROL ONE'S BODY SATISFACTORILY

More graceful than the preschooler because of a lower center of gravity and longer legs, the school age child has increased coordination allowing for motor activities such as bicycle riding, climbing, and sports. Opportunities should be made available for a wide variety of motor skill activities so that the child can practice and perform for both skill attainment and enjoyment.

While muscles grow in size and strength, they are still immature in function as compared with an adolescent's muscles and are more readily injured by strain. This, plus the fact that the heart is proportionately smaller than at any other time, are two of the major reasons why strongly competitive sports are controversial for this age group (Breckenridge and Vincent, 1965).

Motor Ability Motor ability in the school age child is based on strength, reaction time, speed, precision, coordination, and flexibility. Strength is usually determined by hand grip and measurably increases during the school years. Males have greater hand grip than females, and Mexican Americans have less strength in their hand grip than do Anglo-Americans and black Americans. The hand grip of black American females is greater than Mexican-American or Anglo-American females (Goss, 1968).

Speed of reaction time is shown through activities such as jumping, tapping, finger tapping, moving small objects, and removing and replacing pegs in boards. Females are generally better at this than males, and speed improves with age between 6 and 9 years (Connally et al., 1968). There is a noticeable increase in speed particularly in relation to running and hopping in both males and females during the elementary school years. Greater balance, steadiness, increased speed in performance and aiming abilities are indicative of increasing precision and coordination. Denckla (1973, 1974) found that older children (8 years or older) per-

FIGURE 5-5   by Debra Hymovich

form coordination tasks more rapidly than the 5- to 8-year-olds. The ability to perform simple coordination tasks follows the brain growth curve and is reflective of brain maturation.

Symmetrical balancing and hopping were achieved by those children 8 years and older. Girls performed alternating heel-toe and finger

FIGURE 5-6   by Debra Hymovich

successive tasks significantly earlier than boys. Denckla (1974) feels that this is probably secondary to better integration of spatial directional and speed sequencing task completion. While the correlation between motor skills and cognitive maturity is unclear, it has been noted that mentally retarded children show motor skill performance consistent with their mental age, not their chronological age (Angle, 1975). The cognitive ability to plan ahead has been suggested as contributing to the improvement noted in speed of motor skill performance (Kerr, 1975).

When a child enters school, the ability to sit down and keep still becomes important. This is particularly important to the classroom teacher. A low correlation has been found between impulse control and intelligence. Yet, inability to inhibit motor activity during the childhood years has been shown to be predictive of future avoidance of intellectual activities. Restless, impulsive children may be helped if provided with opportunities for movement as well as calm reminders to think before answering (Kahana and Kahana, 1970).

Learning to write is a key task for the school age child and is highly dependent upon motor control, particularly eye-hand coordination. Handwriting shows continual development throughout the school years. Skill in writing is not highly correlated with intelligence or other academic achievement (Herrick and Okada, 1963).

By 7 years of age, visual acuity should be 20/20, and depth sense develops as visual acuity becomes sharper. Depth sense requires coordination of both eyes as well as the ability of the brain to fuse images. Fusion ability is believed to be present by 6 years of age (Lowrey, 1973).

Bowel and Bladder Control   By school age, bowel and bladder control are generally present in all children; however, nocturnal enuresis (bedwetting) may be present in about 10 to 15 percent of otherwise normal 5-year-olds and may be present in about 1 percent of normal 15-year-olds. Nocturnal enuresis is generally more common in boys than in girls and there is a familial tendency. Usually there is no organic basis; delayed maturation of bladder control is the usual cause. Diurnal enuresis is less common than nocturnal enuresis, and, if persistent, usually indicates a pathological disturbance. Children who have acquired good control may still have occasional lapses in nighttime control for several years associated with fatigue or emotional upsets. Excitement, extreme urgency, or engrossment in play may also cause loss of daytime control. Development of bladder control may also be delayed because of inadequate toilet training (Vaughn and McKay, 1975).

Bowel control should be well established by middle childhood. Encopresis, the involuntary passage of feces, commonly refers to fecal soiling without voluntary control of bowel movements or physical signs of retention. This may be present from infancy or it may arise after establishment of a normal bowel control (Vaughn and McKay, 1975). (See "Clinical Applications" later in this chapter.)

LEARNING TO UNDERSTAND AND RELATE TO THE PHYSICAL WORLD

Cognitive Development   School entry occurs at a significant point in the child's cognitive development. The growing peer group influence, a lessening of the influence of the family, and the child's own decreasing egocentricity allow for the development of new ways of thought and judgment. This stage is characterized by considerable growth in thinking, imagination, and language, all of which expand the child's ability to understand the world.

The years 7 to 11 are the period of cognitive development that Piaget has termed "concrete operations." During this period the child begins to understand and use the principles of relationships between things and ideas; to act on or do something to objects, symbols, and ideas; and to think about concrete things in systematic ways. The school age child can count, order, classify, use symbols, apply rules, and think

FIGURE 5-7   by Debra Hymovich

in terms of cause and effect. With the development of the concept of permanence, termed "conservation" by Piaget, the child shows a recognition that while outward appearance of objects or groups might change, the amount, volume, weight, and number can remain the same (Ginsburg and Opper, 1969).

The passage from intuition to logic is assisted by construction of groups within groups. The two most important operations during this period are classifying and ordering. Classifying means that the child can reflect upon and choose the qualities by which to group. The experience of choosing groups of objects with some common element provides the opportunity for internalizing the concept. For example, a group of rocks contains big rocks and little rocks. The rock collector, after classifying rocks as rocks, moves to classifying them as small rocks and large rocks and from there to rough and smooth, dark gray and light gray. From classifying simplistically, the child establishes a system of classifications by which all the parts can be organized into a larger whole. The ability to order experiences and to be aware of their realistic relationship to one another helps to create a notion of certainty. From classifying and ordering of elements, the school age child develops concepts of relations that are essential to formal learning (Maier, 1969).

During this stage of development, the child has a new ability to consider several points of view simultaneously. With this comes an expanding flexibility of thought, as well as the ability to retain one's original thought with a greater awareness of many approaches to problems. By the time a child can develop reversible thought processes and be able to mentally repeat operations in different directions to obtain a given result, there is a shift from an inductive to a deductive mode of thinking (Maier, 1969). This is a key transition in the concrete stage of thinking.

Language Language cannot be separated from cognitive development. It is both a product of the child's intellectual development and a major contributor to it. Articulation increases and vocabulary doubles between the first and sixth grades, while sentences become longer and more complex. The child goes from defining simple words like "orange" to being able to define words like "connection." Socialized speech becomes more frequent as the child becomes less egocentric. Attempts at conveying meaning to others and efforts to look at a situation from another's point of view provide the child with this increase in language skills.

Language reflects the unique culture of middle childhood. Humor is broad and deep and apparently passed from generation to generation. Humor is a product of thinking, language, and imagination; however, imagination is the key to humor. A mode of problem solving and tension reduction, the child's stage of cognitive development determines the level to which a joke can be made or appreciated. During the stage of concrete operations, jokes shift from a long rambling story to a shorter, concise humor, usually having a punch line or surprise ending. Riddles are a favorite for this group. For example: (riddler) "What is black and white and red all over?" (answer) "A newspaper" (riddler) "No, a sunburned zebra." "Stupid jokes" provide tension relief for the school age child. The brunt of the humor in their jokes is not a child, usually, but an older person, thus allowing the child to feel that it is okay not to know everything. Words are considered magical in the sense that they have a certain power over reality and are chanted, with special words considered able to make certain things occur. Word magic, while it is not the exclusive property of children, is very apparent in imagination (Smart and Smart, 1972).

Academic Skills The academic skill of mathematics is based on the development of the child's ability to classify, to begin to abstract, to order, to relate, and to learn number concepts. While preschool children frequently know how to count, they will have no concept of numbers. According to Piaget, mastery of the principles of conservation of quantity, particularly permanency and continuity, is essential to development of the number concept (Maier, 1969). Ability to deal with spatial imagery and to discriminate between objects, as well as the ability to reflect, rather than to impulsively act, aids in the child's developing the skills of mathematics.

Reading is an academic skill which is dependent on language and speech development as well as on the ability to code and decode its graphically represented form. A positive correlation between reading readiness and conservation has also been demonstrated and suggests the use of conservation tasks to predict readiness for reading (Brekke et al.,

FIGURE 5-8   by Debra Hymovich

CHILD AND FAMILY DEVELOPMENT

1973). Vision and auditory perception, as well as curiosity, motor skills, an aesthetic appreciation of books and stories, and the ability to attend to a task, are also of importance.

Because reading is so fundamental in our society, many parents and others feel that the earlier a child learns to read, the better off he or she will be; however, there is questionable value in formal reading instruction for the preschooler (Brekke et al., 1973). As reading does depend on the previously listed developmental factors, it should be noted that this is a highly individual task. Reading failure can cause serious problems because of its highly public nature, particularly in relation to school achievement. Individual children learn at their own rate and should be allowed to learn at the most appropriate time for them, not just because all the children in first grade or in kindergarten are at this point supposed to be attaining a specific reading skill. A sense of competency is enhanced when the children are allowed to proceed at the pace most appropriate for their individual development levels.

Concept of Death   Children's concept of death solidifies with age and cognitive development. As children experience their world and are increasingly able to differentiate between inanimate and animate objects, they begin to believe that death is final and inevitable. The acquisition of time, space, quantity, and causality concepts forms the framework for understanding death as a natural and inevitable occurrence (Kastenbaum, 1972).

Nagy (1948), in a classic study of Hungarian children, found that the school age child tended to personify death (e.g., an angel, a frightened clown). This personification was further reflected in their games (e.g., run fast enough to outrun death). Nagy felt that personification provided protection for children from the reality of their own vulnerability.

While recent studies (Gartley and Bernasconi, 1967; Koocher, 1973) have not demonstrated this personification of death, Melear (1973) did find that the 4- to 10-year-olds he studied attributed biological functionings to the dead. Lack of personification may be due to cultural differences in coping structures, lack of experience with death, or early religious teachings and television (Gartley and Bernasconi, 1967; Koocher, 1973). Because a child's concept of death and cognitive development have been shown to be related, explanations of death should be simple and based on the child's cognitive level and past experience.

Moral Judgment and Behavior   Moral judgment and behavior develop with increased social and cognitive sophistication. Piaget essentially felt that the important aspect in morality was the tendency to accept and

by Debra Hymovich

Figure 5-9 This boy is burying a dead bird.

follow a system of rules that regulate personal behavior (Ginsburg and Opper, 1969). During the more egocentric stages, knowledge of the rules was minimal, with the child's own set of rules being developed and followed. At that point, having a good time and winning were equivalent. During the phase of concrete operations, children are developing a sense of cooperation, with a firmer grasp of rules. Cooperation has been interpreted to mean agreement with a partner about a common set of rules that are to be followed. Competition is present in that both parties attempt to win. Our society, particularly the middle-class urban society, generally defines success and adequacy in terms of competition, of doing better than someone else. It is tragic to note that some children feel that in order to succeed they have to be best, all of which can program failure, resulting in a sense of inadequacy and inferiority.

Children of 7 years become capable of cooperation because of decreased egocentricity and the ability to separate their own viewpoint from that of another. Cooperation in the early portion of this period generally is in following rules together, a mutuality; it is not cooperation to the point of collaboration to achieve an end goal for one person.

A phase of genuine cooperation, assisting someone else to win, or a collaborative effort to achieve a common goal, is not really established before 11 or 12 years of age (Maier, 1969). It is at that point that a thorough mastery of the rules has been achieved.

Confidence is developed further through the development of mutual respect of others and an awareness of the necessity of obedience. It is at this point that the moral values tend to be internalized. A sense of time and its relationship to events, in addition to being able to pull together previously acquired and practiced standards, assists in the internalization of moral values. The child internalizes comments by parents and elders as well as their standards and expectations. Hearsay and knowledge, plus practice, are assembled into a system that is internalized and by

FIGURE 5-10

by Debra Hymovich

which behavior is determined. The key adults in a child's life strengthen the integration of this system by their interpretations of his or her behavior. The growth of a moral outlook can be retarded through lack of explanation and guidance by key adults as well as adults dominating the child's sense of judgment.

Kohlberg (1972) believes that moral judgment is primarily a function of rational operations as well as the ability to empathize and the capacity for guilt. Moral judgment is the result of the individual's ability to perceive reality and utilize experiences. Morality requires a logical reasoning ability.

Moral development is determined by the amount and variety of the social experience as well as the opportunity to encounter other viewpoints and try different roles. Parents who seek the child's view and who assist in comparing viewpoints have been shown to have children with advanced moral judgment.

The school age child is functioning in the preconventional level of moral development (Kohlberg, 1971). At this level the individual responds to cultural rules and labels of good and bad. Right and wrong are defined in terms of punishment and reward. Children in stage one of this level have a punishment and obedience orientation, while stage two implies that the right action satisfies self and occasionally others. Piaget's concept of cooperation fits into this category.

The development of mutual respect is derived as a result of cooperation among children. Maier (1969) indicates that mutual respect is when two individuals attribute to each other equivalent personal value and do not confine themselves to evaluating each other's specific actions. Friendships based on esteem demonstrate mutual respect within them. The concept of mutual respect leads to a new form of moral feeling that is very different from the earlier stage of obedience due to external reasons. A whole new series of feelings previously unknown are demonstrated. Cheating is forbidden not because it is bad, but because it violates agreement among individuals; it is not fair play, it is outside the rules. Implications of lying and deceit are also recognized during this stage. Because rules among peer groups are the key to mutual respect, it is easy to see why deceit among friends is considered much more serious than lying to adults.

Religious Concepts   Religion and philosophy, while not as important to the school age child as to the adolescent, do occupy the school age child and in fact lay the foundation for his or her adolescent queries. A religious concept is the product of social interaction and cognitive development (Smart and Smart, 1972).

FIGURE 5-11   by Debra Hymovich

DEVELOPING SELF-AWARENESS AND A SATISFYING SENSE OF SELF

Mastery of neuromuscular and cognitive tasks is necessary for a sense of competency in the child. Based on successful completion of Erikson's stages of trust, autonomy, and initiative, the child is now in a situation where some concept of control over the environment has been developed. The basis for freedom of choice, hopefully successful choice, within a structured setting has been established. Curiosity and a desire for novelty stimulate learning and a sense of industry. All are related to a feeling of competence. One cannot view academic achievement as evidence of the satisfactory resolution of the crisis of industry versus inferiority. Peer interaction, the interaction with family and teacher, the interaction with the larger environment, and expectations of the social structures of school and church all bear on the ability to reach successful completion of this developmental stage.

Industry versus Inferiority   Mastery is the major theme of this developmental stage. According to Erikson (1963), this stage is polarized, with a sense of industry at one end and a sense of inferiority at the other. Between the ages of 7 to 11 years, the child is trying to resolve feelings of inferiority which are in essence caused by the fact of childhood. The method of resolution is to take advantage of all opportunities to learn by doing and to experiment with the skills and tools available (Maier, 1969). Abundant energies are devoted to self-improvement and conquest of people and things, with the drive to succeed always including a sense of the threat of failure. The threat of failure impels the child to work diligently to avoid the sense of inferiority that is felt when work is unsatisfactory. While a sense of inferiority and inadequacy is the unfavorable outcome of the sense of industry, children generally have some protection against overwhelming feelings of inferiority. A certain cognitive deceit provides a useful function in maintaining a sense of adequacy in the face of actual adult superiority. Excessive and unsuccessful competition with peers and siblings and failure in school can result in damage. Thus, it can be seen that in order to successfully complete this developmental task, a certain amount of success, both in peer relationships and in school or academic achievement, must be attained.

Self-Awareness Gellert's study (1962) of children's concepts of body parts and their functioning sheds some light on the developing awareness of self. Children usually know by the age of 7 years that the heart is

FIGURE 5-12 (*Courtesy of the University of Colorado School Nurse Practitioner Program.*)

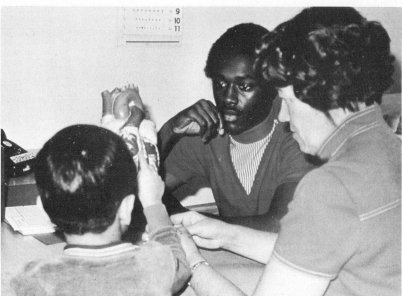

an important part of the body and they explain what the heart does in terms of describing how it beats and by vague statements that we need it in order to live; older children increasingly associate heart function with breathing, usually in a confused manner, and then with pumping blood. By age 13 most children explain what the heart does in terms of its pumping blood around the body. Almost one-half the children between the ages of 7 and 11 years thought the lungs were located in the neck, throat, or head. It was not until they were past the age of 10 years that the majority placed the lungs in the thoracic region. Below the age of 7 years, only one child reported the lungs had something to do with breathing; many younger children gave responses such as you need them to chew. By the age of 9 and 10 years, the majority were able to associate the activity of the lungs with breathing. Only about 15 percent of the children interviewed associated lung function with providing oxygen to the blood. Little was known about the nervous system before 9 years. By age 11 more than one-half the subjects were able to make accurate statements about the function of nerves.

In a study of 106 school age youngsters, Gellert et al. (1971) studied children's awareness of their bodily appearance by asking the children to identify themselves from pictures. They made several tentative conclusions about this group of white (87 percent) and Puerto Rican (13 percent) working and middle-class children; their conclusions are as follows.

1 From the age of 5 years on, children recognize front and profile perspectives of themselves in full-length photographs or mirror reflections.
2 Children below 7 years rarely recognize pictures of their physique from all three perspectives (anterior, posterior, and side) if they cannot see the head portion of the figures.
3 Between 9 and 10 years, children with relatively average body-builds can distinguish between anterior and posterior views of themselves and those of mature adults even when the head is not visible. From 10 to 12 years they can also distinguish their profile views.

Boys tended to refer to the chest, ribs, and bones as distinguishing features, while girls were more likely to refer to breasts, hips, thighs, and buttocks.

Self-Concept Children's self-concepts are developed by seeing themselves as others see them and through a sense of belonging to peer groups. Feelings of being liked or accepted by peers also contribute to their sense of self-worth. A lack of acceptance correlates with a lack of worth or esteem.

Competing against peers is a way of measuring up to standards and is another aspect of the development of self-concept. Successful competition with age mates assists the child in achieving a sense of adequacy. Academic achievement and self-esteem are also related. Self-esteem may be a major determinant in academic achievement (Williams and Cole, 1968). In his study, Coopersmith (1959) obtained a positive relationship between self-concept and academic achievement. Children with poor academic performance demonstrated a more negative view toward self than children with adequate performance (Black, 1974).

Self-appraisal has been shown to be significantly related to the group's appraisal, with communication from significant others affecting the child's self-concept (Williams and Cole, 1968). Peer acceptance is also important. Children with low degrees of social acceptance have shown more restless and showing-off types of behavior, while children with greater social acceptance exhibit more attentive and cooperative behaviors (Brown and Brown, 1976).

Self-concept is also related to social class, race, and sex and is shaped by people of all ages, including peers. With accumulation of experience and cognitive maturation, a child has a better understanding of the full meaning of being a member of a social class, a specific race, or a sex (Smart and Smart, 1972).

Locus of Control   In middle childhood, the child is developing a sense of control over the environment and learning to make viable choices between alternatives. In essence, the child perceives the extent as well as the location of control. Locus of control, or the perceived source of reinforcement for behavior, may be internal or external. The child with an internal locus of control believes that events are caused by self, while the child with an external locus of control believes that events are caused by others or by fate. There is variation in internal or external locus of control according to age as well as social class. Locus of control relates to achievement behavior and to the ability to delay gratification. If children believe that what they do will end in the expected result, they are more able to delay gratification and much more likely to develop a sense of competency. It is at this stage that children are searching for a meaning or an explanation of why things work. In asking questions, some of their sense of adequacy is enhanced, particularly if they get an answer or are allowed to discuss the questions they are asking.

Gender Identity and Sex Role By 5 years of age, gender identity and sex-role preference should be well established. Major activities during this period are often segregated into feminine and masculine roles, and boy-girl relationships are generally kept at a minimum. Our society is fairly flexible in allowing greater latitude to girls in terms of their sex-role behavior during childhood than to boys. It is not always acceptable for a boy to play with dolls, but a girl can be a "tomboy." Girls have greater range of play preferences than do boys, and boys generally will stick to masculine play activities. Our society has very definitely labeled certain activities masculine or feminine, and as children encounter these activities their gender concept will be influenced. The increasing awareness of this labeling has produced some changes, however, particularly in the areas of achievement motivation and success orientation. Children's evaluation of the sex role and the behavior appropriate to it will definitely affect their achievement behavior. It has been demonstrated that children, when given tasks defined as neuter, masculine, and feminine, will do best in the group that is appropriate for their sex and worse in the one that is inappropriate for their sex (Stein et al., 1971).

Feelings Expression of feelings is related to self-concept as well as to sex role. Girls are allowed considerable latitude in expressing feelings, while boys tend to be more restricted. For example, girls are permitted to cry if hurt, but boys are expected to be "brave" and not cry. This tends to be culturally as well as societally determined and is showing change over time.

LEARNING TO RELATE TO OTHERS

Social development is dependent upon the child's interaction with the expanding environment. While the family continues to be a major source for learning love and protection, the social and cultural institutions begin to be more important. Mass media, particularly television, also expand contacts outside the immediate home and neighborhood.

Communication Skills Articulation skills continue to develop so that by 7 or 8 years of age most children are operating close to an adult level. Children are now at a cognitive level that allows them to see things from another point of view, increasing their ability to conduct meaningful two-way conversations.

Family Relationships Relationships with parents may be difficult during the school age period. It is often more difficult for the parents, however, than for the child. It has been shown that the lowest point in satisfaction in family life for the husbands and wives comes when the oldest child is between 6 and 13 years (Burr, 1970). The satisfaction with children is also at the lowest point during this phase. Our mobile society and rapid change in expectations of individuals, and family, have caused roles to be constantly redefined. With the loss of the influence of the extended family, questions arise concerning parenting. What do parents want their children to become? What is the best way to help the child get there? How can a parent do it? How does the child meet the parents' standards?

Families are important to the school age child in two major areas. These are stimulation of cognitive development and the development of a sense of adequacy. Families promote intellectual growth by stimulating

FIGURE 5-13   by Debra Hymovich

a desire for achievement and through offering experiences by which growth can occur. This is essential in the development of a sense of industry. The higher the value a parent places on intellectual achievement, the more likely a sharing will take place with the child, an encouragement of the child, as well as interest in the child.

Children's belief in their own ability to control what happens to them is related to parents being consistent, warm, supportive, praising, and protective rather than dominating, rejecting, or critical. Some studies have suggested that the father's attitudes are more influential than the mother's in this regard (Davis and Phares, 1969; Parke, 1969; Perry and Parke, 1975).

Peer Interaction   Values, behavior, and attitudes are challenged and refined as the child comes into contact with his or her peer group. This can be a particularly difficult time for the child if the family and group values are in strong opposition. One can easily observe group influence in the school age child's tastes, dress, and modes of speech and action. Childhood games, humor, language, and motor coordination are learned through practice and imitation of group members.

Popularity in a group is due to many different reasons. Popular

FIGURE 5-14

by Debra Hymovich

FIGURE 5-15   by Elizabeth Tong

children have been found to expend much energy for group-approved purposes. Leaders within a group have been shown to be healthier, more aggressive, more intelligent, more active, and more gifted and are higher achievers. They generally are more socially adept and better adjusted and excel in physical, mental, or social development. The greatest contribution that peers make to children's development is a greater understanding of their social group (Smart and Smart, 1972).

SEXUALITY   Most interaction is with a same-sex group. Latency has traditionally been viewed as the time when sexual development halts because of the increasing range of interests and learning about the world and the external environment. Sexual interest is still present, however. It has been shown that there is no period in which the majority of boys and the great majority of girls are not interested in the opposite sex (SIECUS, 1976). Generally, an attachment to one's own sex occurs between 9 and 12 years and there is some exchange of genital manipulation and exploration during this period. Trauma results from adult responses that indicate this exploration of sexuality is dirty or evil. For boys, this period is probably a period of consolidating masculine identity rather than a true homosexual activity.

Much of the child's information gap is filled in by the peer group. Once the child reaches school age, sex education and sex-role learning are carried out largely by sex-segregated groups of children of similar ages, although there is some evidence that elementary school children are no longer as rigidly separated into same-sex groups as they once were (Udry, 1971).

FAMILY DEVELOPMENT

MEETING THE BASIC PHYSICAL NEEDS OF THE FAMILY

Providing for parental privacy and children's activities is often difficult during this period, especially for families living in crowded homes with no yards, few playgrounds, and busy streets. In lower-class neighborhoods, parents may find their only solution is letting their children roam the streets. Settlements and social clubs have programs, but these are often inadequate. Upper-class families usually have adequate space for the needs, interests, and privacy of both parents and children. Middle-class families, except those in apartments, usually have sufficient space, and many choose to move to the suburbs at this time to provide for more space.

In low- and moderate-income families, food, clothing, and medical costs are a large part of the budget. Other expenses include those fixed costs such as house payments or rent, car, utilities, and insurance. In addition, expenses for school lunches, allowances, dues, recreation, and the like eat into the family budget.

Older school age children may get occasional jobs in the neighborhood. Many mothers work; in fact, Waldman (1975, p. 64) reports that over half the mothers of school age children are working, most of them full time.

ASSISTING EACH FAMILY MEMBER DEVELOP HIS OR HER
INDIVIDUAL POTENTIAL

During the early school years, the family remains a strong influence in the child's continuing development. This is the setting where most children continue to learn values and competencies they will then try out with their peers.

FIGURE 5-16   by Elizabeth Tong

The child's school achievement depends on family factors, such as parental pressure for achievement, language models, guidance with academic studies, work habits, activities (stimulation) in the home for exploring the larger environment, and the intellectual interests and activities in the home (Bloom, 1965, p. 23, reported in Duvall, 1977).

In a nationwide study of mothers of first graders (Gallup, 1969, pp. 49–50) mothers of high-achieving children read aloud more to their children, talk longer with their children about school and other things of interest to the children, permit less use of television, play more mentally stimulating games, and see college as essential more often than do mothers of low-achieving children.

Parental tasks during this period are to help their youngsters develop their tools and skills, teach them the work principles and pleasures of work completion, help them adjust to the laws and rules outside the family, and help them develop their conscience and maintain their ideals while understanding the values of others.

During the middle years of childhood, parents readjust their own lives somewhat. Some may return to school, others revive old interests in hobbies and sports they share with their children. Mothers may resume old friendships, join clubs, or return to work. The child's widening social contacts also influence their parents' socialization as parents become involved in some group activities such as the PTA or scouting (Kestenberg, 1970).

Parents continue to serve as role models for their elementary school age children, although this role is now shared with other adults, especially the children's teachers. Some researchers suggest that in father-absent homes, boys may fail to develop appropriate sex-role behavior. Recent studies of boys reared in father-absent homes indicate a lack of masculinity or exaggerated attempts to prove masculinity, general immaturity, inadequate peer adjustment, dependency, and lack of social responsibility (Biller, 1971; Biller and Davids, 1973); these boys perform below grade level on measures of academic achievement, score higher on tests of verbal rather than mathematical ability (Carlsmith, 1964), score lower than average on tests of intellectual performance (Blanchard and Biller, 1971), and are more likely to become school dropouts and delinquents (Anderson, 1968).

Among the effects of father absence on girls, the following findings have been reported: these girls are more likely to have emotional problems and difficulties in school and to engage in antisocial "acting-out" behavior (Heckel, 1963) and that high school age daughters of widows tend to be shy and withdrawn and to begin dating later than most girls (Hetherington, 1972).

Interpreting these findings is difficult because father-absence cannot be isolated from other variables such as the mother's behavior and attitude, the cause of father absence, the personalities of the children, and interviewer bias. It is also important to keep in mind that many children do not manifest the behaviors described above. Many single mothers are able to compensate for the father's absence by providing for adult male models for their children through their friends and relatives and by arranging for participation in organized group activities such as scouting or team activities. From the studies of modeling behavior Bandura et al. (1963) conclude that when children are exposed to multiple role models, they select one or two as their primary models but do not imitate all the behaviors of any single individual. In fact, even when a father is present he may not serve as a significant role model for masculine behavior.

PROVIDING EMOTIONAL SUPPORT AND COMMUNICATING EFFECTIVELY WITH ALL FAMILY MEMBERS

According to two major studies recently published (Burr, 1970; Rollins and Feldman, 1970), marital satisfaction is at a low ebb during the school age period of family development. In Burr's study, ($N = 1471$ middle-class couples) parents indicated low levels of satisfaction with finances, sex, companionship, task performance, and relationships with children. In the Rollins and Feldman study of 1598 couples, fewer parents reported satisfaction in marriage "all the time" during this school age stage than at any other time in their child-rearing years. Significantly more wives also reported showing negative emotions, such as feeling resentful, misunderstood, or not needed, more often than at other times in their marriage.

As peer pressures and standards begin to take precedence over those of parents, children become increasingly independent of their parents. It becomes necessary at this stage for parents to learn to accept what may seem to them their school child's total rejection while at the same time the parents must not desert their child. Friedman and Friedman (1977) describe the parental task at this stage as "being there when needed without intruding unnecessarily."

Parents may react to their child's increasing assertion of independence by feeling hurt, angry, or disappointed. They may become more demonstrative or possessive as their school age child becomes more involved with peers than family. They may quiz the child about what is bothering him or her or yell at him or her for lack of filial devotion. Such measures are more likely to increase the child's participation with the gang (Stone and Church, 1973).

Although school children tend to overdo their independence from the home and family, the family continues to be an important emotional refuge, as well as a source of learning, entertainment, and companionship. They still need a great deal of parental support, unobtrusive support that is given with understanding and respect for the child's feelings and pride.

Communication problems may become more prominent at this stage as each child is struggling to establish his or her separate identity within the family (Koch, 1960). Sibling jealousies and conflicts reflect their struggle for parental attention, affection, recognition, status, and competition for other family resources (i.e., the television set). There are also periods of joint activities, sharing with each other, and "more or less harmonious sharing in wide-family enterprises and chores" (Stone and Church, 1973).

At the same time, sibling relationships also have an impact on the child's behavior because they serve as role models. Studies designed to look at the significance of birth order are difficult to interpret because of the multiple variables influencing birth order and the number of possible sibling combinations. However, several trends have been identified although they do not necessarily hold true for any specific family. Firstborn children tend to be more achievement-oriented, cooperative, and conforming to social pressures, to experience guilt feelings, and to encounter psychological problems. One possible explanation for this difference between first- and later-born children is the greater tension and anxiety often felt by parents of firstborns.

Children's perceptions of the child-rearing practices of their parents have been the subject of a number of investigations. Becker (1964) reviewed many of these studies and reported the following findings:

> ...(a) mother is usually seen as more loving and nurturant than father; (b) father is perceived as being stricter; (c) mothers are viewed as using more psychological control, especially with girls; (d) fathers are viewed as using more physical punishment, especially with boys; (e) the opposite-sexed parent is rated as more likely to grant autonomy than the same sexed parent; (f) boys feel they get punished more than other members of the family; (g) the same-sexed parent is seen as being less benevolent and more frustrating, particularly by older children; and (h) father is viewed as more fear-arousing. (p. 172)

Becker also points out that certain parental actions may produce opposite effects; for example, boys reared by strict discipline may become either extremely nonaggressive or extremely aggressive. Perhaps one of the most useful concepts is that there are certain risks with each form of discipline even though they result in the behavior the parent wants. Permissiveness may foster children who are outgoing, assertive, sociable, and intellectually striving, but it may also lead to less persistence and more aggressiveness. Strict discipline may result in children who are obedient and well-controlled, but they may also become fearful, dependent, and submissive. Pearlin (1971) found that parental pressure on working-class children to succeed in school resulted in cheating rather than working hard.

According to Gecken (1964), the longer couples have been married, and the older their offspring, the more the father cooperates with the mother in disciplining the children and in guiding their leisure activities. "The father who does not increase, or at the very least maintain, his participation in the activities of children as they mature is symptomatic of serious family malfunctioning" (Benson, 1968, p. 62).

A study of third- to sixth-grade boys (Zimmerman and Cervantes, 1960) found that children of parents who were both coercive and autonomy granting were successfully assertive in both academic and social settings. These data suggest that school children need both firm controls from their parents and a chance to prove themselves autonomous.

Armentrout and Burger (1972) asked fourth to eighth graders to describe the kinds of control they felt their parents used. From the fourth to the sixth grade, the children described a steady decrease in psychological control and an increasing use of rules. The establishment and enforcement of rules then decreased between the sixth and the eighth grades. The researchers hypothesize that as parents recognize the increasing autonomy of their children they replace psychological control techniques designed to make the child dependent on them with rule making and limit setting, and that once control has been established, rules can be relaxed somewhat.

Maintaining a Sense of Autonomy and Self-Worth Throughout this period, parents face the task of providing opportunities for their children to do things that are within their capabilities. Parents need to recognize children's commitment to the peer group and understand the importance of the group for the child's growth toward independence while trying to combat the negative teachings of the gang. Here, as at all ages, parents must be prepared to let the child try out some activities that the parents know will not be successful, to let the child make some mistakes and hopefully learn from making them. Overly cautious parents may be apt to curtail their child's activities for fear he or she may be injured.

Parents who are willing to let their children risk failure also need to be able to "support the child through the pain of failure and to help him learn the lessons it teaches, without rubbing it in" (Stone and Church, 1973, p. 380).

Relating to Members of the Extended Family Communications with relatives who live far away is usually maintained through letter writing, telephoning, visiting, gift giving, and sharing services when needed. School-aged children are old enough to visit relatives for a period of time without becoming homesick. They are able to take care of their own needs and interests now without continuous supervision.

MAINTAINING AND ADAPTING FAMILY ORGANIZATION AND MANAGEMENT TO MEET CHANGING NEEDS

Many established routines revolve around school and extracurricular activities as well as the work responsibilities of the parents. During middle childhood, children are generally expected to become more involved in helping with household chores.

When crises or unexpected events occur, these children become increasingly able to share in the responsibility of managing some tasks not ordinarily a part of their routine.

FIGURE 5-17   by Elizabeth Tong

FIGURE 5-18   by Debra Hymovich

FUNCTIONING IN THE COMMUNITY

As their child's world expands into the community, the parents are also likely to become more involved in community activities related to their children's needs and interests. Parents may be pressured to become actively involved in parent-teacher associations, youth groups, and "athletic and cultural functions" in which their children are taking part. As the family members carry out this task of wider community involvement, they mature together (Duvall, 1977).

When left to themselves, children make friends with a variety of different children. Parents believe "undesirable friends" can be discouraged when the other children tend toward violence or engage in disturbing or compulsive sex play or in lawless behavior when they are together (Brenton, 1975, p. 21). Allowing children to have contact with children from different social class, racial, and ethnic backgrounds broadens their personal experiences of the real world and helps them learn ways of coping with a variety of life situations.

EFFECT OF SELECTED VARIABLES ON DEVELOPMENT DURING MIDDLE CHILDHOOD

SEX DIFFERENCES

Differences between the sexes due to physical growth and development have previously been mentioned. There have been numerous studies of sex differences in achievement, aspiration, interests, and behaviors. In general, boys have shown a greater need for achievement (Walter and Margolf, 1951), have expected success at new tasks, have tended to project blame for intellectual failure to others (Crandall et al., 1962), and associated moral transgressions with fear rather than guilt (Hoffman, 1975). Girls, on the other hand, have been shown to value intellectual attainment more than boys, tended to assume blame for intellectual failure (Crandall et al., 1962), demonstrated greater consideration for others, and associated moral transgressions with guilt (Hoffman, 1975).

In a review of the literature, Maccoby and Jacklin (1974) found that differences in socializing abilities were primarily a matter of degree, with boys being highly oriented toward peer groups and congregating in larger groups whereas girls tended to associate in small groups of age mates. The sexes were also noted to be similar in overall self-satisfaction and self-confidence, equally proficient at discrimination and learning, and equally motivated for achievement, although boys tended to need an ego challenge for motivation. In addition, girls are observed to have greater verbal ability than boys, while boys have better visual-spatial abilities, are better at mathematics, and are more aggressive.

Boys' better spatial perception and orientation provide for their greater abilities in the areas of arithmetical reasoning and general information. Their problem-solving ability is generally greater than girls, which is probably due to their ego involvement (challenge) and their ability to utilize their visual-spatial cues effectively, as well as their arithmetical reasoning ability. In addition, boys tend to have a more favorable attitude toward problem solving, which is probably due to their ego challenge (Garai and Scheinfeld, 1968).

Aggressive behavior is attributed to the male role by both boys and girls (Sandidge and Friedland, 1975). This is probably the consequence of a society where aggression and competitiveness are rewarded in males. Mothers and fathers expect more aggression in their sons, and mothers have been noted to be more tolerant of both verbal protest and physical aggression toward them by sons (Baumrind and Black, 1967; Lambert et al., 1971; Rothbart and Maccoby, 1966; Sears et al., 1957; Tasch, 1952).

Boys have generally demonstrated a stronger and more distinctly traditional sex-role typing than girls (Hall and Keith, 1964). This is probably due to the greater amount of social pressure placed on boys against inappropriate sex typing. Girls generally have greater latitude in their activities. For example, girls can read both girls' and boys' books while boys should only read boys' books; girls can be tomboys, but boys should not play with dolls (Fling and Manosevitz, 1972; Hartley and Hardesty, 1964; Hartup and Moore, 1963; Lansky, 1967).

Generally, sex differences are based in the socialization process of children. As our society expands and changes its expectations of both the male and the female, it is anticipated that the differences noted will diminish.

Sex Differences and Achievement Behavior   While achievement behavior does show some sex differences, there are probably fewer differences for the school age child than for the adolescent. In the areas of visual-spatial abilities, males (adolescent and adults) have been shown to perform better than females; however, these findings have been inconsistent in childhood (Keogh and Ryan, 1971; Maccoby and Jacklin, 1974; Saarni, 1973; Witkin et al., 1967). In the areas of mathematical and verbal abilities fewer differences are consistently found until 11 or 12 years of age (Maccoby and Jacklin, 1974). This finding is also true in the area of risk taking. No significant differences between the sexes have been found before 10 or 11 years of age (Kopfstein, 1973; Slovic, 1966).

It has been hypothesized that boys and girls are motivated toward different types of achievement. That is, males achieve for the sake of achieving—task orientation—while females achieve for approval and affection—person orientation (Katkovsky et al., 1964). Maccoby and Jacklin (1974) do not feel that the existing research data support this hypothesis. They conclude that females are not affected by social reinforcement any more than are males. They do not feel that either sex showed greater sensitivity to others, either their needs or emotional states, or that praise affected one sex greater than the other. While they do not feel that either sex was more achievement motivated than the other, it was noted that males were more moved to achieve in a directly competitive situation.

Boys' belief in self-responsibility has generally been correlated well with scores on academic achievement tests. It is interesting to note, however, that boys' standards of excellence in terms of achievement are much more realistic than those of girls. Some characteristics of superior achievers are independence, increased persistence at tasks, high peer competition, fewer positive feelings towards siblings, and greater guilt feelings than average. A high self-esteem and positive self-concept are closely related to achievement behavior (Crandall et al., 1965).

TEMPERAMENT

The temperamental characteristics described by Thomas et al. (1968) affect school behavior as well as that in the home and need to be taken into account by teachers as well as parents. For the "difficult" child school entry and achievement were often major hurdles. "Easy" children did all right as long as the home and school environments were relatively close in terms of values, beliefs, and behaviors, but when markedly different created problems. For example, children who were socialized to be unaggressive and meticulously clean would be termed sissies in school.

"Slow to warm up" children had particular problems with school entry and may be seen as intellectually inferior by the teacher because of their unaggressiveness.

Finally, the child with a short attention span and a high activity level is likely to be labeled "brain damaged" and put on medication, while many can be handled appropriately with some modification of the classroom environment.

BIRTH ORDER AND ORDINAL POSITION

Studies have substantiated that firstborn and only children show greater educational attainment (Adams, 1972; Bradley, 1968). They attend college in greater numbers, are more likely to meet teachers' expectations, and exhibit more information-seeking behavior. They are seen by others as serious and low in aggression, which may increase achievement motivation and enhance performance (Bradley, 1968). Their superior academic achievement was more pronounced when siblings were close in age (Chittenden et al., 1968).

HEALTH

Central Nervous System Dysfunction   Of school children of average intelligence, 5 to 10 percent will have a specific learning problem and/or hyperactivity or other neurodevelopmental problems severe enough to require special assistance (Peters et al., 1973). Learning disabilities have been correlated with hyperactivity, as have behavior problems and immaturity (Safer and Allen, 1976).

The *hyperactive behavior syndrome* is characterized by: (1) distractibility, (2) short interest span, (3) motor restlessness, (4) impulsivity, (5) low frustration tolerance, (6) emotional lability, and (7) poor peer interaction. The key characteristic in the hyperactive behavior syndrome is distractibility, which means the child is overly sensitive to environmental stimuli (tactile, auditory, or visual). Stimuli cannot be screened out. Being interested in something will affect the length of the attention span. Motor restlessness is difficult to measure, but generally is defined as an increased amount of motor activity. Impulsivity is the characteristic usually described by parents as "he acts before he thinks." The stimulus for the child's action is internal and not obvious to the observer. A low frustration tolerance is common. The child has strong reactions to minor upsets. Responses to frustration are out of the expected proportion. Emotional lability is a rapid emotional shift probably larger in degree than the actual feelings of the child. The last characteristic, that of poor peer interaction, is of significance because of the long-term psychosocial consequences. These children generally have trouble establishing and maintaining social relationships. They appear unpredictable and aggressive and their behavior tends to isolate them.

CULTURAL FACTORS

Our heterogeneous society provides an educational system that is traditionally white, Anglo-Saxon, Protestant, and imbued with middle-class values. Children can thus have difficulties in achieving their developmental tasks when the forms of discipline and the expectations of the school system differ from the child's home environment.

These values can pose difficulties for the child placed in a highly competitive, future goal-oriented educational setting. In Texas alone, nearly half the Mexican-American students will leave school before graduation (Schulman et al., 1973). Behavior problems are less frequently a concern of Mexican Americans than in white children, however (Touliatos and Lindholm, 1976). A conflict of culture and values could disrupt the educational learning process.

STRESS AND CRISIS

Mobility The mobility of families is increasing. This means that schools are one of the major resocializing and reintegrating forces in the school child's life disrupted by a family move. The experience of being the "new kid on the block" may result in withdrawal behavior and reluctance to establish new close relationships for fear they may only again be disrupted.

Divorce and Marital Stress Divorce and marital stress may be the cause of apparent daydreaming in the classroom. It is quite common for children of separating or feuding parents to worry about their role in either causing the split or ways they can magically make it better. Frequent illness complaints, exacerbations of chronic illness, or academic problems may be reflecting a wish: "If I'm having trouble, they will have to pay attention to me and take their minds off their own arguments." The number of divorces surpassed 1 million in 1975 (Stack, 1976).

Disorganized Family Environment While the family environment has a lessened impact on the school age child, a disorganized family environment, particularly that caused by marital separation and divorce, has been shown to cause a wide spectrum of responses, especially in the early elementary age child. Kelly and Wallerstein (1976) have described the 7- and 8-year-old as being immobilized by parental sufferings. Initial responses include a pervasive sadness, fear, feelings of deprivation, strong desire for recognition, strong sense of loss in relation to the father, and considerable anger toward the mother for divorce, as well as fear of the powerful mother image. This group of children did not see themselves as the cause of the divorce but felt that the parent had left them. They had much difficulty in complying with demands to align themselves with one parent or another and frequently retained loyalty in secret and at great cost. Behaviors noted in school settings included crying, temper tantrums, sadness, and fearfulness.

In a study of older elementary children (Wallerstein and Kelly, 1976), conscious and intense anger was observed; however, it is significant to note that these children attempted to master feelings through activity and play. The anger was generally directed toward the person initiating the divorce. They exhibited a sense of outrage at what they considered to be immoral and irresponsible behavior. Fears were usually about being forgotten or abandoned, and their sense of identity was shaken. They were lonely and conflicts arose because of loyalties, while their attempts to refrain from choosing sides caused greater feelings of loneliness. Definite changes were noted. In school, academic performance and peer relationships deteriorated. Frequently, the behavior seen at school was the direct opposite of what was seen at home.

Illness, Hospitalization, and Death Illness, hospitalization, or death of a parent or sibling of a school child may manifest itself in altered school behavior or performance. One study of school absenteeism noted that the group of excessively absent children was more likely to have a parent who had been hospitalized in the past year for reasons other than childbirth. The same was true in a study of frequent school clinic utilizers (Van Arsdale, 1972).

School-aged children are prone to some of the same separation anxieties as younger children and to similar unrealistic as well as real fears. However, their individual sense of reality and their ability to communicate with adults helps them in handling these feelings. Regression in behavior occurs in the hospitalized youngster at this as well as at other ages. Of particular concern to these children is their separation from peers and missing school.

LIFE-THREATENING ILLNESS The threat of a potentially fatal illness can have a tremendous impact on a child's development. In addition, a life-threatening illness can cause much anxiety for the child and family. Frequent separations from family and peers due to hospitalizations, painful treatments, disfigurement, and loss of normal activity are all causes for fear and anxiety in the child. Family responses to the illness can cause feelings of isolation and hinder meaningful communication between parents and child (Binger et al., 1969). The anxiety felt by members of the helping profession can further increase the child's anxiety and feelings of isolation (Spinetta et al., 1973).

Because of the chronicity of many of these potentially fatal illnesses, the child, family, peers, and schools must cope with an almost constant stress. Interaction with peers may be limited or nonexistent if the child is unable to attend school, even irregularly, thus hindering social as well as cognitive development. The frequent hospitalizations as well as the debilitating effects of the disease and treatment process interrupt the educational process and cognitive development. School phobia is not infrequent (Lansky and Lawman, 1974). Family responses to the illness (anxiety, fear, overprotectiveness, guilt, resentment, and anger) can affect both psychological as well as social development. Marital discord, over-indulgent grandparents, and resentful siblings are possible family symptoms of the stress.

MASS MEDIA

See discussion in Chapter 1.

CLINICAL APPLICATIONS

Health Maintenance Activities: Collaboration with the Schools

After children reach age 4 to 5 years, families are not accustomed to using the physician's office or clinic for routine health maintenance activities. Most contacts with primary care providers for the school age group are for acute illness, except for an occasional physical examination clearance for participation in athletics or for attending summer camp. Yet, assessment and facilitation of the overall growth and development of the child should be an integral part of routine health maintenance procedures. In order to accomplish this optimal care, it will be necessary for primary health care providers to reach out to schools to develop creative approaches to health maintenance and problem-solving activities, since the school allows access to large numbers of children on an ongoing basis.

Although a great deal of screening and anticipatory guidance of both children and their parents can take place within the schools, many of the identified problems will need referrals to the appropriate health care provider either without or within the school team.

RATIONALE FOR APPROACHING THE CARE OF THE SCHOOL AGE
CHILD IN RELATION TO THE SCHOOL

Because almost all children attend school, it has a unique contribution to make in the overall development of the child. With the advent of recent legislation mandating equal educational opportunities for the handi-capped, this influence will spread to virtually every individual in our society. The simple logistics of individual versus group health promotion activities make it obvious that the primary health care provider can reach many more children and families by working with school personnel who, in turn, see more children on a daily basis than health care pro-viders could ever impact on a one-to-one basis.

Since one of the major goals of pediatric care is to help children grow and develop into individuals who can effectively self-manage their health, the role of education becomes central. This is another important reason for becoming involved with schools. Improving existing health resources and technology will increase health status only slightly. The majority of morbidity and mortality in our country today has its roots in life-style and decision-making choices that are often developed in the school age period (Preventive Medicine USA, 1976).

There are increasing resources in public schools today to deal with health education, health-related problems, and health problem detec-tion. The health care provider needs to learn how to work effectively with school nurses, aides, health educators, social workers, psychol-ogists, counselors, educational diagnosticians, and special educators. Many routine screening activities are now carried out in schools. Phys-ical health screening procedures often lend themselves to the school setting, especially if done by qualified personnel, and follow-up activities are initiated in the event a problem is discovered. Vision, hearing, growth, and scoliosis have been suggested as routine screening proce-dures appropriate for school programming. The value of the routine school physical examination is at best questionable. Tuberculosis screening is now rarely indicated, except in endemic areas or as an epidemiologic investigation. Some practitioners are now requesting regular teacher reports on their young clients beginning school. The pur-pose of these reports is to detect early difficulties in academic or social achievement. Early intervention could prevent a malicious cycle of fail-ure and poor self-image.

Helping Prepare Children and Parents for Separation

School entry represents a separation task for both the child and the par-ents. Successful anticipatory guidance during the preschool years should result in accomplishing the separation without difficulty. The primary care provider, having followed the family and child for several years, will know which families might be at high risk for difficulties in separation. School and health care personnel could jointly develop preschool "guided observation" courses to help parents become aware of the developmental needs of a child approaching school age. Groups for parents of entering kindergarten children could cover the social and academic stresses the child will be expected to encounter. Predicting the inevitable spread of upper respiratory infections that attend the grouping of young children might cause less concern for the inexperienced young parent.

Fostering a Positive Self-Concept in the Child

The task of industry versus inferiority, discussed earlier in this chapter, needs to be monitored by the provider of health care. The only way this can be accomplished is through regular, direct communication with the child's teachers. The feelings of self-confidence, positive self-concept, and success in competitive situations that develop or fail to develop during this critical time period can have long-lasting effects.

Planning Educational Programs for Parents, Children, and Teachers

Education for parents of school age children could be jointly developed by school and primary health care providers in a community. Included could be sessions on expected developmental events which often cause family concerns, including "stealing," "lying," the denigration of parent knowledge by the child in favor of the "always correct" teacher, and the "enrichment" of the child's vocabulary reflecting out-of-family contacts. Also, general courses for adults of the community dealing with some of the crisis events discussed below (e.g., divorce education) could be jointly developed.

Parents may need help in understanding the capabilities as well as limitations of their school age children. To help the children accomplish their developmental tasks, parents can be advised to involve their child in family decision making, responsibilities, and opportunities. Involvement in family discussions and joint planning including all family members is one way of helping these children to gain first-hand experience in the democratic process.

Smith and Brache (1963) designed an experimental program involving parents and teachers that significantly raised the achievement level of culturally deprived elementary children in Michigan. It was suggested that parents read to their children daily; listen to their children read; provide a regular quiet time each day for reading and study; provide pencils, paper, a notebook, and a dictionary for home study; and show their children that they value school achievement. In this study these

FIGURE 5-19 Children learning to be active participants in their health care. (*Courtesy of the University of Colorado School Nurse Practitioner Program. School nurse practitioners are engaged in orienting children/adolescents to stronger, more assertive health consumer roles. Specially designed materials and curricula are used by SNPs for these purposes.*)

suggestions were supplemented by booklets explaining techniques of reading aloud, helping children improve their study habits, and ways of developing favorable attitudes toward school.

The *health education* of school age children should focus on increasing the responsibility they feel to be involved in their own health care. In the practitioner's office or clinical setting this will include interviewing the school age child as well as the parents to assess the child's understanding of the presenting complaint and to reinforce appropriate ways of reacting to and handling it. In the school, the primary care provider should work with the nurse or teachers to help allow children to begin to make decisions about when they need to go to the nurse (Lewis and Lewis, 1977). Other school noncurricular approaches to health education include establishing programs for target groups with specific health or developmental needs (see below).

Sex education, begun in the preschool years, needs to continue throughout this school age period. Parents need to know what they believe are the morally and psychologically relevant standards for adult sexuality. They also need to know what to tell their children and how and when to tell them. School children do not give their parents as many clues to their questions as they did in the earlier years because they have picked up adults' attitudes which tend to make the child reluctant to express feelings or questions about sexuality. Parents can anticipate their child is picking up attitudes, information, and misinformation from peers, and if they wish their views to have priority, they should continue their instruction during the early phase of this stage. If frank discussion between child and parent is difficult, alternatives are available, such as books designed for young readers (e.g., Child Study Association, 1965), relatives, friends, clergy, health professionals, or teachers. The key to finding the appropriate person is that they have the requisite knowledge and sensitivity for the task.

Because of the increasing divorce rate a form of *divorce education* for school children may be warranted. A minimal effort in this direction would be in-service education for teachers on the impact and meaning of divorce for children. Teachers need support in order to deal effectively with children's feelings without invasion of the privacy of the particular child or family.

Teachers need help and support from the health care providers in being comfortable discussing death, illness, or hospitalization. There is more and more material available on death education for all age groups (Berg and Daugherty, 1973).

Enhancing Child Development through Extracurricular School Activities

ORGANIZED ATHLETICS

Organized athletics for older school age children of both sexes is often an area of concern for parents and not infrequently the subject of debate by proponents and antagonists of sports activities for the school age youngster (Sayre, 1975).

Many feel that the organization by adults of younger children's play activities into "leagues," with coaches, playoffs, championships, and even "cheerleaders," is a deplorable development and fraught with the dangers of undue psychological stress. Others argue that the "world" is competitive and that trying to accomplish a goal outweighs disadvantages if they are present.

The most important aspect of the primary care provider's participation in this aspect of the school age child's life is the prevention of any psychological or physical trauma that could have longer-lasting effects on the child's future functioning. The primary care provider's role and function with regard to these issues are twofold. The first responsibility is to the child and then to his or her family. There needs to be a judgment made about the developmental level and capabilities of the child and the child's desires. A separate assessment is made of the parental desires, expectations, and motivations. The primary care provider needs to make these assessments, and then counsel with the parents concerning any differences present.

A second function of the primary care provider is with school per-

FIGURE 5-20

by Debra Hymovich

sonnel or recreation (voluntary) personnel directly associated with the organized sports activities of a community. To what degree are those individuals knowledgeable about the sport under consideration? To what degree are those individuals knowledgeable about the physical and emotional maturity level of the children under their care and supervision? A checklist of questions to answer in helping to assess the question of participation of a school age child in an organized sporting activity includes the following. (1) Is there going to be good instruction and supervision in the activity? (2) Is the coach knowledgeable as well as a good "teacher" for the age group under consideration? (3) During practice and game sessions, if equipment is to be used, is it appropriate in size and safety requirements? (4) Is the playing area safe? Is the ground level? Is there broken glass or obstructions? (5) Are there any physical or health factors that need to be taken into account? (6) Are there any psychological factors that need to be taken into account? (7) Is the child already under a great deal of stress and likely to see participation as one more unrealistic expectation? (8) Will there be opportunity for the development of physical fitness (strength and endurance) appropriate to the age and development of the child? (9) If individual children are to be matched, is there assurance that they are appropriately matched in both size and skill?

Management of Common Stage-Related Problems

SPECIFIC SCHOOL-RELATED PROBLEMS: UNDERACHIEVEMENT,
SCHOOL FAILURE, AND LEARNING DISABILITIES

In a recent survey of parents of 2000 randomly selected school children, about 25 percent reported that their children have had some school problems (Haggerty et al., 1975). Many of these problems were characterized as "trouble reading," "trouble learning," "can't sit still," "won't learn," "daydreaming," "underachiever," and so on. Of those reporting trouble with school work, about 45 percent had academic and reading problems. Behavioral problems were thought by parents to be the cause of the trouble in about one-third of the cases. The current extent of school learning or behavior complaints presented to clinicians demands a close working relationship with schools, since both problem definition and resolution often depend upon the school environment and resources.

A Working Classification of School Problems The labels, diagnoses, and syndromes used to describe children with school problems include such terms as school failure, underachievement, learning disability, minimal cerebral dysfunction, psychoneurologic learning disability, mild mental retardation, dyslexia, dysgraphia, dyscalculia, adjustment reaction of childhood, and emotional disturbance.

A recent review has called attention to the multiple factors influencing a child's learning (Meier, 1976, pp. 92–95). The author finds that a working classification can aid the primary care provider in approaching the evaluation and care of such children. A school problem can, in reality, be any problem (family, health, or classroom behavior) that relates to, or is manifested in, school. A subset of these school problems can be characterized as *learning problems.* Such children are brought to attention because they are not learning up to the level expected of them by some adult (teacher or parent). The first task is to define the reality of that concern. By comparing a child's learning ability or potential with current achievement, one can determine whether performance is below that which one should reasonably expect, or whether the child is achieving at a level commensurate with ability. For example, a child with borderline or dull-normal intelligence may be achieving at a level equal to his or her mental age but below that of classmates. A child with average abilities is sometimes seen as a slow learner in a class where the mean intelligence scores, if measured, would be in the above-average or superior ranges.

Children with *learning disabilities* are those who are not achieving at a level equal to their overall normal abilities and, in addition, have demonstrable deficiencies in one or more subareas of cognitive functioning. Such functions are a key to new learning. These cognitive function areas often are at an age level much below the mean mental age of the child. For example, a 9-year-old child may have normal overall ability, but score like a 4-year-old on a test of auditory memory. This means that the child's rate of new learning is handicapped by the cognitive function of auditory memory. It is closer to that of a 4-year-old child. Most learning problems or learning disabilities are problems in central auditory or visual processing, such as attention and short-term memory rather than actually a "perceptual" distortion ("seeing" it wrong). By official definitions, a child with a learning disability must not have an obvious sensory or motor defect, be emotionally disturbed, or suffer from cultural deprivation. With regard to these latter stipulations, it is virtually impossible to find a school or family environment that has not in some way contributed to an emotional overlay and failure cycle in a child with a learning disability. Likewise, children from the lower socioeconomic classes who suffer cultural deprivation are also children who may be at higher risk for neurodevelopmental delays secondary to perinatal stresses.

Learning disabilities may be subcategorized as being either *developmental*, in which the child will eventually overcome the deficits required for new learning, or as *specific*, in which it is probable that the child will always have the deficit. Remediation is always indicated (see later) in order to prevent the failure syndrome.

It should also be noted that a child who is frankly *retarded* may also display wide variability in cognitive function, but on close examination, none are in the normal range. Such a child should not be thought of as having a learning disability, since the latter implies the potential for normal achievement.

The term hyperactive has been associated with learning problems. The *hyperactive child syndrome* is characterized by excessive motor activity, short attention span, impulsiveness, and distractibility. While hyperactivity is often a complaint of either parents or teachers, it should be remembered that it is sometimes a description of behavior, but never a diagnosis. Some of the syndrome's characteristics may also, but not always, be features of a learning problem. A common error is the labeling of aggressive behavior as hyperactive. It is essential to obtain details of specific behaviors in the history of a child presenting with hyperactivity.

Approach to the Evaluation and Management of a Child with School Problems The outcome of an evaluation of a child presenting with school problems is not an etiologic diagnosis. Diagnoses are sometimes crucial to defining important physical reasons for school problems (e.g., neurofibromatosis, Turner's syndrome, or post-cytomegalic inclusion disease). However, in most instances, the diagnosis alone will not necessarily help the child. It is necessary to develop a matrix of strengths and weaknesses for the child, the family, and the school resources. This matrix is then used to suggest the best or alternative methods of ongoing management and care. By specifying expected results and by follow-up it will also be possible to modify intervention plans (see Figure 5-21).

If the matrix is kept in mind, the primary care provider is required to contact the school in all phases of the evaluation and follow-up of the child. The first step in the evaluation is to determine how each party (child, family, and school) defines the problem, noting the language and terms used. Later, in communicating the results of the evaluation, it is important to relate them in terms that each used to define the original complaints.

The second step is the collection of a complete data base including all pertinent social, school, developmental, and medical history. Direct observation in class and/or reports from the child's teachers will be

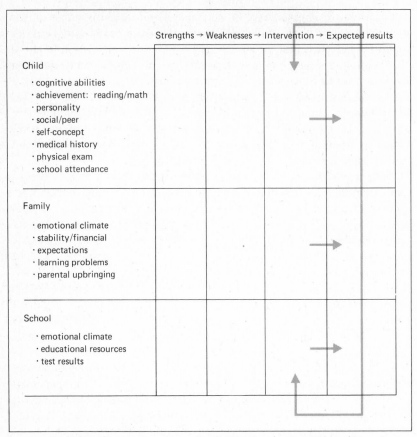

FIGURE 5-21 Matrix of care for child with school problems. The primary care provider may find the above matrix of use as a guide in constructing a profile of function for a child presenting with school problems. Each of the factors noted in the left columns are investigated and strengths (positive features) and weaknesses (negative features) of each are briefly described. This profile should yield the skeleton of the data needed to plan an intervention program with identifiable expected results or outcomes. The degree to which actual outcomes approach those desired will dictate modification or continuation of intervention plans.

valuable. The complete and detailed results of the child's individual testing and achievement will also be important. School resources need to be defined as do the criteria used to make them available to children. No child should be considered to be completely evaluated unless thorough physical and neurologic examinations are done, along with a recent test of vision and hearing acuity. Interpretation of psychoeducational testing is problematic for the untrained primary care provider. It is mandatory, therefore, for the school and care provider to work together. A glossary of frequently used tests and terms is presented in Appendix B. The educational implications of a test profile is what is important rather than the test results themselves.

The third step is to synthesize all the available information into a profile of strengths, weaknesses, and proposed plans for intervention (see Figure 5-21). A summary conference with the parents and child is used to delineate the nature of the difficulties and the plans for remediation. The use of terms such as "minimal brain dysfunction" adds little to parental understanding. The child is often concerned that he or she is "dumb," "retarded," "lazy," or "crazy." A simple reassurance that all children learn differently, that there is a real reason why new learning is difficult for them, and that the child, teachers, and parents are going to be working on the problem will often result in a measurable decrease in the anxiety and tenseness displayed by the child. In summarizing with school personnel, their role in decision making regarding specific resources or approaches must be respected. If a child is predominantly a visual learner (for example, has an auditory memory problem), then reading remediation should probably not be based on a system using entirely auditory processing channels.

The main principles of academic remediation are: (1) the child should be able to succeed without undue frustration; (2) the remediation should be specific (e.g., if a child has a reading problem, then the remediation exercises should deal with reading, not motor activities); and (3) most of the educational remediation should take place in the school and not in the home, thus permitting more appropriate activities between the parent and child (Kinsbourne, 1977). In working with school personnel to develop remediation progress, it is best to use inquiry techniques: "What do you think would be the best program?" rather than the directive "I want the child in a resource room for reading and math."

Review of the expected results of specific interventions should be measured against both short-term and long-term goals developed for each case. Examples of typical short-term goals include improved child behavior and attention, improved parent-child and/or teacher-child interaction, and an interruption of the failure cycle. Long-term goals may include improvement in overall academic achievement, improved family functioning, and appropriate long-term school placement. Long-term goals may also include the development in the child and family of skills necessary to cope with a static handicap or difficult situation.

The outcome of prompt recognition and appropriate intervention in cases of school problems should ultimately result in fewer dropouts, less delinquency (Tarnapol, 1970), and a decrease in the overall costs to society of the children who grow up "failing."

School Phobia   Many cases of school phobia can be and are handled by school personnel without any interaction with the primary care provider. Many children are seen and followed in a primary care setting for numerous somatic complaints without the question of school attendance ever arising. The need for a cooperative approach to the management and prevention of school phobia is apparent (Nader et al., 1975).

DEFINITIONS   School phobia does not mean a fear of school. The term applies to a variable-symptom picture consistent with underlying anxiety in a child who is excessively absent from school. It differs from truancy in that the child, if not in school, is at home. A truant child does not go home when out of school during the day.

ASSESSMENT AND MANAGEMENT   As soon as the possibility of the diagnosis of school phobia is raised, then an emergent aspect to the case arises. The longer the child remains out of school, the more difficult it will be to eventually get him or her back to school. Therefore, a fairly rapid assessment needs to be done for three areas. The first is the child: is there any illness, real or psychogenic? The second is an analysis of family communication systems: who is helping or not helping the child go back to school? The third relates to school factors: what are the child's abilities, grades, and peer interactions?

Management will not be successful unless parents, child, and key school personnel are included in an active treatment plan. The nurse, teacher, and principal need to be sure of the absence of any serious unrecognized medical problem. It is very important for the child not to be sent home due to illness complaints. Ongoing communication is essential not only to assess the outcome and success of management, but also to minimize the "resocialization" trauma due to the previous prolonged school absence. Counselors and other school personnel can be very supportive to the child for whom the return to school is truly terrifying and anxiety laden.

INDICATIONS AND PROCEDURES FOR REFERRAL   In preadolescent school phobia, referral may be required because more severe family or marital problems are interfering with a successful resolution of the problem. Referral of adolescent school phobia is almost always because of more serious psychopathology in the child (depression or schizophrenia). Widely divergent parental opinions which seem unresolvable in a reasonable period after initial counseling will require referral to some type of family counseling service.

Referral resources are determined by geographic, financial, and interpersonal trust factors. The family will require a great deal of support and confidence that their problem can be solved with the appropriate help. Direct communication between the primary care provider and the source of referral (private psychiatrist, child development or mental health clinic, social worker, psychologist, family service agency, and so on) is mandatory until it is known for sure that the family has been seen and treatment initiated. Someone must keep in contact with the family and school at least until the child has returned to school.

PREVENTION OF SCHOOL PHOBIA The primary care provider will need to be alert to family or life situations in which school phobia might develop. These could include: a child perceived as "delicate" or vulnerable; a chronically ill child; or a child who experienced prematurity or serious or frequent illnesses as an infant. Others might include: an observed overprotective parent-child interaction pattern; parental illness, hospitalization, death, separation, divorce, or other family crisis. An appropriate schedule for the development of child independence is suggested by Schmitt (1971, p. 440): "... being left alone by six months of age with adults other than the parents; being left with a sitter during waking hours by age two years; leaving the child in places other than at home by three years."

The primary care provider may also help to prevent school phobia in children by working as a school consultant. By alerting local school officials to the loss of student attendance and revenues, interest will be focused on this problem. A regular and periodic review of school absence data, including total days absent and pattern of "instances" of absence, should permit early identification of children developing a school phobia picture. The primary care provider can support school personnel in doing as much as they can before calling on outside help, since often it is the school itself that has the practical benefit of resolving the problem early. Other preventive activities based in the school could include discussions and meetings for groups of parents of kindergarten children who have had older siblings with excessive absenteeism. The topics would range from "usual and expected separation difficulties," to "common illnesses caught at school and how to manage them," to "the importance and meaning of school attendance." For "hard-core" families, more in-depth assessment of the family problems would be required in order to effectively intervene. The primary care provider could assist school personnel in outlining in-depth assessment procedures.

PSYCHOGENIC COMPLAINTS

One of the most frequently occurring complaints to school nurses is stomachache. After minor trauma, headache and stomachache were the most common reasons noted for visiting the nurses' office in school (McKevitt et al., 1977). Apley (1959), in another epidemiologic study, noted that its incidence in boys of school age was about 9 percent and for girls about 12 percent. Frequently, no specific serious organic problem can be detected. In fact, it may not be unusual for a child to present with abdominal pain, be diagnosed and treated for a viral gastroenteritis, recover because some school stress was removed, and yet the physician and patient are unaware of the real nature of the problem.

Because of the frequency of this troublesome symptom, and the potential dysfunction for the child's school participation due to the symptom, it pays the primary care provider to remain in close contact with the child's school in both the diagnostic and treatment phases of psychogenic somatic complaints.

Initial definitions of types of psychogenic complaints will help to clarify diagnostic considerations and decisions about evaluation and treatment.

Psychogenic pertains to symptoms or complaints secondary to psychological factors or caused by psychological factors. *Psychosomatic* refers to psychological processes that are associated with demonstrable somatic disease or pathological processes. *Conversion* symptoms are the result of a psychological mechanism in which an idea, fantasy, or wish is expressed in bodily terms rather than in verbal terms. The symptom is experienced by the individual physically rather than mentally (Engel, 1970). The process is not considered to be under voluntary control. *Malingering* is the presentation of a symptom or complaint by the child in order to accomplish a specific goal. The symptom complex or complaint is not based on a real perception, and is presumed to be under voluntary control.

Diagnostic and Management Considerations   Several factors are presumed to predispose a child to the likelihood of developing psychogenic symptoms. Some may be known, in a given case, by the primary health provider, but others would have to be determined from the family and school personnel. Some of these predisposing factors include developmental delays, a dependent child, illness in the family, an overachiever, an underachiever, and the child with poor peer relationships and low self-esteem.

It is necessary to differentiate a psychogenic symptom or complaint by the type (psychosomatic, conversion, or malingering) before initiating a treatment approach. Examples of classic *psychosomatic* complaints include that portion of symptom precipitation of asthma ascribed to emotional factors, and abdominal complaints associated with somatic changes (e.g., ulcer and increased motility of the gut). A minor degree of this example experienced by almost everyone is the feeling of "butterflies" in the stomach associated with anxiety over tests or a speech to be delivered in front of a large audience. This analogy is sometimes helpful in explaining to parents or children how a feeling can cause a real physical symptom. Close collaboration between health care provider and school is required in order that the school does not either unduly precipitate a psychosomatic illness, or that the child becomes too protected and suffers educational and social isolation.

In analyzing a complaint thought to represent a *conversion* symptom, several criteria need to be met before that conclusion is justified. These are: (1) There is often a precipitating event. (2) There is often a model for the complaint or symptom. This can be a close relative or friend, or it can be a previous illness the child has experienced. (3) There is evidence that the symptom results in a great deal of "secondary" gain or attention paid to the child as a result of the symptom. (4) The symptom is often presented in a very immature, dependent, or cute manner. The severity of the complaint is not matched by an appropriate feeling tone (e.g., a smiling child complaining of a "bad stomachache"). (5) Finally, the symptom complex is not coincident with anatomical or physiologic facts or function.

After a thorough evaluation including a complete history and physical examination, but only necessary laboratory tests, the major therapeutic effort is to reassure and to arrange follow-up not dependent on the presence of a symptom. The follow-up should be scheduled on a regular basis, and anything may be discussed with the child *except* the symptom. The complaint is ignored and the child is told that "these things eventually get better and go away" and that the child can "be brave and keep going even if uncomfortable." The question of symptomatic medication for relief of pain is often raised. Medication often reinforces sick-role behavior; however, if the symptom seems severe enough to limit functioning, symptomatic medication on an "as needed" basis may be used.

It should be the responsibility of the child to decide when to use it, and parents or teachers should not inquire about the health status of the child. The child should not be asked "how's your headache today?"

There are two main issues in dealing with a child thought to be *malingering*. One is the reaction of parents, health care providers, peers, and school personnel to the negative idea of fabrication. The other issue helps to counteract this reaction. It is the answer to the question: What is the child's goal in complaining? It often represents, at least in school, an acceptable "ticket" out of a stressful situation. Management then depends on an in-depth analysis of the causes of that stressful reason or environment. "In-depth" is stressed because the apparent or stated reason ("I don't like Mrs. Jones, the math teacher") is often not the real reason (a learning disability for math). School personnel, with the primary care provider's assistance, are often able to be quite supportive to children with psychogenic somatic complaints.

RESPIRATORY ILLNESS, STREPTOCOCCAL INFECTIONS, AND OTITIS MEDIA

Many symptoms of the most common pediatric illnesses do not come to the attention of the primary care provider. Recent household interviews conducted as part of the National Health Survey reveal that respiratory conditions affect over 30 million children yearly.

Two complications of upper respiratory infection, namely streptococcal infection and otitis media, have special implications for the school age child. Both represent serious health hazards, especially among low-income groups who have more nutritional and other health problems. This group also has less access to appropriate detection, treatment, and follow-up services from health care providers. Streptococcal infections can result in loss of school days as well as the morbidity associated with poststreptococcal illnesses. Otitis media, if chronic or repeated, also has well-documented functional (hearing loss) and educational (poor achievement) consequences (National Academy of Science, 1973).

Primary health care providers could support efforts with schools in the community fortunate enough to have school nurses or nurse practitioners to develop their skills to assist in the detection and follow-up of these problems. Primary care providers and health departments could make streptococcal screening culture facilities available to school nurses and prepare them to culture children meeting agreed-upon criteria. Symptomatic children with positive cultures could then be referred to primary care resources for treatment. Likewise, nurses and nurse practitioners could observe and interpret the physical findings associated

MIDDLE CHILDHOOD

with acute and chronic otitis. The school often provides good facilities for auditory acuity screening which could be done at the request of the primary care provider noting the repeated occurrence of otitis media.

ACCIDENTS

Accidents remain the chief cause of death among children 5 to 14 years of age. Motor vehicle accident–associated mortality was 10.6 per 1000 in 1973. For all other accidents, the rate was 10.2 per 1000 children (Newberger et al., 1976). Estimates range from 3 to 10 million children who are disabled either temporarily or permanently from accidents. About one-third the accidents that happen to children occur at school, and it is estimated that over 2 million school days are lost annually due to accidents. Low-income children seem to be at higher risk for accidents.

Primary care providers and schools have been relatively unsuccessful in moving from simple accident protection and treatment programs to education and prevention of accidents. The latter requires a better understanding of the factors which are likely to contribute to an accident and ways to influence these predisposing factors. It is evident that age and sex, the particular injuring agents, and the physical and social environment of the child are important factors in approaching the prevention of accidents.

Preventive efforts by others could possibly be more effective than those of the individual clinician alone. Primary care providers could assist schools and other community agencies by helping identify the major causes of accidental mortality and morbidity in a particular community and school. Local or regional offices of the National Safety Council will be of assistance. By becoming actively involved with community groups such as the school, the primary care provider can help ensure a safe environment for the developing school age child. Special attention should be given to the following areas: (1) motor vehicle accidents (local statistics on ages, drivers, locations, and circumstances of both driver and pedestrian accidents); (2) bicycle accidents (same); (3) school accidents (frequency by type of injury, location, circumstances, and resulting loss of school attendance; most schools are required to report all accidents on an annual basis to their state education agency); (4) drownings—especially important in coastal, lake, or resort areas (Does the local school in such areas have a graduation requirement for demonstrating the water skills necessary to avoid drowning?); (5) firearms; and (6) sports and recreational activities (What are the local provisions for preparation and safety of youthful participants?).

CHILD AND FAMILY DEVELOPMENT

ENURESIS

By definition, enuresis, or the involuntary discharge of urine, occurs only in school age or older children. Several authors state that the diagnosis should not be made in girls before age 5 and in boys before age 6. However, daytime wetting in school, or diurnal enuresis, only rarely occurs, and is usually associated in younger school age children with stress or preoccupation with play. Persistent daytime wetting usually suggests a pathologic condition. Primary enuresis (those children never consistently dry) is contrasted with secondary enuresis (those children who were dry for at least 3 months then "relapsed"). Boys and families from lower socioeconomic and educational status seem to be more affected.

Many factors influence the presence of enuresis. It is important for the primary care provider to realize that the presence of enuresis in itself is not tantamount to diagnosing a psychological problem or personality disorder. While the symptom of enuresis may be one of many manifestations of emotional illness, the others need to be readily identifiable before attributing the enuresis solely to an emotional cause. Cohen (1975), in his review of enuresis, states:

> The theory that enuresis represents an hereditary delay in the development of adequate neuromuscular maturation to maintain consistent bladder control is supported by: (1) the demonstration of a small functional bladder capacity in enuretic children; (2) increased frequency of voiding and urgency to void in enuretic children; (3) the undeniable hereditary aspect of enuresis; and (4) the high incidence of spontaneous cures or developmental maturation.

Because it rarely occurs in school and usually is not related to school factors, there needs to be little or no interaction with the school in the evaluation or management of enuresis. Those children with the rare diurnal enuresis may need to have their primary care provider ensure adequate access to lavatory facilities, privacy for changing or drying clothes, if necessary, and guarding from ridicule by staff or peers.

Most cases of enuresis can be totally and effectively evaluated and treated by the primary care provider. A thorough history, physical examination, and routine urinalysis will usually identify those few who may need more invasive procedures or referrals to subspecialists. Contrast radiographic studies are only indicated if there is significant evidence of functional or anatomical pathology by history or examination.

Whether the primary care provider utilizes behavior modification and conditioning devices, support and counseling, and/or medication, the guiding principles of treatment are twofold: (1) the enuresis will eventually stop, and (2) the child will feel increasingly responsible and be an important participant in what treatment program is developed. An important first step is to determine who (child, parent, or health care provider) is most concerned and worried about the symptom. The vigor with which treatment is pursued will depend upon the age and capabilities of the given child and family, and also the degree to which other areas of the child's development are affected by the presence of the symptom. Imipramine (Kardish et al., 1968) has been reported to be effective in about one-half those children over 12 years of age who take the medication (25 to 50 milligrams) about 30 minutes before bedtime. Too much emphasis on the symptom and elaborate rituals about going to the bathroom, bladder exercises, rewards, and so on, only exacerbate the symptom and prolong the uncomplicated natural history and resolution of the symptom.

ENCOPRESIS

Fecal soiling is not rare in pediatric practice, but its presence in the school age child is more unusual and usually indicative of an abnormal persistence of rebellious resistance to parental authority, a phase of development normally found in the 2-year-old child. Fecal soiling at school age may only be occasional or it may occur daily or even several times a day. It rarely occurs at school, but may occur on the way home or near the end of the school day. When occurring at school or at home it usually is easily noticeable because of the odor, and not infrequently creates feelings of disgust, strife, and ridicule. As a result, the child often hides movements or soiled clothes, which in turn further aggravates adult reaction.

Most organic causes of constipation and fecal retention are diagnosed before school age. Encopresis in the school age child is a symptom of anxiety, anger, or feelings of deprivation of love and caring from parents. Faulty bowel training in normal children or lack of training in environmentally deprived children or children of lowest mental abilities may also be causative factors (Levine and Bakow, 1976).

Management of the school age child with fecal soiling will center on the alleviation, if possible, of the contributing emotional factors. Regular bowel habit patterns need to be established, and supportive counseling is always indicated. The active involvement of the child in the treatment plan is important, but parental involvement in counseling is usually mandatory in order to overcome this symptom. Psychiatric referral may be helpful. The primary care provider can approach the problem with the realization that eventually the symptom will disappear. The crucial issue is whether the associated factors can also be improved in order that the child grow to an optimal emotional and social functional state. School personnel will often need a great deal of support from the health care provider to, in turn, be supportive of such a child, and to avoid unwittingly reinforcing the symptom.

PARENT-CHILD RELATIONSHIPS

Whenever difficulties occur in the parent-child relationship, a thorough family history is indicated. Observations of the relationship during the office visit also provide clues to the potential problem. The health provider then needs to identify the parenting style for the parents and encourage them to talk about their ideas about parenting. In keeping with Missildine's "mutual respect balance," Colley (1978) recommends the following guidelines.

1 Give attention to the child for positive behavior and not just negative behavior.
2 Clearly define limits for the child.
3 Be firm and consistent in enforcing limits but avoid lecturing, scolding, belittling, or moralizing.
4 Isolate all children involved in an uproar until they think they can settle the argument peacefully.
5 The child should be made to pay for anything broken, stolen, marred, or lost. "Restitution can be made by extra work or deduction from allowance."
6 The child's chores should be clustered around one time period so he or she is not on constant call.
7 There should be a specified study time without the radio or television. This should begin about the third grade.
8 Leave the child alone on things that are his or hers.
9 Do not cater to the child, especially after the preschool years.
10 Train the child in self-respect by setting limits on self-belittling.
11 Parents need a time away from their children.

Early intervention can usually modify a potential family imbalance. Families with long-standing imbalance often find themselves invested in trying to maintain this imbalance and therefore do not follow the guidelines consistently. Parents who are self-belittling or lack inner self-control need help in working through this before they can be expected to help their children modify their behavior.

When disruptions in family relationships occur, the health professional is in a position to facilitate the family members in expression and working through their feelings toward each other. The goal of such discussions is to help them develop positive feelings toward each other (Brown, 1978).

Parent guidance may include a variety of approaches, including education, clarification, advice, persuasion, permission, facilitation, channeling or manipulating feelings, modeling behavior, or psychotherapeutic techniques (Arnold, 1978). The choice of intervention depends upon the nature of the problem, as well as the parents' personalities, strengths, and expectations.

Guidance may be indirect, in which the health professional acts as a sounding board, reflector, or clarifier for the family, or it may be of a more direct nature. Advice can be given directly, suggested as a request, or by suggesting contingencies, i.e., "if you wish to stop his tantrums, it would be necessary to stop giving in to him each time he has one." The degree of directiveness should depend upon the wishes of the parents.

Arnold (1978) suggests that when the professional is suggesting the parents do things the child probably will not like, such as being firmer, inflicting punishment, or depriving the child of something pleasant but harmful, that this advice be given in front of the child. In this way the professional takes some of the blame rather than the parents, and the parents, especially those who are ambivalent or guilt ridden, are more likely to carry out the suggestion. On the other hand, if the professional is suggesting something the child will find pleasant, such as relaxing restrictions, this should be done privately without having the child present. Thus, the parents can take full credit for these pleasant changes and will not be in a bind if they are not carried out.

Parents should have developed habits of praising and encouraging their children long before their children reach school age. However, it behooves the clinician to assess this aspect of parent-child communication, particularly if the child is having difficulty in school. Douglas (1964) found that among English families whose children were doing well in school, parental encouragement was the single best predictor of academic achievement. Parents can be encouraged to learn about their child's school progress (strengths and weaknesses) in order to set realistic expectations that are neither too high nor too low for their children. Children who see their parents reading, discussing, and listening to others will tend to imitate these activities. Such participation should be welcomed and encouraged by parents. In addition, parents should plan or select activities that will challenge their child's mental abilities, thus fostering cognitive development. In doing this the parents need to provide means for assisting their children solve these new problems by providing a place for them to study, reference materials, and time for discussion. Trips to places such as museums and zoos provide opportunities for stimulating cognitive growth.

Parents may need help in understanding the importance of the peer group and its role in fostering growth toward independence. In helping their youngsters develop, parents need to let them try some things they know will not be successful, to let them make some mistakes, and hopefully to learn from mistakes. Parents will need to support their child through their failures and learn from their mistakes without saying, "I told you so."

Anticipatory guidance can help parents understand the behavior patterns of the school age child and set appropriate limits. Since interests often shift rapidly at this time, parents might be wise to let their child select one or two activities to pursue rather than having too many at once.

Helping Families Cope with Stress and Crisis

CHRONIC AND HANDICAPPING CONDITIONS

The distinguishing features between the terms disease (the pathophysiological process underlying the condition), disability (the direct behavioral manifestation of the illness), and handicap (the socially determined limitation of performance of specific activities) (Pless and Pinkerton, 1975) are important, for it is often the degree to which the "disability" and the "handicap" interfere with normal school age activities that spell the ultimate adjustment to having a chronic illness.

It is estimated that there are over 6 million school age children with handicaps in the United States, with perhaps only 50 percent actually receiving services (see Table 5-2). Federal legislation has recently mandated equal public school educational opportunity for all handicapped children in what is termed the "least restrictive" environment. This means that a disabled child will be placed in as normal a classroom setting as it is possible to do. This will demand closer working relationships between providers of health care and schools.

Several areas of activity and cooperation between health care providers and schools are immediately apparent when considering care of children with chronic illnesses and handicaps. The first area is *detection* of the child and *notification* of the school where the child likely will be educated. In some states, school programs are being developed for disabled or handicapped children as young as 3 years of age. A second area is the joint *planning* of services and of an educational program. This will require sharing, with parental permission, appropriate information with

TABLE 5-2
Estimated Number of Handicapped Children Served* and Unserved
by Type of Handicap

Condition	1974–1975 Total handicapped children served and unserved†	Percentage served
Total age 0–19	7,886,000	50
Total age 6–19	6,699,000	55
Total age 0–5	1,187,000	22
Speech impaired	2,293,000	81
Mentally retarded	1,507,000	83
Learning disabilities	1,966,000	12
Emotionally disturbed	1,310,000	18
Crippled and other health-impaired	328,000	72
Deaf	49,000	71
Hard of hearing	328,000	18
Visually handicapped	66,000	59
Deaf-blind and other multihandicapped	40,000	33

* Estimated total numbers of handicapped children served—obtained from State Education Agency's (SEA) Fall and Winter 1975. Information by type of handicap was not available and is projected from data provided by SEA's for school year 1972–73.
† Total number of handicapped children ages 0 to 19 provided on basis of estimates obtained from various sources, including national agencies and organizations and state and local directors of special education. According to these sources, the incidence levels by types of handicap are as follows: speech impaired 3.5%, mentally retarded 2.3%, learning disabled 3.0%, emotionally disturbed 2.0%, crippled and other health-impaired 0.5%, deaf 0.08%, hard of hearing 0.5%, visually handicapped 0.1%, deaf-blind and other multihandicapped 0.06%. The total number of handicapped children in the above categories represents 12.035% of all school age children from 6 to 19 and 6.018% of all children age 0 to 5 years. The population figures to which the incidence rates were applied were obtained from the Bureau of Census and reflect the population as of July 1, 1974.
SOURCE: Committee on School Health, *School health: A guide for health professionals.* Evanston, Ill., American Academy of Pediatrics, 1977. (Reprinted with permission.)

the school. The information cannot contain medical jargon, and it should be relevant to the educational management and needs of the child.

The school needs to receive the following information: the diagnosis and a brief description, in plain terms, of what it means; the frequency and nature of ongoing treatment and/or medication; and notation of any special modification of the school program related to the above items. Other information should include a description of the child's receptive and expressive communication skills, and, if known, the academic level and learning style (e.g., impulsiveness, attention span). Special modifications of the academic program that are needed in connection with this information should be noted. Finally, the child's realistic limitations in the following daily living activities should be noted: mobility, use of upper extremities, dressing, feeding, grooming and hygiene; and awareness of safety hazards. Opportunity for continuous dialogue should be established at the initial contact.

Another area of joint activity in relation to chronic illness is that of the mutual education of both educators and health care providers. The latter can learn how educational programs can facilitate the handicapped child's learning of life skills and coping with the chronic condition. Educators, in turn, will become more comfortable in working with children with chronic conditions if they understand the nature of the problems and the extent of the limitations.

A final area of activity between health care providers and educators is the assessment of outcomes of care for chronically ill children (Starfield, 1974). Many of the objectives of health care may best be assessed by independent (teacher) observations of a child's daily behavior among peers and when engaged in the work tasks of school. Frequency of absence may reflect the degree to which the condition is interfering with a normal activity such as going to school. The self-concept and anxiety of children with chronic conditions could also be monitored in the school setting.

Since siblings of the chronically ill are likely to be affected in a variety of ways, they should be considered at risk for potential problems. Among the reported difficulties are curtailment of social activities, reluctance to invite friends home (Kew, 1975), increased somatic complaints, and deterioration in school performance (Pless and Pinkerton, 1975).

Obesity Depending upon the definition employed, the measurements used, and the populations investigated, between 2 and 20 percent of school age children will be found to be obese (Neumann, 1977). This state is likely to persist into adulthood for most obese school age children.

It has been suggested that prevention of obesity is the only approach that is likely to hold promise, since most approaches toward treatment have proven unsuccessful. The negative social attitudes often surrounding the obese school age child far outweigh the actual physical health hazards. These negative reactions of peers, teacher, and, at times, even parents, reinforce a low self-esteem that may already be present.

A joint approach between health care providers and schools could build on the little evidence that exists to indicate that moderate success can sometimes be obtained (Seltzer and Mager, 1970). The approach

FIGURE 5-22 *(Courtesy of the University of Colorado School Nurse Practitioner Program.)*

utilizes several key ideas: (1) self-help groups of obese children are organized; (2) educational materials developed to improve self-concept are utilized in these groups; (3) exercise and activity are included through specialized physical education programs; and (4) very little emphasis is placed on diet or monitoring of weight. Before participating in the school groups, each child should be carefully screened by school personnel and by the primary care provider for any unmet health or psychological needs. Ongoing support and communication will be needed for such programs to be continued in the school setting.

Asthma   Childhood asthma is one of the most common chronic physical illnesses affecting school children. It is the single illness most frequently identified as accounting for a large proportion of school absenteeism. While asthmatics vary in the seriousness of their illness, primary care providers are often acutely aware of the need for better understanding by parents and children of the prevention of the acute asthmatic attacks and better understanding of appropriate management of an attack of asthma

FIGURE 5-23   Health education class for asthmatic children with consulting practicing pediatrician participating.

FIGURE 5-24   Children and parents learning breathing exercises from the pediatric allergy fellow in the health education program for asthmatic children.

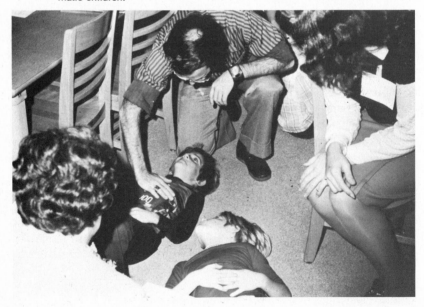

in order to avoid emergency office or hospital visits, or even hospitalization.

Because of the relatively high incidence of asthma, a school of 600 to 800 children may have 30 to 40 children with the illness. Recently, a health education program (Parcel and Nader, 1977) has been developed that is aimed at this target group, and joins the resources of health care providers and educational personnel in the following tasks: (1) to improve the child's and parents' knowledge of asthma and its pathophysiology; (2) to increase the child's and parents' ability to manage (prevent and treat) episodes of an acute asthmatic attack; and (3) to increase self-concept and belief that the child has control over the management of the condition.

Life-Threatening Illness   The child should be encouraged to maintain as normal a life as possible. This does not mean avoidance of discussion of the illness either within the family or between the parents and child. Stress and anxiety can be better coped with if the child can discuss the source and explore the feelings that the illness triggers. Open communication can decrease the sense of isolation that so often occurs (Koch et al., 1974; Samamiego et al., 1977). As has been noted previously, school age children understand death within the framework of their cognitive development. Not only can they be aware of the fact of personal death but this knowledge can be expressed both overtly and covertly (Waechter, 1971). Studies have also shown that even when the diagnosis is kept from the child, the knowledge of impending death is realized (Binger, et al., 1969; Spinetta, 1974).

Returning to and attending school as regularly as possible is important in achieving a sense of normalcy for the child. It is important that the teacher understand the nature of the illness and know the realistic limits of the child. In addition, the teachers need to be able to deal with their own personal feelings about death and dying. Assistance may also be needed in preparing classmates for the ill student's return. The school's support services (e.g., social worker, school nurse, counselor) can be of considerable assistance both to the teacher and to the health care provider. The school nurse, with knowledge of both educational and health care systems, can facilitate communication between educators and medical personnel. Maintenance of communication between all those concerned throughout the child's illness provides a support system and increases their ability to cope with the stress.

Hospitalization   Honesty and fairness are high in the value system of the school age child. Therefore, it is important to be honest in preparing and

CHILD AND FAMILY DEVELOPMENT

reassuring them in order to maintain the child's trust. Korsch (1975) indicates that depending on personality, anxiety level, and family patterns in terms of planning and discussing ahead, children may need a few days to even a few weeks preparation time. In general, information tends to be reassuring rather than frightening. However, the child's expressed concern and questions to parents and staff should be the guide in deciding how much to tell.

Provisions for continuing peer contact through letters, cards, and visiting should be made if the child is hospitalized or must remain at home for any length of time. It is also important to arrange for the child to keep up with school work in order not to fall behind the others.

Child Abuse   Several estimates indicate that school age children account for 20 to 30 percent of the total cases of child abuse reported annually. The school can be an important resource—not only for detection, screening, and reporting of child abuse, but also as a resource for monitoring child behavior and providing ongoing support for a child and his or her family. The primary care provider can inquire about the existence of a school policy on how suspected cases of child abuse are to be handled. Most states mandate such reporting, and all reports made in good faith are guaranteed immunity and confidentiality. A team approach is advised, including the teacher, an administrative officer, and the school nurse if one is available. Primary care providers may wish to be available as consultants to help arrange for the further family and child evaluations and treatment that are often required.

Appendix A:
NCHS Growth Charts

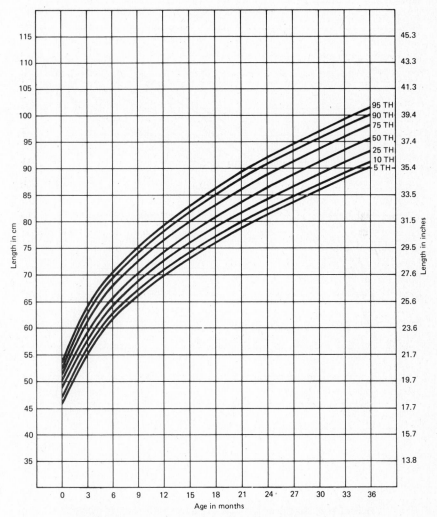

FIGURE A-1 Girls' length by age percentiles: ages birth–36 months. (*NCHS growth charts reprinted with permission from Monthly Vital Statistics Report, vol. 25, no. 3, June 22, 1976.*)

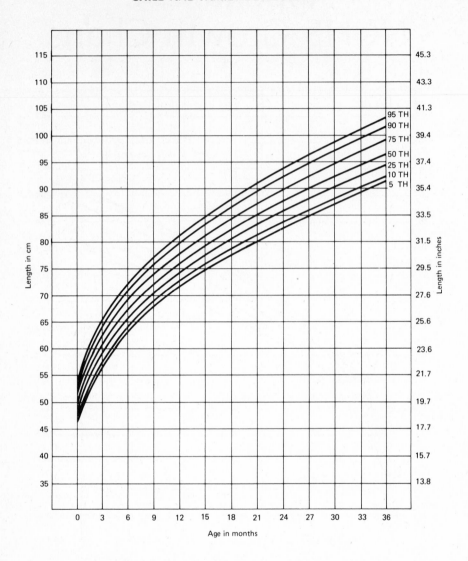

FIGURE A-2 Boys' length by age percentiles: ages birth–36 months. (*NCHS growth charts reprinted with permission from Monthly Vital Statistics Report, vol. 25, no. 3, June 22, 1976.*)

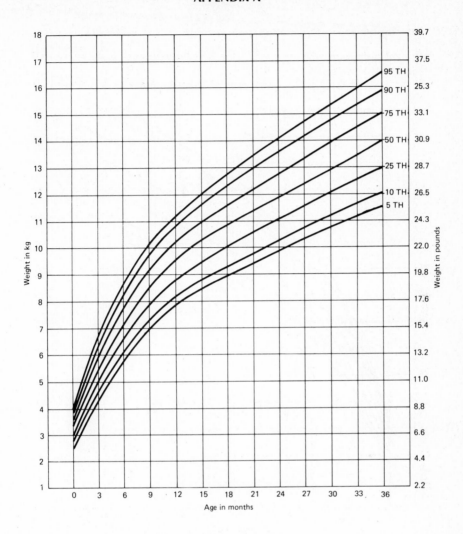

FIGURE A-3 Girls' weight by age percentiles: ages birth–36 months. (*NCHS growth charts reprinted with permission from Monthly Vital Statistics Report, vol. 25, no. 3, June 22, 1976.*)

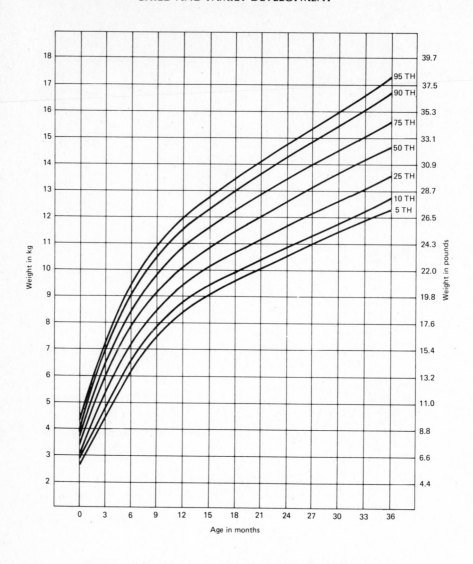

FIGURE A-4 Boys' weight by age percentiles: ages birth–36 months. (*NCHS growth charts reprinted with permission from Monthly Vital Statistics Report, vol. 25, no. 3, June 22, 1976.*)

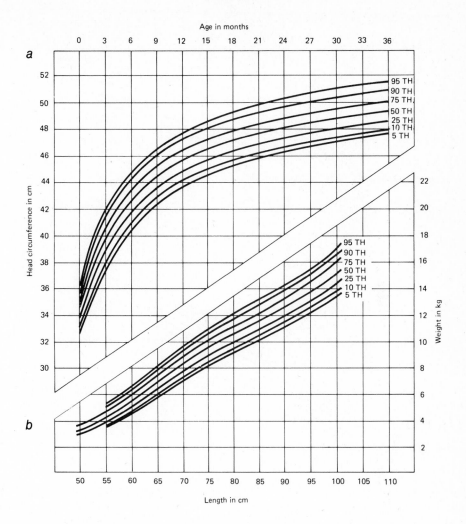

FIGURE A-5 (a) Girls' head circumference by age percentiles: ages birth–36 months. (b) Girls' weight by length percentiles: ages birth–36 months. (*NCHS growth charts reprinted with permission from Monthly Vital Statistics Report, vol. 25, no. 3, June 22, 1976.*)

CHILD AND FAMILY DEVELOPMENT

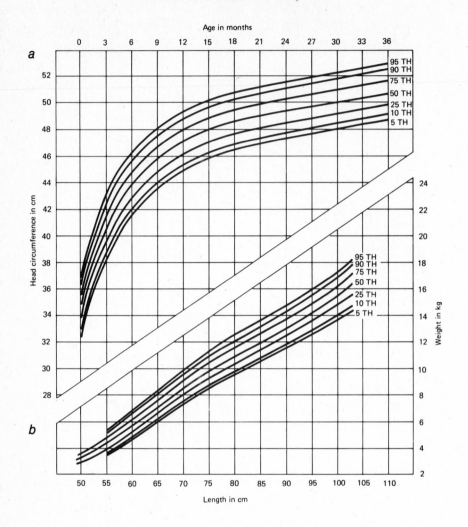

FIGURE A-6 (a) Boys' head circumference by age percentiles: ages birth–36 months. (b) Boys' weight by length percentiles: ages birth–36 months. (NCHS growth charts reprinted with permission from Monthly Vital Statistics Report, vol. 25, no. 3, June 22, 1976.)

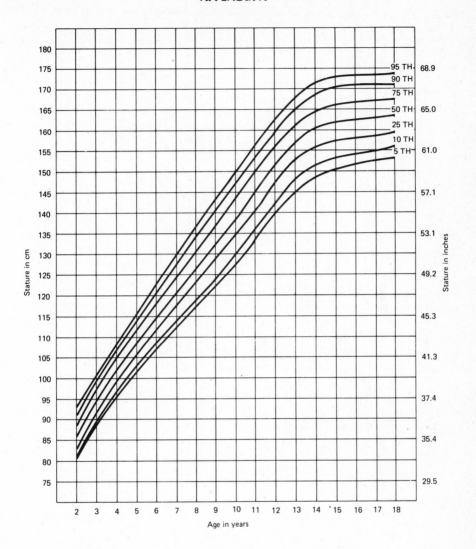

FIGURE A-7 Girls' stature by age percentiles: ages 2 to 18 years. (*NCHS growth charts reprinted with permission from Monthly Vital Statistics Report, vol. 25, no. 3, June 22, 1976.*)

CHILD AND FAMILY DEVELOPMENT

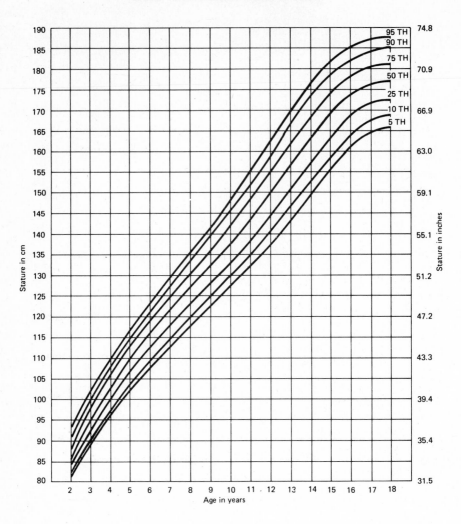

FIGURE A-8 Boys' stature by age percentiles: ages 2 to 18 years. (*NCHS growth charts reprinted with permission from Monthly Vital Statistics Report, vol. 25, no. 3, June 22, 1976.*)

APPENDIX A

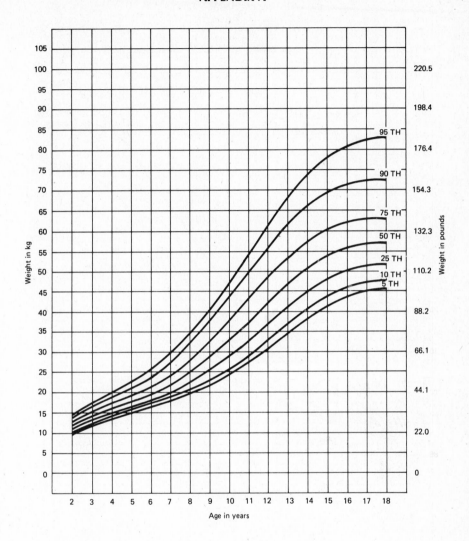

FIGURE A-9 Girls' weight by age percentiles: ages 2 to 18 years. (*NCHS growth charts reprinted with permission from Monthly Vital Statistics Report, vol. 25, no. 3, June 22, 1976.*)

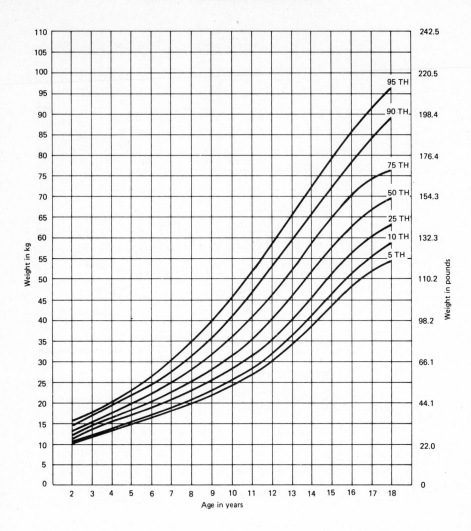

FIGURE A-10 Boys' weight by age percentiles: ages 2 to 18 years. *(NCHS growth charts reprinted with permission from Monthly Vital Statistics Report, vol. 25, no. 3, June 22, 1976.)*

APPENDIX A

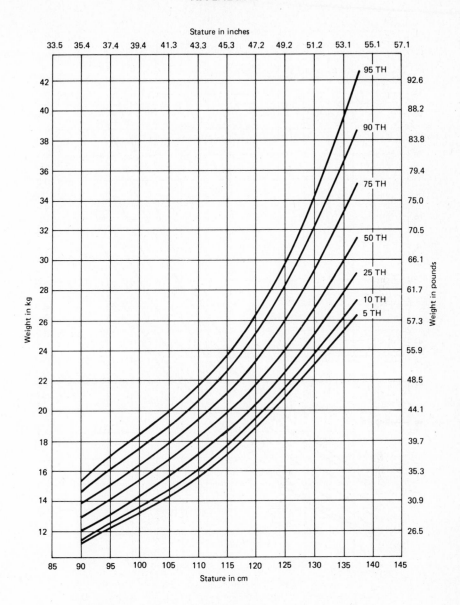

FIGURE A-11 Weight by stature percentiles for prepubertal girls. (*NCHS growth charts reprinted with permission from Monthly Vital Statistics Report, vol. 25, no. 3, June 22, 1976.*)

CHILD AND FAMILY DEVELOPMENT

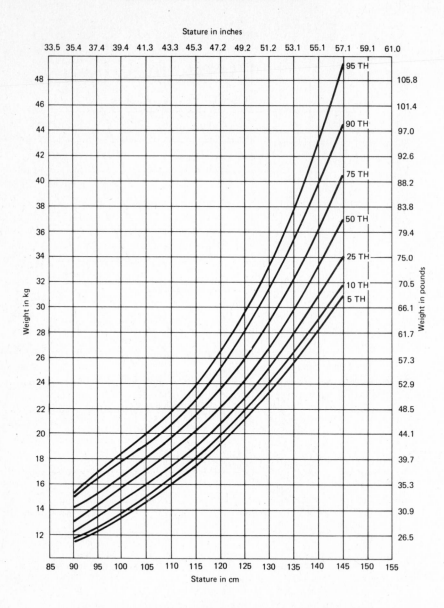

FIGURE A-12 Weight by stature percentiles for prepubertal boys. *(NCHS growth charts reprinted with permission from Monthly Vital Statistics Report, vol. 25, no. 3, June 22, 1976.)*

Appendix B:
Commonly Used
Psychoeducational
Tests

TABLE 1

Ability Measures

Wechsler scales (measures verbal and performance abilities)
    WAIS — Wechsler Adult Intelligence Scale, ages 16-0 through adult
    WPPSI — Preschool and Primary Scale of Intelligence, ages 4-0 to 6-0
    WISC-R — Wechsler Intelligence Scale for Children, revised, ages 6-10 to 16-11

Verbal:
1. Information: "From what animal do we get milk?" "Who discovered America?," etc.,
   obviously involves experience and culture as well as "intelligence"
2. Comprehension: "What is the thing to do if you cut your finger?" "Why are criminals
   locked up?," also influenced by culture and background and involves increasingly
   complex language reception and expression
3. Arithmetic: "Story" problems in increasingly difficult sequence require "following" a
   complicated story and remembering an oral sequence
4. Similarities: "In what way are a cat and mouse alike?", etc., tests ability to categorize
   and abstract
5. Vocabulary: Is simply a list of words from bicycle to imminent and aseptic, scored
   relative to age standards
6. Digit span (optional): Tests memory for an increasingly long span of digits, i.e., an
   auditory sequencing and memory task

Performance:
1. Picture completion: This requires child to notice what is missing from a picture, i.e., a
   cat with whiskers missing: checks figure/ground abilities and visual discrimination

TABLE 1
Ability Measures (Continued)

Performance: (Continued)

2 Picture arrangement: A set of pictures is arranged into a story, testing visual sequencing

3 Block design: Tests the ability to assess two-dimensional spatial relationships and manipulate these, a test of nonverbal abstraction

4 Object assembly: Putting together a puzzle, i.e., a car: must be able to organize parts into a whole

5 Coding: Requires translating a code and is a speed test so motor abilities are important as well as perception, spatial relations, visual memory, and attention

6 Mazes (optional): A test involving complicated oral directions, planning ahead visually and motor coordination

Binet (Stanford-Binet, Form L-M)
  Ages 2-0 through adult
Yields mental ages and verbal and performance abilities at 20 levels: test is considered to be more verbal than the Wechsler scales

Leiter (Leiter International Performance Scale)
  Ages preschool through adult
This test was developed as a measurement for the deaf as it is a nonverbal measurement. It is often used for those who speak a foreign language or those in whom verbal training is suspect, those for whom the Binet and Wechsler scales would not be appropriate as they are highly dependent on verbal skills, e.g., understanding and interpreting words.

TABLE 2
Language Measures

ITPA (Illinois Test of Psycholinguistic Ability)
Ages 2-3 to 10-3
Used to delineate specific language abilities. Serves as a model for evaluating learning processes and programming remedial approaches. Test yields overall language age and specific age levels for each of the following language skills:

1 Auditory reception: Assesses ability to derive meaning from verbally presented material. The response is kept at the level of "yes" or "no"; sample: "Do dogs eat?" "Do wingless birds soar?"
2 Visual reception: Assesses ability to gain meaning from visual symbols; stimulus picture on one page, four responses on second page: "See this?" (3 seconds) "Find one here"
3 Auditory-vocal association: Taps ability to relate concepts presented orally. "I cut with a saw. I pound with a ——" to which a child responds verbally with the word necessary to complete the sentence
4 Visual motor association: Taps ability to relate concepts presented visually. "What goes with this?" (pointing to a stimulus picture, e.g., a sock) "Which of these (pointing to four optional pictures, one of which is a shoe) goes with this?"
5 Verbal expression: Assumes ability of child to express concepts vocally; shown four familiar objects (ball, envelope, button, etc.) and asked "tell me all about this"
6 Manual expression: Assesses ability to express ideas manually; pictures of common objects, e.g., comb and mirror, are shown one at a time and child is asked "show me what to do with a comb and mirror"
7 Grammatic closure: Assesses ability to make use of redundancies of oral language in acquiring automatic habits for handling syntax and grammatic inflections: "Here is a dog; here are two ——"
8 Auditory closure: Assesses a child's ability to fill in missing parts which were deleted in auditory presentation and produce a complete word: "What am I talking about? bo/le? tele/one?"
9 Sound blending: Assesses ability to synthesize separate parts of the word and produce integrated whole; sounds are spoken singly (e.g., sh-oo) and child is asked to tell what the word is
10 Visual closure: Assesses child's ability to identify a common object from an incomplete visual presentation. Four scenes are presented separately each containing 14–16 examples of specified object (e.g., a dog) seen in varying degrees of concealment: "How quickly can you point to all the dogs?" (30 seconds)
11 Auditory sequential memory: Assesses ability to reproduce from memory sequences of spoken digits increasing in length from two to eight digits
12 Visual sequential memory: Assesses ability to reproduce sequences of nonmeaningful figures from memory; child is shown sequence of figures for 5 seconds and asked to put corresponding chips in same order

Detroit (Detroit Test of Learning Aptitude)
Ages 3-0 through adult
Test yields a general mental age as well as a series of subtest mental ages. There are 19 subtests, usually 9–13 are recommended at the discretion of the examiner. Subtests that reflect commonly occurring learning disabilities include motor speed and precision, auditory attention span for unrelated words, visual attention span for objects, auditory attention span for related syllables, visual attention span for letters, oral directions, pictorial absurdities, and pictorial opposites.

TABLE 3
Achievement and Visual Motor Function Measures

WRAT (Wide Range Achievement Test)
Level I — 5-0 to 11-11
Level II — 12 through adult
Measures achievement in the basic school subjects of reading, written spelling, and arithmetic computation. Scores are reported in grade equivalent, standard scores and percentiles. Standard scores should correlate with IQ scores. Prespelling consists of copying marks and writing own name. Spelling consists of writing dictated words ranging from "go" to "occurrence" at level I and from "cat" to "iridescence" at level II. Prereading has three parts: (1) naming two letters in previously written name; (2) identifying 10 letters by form; (3) naming 13 (printed on form) letters. Reading: pronouncing 75 words from "cat" to "aborigines" and "milk" to "synecdoche." Arithmetic consists of an oral part: counting 15 dots aloud and answering simple "story" problems, reading digits and telling which is more. Written part is 43 computation problems.

PIAT (Peabody Individual Achievement Test)
Ages preschool to 18 years
Measures achievement in mathematics, reading recognition and reading comprehension, spelling, and general information. Mathematics consists of 84 multiple choice questions ranging from recognizing numerals to concepts in geometry and trigonometry. Reading recognition also has 84 items from readiness matching of letters through high school level words such as "macrocosm." Reading comprehension begins at item 19 (using the first 18 from "Recognition" as beginning reading). The student reads a sentence silently and then chooses from four pictures the one which best represents the meaning of the sentence. Spelling words are pronounced and used in sentences by the examiner and the student chooses the correct spelling from among four choices after item 14. The earlier items require matching letters and selecting the correct letter for sounds given by the examiner. General information: questions read aloud by the examiner are answered orally by the student. This subtest measures "general encyclopedic knowledge ranging across science, social studies, the fine arts and sports" according to the authors. Rationale for this test is to sample the extent an individual has acquired knowledge regarding humans and environments since schools focus directly on teaching such knowledge.

PPVT (Peabody Picture Vocabulary Test)
This is a test of vocabulary and is not a good measure of general intelligence as purported. Vocabulary is considered to be a good indicator of a person's intelligence but is not a good measure as it is so influenced by education, opportunity, and even inclination. This test is also biased against blacks, foreigners, and others who are not middle-class white Americans without learning disabilities.

Bender (The Bender Gestalt Test for Young Children)
Ages 5-0 to 11-11
Generally used as maturational test in visual motor gestalt function to explore retardation, regression, loss of function, and organic brain defects. The test consists of nine figures to be copied as the child sees them. Requires child to be able to perceive a two-dimensional figure, integrate it with previous experiences dealing with space, and produce the "gestalt" on paper via small motor coordination. Koppitz scoring system is well validated and yields an expected age placement, expected grade placement, as well as indicators of organic involvement and emotional indicators.

APPENDIX B

TABLE 3
Achievement and Visual Motor Function Measures *(Continued)*

VMI (Developmental Test of Visual Motor Integration)
   Ages 2 to 15
The VMI is a series of 24 geometric forms to be copied, without erasing, using pencil and test booklet. The forms are arranged in order of increasing difficulty. The test can be administered to children individually or in groups between 2 and 15 but was primarily designed for preschool and early primary grades.

SORT (Slosson Oral Reading Test)
   Ages primary grades through high school
This measures oral reading (naming words) from primer through high school levels. It correlates well with Gray Oral Reading Test and is very quickly administered.

Bibliography

Abel, J. D. The family and child television viewing. *J. Marriage Fam.*, 1976, *38*, 331–335.

Abramowicz, M., & Kass, E. Pathogenesis and prognosis of prematurity. *N. Engl. J. Med.*, 1966, *275*, 878–885, 938–943, 1001–1007, 1053–1059.

Ackerman, N. *The psychodynamics of family life.* New York: Basic Books, 1958.

Acosta, P., & Aranda, R. Mexican-American low-income groups. In S. Foman & T. Anderson (Eds.), *Practices of low-income families in feeding infants and small children, with particular attention to cultural sub-groups.* Rockville, Md.: U.S. Dept. Health, Education and Welfare, 1972, pp. 75–87.

Acton, R. L. Management and supportive care during pregnancy. In J. P. Clausen, M. H. Flook, & B. Ford (Eds.), *Maternity nursing today.* New York: McGraw-Hill, 1977, pp. 251–280.

Adams, A. B. Choice of infant feeding techniques as function of maternal personality. *J. Consult. Psychol.*, 1959, *23*, 143–146.

Adams, B. N. Structural factors affecting parental aid to married children. *J. Marriage Fam.*, 1964, *26*, 327–331.

Adams, M. Early concerns of primigravida mothers regarding infant care activities. *Nurs. Res.*, 1963, *12*, 72–77.

Adams, N. Birth order: A critical review. *Sociometry*, 1972, *35*(3), 411–439.

Ainsworth, M. D. Patterns of attachment shown by the infant in interaction with his mother. *Merrill-Palmer Q.*, 1964, *10*, 51–58.

——— *Infancy in Uganda: Infant care and the growth of love.* Baltimore: Johns Hopkins Press, 1967.

BIBLIOGRAPHY

——— Object relations, dependency, and attachment: A theoretical review of the mother-infant relationship. *Child Dev.*, 1969, *40*, 969–1025.

———, & Bell, S. M. Some contemporary patterns of mother-infant interaction in the feeding situation. In A. M. Ambrose (Ed.), *Stimulation in early infancy*. London: Academic Press, 1969.

———, & ——— Attachment, exploration, and separation: Illustrated by the behavior of one-year-olds in a strange situation. *Child Dev.*, 1970, *41*(1), 49–67.

Aladjem, S., & Brown, A. (Eds.). *Perinatal intensive care*. St. Louis: Mosby, 1977.

Aldous, J. Occupational characteristics and males' role performance in the family. *J. Marriage Fam.*, 1969, *31*, 707–712.

Allen, F., Hart, B., Buell, J., Harris, F., & Wolf, M. Effects of social reinforcement on isolate behavior of a nursery school child. *Child Dev.*, 1964, *35*, 511–518.

Altshuler, A. *Books that help children deal with a hospital experience*. Washington, D.C.: U.S. Government Printing Office, DHEW, 1974.

Alvord, J. R. The home token economy: A motivational system for the home. *J. Corr. Psychiatry Social Ther.*, 1971, *17*, 1–8.

American Academy of Pediatrics Committee on Accident Prevention. Auto safety for the infant and young child. *News Comments*, 1974, *25*, 2.

American Academy of Pediatrics Committee on Nutrition. On the feeding of solid foods to infants. *Pediatrics*, 1958, *21*, 685–692.

Ames, L. B. The development of the sense of time in the young child. *J. Genet. Psychol.*, 1946, *68*, 97–125.

——— The sense of self of nursery school children as manifested by their verbal behavior. *J. Genet. Psychol.*, 1952, *81*, 193–232.

———, & Ilg, F. L. Developmental trends in writing behavior. *J. Genet. Psychol.*, 1951, *79*, 29–46.

———, & Learned, J. Imaginary companions and related phenomena. *J. Genet. Psychol.*, 1946, *69*, 147–167.

Anders, T., & Weinstein, P. Sleep and its disorders in infants and children: A review. *Pediatrics*, 1972, *50*, 312–324.

Anderson, R. E. Where's dad? Paternal deprivation and delinquency. *Arch. Gen. Psychiatry*, 1968, *18*, 641–649.

Anderson, T. A. Commercial infant foods: Content and composition. *Pediatr. Clin. North Am.*, 1977, *24*, 37–47.

Andry, R. G. *Delinquency and parental pathology*. London: Methuen, 1960.

Angell, R. C. *The family encounters the depression*. New York: Scribner's, 1936.

Angle, C. R. Locomotor skills and school accidents. *Pediatrics*, 1975, *56*, 819–822.

Apley, J. *The child with abdominal pain*. Oxford: Blackwell Scientific, 1959.

Arey, L. *Developmental anatomy*. Philadelphia: Saunders, 1974.

Armentrout, J. A., & Burger, G. K. Children's reports of parental child-rearing behavior at five grade levels. *Dev. Psychol.*, 1972, *7*, 44–48.

Arnold, L. E. Strategies and tactics of parent guidance. In L. E. Arnold (Ed.),

Helping parents help their children. New York: Brunner/Mazel, 1978, pp. 3–21.

Arnstein, H. *Your growing child and sex.* New York: Bobbs-Merrill, 1967.

Augenbraun, B., Reid, H., & Friedman, D. Brief intervention as a preventive force in disorders of early childhood. *Am. J. Orthopsychiatry,* 1967, *37*, 697–702.

Ayllon, T., Layman, D., & Kandel, H. A behavioral-educational alternative to drug control of hyperactive children. *J. Appl. Behav. Anal.,* 1975, *8*, 137–146.

Azrin, N. H., & Foxx, R. M. *Toilet training in less than a day.* New York: Simon & Schuster, 1974.

Backer Dirks, O., Jongeling-Eijndhoven, J., Flissebaalje, T. D., & Gedalia, I. Total and free ionic fluoride in human and cows milk as determined by gas liquid chromotography and the fluoride electrode. *Caries Res.,* 1974, *8*, 181–186.

Baker, A. A. *Psychiatric disorders in obstetrics.* Oxford: Blackwell Scientific, 1967.

Baldwin, A. L. *Theories of child development.* New York: Wiley, 1967.

Bandura, A. *Principles of behavior modification.* New York: Holt, 1969.

————— (Ed.), *Psychological modeling.* Chicago: Aldine-Atherton, 1971.

—————, Ross, D., & Ross, S. A. A comparative test of the status envy, social power, and secondary reinforcement theories of identificatory learning. *J. Abnorm. Social Psychol.,* 1963, *67*, 527–534.

—————, & Walters, R. H. *Adolescent aggression.* New York: Ronald Press, 1959.

—————, & ————— *Social learning and personality development.* New York: Holt, 1963.

Bank, S., & Kahn, M. D. Sisterhood-brotherhood is powerful: Sibling sub-systems and family therapy. *Fam. Process,* 1975, *14*, 311–337.

Barbero, G. Failure to thrive. In M. H. Klaus, T. Leger, & M. A. Trause (Eds.), *Maternal attachment and mothering disorders: A round table.* Sausalito, Calif.: Johnson & Johnson Baby Products Co., 1975, pp. 9–11.

Barltrop, D. The prevalence of pica. *Am. J. Dis. Child.,* 1966, *112*, 116–123.

Barnard, K. E., & Douglas, H. B. (Eds.). *Child health assessment, Part 1: A literature review* [DHEW Pub #(HRA) 75-30]. Bethesda, Md.: U.S. Dept. Health, Education & Welfare, 1974.

Barnes, F. (Ed.). *Ambulatory maternal health care and family planning services— American Public Health Association—Maternal and Child Health Section.* Crawfordsville, Ind.: Donnelley, 1978.

Barnett, C. R., Leiderman, P. H., Grobstein, R., & Klaus, M. Neonatal separation: The maternal side of interactional deprivation. *Pediatrics,* 1970, *45*, 197–205.

Barsch, R. H. *The parent of the handicapped child.* Springfield, Ill.: Charles C Thomas, 1968.

Bartlett, M. H., Johnston, A., & Meyer, T. C. Dial access library—patient information service. *N. Engl. J. Med.,* 1973, *288*(19), 994–998.

Bates, J., Skilbeck, W., Smith, K., & Bentlev, P. Intervention with families of gender disturbed boys. *Am. J. Orthopsychiatry,* 1975, *45*, 150–157.

Battle, C. U. Disruption in the socialization of a young, severely handicapped child. *Rehabil. Lit.,* 1974, *35*(5), 130–140.

Baumrind, D. Effects of authoritative parental control on child behavior. *Child Dev.*, 1966, *37*(4), 887–907.

—— Current patterns of parental authority. *Dev. Psychol.*, 1971, *4*, 1–103.

——, & Black, A. E. Socialization practices associated with dimensions of competence in preschool boys and girls. *Child Dev.*, 1967, *38*, 291–327.

Bayer, L. M., & Bayley, N. *Growth diagnosis*. Chicago: University of Chicago Press, 1959.

——, & Synder, M. Illness experience in a group of normal children. *Child Dev.*, 1950, *21*, 93–190.

Bayley, N. The development of motor abilities during the first three years. *Monogr. Soc. Res. Child Dev.*, 1935, *1* (Serial No. 1).

—— *Bayley scales of infant development: Birth to two years.* New York: Psychological Corp., 1969.

——, & Schaefer, E. Relationships between socio-economic variables and the behavior of mothers toward young children. *J. Genet. Psychol.*, 1960, *96*, 61–77.

Beal, V. Termination of night feeding in infancy. *J. Pediatr.*, 1969, *75*, 690–692.

Becker, W. C. Consequences of different kinds of parental discipline. In M. L. Hoffman & L. W. Hoffman (Eds.), *Review of child development research* (Vol. 1). New York: Russell Sage Foundation, 1964, pp. 169–208.

Behrle, F., Elkin, M., & Laybourne, P. Evaluation of conditioning device in treatment of nocturnal enuresis. *Pediatrics*, 1956, *17*, 849–854.

Bell, R. Q., & Costello, N. S. Three tests for sex differences in tactile sensitivity in the newborn. *Biol. Neonatol.*, 1964, *7*, 335–347.

——, & Harper, L. *Child effects on adults.* Hillsdale, N.J.: Lawrence Erlbaum, 1977.

Bell, S. M. the development of the concept of object as related to infant-mother attachment. *Child Dev.*, 1970, *41*, 291–311.

Bellman, M. Studies on encopresis. *Acta Paediatr. Scand.*, Supplement, 1966, *170*, 1–138.

Bender, L. Schizophrenia in childhood. *Nerv. Child*, 1942, *1*, 138–140.

—— Childhood schizophrenia: Clinical study of 100 schizophrenic children. *Am. J. Orthopsychiatry*, 1947, *17*, 40–56.

Benedek, T. The psychosomatic implications of the primary unit: Mother-child. *Am. J. Orthopsychiatry*, 1949, *19*, 642–654.

—— Parenthood as a developmental phase. *J. Am. Psychoanal. Assoc.*, 1959, *7*, 389–417.

—— Motherhood and nurturing. In E. J. Anthony & T. Benedek (Eds.), *Parenthood—Its psychology and psychopathology*. Boston: Little, Brown, 1970a, pp. 153–165.

—— The psychobiology of pregnancy. In E. J. Anthony & T. Benedek (Eds.), *Parenthood—Its psychology and psychopathology*. Boston: Little, Brown, 1970b, pp. 137–151.

—— Fatherhood and providing. In E. J. Anthony & T. Benedek (Eds.), *Parenthood—Its psychology and psychopathology*. Boston: Little, Brown, 1970c, pp. 167–183.

Benfield, D. G., Leib, S. A., & Reuter, J. Grief response of parents after referral of the critically ill newborn to a regional center. *N. Engl. J. Med.*, 1976, *294*, 975–978.

Benson, L. *Fatherhood a sociological perspective.* New York: Random House, 1968.

Berg, D. W., & Daugherty, G. G. Teaching about death. *Today's Educ.*, 1973, *62*, 46–47.

Berggreen, S. M. A study of the mental health of the near relatives of twenty multihandicapped children. *Acta Paediatr. Scand.*, Supplement, 1971, *215*, 1–24.

Bergman, A., & Stamm, S. The morbidity of cardiac nondisease in school children. *N. Engl. J. Med.*, 1967, *276*, 1008–1013.

Bergmann, T. *Children in hospital.* New York: International Universities Press, 1965.

Bergner, L., & Susser, M. Low birth weight and prenatal nutrition: An interpretative review. *Pediatrics*, 1970, *46*, 946–966.

Bijou, S. W. Behavior modification in the mentally retarded. *Pediatr. Clin. North Am.*, 1968, *15*, 969–987.

———, & Baer, D. M. *Child development* (Vol. 2). New York: Appleton-Century-Crofts, 1965.

Biller, H. B. *Father, child and sex role.* Lexington, Mass.: Heath, 1971.

———, & Davids, A. Parent-child relations, personality development and psycho-pathology. In A. Davids (Ed.), *Abnormal child psychology.* Monterey, Calif.: Brooks/Cole, 1973, pp. 48–76.

Billingsley, A. *Black families in white America.* Englewood Cliffs, N.J.: Prentice-Hall, 1968.

Binger, C. M., Ablin, A. R., Feverstein, R. C., Kushner, J. H., Zoger, S., & Mikkelsen, C. Childhood leukemia: Emotional impact on patient and family. *N. Engl. J. Med.*, 1969, *280*, 414–418.

Birch, H. G. (Ed.). *Brain damage in children: The biological and social aspects.* Baltimore: Williams & Wilkins, 1964.

———, & Gussow, J. *Disadvantaged children: Health, nutrition and school failure.* New York: Harcourt Brace Jovanovich, Inc., 1970.

Bishop, B. A guide to assessing parenting capabilities. *Am. J. Nurs.*, 1976, *76*, 1784–1787.

Black, F. W. Self-concept as related to achievement and age in learning disabled children. *Child Dev.*, 1974, *45*, 1137–1148.

Blanchard, R. W., & Biller, H. B. Father availability and academic performance among third grade boys. *Dev. Psychol.*, 1971, *4*, 301–305.

Blood, R. O., Jr. The husband-wife relationship. In F. I. Nye & L. W. Hoffman (Eds.), *The employed mother in America.* Chicago: Rand McNally, 1965.

———, & Wolfe, D. M. *Husbands and wives: The dynamics of married living.* New York: Macmillan, 1960.

Bloom, B. S. Early learning in the home. First B. J. Paley Lecturer, University of California, Los Angeles, July 18, 1965 (mimeographed).

Bordley, J. Office detection of hearing defects in children. *Pediatrics*, 1959, *21*, 980–988.

Bossard, J. H. S. The law of family interaction. *Am. J. Sociol.*, 1945, *50*, 292–294.

———, & Carter, W. Large and small families—A study in contrast. *J. Am. Soc. Chartered Life Underwriters*, 1958–1959, *13*, 221–240.

Boulette, T. R. Parenting: Special needs of low-income Spanish-surnamed families. *Pediatr. Ann.*, 1977, 6(9), 613–619.

Bowden, B. D. The effects of digital and dummy sucking on arch widths, overbite, and overjet: A longitudinal study. *Aust. Dent. J.*, 1966, *11*, 396–404.

Bowlby, J. *Maternal care and mental health.* Geneva: World Health Organization, 1951.

Bradford, R. L. Nutrition during pregnancy and the postpartum period. In J. P. Clausen, M. H. Flook & B. Ford (Eds.), *Maternity nursing today.* New York: McGraw-Hill, 1977.

Bradley, N. C. The growth of the knowledge of time in children of school age. *Br. J. Psychol.*, 1947, *38*, 67–78.

Bradley, R. W. Birth order and school-related behavior: A heuristic review. *Psychol. Bull.*, 1968, 70(1), 40–51.

Braen, B. B., & Forbush, J. B. School-age parenthood—A national overview. *J. School Health*, 1975, *45*, 256–262.

Branstetter, E. The young child's response to hospitalization—Separation anxiety or lack of mothering care? *Am. J. Publ. Health*, 1969, *59*, 92–96.

Brant, H. A. Preparation of multigravid patients. *Psychosomatic medicine in obstetrics and gynaecology.* Basel: Karger, 1972, pp. 78–80.

Brazelton, T. Sucking in infancy. Pediatrics, 1956, *17*, 400–404.

——— Psychophysiologic reactions in the neonate. *J. Pediatr.*, 1961, *58*, 508–510.

——— A child oriented approach to toilet training. *Pediatrics*, 1962, *29*, 121–128.

——— *Infants and mothers: Differences in development.* New York: Dell, 1969.

——— *Neonatal behavioral assessment scale.* (Clinics in developmental medicine, No. 50). Philadelphia: Lippincott, 1973.

——— Anticipatory guidance. *Pediatr. Clin. North Am.*, 1975a, *22*, 533–544.

——— Mother-infant reciprocity. In M. H. Klaus, T. Leger, & M. A. Trause (Eds.), *Maternal attachment and mothering disorders: A round table.* Sausalito, Calif.: Johnson & Johnson Baby Products Co., 1975b, pp. 51–54.

——— Early parent-infant reciprocity. In V. C. Vaughn & T. B. Brazelton (Eds.), *The family—Can it be saved?* Chicago: Year Book Medical Publishers, 1976, pp. 133–141.

Breckenridge, M. E., & Vincent, E. *Child development.* Philadelphia: Saunders, 1965.

Brekke, W., Williams, J., & Harlon, S. D. Conservation and reading readiness. *J. Genet. Psychol.*, 1973, *123*, 133–138.

Brenner, A., & Samelson, N. Kindergarten behavior and first grade achievement: A case study of exploration. *Merrill-Palmer Q.*, 1959, *5*, 140–155.

Brent, R. L., & Harris, M. I. (Eds.). *Prevention of embryonic, fetal, and perinatal disease.* DHEW Publication (NIH) 76-853, 1976.

Brenton, M. *Playmates: The importance of childhood friendships.* New York: Public Affairs Committee, 1975.

Brewer, T. Human pregnancy nutrition: A clinical view. *Obstet. and Gynecol.,* 1967, *30*, 605–607.

Brim, O. G. The parent-child relation as a social system: I. Parent and child roles. *Child Dev.,* 1957, *28*(3), 343–364.

———— *Education for childrearing.* New York: Russell Sage Foundation, 1959.

Brody, S. *Patterns of mothering.* New York: International University Press, 1956.

———— Self-rocking in infancy. *J. Am. Psychoanal. Assoc.,* 1961, *8*, 464–491.

Bromwich, R. M. Focus on maternal behavior in infant intervention. *Am. J. Orthopsychiatry,* 1976, *43*, 439–446.

———— Stimulation in the first year of life: A perspective on infant development. *Young Child.,* 1977, *32*, 71–82.

Bronfenbrenner, U. Is early intervention effective? In B. Friedlander, G. Sterritt, & G. Kirk (Eds.), *Exceptional infant.* (Vol. 3) *Assessment and intervention.* New York: Brunner/Mazel, 1975.

———— Who cares for America's children? In V. C. Vaughn & T. B. Brazelton (Eds.), *The family—Can it be saved?* Chicago: Year Book Medical Publishers, 1976, pp. 3–32.

Brooks, D. J., Jr. *A study to determine the employment potential of mothers receiving aid to dependent children assistance.* Chicago: Cook County Department of Public Aid, 1964.

Brooks, M. R. A stimulation program for young children performed by a public health nurse as part of well baby care. In *ANA Clinical Sessions.* New York: Appleton-Century-Crofts, 1971, pp. 128–139.

Brooks, M. S., Rennie, D. L., & Sondag, R. F. Reaction of mothers to literature on childrearing. *Am. J. Publ. Health,* 1964, *54*, 803–811.

Broussard, E. R. Neonatal prediction and outcome at 10/11 years. Unpublished paper presented at the 128th Annual Meeting of the American Psychiatric Association, Anaheim, California, May 8, 1975.

———— Evaluation of televised anticipatory guidance to primiparae. *Community Ment. Health J.,* 1976, *12*(2), 203–210.

————, & Hartner, M. S. S. Further considerations regarding maternal perception of the first born. In J. Hellmuth (Ed.), *Exceptional infant* (Vol. 2) *Studies in abnormalities.* New York: Brunner/Mazel, 1971, pp. 432–449.

Brown, F., Lieberman, J., Winson, J., & Pleshette, N. Studies in choice of infant feeding by primiparas. I. Attitudinal factors and extraneous influences. *Psychosom. Med.,* 1960, *22*, 421–429.

Brown, J. H., & Brown, C. S. Concomitants of social acceptance: Exploratory research and implications for treatment. *Am. J. Orthopsychiatry,* 1976, *46*, 470–476.

BIBLIOGRAPHY

Brown, P., & Elliott, R. Control of aggression in a nursery school class. *J. Exp. Child Psychol.*, 1965, *2*, 103–107.

Brown, S. L. Functions, tasks, and stresses of parenting: Implications for guidance. In L. E. Arnold (Ed.), *Helping parents help their children*. New York: Brunner/Mazel, 1978, pp. 22–34.

Bruch, H. Parent education or the illusion of omnipotence. *Am. J. Orthopsychiatry*, 1954, *24*, 723–732.

Buhler, K. *The mental development of the child*. New York: Harcourt Brace Jovanovich, Inc., 1930.

Burchinal, L., Gardner, B., & Hawkes, G. R. Children's personality adjustment and the socioeconomic status of their families. *J. Genet. Psychol.*, 1958, *92*, 149–159.

Burdé, B., & Reames, B. Prevention of pica: The major cause of lead poisoning in children. *Am. J. Pub. Health*, 1973, *63*, 737–743.

Burgess, E. W. The family as a unity of interacting personalities. *Family*, 1926, *7*, 3–9.

———— The family and sociological research. *Social Forces*, 1947, *26*, 1–6.

Burke, B. S., Stevenson, S. S., Worcester, J., & Stuart, H. C. Nutrition studies during pregnancy: V. Relation of maternal nutrition to condition of infant at birth: Study of siblings. *J. Nutr.*, 1949, *38*, 453–467.

Burr, W. R. Satisfaction with various aspects of marriage over the life cycle: A random middle class sample. *J. Marriage Fam.*, 1970, *32*, 29–37.

Burstein, I., Kinch, R., & Stern, L. Anxiety, pregnancy, labor, and the neonate. *Am. J. Obstet. Gynecol.*, 1974, *118*, 195–199.

Burton, L. *The family life of sick children*. London: Routledge & Kegan Paul, 1975.

Butler, N. Late postnatal consequences of fetal malnutrition. In M. Winick (Ed.), *Current concepts of nutrition* (Vol. 2) *Nutrition and fetal development*. New York: Wiley, 1974.

————, & Alberman, E. D. Perinatal problems. *The second report of the 1958 British Perinatal Mortality Survey*. Edinburgh: Livingstone, 1969, p. 49.

Buxton, C. L. *A study of psychophysical methods for relief of childbirth pain*. Philadelphia: Saunders, 1962.

Cain, A., Fast, I., & Erikson, M. Children's disturbed reactions to the death of a sibling. *Am. J. Orthopsychiatry*, 1964, *34*, 741–752.

Caldwell, B. M. Effects of infant care. In M. L. Hoffman & L. W. Hoffman (Eds.), *Review of child development research* (Vol. 1). New York: Russell Sage Foundation, 1964, pp. 9–87.

————, Wright, C. M., Honig, A. S., & Tannenbaum, J. Infant day care and attachment. *Am. J. Orthopsychiatry*, 1970, *40*, 397–412.

Caplan, G. *Concepts of mental health and consultation*. Washington, D.C.: U.S. Government Printing Office, DHEW, 1959.

———— *An approach to community mental health*. New York: Grune & Stratton, 1961. (Excerpts reprinted with permission.)

CHILD AND FAMILY DEVELOPMENT

—————— *Principles of preventive psychiatry.* New York: Basic Books, 1964.

——————, Mason, E. A., & Kaplan, D. M. Four studies of crisis in parents of prematures. *Community Ment. Health J.*, 1965, *1*, 149–161.

—————— Psychological aspects of pregnancy. In H. I. Leif (Ed.), *The psychologic basis of medical practice.* New York: Harper & Row, 1973.

Carey, W. B. A simplified method for measuring infant temperament. *J. Pediatr.*, 1970, *77*, 188–194.

—————— Night waking and temperament in infancy. *J. Pediatr.*, 1974, *84*, 756–758.

Carlsmith, L. Effect of early father-absence on scholastic aptitude. *Harvard Educ. Rev.*, 1964, *34*, 3–21.

Carr, J. Young children with Down's syndrome: Their development, upbringing, and effect on their families. *Institute for Research into Mental and Multiple Handicap* (Monograph No. 4). London: Butterworths, 1975.

Casler, L. Maternal deprivation: A critical review of the literature. *Monogr. Soc. Res. Child Dev.*, 1961, *26*, 1–64.

Chabon, I. *Awake and aware.* New York: Delacorte Press, 1966.

Chamberlin, R. W. Approaches to child rearing: Their identification and classification. *Clin. Pediatr.*, 1965, *4*, 150–159.

—————— Early recognition and modification of vicious circle parent-child relationships. *Clin. Pediatr.*, 1967, *6*, 469–479.

—————— Management of preschool behavior problems. *Pediatr. Clin. North Am.*, 1974, *21*, 33–47. (With permission.)

—————— The use of teacher checklists to identify children at risk for later behavioral and emotional problems. *Am. J. Dis. Child.*, 1976, *130*, 141–145.

—————— Parenting styles, child behavior, and the pediatrician. *Pediatr. Ann.*, 1977, *6*, 584–591. (With permission.)

—————— Anticipatory guidance: The role of the physician in parent education. In R. A. Hoekelman et al. (Eds.). *Principles of pediatrics,* New York: McGraw-Hill, 1978, pp. 168–173. (Excerpts reprinted with permission.)

—————— Relationships between child rearing styles and child behavior over time. *Am. J. Dis. Child.*, 1978, *132*, 155–160.

——————, & Radebaugh, J. Delivery of primary health care union style. *N. Engl. J. Med.*, 1976, *294*, 641–645.

Charney, E. Patient-doctor communication. Implications for the clinician. *Pediatr. Clin. North Am.*, 1972, *19*, 276–279.

Chess, S., Korn, S., & Fernandez, P. *Psychiatric disorders of children with congenital rubella.* New York: Brunner/Mazel, 1971.

——————, Thomas, A., & Birch, H. G. *Your child is a person.* New York: Viking, 1965.

Childers, P., & Wimmer, M. The concept of death in early childhood. *Child Dev.*, 1971, *42*, 1299–1301.

BIBLIOGRAPHY

Child Study Association. *Parents' guide to facts of life for children.* New York: Maco, 1965.

Chilman, C. *Growing up poor.* Washington, D. C.: U.S. Government Printing Office, DHEW, 1966.

Chittenden, E. A., Foan, M. W., Zweile, D. M., & Smith, J. R. School achievement of first and second born siblings. *Child Dev.*, 1968, *39*, 1223–1228.

Clark, A. L., & Affonso, D. D. *Childbearing: A nursing perspective.* Philadelphia: Davis, 1976.

Clark, K., & Clark, M. Racial identification and preference in Negro children. In T. M. Newcomb & E. L. Hartley (Eds.), *Readings in social psychology.* New York: Holt, 1947, pp. 169–178.

Clark School for the Deaf. Studies in the psychology of the deaf. *Psychol. Monogr.*, 1940, *52* (Whole No. 232).

Clarke-Stewart, K. A. Interactions between mothers and their young children: Characteristics and consequences. *Monogr. Soc. Res. Child Dev.*, 1973, *38* (Whole No. 153).

Clausen, J. A. Family structure, socialization and personality. In L. W. Hoffman & M. L. Hoffman (Eds.), *Review of child development research* (Vol. 2). New York: Russell Sage Foundation, 1966, pp. 1–54.

———— (Ed.). *Socialization and society.* Boston: Little, Brown, 1968.

Clayton, T. E. *Teaching and learning—A psychological perspective.* Englewood Cliffs, N.J.: Prentice-Hall, 1965.

Cobrink, W. R., Hood, J., & Chusid, E. The effect of maternal narcotic addiction on the newborn infant. *Pediatrics*, 1959, *24*, 288–304.

Cohen, L. J., & Campos, J. J. Father, mother, and stranger as elicitors of attachment behaviors in infancy. *Dev. Psychol.*, 1974, *10*, 146–154.

Cohen, M. Enuresis. *Pediatr. Clin. North Am.*, 1975, *22*(3), 545–560.

Cohen, R. L. Some maladaptive syndromes of pregnancy and the puerperium. *Obstet. Gynecol.*, 1966, *27*, 562–570.

————, et al. The incidence of significant stress as perceived by pregnant women. Personal communication, reported by S. Horsley, Psychological management of the pre-natal period. In J. G. Howells (Ed.), *Modern perspectives in psycho-obstetrics.* New York: Brunner/Mazel, 1972, p. 312.

Coleman, R., & Provence, S. Environmental retardation in infants living in families. *Pediatrics*, 1957, *19*, 285–292.

Collen, F. B., & Soghikian, K. A health education library for patients. *Health Serv. Rep.*, 1974, *89*(3), 236–243.

Colley, K. D. Growing up together: The mutual respect balance. In L. E. Arnold (Ed.), *Helping parents help their children.* New York: Brunner/Mazel, 1978, pp. 46–54.

Colman, A. D., & Colman, L. L. *Pregnancy: The psychological experience.* New York: Herder & Herder, 1971.

———, & ——— Pregnancy as an altered state of consciousness. *Birth Fam.*, 1973–1974, *1*(1), 7–11.

Committee on Nutrition. On the feeding of solid foods to infants. *Pediatrics*, 1958, *21*, 685–692.

Cone, B. A. Puerperal depression. *Psychosomatic medicine in obstetrics and gynaecology.* 3d Int. Congress, London, 1971. Basel: Karger, 1972, pp. 355–357.

Conn, J. H. Sexual curiosity of children. *Am. J. Dis. Child.*, 1940, *60*, 1110–1119.

——— Children's awareness of the origin of babies. *J. Child Psychiatry*, 1948, *1*, 140–176.

———, & Konner, L. Children's awareness of sex differences. *J. Child Psychiatry*, 1947, *1*, 3–57.

Conn, R. Using health education aides in counseling pregnant women. *Public Health Rep.*, 1968, *83*, 979–982.

Connally, K., Brown, K., & Bassett, E. Developmental changes in some components of a motor skill. *Br. J. Psychol.*, 1968, *59*, 305–314.

Connely, J. Viral and drug hazards in pregnancy. *Clin. Pediatr.*, 1964, *3*, 587–595.

Cooper, M. *Pica.* Springfield, Ill.: Charles C Thomas, 1957.

Coopersmith, S. A method for determining types of self-esteem. *J. Educ. Psychol.*, 1959, *59*, 87–94.

Cornell, E., & Gottfried, A. Intervention with premature human infants. *Child Dev.*, 1976, *47*, 32–39.

Cornell, M. M. Psychological variables related to infant feeding patterns. *Dissert. Abstr.*, 1969, *29B3*, 3479B, no. 69-04522.

Counihan, D. Stuttering: Etiology and prevention. *Clin. Pediatr.*, 1964, *3*, 229–232.

Craig, M. M., & Glick, S. J. *A manual of procedures for applications of the Glueck prediction table.* London: University of London Press, 1965.

Crain, A. J., Sussman, M. B., & Weil, W. B. Effects of a diabetic child on marital integration and related measures of family functioning. *J. Health Hum. Behav.*, 1966, *7*, 122–127. [Also in Crawford, C. O. (Ed.), *Health and the family: A medical-sociological analysis.* New York: Macmillan, 1971, pp. 243–256.]

Crandall, V. C., Katkowsky, W., & Crandall, V. J. Children's beliefs in their own control of reinforcements in intellectual-academic achievement situations. *Child Dev.*, 1965, *36*, 91–109.

———, ———, & Preston, A. Motivational and ability determinants of young children's intellectual achievement behaviors. *Child Dev.*, 1962, *33*, 643–661.

Cranley, M. S. When a high-risk infant is born. *Am. J. Nurs.*, 1975, *75*, 1696–1699, 1714.

Craven, R. F., & Sharp, B. H. The effects of illness on family functions. *Nurs. Forum*, 1972, *11*(2), 186–193.

Creak, M. Schizophrenia syndrome in childhood: Progress report of a working party. *Cerebral Palsy Bull.*, 1961, *3*, 501–504.

BIBLIOGRAPHY

Cullberg, J. Mental reactions of women to perinatal death. *Psychosomatic medicine in obstetrics and gynaecology.* 3d Int. Congress, London, 1971, Basel: Karger, 1972, pp. 326–329.

Curry, N., & Armand, S. (Coordinators) *Play: The child strives toward self-realization.* Washington, D.C.: National Association for the Education of Young Children, 1971.

D'Arcy, E. Congenital defects 1. Some findings concerning the impact on the family. *Nurs. Times,* 1969, *65,* 1421–1422.

Davids, A., DeVault, S., & Talmidge, M. Anxiety, pregnancy and childbirth abnormalities. *J. Consult. Psychol.,* 1961, *25,* 74–77.

Davidson, M., Kuggler, M., & Bauer, C. Diagnosis and management in children with severe and protracted constipation and obstipation. *J. Pediatrics,* 1963, *62,* 261–275.

Davies, D. P., Gray, O. P., Ellwood, P. C., & Abernathy, M. Cigarette smoking in pregnancy: Association with maternal weight gain and fetal growth. *Lancet,* 1976, *1,* 385–387.

Davis, A., & Havighurst, R. J. Social class and color differences in child-rearing. In C. Kluckhohn, H. A. Murry, & D. Schneider (Eds.), *Personality in nature, society and culture* (2d ed.). New York: Alfred Knopf, 1953, pp. 308–320.

Davis, F. *Passage through crisis.* Indianapolis: Bobbs-Merrill, 1963.

Davis, J. A. *Stipends and spouses: The finances of American arts and sciences graduate students.* Chicago: University of Chicago Press, 1962.

Davis, R. E., & Ruiz, R. A. Infant feeding method and adolescent personality. *Am. J. Psychiatry,* 1965, *122,* 673–678.

Davis, W. L. & Phares, E. J. Parental antecedents of internal-external control of reinforcement. *Psychol. Rep.,* 1969, *24,* 427–436.

Dawe, J. A study of the effect of an educational program upon language development and related mental functions in young children. *J. Exp. Educ.,* 1942, *11,* 200–209.

deHirsh, K., Jansky, J., & Longfield, W. L. *Predicting reading failure.* New York: Harper & Row, 1966.

Deisher, R., & Goers, S. A study of early and later introduction of solids into the infant diet. *J. Pediatr.,* 1954, *45,* 191–199.

DeLissovoy, V. Head banging in early childhood: Home observations. *Child Dev.,* 1962, *33,* 43–56.

DeMyer, M., Bryson, C., & Churchill, D. The earliest indicators of development: Comparison of symptoms during infancy and early childhood in normal, subnormal, schizophrenic and autistic children. In J. Nurnberger (Ed.), *Biological and environmental determinants of early development.* Baltimore: Williams & Wilkins, 1973.

Denckla, M. B. Development of speed in repetitive and successive finger movements in normal children. *Dev. Med. Child Neurol.,* 1973, *15,* 635–645.

——— Development of motor coordination in normal children. *Dev. Med. Child Neurol.,* 1974, *16,* 729–741.

Denhoff, E., & Holden, R. H. The significance of delay and development in the diagnosis of cerebral palsy. *J. Pediatr.,* 1951, *38,* 452–456.

Dennis, W. Infant development under conditions of restricted practice and of minimum social stimulation. *Genet. Psychol. Monogr.*, 1941, *23*, 143–189.
—— Causes of retardation among institutionalized children: Iran. *J. Genet. Psychol.*, 1960, *96*, 47–59.

Department of Health, Education, & Welfare. *Ten-state nutritional survey 1968-1970.* Washington, D.C., Center for Disease Control, Health Services and Mental Health Administration, 1972.

Deutsch, M. The role of social class in language development and cognition. *Am. J. Orthopsychiatry*, 1965, *35*, 78–88.

Deutsh, H. *The psychology of women* (Vol. 1). New York: Grune & Stratton, 1944.
—— *The psychology of women* (Vol. 2). New York: Grune & Stratton, 1945.

Devereux, E. C., Bronfenbrenner, U., & Suci, G. J. Patterns of parent behavior in the United States of America and the Federal Republic of Germany: A cross-national comparison. *Int. Social Sci. J.*, 1962, *14*, 488–506.

Dewsbury, A. R. Family violence seen in general practice. *Health J.*, 1975, *6*, 290–294.

Dickens, H. O., Mudd, E. H., Garcia, C. R. et al. One hundred pregnant adolescents, treatment approaches in a university hospital. *Am. J. Public Health*, 1973, *63*, 794–800.

Dingle, J., Badger, G., & Jordan, W. *Illness in the home: A study of 25,000 illnesses in a group of Cleveland families.* Cleveland: Western Reserve University Press, 1964.

Dollard, J. *Caste and class in a southern town.* New Haven: Yale University Press, 1973.

Douglas, J. W. B. *The home and the school.* London: Macgibbon & Kee, 1964.
——, Ross, J. M., & Simpson, H. R. *All our future.* London: Davies, 1968.

Downs, F. S., & Fernbach, V. Experimental evaluation of a prenatal leaflet series. *Nurs. Res.*, 1973, *22*(6), 498–506.

Drabman, R. S., & Thomas, M. H. Does watching violence on television cause apathy? *Pediatrics*, 1976, *57*, 329–331.

Dreikurs, R. R. *Fundamentals of Adlerian psychology.* Chicago: Alfred Adler Institute, 1953.

Drillien, C. M. *The growth and development of the prematurely born infant.* Baltimore: Williams & Wilkins, 1964.
—— Studies in mental handicap. II. Some obstetric factors of possible aetiological significance. *Arch. Dis. Child.*, 1968, *43*, 283–294.

Drotar, D., Baskiewicz, A., Irvin, N., Kennell, J., & Klaus, M. The adaptation of parents to the birth of an infant with a congenital malformation: A hypothetical model. *Pediatrics*, 1975, *56*, 710–717.

Drugs in breast milk. *Med. Lett.*, 1974, *16*, 25–27.

Dunbar, F. A psychosomatic approach to abortion and the abortion habit. In H. Rosen (Ed.), *Therapeutic abortion.* New York: Julian Press, 1954.

Dunn, H. G., McBurney, A. K., Ingram, S., & Hunter, C. M. Maternal cigarette smoking during pregnancy and the child's subsequent development. 1. Physical growth to the age of 6½ years. *Can. J. Publ. Health*, 1976, *67*(6), 499–505.

BIBLIOGRAPHY

Dunning, J. M. Current status of fluoridation. *N. Engl. J. Med.*, 1965, *272*, 30–35.

Duvall, E. M. *Family development* (4th ed.). Philadelphia: Lippincott, 1971.

────── *Marriage and family development.* Philadelphia: Lippincott, 1977.

Dyer, E. D. Parenthood as crisis: A restudy. *Marriage and Family Living*, 1963, *25*, 196–201.

Eastman, N. J., & Jackson, E. Weight relationships in pregnancy. I. The bearing of maternal weight gain and pre-pregnancy weight on birthweight in full term pregnancies. *Obstet. Gynecol. Surv.*, 1968, *23*, 1003–1025.

Eicheinwald, H. F. Congenital toxoplasmosis: A study of one hundred fifty cases. *Am. J. Dis. Child.*, 1957, *94*, 411–412.

Eichorn, D., & Bayley, N. Growth in head circumference from birth through young adulthood. *Child Dev.*, 1962, *33*, 257–271.

Eiduson, B., Cohen, J., & Alexander, J. Alternatives in child rearing in the 1970s. *Am. J. Orthopsychiatry*, 1973, *43*, 720–731.

Eisenberg, L. The clinical use of stimulant drugs in children. *Pediatrics*, 1972, *49*, 709–715.

Elder, G. H., Jr., & Bowerman, C. E. Family structure and child-rearing patterns: The effect of family size and sex composition. *Am. Sociol. Rev.*, 1963, *28*, 891–905.

Elder, J. W. National loyalties in a newly independent nation. In D. E. Apter (Ed.), *Ideology and discontent.* New York: Free Press, 1964, pp. 77–92.

Elmer, E. Failure to thrive: Role of the mother. *Pediatrics*, 1960, *25*, 717–725.

────── *Children in jeopardy.* Pittsburgh: University of Pittsburgh Press, 1967.

──────, & Gregg, G. S. Developmental characteristics of abused children. *Pediatrics*, 1967, *40*, 596–602.

Emde, R. N., Gaensbauer, T. J., & Harmon, R. J. Emotional expression in infancy: A biobehavioral study. *Psychol. Iss.*, 1976, *10*(1), Monograph 37.

Emmerich, W. The parental role: A functional-cognitive approach. *Monogr. Soc. Res. Child Dev.*, 1969, *34*(Serial no. 132).

Engel, G. L. Conversion symptoms. In C. M. MacBoyde & R. S. Blacklow (Eds.), *Signs and symptoms: Applied physiology and clinical interpretation.* Philadelphia: Lippincott, 1970.

Eppright, F., & Fox, L. Eating behavior of preschool children. *J. Nutr. Educ.*, 1969, *1*, 16–18.

Erickson, M. L. *Assessment and management of developmental changes in children.* St. Louis: Mosby, 1976.

Ericsson, Y. Fluoride excretion in human saliva and milk. *Caries Res.*, 1969, *3*, 159.

──────, Hellstrom, I., & Hofvander, Y. Pilot studies on the fluoride metabolism in infants on different feedings. *Acta Paediatr. Scand.*, 1972, *61*, 459.

Erikson, E. H. *Childhood and society* (2d ed.). New York: W. W. Norton, 1963.

Erlanger, H. S. Social class and corporal punishment in childrearing: A reassessment. *Am. Sociol. Rev.*, 1974, *39*, 68–85.

Espenshade, T. J. The value and cost of children. *Pop. Bull.*, 1977, *32*, 3–47.

Etaugh, C. Effects of maternal employment on children, a review of current research. *Merrill-Palmer Q.*, 1974, *20*(2), 71–98.

Ewing, I. R., & Ewing, A. W. G. The ascertainment of deafness in infancy and early childhood. *J. Laryngol. Otol.*, 1944, *59*, 309–333.

Eysenck, H. S., & Wilson, G. D. *The experimental study of Freudian theories.* London: Methuen, 1973.

Fagot, B. I. Sex differences in toddlers' behavior and parental reaction. *Dev. Psychol.*, 1974, *10*, 554–558.

Falicov, C. J. Sexual adjustment during first pregnancy and post partum. *Am. J. Obstet. Gynecol.*, 1973, *117*, 991–1000.

Fanaroff, A. A., Kennell, J., & Klaus, M. Follow-up on low birth weight infants— the predictable value of maternal visiting patterns. *Pediatrics*, 1972, *49*, 287–290.

Farber, B. Family and crisis: Maintenance of integration in families with a severely mentally retarded child. *Monogr. Soc. Res. Child Dev.*, 1960, *25* (Serial No. 75).

——— *Mental retardation: Its social context and social consequences.* New York: Houghton Mifflin, 1968.

Faulkner, F. Deciduous tooth eruption. *Arch. Dis. Child.*, 1957a, *32*, 386–391.

——— Some physical measurements in the first three years of life. *Arch. Dis. Child.*, 1957b, *33*, 1.

——— Some physical growth standards for white North American children. *Pediatrics*, 1962, *29*, 467–474.

Fein, G. G., & Clarke-Stewart, K. A. *Day care in context.* New York: Wiley, 1973.

Fein, R. A. Men's entrance to parenthood. *Fam. Coord.*, 1976, *25*, 341–348.

Feldman, H., & Rogoff, M. Correlates of changes in marital satisfaction with the birth of the first child. Paper read at the American Psychological Association Meetings, September 3, 1968. Reported in E. Duvall, *Marriage and family development.* Philadelphia: Lippincott, 1977.

Feldman, M. Cluster visits. *Am. J. Nurs.*, 1974, *74*, 1485–1488.

Ferreira, A. The pregnant woman's emotional attitude and its reflection on the newborn. *Am. J. Orthopsychiatry*, 1960, *30*, 553–561.

Field, T. M., Dabiri, C., Hallock, N., & Shuman, H. H. Developmental effects of prolonged pregnancy and the postmaturity syndrome. *J. Pediatr.*, 1977, *90*(5), 836–839.

Fink, S. L. Crisis and motivation: A theoretical model. *Arch. Phys. Med. Rehabil.*, 1967, *48*, 592–597.

Fischman, S. H. The pregnancy-resolution decisions of unwed adolescents. *Nurs. Clin. North Am.*, 1975, *10*, 217–227.

Fling, S., & Manosevitz, M. Sex typing in nursery school children's play interests. *Dev. Psychol.*, 1972, *7*, 146–152.

Flowers, C. E. Discussion. *Am. J. Obstet. Gynecol.*, 1969, *103*, 786–787.

Fomon, S. *Infant nutrition.* Philadelphia: Saunders, 1974.

———, Filer, L. J., Thomas, L. N., Rogers, R. R., & Proksch, A. M. Relationship between formula concentration and rate of growth of normal infants. *J. Nutr.*, 1969, *98*, 241–254.

Fowler, W. Cognitive learning in infancy and early childhood. *Psychol. Bull.*, 1962, *59*, 116–152.

BIBLIOGRAPHY

Fraiberg, S. *The magic years*. New York: Scribner, 1959.

———— Smiling and stranger reactions in blind infants. In J. Hellmuth (Ed.), *Exceptional infant* (Vol. 2) *Studies in abnormalities*. New York: Brunner/Mazel, 1970.

———— Intervention in infancy: A program for blind infants. In B. Friedlander, G. Sterritt, & G. Kirk (Eds.), *Exceptional infant* (Vol. 3) *Assessment and intervention*. New York: Brunner/Mazel, 1975.

Frankel, E. Characteristics of working and non-working mothers among intellectually high and low achievers. *Personnel Guidance J.*, 1964, *42*, 776–780.

Frankenburg, W. K. *Pediatric screening tests*. Springfield, Ill.: Charles C Thomas, 1975.

————, & Dodds, J. The revised Denver developmental screening test: Its accuracy as a screening instrument. *J. pediatr.*, 1971, *79*, 988.

Freeman, R. D. Emotional reactions of handicapped children. *Rehabil. Lit.*, 1967, *28*(9), 274–282.

Freemon, B., Negrete, V. F., Davis, M., & Korsch, B. M. Gaps in doctor-patient communication: Doctor-patient interaction analysis. *Pediatr. Res.*, 1971, *5*, 298–311.

Friedman, A. S., & Friedman, D. B. Parenting: A developmental process. *Pediatr. Ann.*, 1977, *6*(9), 564–572.

Friedman, D. D. Motivation for natural childbirth. In *Psychosomatic medicine in obstetrics and gynaecology*. 3d Int. Congress, London, 1971, Basel: Karger, 1972, pp. 30–34.

Friedman, S. B., Chadoff, P., Mason, J. W., et al. Behavioral observations of parents anticipating the death of a child. *Pediatrics*, 1963, *32*, 610–625.

————, & Hansen, H. Family therapy in pediatrics. *Clin. Pediatr.*, 1968, *7*, 665–669.

Frommer, E. A., & O'Shea, G. Antenatal identification of women liable to have problems in managing their infants. *Br. J. Psychiatry*, 1973, *123*, 149–156.

Fry, J. *The catarrhal child*. London: Butterworths, 1961.

Furham, R. Handling parental pressure for T & A. *J. Pediatr.*, 1959, *54*, 195–199.

Furth, H. G. *Thinking without language: Psychological implications of deafness*. New York: Free Press, 1966.

Gale, R. F. *Developmental behavior: A humanistic approach*. New York: Macmillan, 1969.

Galenson, E., & Raphe, H. The emergence of genital awareness during the second year of life. In Vande Wiele, R. L. Freedman, & R. R. Richart (Eds.), *Sex differences in behavior*. New York: Wiley, 1974, pp. 223–231.

Gallup International survey for the Institute of Development of Educational Activities, an affiliate of the Charles F. Kettering Foundation. How to help your child do well in school. *U.S. News and World Report*, October 6, 1969, pp. 49–50.

Garai, J. F., & Scheinfeld, A. Sex differences in mental and behavioral traits. *Genet. Psychol. Monogr.*, 1968, *77*, 169–299.

Garn, S. M. Body size and its implications. In L. W. Hoffman & M. L. Hoffman

(Eds.), *Review of Child Development Research* (Vol. 2). New York: Russell Sage Foundation, 1966.

———, & Clark, D. C. Nutrition, growth development and maturation: Findings from the Ten-State Nutrition Survey of 1968–1970. *Pediatrics*, 1975, *56*(2), 306–319.

———, & Haskell, J. A. Fat thickness and developmental status in childhood and adolescence. *Am. J. Dis. Child.*, 1960, *99*, 746–751.

Gartley, W., & Bernasconi, M. The concept of death in children. *J. Genet. Psychol.*, 1967, *110*, 71–85.

Gath, A. The mental health of siblings of congenitally abnormal children. *J. Child Psychol. Psychiatry*, 1972, *13*, 211–218.

Gayford, J. J. Wife battering: A preliminary survey of 100 cases. *Br. Med. J.*, 1975, *1*, 194–197.

Gecas, V. & Nye, F. I. Sex and class differences in parent-child interaction: A test of Kohn's hypothesis. *J. Marriage Fam.*, 1974, *36*, 742–749.

Gecken, K. F. Expectations concerning husband-wife responsibilities in the home. *J. Marriage Fam.*, 1964, *26*, 349–352.

Gellert, E. Children's conception of the content and functions of the human body. *Genet. Psychol. Monogr.*, 1962, *65*, 293–405.

———, Girgus, J., & Cohen, J. Children's awareness of their bodily appearance, a developmental study of factors associated with the body perception. *Genet. Psychol. Monogr.*, 1971, *84*, 109–174.

Gesell, A., & Amatruda, C. S. *The embryology of behavior.* Westport, Conn.: Greenwood Press, 1945.

———, Halverson, H. M., Thompson, H., Ilg, F., Castner, B., Ames, L., & Amatruda, C. *The first five years of life.* New York: Harper & Row, 1940.

———, & Ilg, F. L. *Child development: An introduction to the study of human growth.* New York: Harper, 1949.

———, ———, & Ames, L. B. *Youth: The years from ten to sixteen.* New York: Harper, 1956.

———, ———, & ——— *Infant and child in the culture of today* (Rev. ed.). New York: Harper & Row, 1974.

Gilman, R., & Knox, D. Coping with fatherhood: The first year. *Child Psychiatry Hum. Dev.*, 1976, *6*, 134–148.

Gingold, J. One of these days—Pow, right in the kisser. *Ms.*, 1976, *5*, 51–52ff.

Ginsberg, E. *Life styles of educated women.* New York: Columbia University Press, 1966.

Ginsburg, H., & Opper, S. *Piaget's theory of intellectual development: An introduction.* Englewood Cliffs, N.J.: Prentice-Hall, 1969.

Glasser, P. H., & Glasser, L. N. (Eds.), *Families in crisis.* New York: Harper & Row, 1970.

Glueck, S., & Glueck, E. T. *Family environment and delinquency.* London: Kegan Paul, 1962.

Goldberg, S. B. Family tasks and reactions in the crisis of death. *Social Casework*, 1973, *54*, 398–405.

BIBLIOGRAPHY

Goldblatt, P. B., Moore, M. E., & Stunkard, A. J. Social factors in obesity. *JAMA*, 1965, *192*, 1039–1044.

Goodman, M. E. *Race awareness in young children.* Cambridge, Mass.: Addison-Wesley, 1952.

Goodrich, F. W. The problem of anxiety in obstetrics. *Child Fam.*, 1965, *4*, 62–73.

Gordon, I. J. *Baby learning through baby play.* New York: St. Martin's Press, 1970.

———— *Toddler learning through toddler play.* New York: St. Martin's Press, 1972.

Gordon, R. E., & Gordon, K. K. Social factors in the prevention of postpartum emotional problems. Mimeographed paper presented at the 1967 AOA Annual Meeting, Washington, D.C., 1967.

————, Kapostins, E. E., & Gordon, K. K. Factors in postpartum emotional adjustment. *Obstet. Gynecol.*, 1965, *25*, 158–166.

Goss, A. M. Estimated versus actual physical strength in three ethnic groups. *Child Dev.*, 1968, *39*, 283–291.

Gothberg, L. C. The mentally defective child's understanding of time. *Am. J. Ment. Defic.*, 1949, *53*, 441–455.

Gozzi, E. Pediatric nurse practitioner at work. *Am. J. Nurs.*, 1970, *70*, 2371–2374.

Gralewicz, A. Play deprivation in multihandicapped children. *Am. J. Occupat. Ther.*, 1973, *27*(2), 70–72.

Green, M., & Solnit, A. J. Reactions to the threatened loss of a child: A vulnerable child syndrome. Pediatric management of the dying child, Part III. *Pediatrics*, 1964, *34*, 58–66.

Green, R. *Sexual identity conflict in children and adults.* New York: Basic Books, 1974.

————, Newman, L., & Stoller, R. Treatment of boyhood "transsexualism." *Arch. Gen. Psychol.*, 1972, *26*, 213–218.

Greenberg, M., & Morris, N. Engrossment: The newborn's impact upon the father. *Am. J. Orthopsychiatry*, 1974, *44*, 520–531.

Grimm, E. R. Psychological and social factors in pregnancy, delivery, and outcome. In S. A. Richardson & A. F. Guttmacher (Eds.), *Childbearing—Its social and psychological aspects.* Baltimore: Williams & Wilkins, 1967.

Gruenberg, S. *The wonderful story of how you were born.* Garden City, N.Y.: Doubleday, 1970.

Grunwaldt, E., Bates, T., & Guthrie, D. The onset of sleeping through the night in infancy. *Pediatrics*, 1960, *26*, 667–668.

Gutelius, M. F., Kirsch, A. D., MacDonald, S., Brooks, M. R., McErlean, B. A., & Newcomb, C. Promising results from a cognitive stimulation program in infancy. A preliminary report. *Clin. Pediatr.*, 1972, *11*, 585–593.

————, Millican, F. K., Layman, E. M., Cohen, G. J., & Dublin, C. C. Nutritional studies of children with pica I: Controlled study evaluating nutritional status II: Treatment of pica with iron given intramuscularly. *Pediatrics*, 1962, *29*, 1012–1023.

Haggerty, R. J., Roghmann, K. J., & Pless, I. B. *Child health and the community.* New York: Wiley, 1975.

Hall, C. S. *A primer of Freudian psychology*. New York: Mentor, 1954.

Hall, M., & Keith, R. A. Sex role preference among children of upper and lower social class. *J. Social Psychol.*, 1964, *62*, 101–110.

Hamburg, D. A. Coping behavior in life-threatening circumstances. *Psychother. Psychosom.*, 1974, *23*, 13–25.

Hamilton, J. A. *Postpartum psychiatric problems*. St. Louis: Mosby, 1962.

Hammar, S. Obesity: Early identification and treatment. In P. Collipp (Ed.), *Childhood obesity*. Acton, Mass.: Publishing Sciences Group, 1975.

Handel, G. Sociological aspects of parenthood. In D. P. Hymovich & M. U. Barnard (Eds.), *Family health care* (Vol. 1) *General perspectives* (2d ed.). New York: McGraw-Hill, 1979, pp. 31–56.

Hansen, M. F., & Aradine, C. R. The changing face of primary pediatrics. *Pediatr. Clin. North Am.*, 1974, *21*, 245–256.

Hanshaw, J. B. Congenital and acquired cytomegalovirus infection. *Pediatr. Clin. North Am.*, 1966, *33*, 279–293.

Hardgrove, C., & Warrick, L. H. How shall we tell the children? *Am. J. Nurs.*, 1974, *74*, 448–450.

Harper, P. *Preventive pediatrics: Child health and development*. New York: Appleton-Century-Crofts, 1962.

Harper, R. G., Garcia, A., & Sia, C. Inguinal hernia: Common problem of premature infants weighing 1,000 grams or less at birth. *Pediatrics*, 1975, *56*, 112–115.

Harrington, E. A major pitfall: Inadequate assessment of the patients' needs resulting in inappropriate treatment. *Pediatr. Clin. North Am.*, 1965, *12*, 156–173.

Harris, P. L. Development of search and object permanence. *Psychol. Bull.*, 1975, *82*, 332–344.

Harris, T. "*I'm ok, you're ok.*" (Rev. ed.) New York: Harper & Row, 1969.

Hart, B. Gonadal androgen and sociosexual behavior of male mammals: A comparative analysis. *Psychol. Bull.*, 1974, *81*, 383–400.

Hartley, R. E., & Hardesty, F. P. Children's perceptions of sex roles in childhood. *J. Genet. Psychol.*, 1964, *105*, 43–51.

Hartman, C. C. Psychotic mothers and their babies. *Nurs. Outlook*, 1968, *16*, 32–36.

Hartup, W. W., & Moore, S. B. Avoidance of unappropriate sex-typing by young children. *J. Consult. Psychol.*, 1963, *27*, 467–473.

Harwood, A. The hot-cold theory of disease. *JAMA*, 1971, *216*, 1153–1158.

Hattendorf, K. W. A study of the questions of young children concerning sex. *J. Social Psychol.*, 1932, *3*, 37–65.

Hattwick, L. Sex differences in behavior of nursery school children. *Child Dev.*, 1937, *8*, 343–355.

———, & Sanders, M. Age differences in behavior at the nursery school level. *Child Dev.*, 1938, 9, 27–47.

Havighurst, R. J. *Developmental tasks and education* (3d ed.). New York: McKay, 1972.

Hawkes, R., Burchinal, L., & Gardner, B. Size of family and adjustment of children. *J. Marriage Fam. Living*, 1958, *20*, 65–68.

Hawkins, R. P., Peterson, R. F., Schweid, E., & Bijou, S. W. Behavior therapy in the home: Amelioration of problem parent-child relations with the parent in a therapeutic role. *J. Exp. Child Psychol.*, 1966, *4*, 99–107.

Heagarty, M. G., Glass, G., & King, H. Care of the well-child: Sex and the preschool child. *Am. J. Nurs.*, 1974, *74*, 1479–1482.

Health Education Materials. New York; Health Insurance Institute (n.d.).

Heber, R., & Garber, H. The Milwaukee project: A study of the use of family intervention to prevent cultural-familial mental retardation. In B. Friedlander & G. Sterritt (Eds.), *Exceptional infant* (Vol. 3). New York: Brunner/ Mazel, 1975, pp. 399–432.

Heckel, R. V. The effects of fatherlessness on the preadolescent female. *Ment. Hyg.*, 1963, *47*, 69–73.

Heer, D. M. The measurement and bases of family power: An overview. *Marriage Fam. Living*, 1963, *25*, 133–139.

Heider, G. M. Adjustment problems of the deaf child. *Nerv. Child*, 1948, *7*, 38–44.

Heilbrun, A. B., Jr. Maternal child rearing and creativity in sons. *J. Genet. Psychol.*, 1971, *119*, 175–179.

Heinstein, M. I. Behavioral correlates of breast-bottle regimes under varying parent-infant relationships. *Monogr. Soc. Res. Child Dev.*, 1963, *28(4)*, 1–61.

Helfer, R., & Kempe, H. (Eds.). *The battered child.* Chicago: University of Chicago Press, 1968.

Hendrix, M. J., LaGodna, G. E., & Bohen, C. A. The battered wife. *Am. J. Nurs.*, 1978, *78*, 650–653.

Hennan, D. K., Stookey, G. K., & Muhler, J. C. Prevalence and distribution of dental caries in preschool children. *J. Am. Dent. Assoc.*, 1969, *79*, 1405.

Herrick, V. E., & Okada, N. The present scene: Practices in the teaching of handwriting in the United States—1960. In V. E. Herrick (Ed.), *New horizons for research in handwriting.* Madison: University of Wisconsin, 1963.

Herzog, A., & Detre, T. Psychotic reactions associated with childbirth. *Dis. Nerv. Sys.*, 1976, *37*(4), 229–235.

Hess, R. D., & Shipman, V. C. Early experience and the socialization of cognitive modes in children. *Child Dev.*, 1965, *36*, 869–886.

————, & ———— Cognitive elements in maternal behavior. In J. P. Hill (Ed.), *Minnesota symposia on child psychology.* Minneapolis: University of Minnesota Press, 1967, pp. 58–81.

————, & ———— Maternal influences upon early learning: The cognitive environments of urban preschool children. In R. D. Hess & R. M. Bear (Eds.), *Early education.* Chicago: Aldine, 1968, pp. 91–103.

Hetherington, E. M. Effects of father absence on personality development in adolescent daughters. *Dev. Psychol.*, 1972, *7*, 313–326.

Hewitt, S., Newson, J., & Newson, E. *The family and the handicapped child.* Chicago: Aldine, 1970.

Hilgard, E. R. *Theories of learning* (4th ed.). New York: Appleton-Century-Crofts, 1975.

Hill, L. Anticipatory guidance in pediatric practice. *J. Pediatr.*, 1960, *56*, 299–307.

Hill, R. Generic features of families under stress. In H. J. Parad (Ed.), *Crisis intervention: Selected readings.* New York: Family Service Association of America, 1965.

———— *Family development in three generations.* Cambridge, Mass.: Schenkman, 1970.

Hirschowitz, R. G. Family coping patterns in times of change. *Int. J. Social Psychiatry*, 1974–75, *21*, 37–43.

Hobbs, D. F., Jr. Parenthood as crisis: A third study. *J. Marriage Fam.*, 1965, *27*, 367–372.

Hodgson, K. W. *The deaf and their problems: A study in special education.* London: Watts, 1953.

Hoekelman, R. A. What constitutes adequate well baby care? *Pediatrics*, 1975, *55*, 313–326.

Hoff, W. Role of community health aide in public health programs. *Publ. Health Rep.*, 1969, *84*, 998–1002.

Hoffman, L. W. Mothers enjoyment of work and effects on the child. In F. I. Nye & L. W. Hoffman (Eds.), *The employed mother in America.* Chicago: Rand McNally, 1965, pp. 95–105.

Hoffman, M. L. Sex differences in moral internalization and values. *J. Personal. Social Psychol.*, 1975, *32*(4), 720–729.

Holt, J., Latouvette, H., & Watson, E. Physiological bowing of the legs in young children. *JAMA*, 1954, *154*, 390–394.

Holt, K. S. The home care of severely retarded children. *Pediatrics*, 1958, *22*, 746–755.

Holter, J. C., & Friedman, S. B. Child abuse: Early case finding in the emergency department. *Pediatrics*, 1968, *43*, 128–138.

Honzik, K. M., & McKee, J. The sex difference in thumb sucking. *J. Pediatr.*, 1962, *61*, 726–732.

Hood, P. N., & Perlstein, M. A. Infantile spastic hemiplegia: Oral language and motor development. *Pediatrics*, 1956, *17*, 58–63.

Hornberger, R., Bowman, J., Greenblatt, H., & Corsa, L. *Health supervision of young children in California.* Berkeley: Bureau of Maternal and Child Health, State of California, Department of Public Health, 1960.

Horowitz, M. N., & Horowitz, N. F. Psychologic effects of education for childbirth. *Psychosomatics*, 1967, *8*, 196–202.

Horsley, S. Psychological management of the pre-natal period. In J. G. Howells (Ed.), *Modern perspectives in psycho-obstetrics.* New York: Brunner/Mazel, 1972, pp. 291–313.

Howard, M. C. *Group infant care programs: A survey.* Washington, D.C.: Cyesis Programs Consortium, George Washington University, 1971.

———— *Model components of comprehensive programs for pregnant school-age girls.* Series No. 4. Washington, D.C.: Consortium on Early Childbearing and Childrearing, 1972.

Howell, M. C. Effects of maternal employment on the child II. *Pediatrics*, 1973a, *52*(3), 327–343.

—— Employed mothers and their families I. *Pediatrics*, 1973b, *52*, 252–263.

Howell, S. E. Psychiatric aspects of habilitation. *Pediatr. Clin. North Am.*, 1973, *20*, 203–219.

Howells, J. G. *Theory and practice of family psychiatry.* New York: Brunner/ Mazel, 1971.

—— Childbirth is a family experience. In J. G. Howells (Ed.), *Modern perspectives in psycho-obstetrics.* New York: Brunner/Mazel, 1972a, pp. 127–149.

—— (Ed.). *Modern perspectives in psycho-obstetrics.* New York: Brunner/ Mazel, 1972b.

Hurlock, E. B. *Developmental psychology* (4th ed.). New York: McGraw-Hill, 1975.

Hymovich, D. P. Parents of sick children: Their needs and tasks. *Pediatr. Nurs.*, 1976, *2*, 9–13.

—— Assessment of the chronically ill child and family. In D. P. Hymovich & M. U. Barnard (Eds.), *Family health care* (Vol. 1) *General perspectives.* New York: McGraw-Hill, 1979, pp. 280–293.

——, & Barnard, M. U. (Eds.), *Family health care* (Vol. 1) *General perspectives.* New York: McGraw-Hill, 1979a.

——, & —— (Eds.), *Family health care* (Vol. 2) *Developmental and situational crises.* New York: McGraw-Hill, 1979b.

Ilg, F. L., & Ames, L. B. *Child behavior.* New York: Dell, 1960.

——, ——, & Apell, R. J. School readiness as evaluated by Gesell developmental, visual and projective tests. *Genet. Psychol. Monogr.*, 1965, *71*, 61–91.

Ireton, H., & Thwing, E. The Minnesota child development inventory in the psychiatric developmental evaluation of the preschool-age child. *Child Psychiatry Hum. Dev.*, 1972, *3*, 103–114.

Irwin, O. C. Infant speech: Effect of systematic reading stories. *J. Speech Hearing Res.*, 1960, *3*, 187–190.

Jabaley, M. E., Hoopes, J. E., Knorr, N. J., & Myer, E. The burned child. In M. Debuskey (Ed.), *The chronically ill child and his family.* Springfield, Ill.: Charles C Thomas, 1970.

Jamieson, B. D. Influences of birth order, family size and sex differences in risk taking behavior. *Br. J. Social Clin. Psychol.*, 1969, *8*, 1–8.

Jason, L., & Kimbrough, C. A preventive educational program for young economically disadvantaged children. *J. Community Psychol.*, 1974, *2*, 134–139.

Jeans, P. C., Smith, M. B., & Stearns, G. Incidence of prematurity in relation to maternal nutrition. *J. Am. Diet. Assoc.*, 1955, *31*, 576–581.

Jelliffe, D. B. Cultural variation and the practical pediatrician. *J. Pediatr.*, 1956, *49*, 661–671.

——, & Jelliffe, P. E. F. An overview. *Am. J. Clin. Nutr.*, 1971, *24*, 1013–1024.

————, & Stanfield, J. P. *Diseases of children in the subtropics and tropics* (3d ed.). London: Edward Arnold, 1978.

Jenkins, G. N., & Ferguson, D. B. Milk and dental caries. *Br. Dent. J.*, 1966, *120*, 472–477.

Jersild, A., & Markey, F. Conflicts between preschool children. *Child Dev. Monogr.*, 1935 (No. 21).

Jessner, L., Blom, G. E., & Waldfogel, S. Emotional implications of tonsillectomy and adenoidectomy on children. *Psychoanal. Study Child*, 1952, *7*, 126–169.

————, Weigert, E., & Foy, J. L. The development of parental attitudes during pregnancy. In E. J. Anthony & T. Benedek (Eds.), *Parenthood—Its psychology and psychopathology*. Boston: Little, Brown, 1970, pp. 209–244.

Johannis, T. B., Jr., & Rollins, J. M. Teenager perceptions of family decision making. *Coordinator*, 1959, *7*, 70–74.

Johnson, J.E., Kirchhoff, K. T., & Endress, M. P. Altering children's distress behavior during orthopedic cast removal. *Nurs. Res.*, 1975, *24*(6), 404–410.

Johnson, W., & Leutenegger, R. *Stuttering in children and adults*. Minneapolis: University of Minnesota Press, 1955.

Johnston, C., & Deisher, R. Contemporary communal child rearing. First analysis. *Pediatrics*, 1973, *52*, 319–326.

Joint Commission on Mental Health of Children. *Mental health: From infancy through adolescence*. New York: Harper & Row, 1973.

Jones, K. L., & Smith, D. W. Recognition of the fetal alcohol syndrome in early infancy. *Lancet*, 1973, *2*, 999–1001.

————, ————, Ulleland, C. N., & Streissguth, A. P. Pattern of malformation in off-spring of chronic alcoholic mothers. *Lancet*, 1973, *1*, 1267–1270.

Jorgensen, V. Clinical report on Pennsylvania Hospital's adolescent obstetric clinic. *Am. J. Obstet. Gynecol.*, 1972, *112*, 816–818.

Kahana, B., & Kahana, E. Roles of delay of gratification and motor control in the attainment of conceptual thought. *Proceedings, 78th Annual Convention, American Psychological Association*, 1970, pp. 287–288.

Kaij, L., & Nilsson, A. Emotional and psychotic illness following childbirth. In J. G. Howells (Ed.), *Modern perspectives in psycho-obstetrics*. New York: Brunner/Mazel, 1972, pp. 364–384.

Kane, F. J., Harman, W. J., Keeler, M. H., & Ewing, J. A. Emotional and cognitive disturbance in the early puerperium. *Br. J. Psychiatry*, 1968, *114*, 99–102.

Kanner, L. Autistic disturbances of affective contact. *Nerv. Child*, 1943, *2*, 217.

Kantor, D., & Lehr, W. *Inside the family*. San Francisco: Jossey-Bass, 1975.

Kantor, M. B., Glidwell, J. C., Mensh, I. N., Domki, H. R., & Gildea, M. C. Socio-economic level and maternal attitudes toward parent-child relationships. *Hum. Organization*, 1958, *16*, 44–48.

Kaplan, D. M. Observations on crisis theory and practice. *Social Casework*, 1968, *49*, 151–160.

————, & Mason, E. A. Maternal reactions to premature birth viewed as an acute emotional disorder. *Am. J. Orthopsychiatry*, 1960, *30*, 539–547.

BIBLIOGRAPHY

———, Smith, A., Grobstein, R., & Fischman, S. E. Family mediation of stress. *Social Work*, 1973, *18*, 60–69.

Kaplan, M. The uses of leisure. In C. Tibbitts (Ed.), *Handbook of social gerontology*. Chicago: University of Chicago Press, 1960.

Kardish, S., Hillman, E. S., & Werry, J. Efficacy of imipramine in childhood enuresis: A double blind control study with placebo. *Can. Med. Assoc. J.*, 1968, *99*, 263–266.

Karlberg, P., Engstrom, I., Lichtenstein, H., & Svennberg, I. The development of children in a Swedish urban community. A prospective longitudinal study. III. Physical growth during the first three years of life. *Acta Paediatr. Scand.*, Supplement, 1968, *187*, 48–66.

Kasius, R. V., Randall, A., Thompkins, W., & Wiehl, D. Maternal and newborn nutrition studies at Philadelphia lying-in hospital. V. Size and growth of babies during the first year of life. *Milbank Mem. Fund Q.*, 1957, *35*, 323–372.

Kastenbaum, R. The kingdom where nobody dies. *Saturday Rev.*, 1972, *55*, 33–38.

Katkovsky, W., Preston, A., & Crandall, V. J. Parents' attitudes toward their personal achievements and toward the achievement behavior of their children. *J. Genet. Psychol.*, 1964, *104*, 67–82.

Kaye, E. *The family guide to children's television: What to watch, what to miss, what to change and how to do it!* New York: Pantheon, 1974.

Kearsley, R., Zelazo, P., Kagan, J., & Hartmann, R. Separation protest in day care and home reared infants. *Pediatrics*, 1975, *55*, 171–175.

Kellner, R. *Family ill health—An investigation in general practice*. Springfield, Ill.: Charles C Thomas, 1963.

Kelly, J. B., & Wallerstein, J. S. The effects of parental divorce: Experiences of the child in early latency. *Am. J. Orthopsychiatry*, 1976, 46(1), 20–32.

Kempe, H., & Helfer, R. *Helping the battered child and his family*. Philadelphia: Lippincott, 1972.

Kendall, D. C., & Calmann, I. E. *Handicapped children and their families*. Part III. Reports of the Carnegie United Kingdom Trust, Dunfermline, 1964.

Kenkel, W. F. *The family in perspective* (3d ed.). New York: Meredith, 1973.

Kennell, J. H., & Bergen, M. Early childhood separations. *Pediatrics*, 1966, *37*, 291–298.

———, Jerauld, R., Wolfe, H., Chesler, D., Kreger, N. C., McAlpine, W., Steffa, M., & Klaus, M. H. Maternal behavior one year after early and extended post-partum contact. *Dev. Med. Child Neurol.*, 1974, *16*, 172–179.

———, Slyter, H., & Klaus, M. H. The mourning response of parents to the death of a newborn infant. *N. Engl. J. Med.*, 1970, *283*, 344–349.

———, Soroker, E., Thomas, P., & Wasman, M. What parents of rheumatic fever patients don't understand about the disease and its prophylactic management. *Pediatrics*, 1969, *43*(2), 160–167.

Keogh, B. K. (Ed.). Early identification of children with learning disabilities. *J. Spec. Educ. Monogr.*, 1969, *4*(3), 309–363.

————, & Ryan, S. R. Use of three measures and field organization with young children. *Percep. Motor Skills*, 1971, *33*, 466.

————, & Smith, C. Early identification of educationally high potential and high risk children. *J. School Psychol.*, 1970, *8*, 285–290.

Kerr, R. Movement control and maturation in elementary grade children. *Percep. Motor Skills*, 1975, *41*, 151–154.

Kessen, W., Williams, E. J., & Williams, J. P. Selection and test of response measures in the study of the human newborn. *Child Dev.*, 1961, *32*, 7–24.

Kestenberg, J. S. The effect on parents of the child's transition into and out of latency. In E. J. Anthony & T. Benedek (Eds.), *Parenthood—Its psychology and psychopathology*. Boston: Little, Brown, 1970, pp. 289–306.

Kew, S. *Handicap and family crisis. A study of the siblings of handicapped children*. London: Pitman, 1975.

Keyserling, M. B. *Windows on day care*. New York: National Council of Jewish Women, 1972.

King, S. H. *Perceptions of illness and medical practice*. New York: Russell Sage Foundation, 1962.

Kinsbourne, M. School learning problems and developmental differences. In R. Hoekelman, et al. (Eds.), *Principles of pediatrics, health care of the young*. New York: McGraw-Hill, 1977.

Kinsey, A. *Sexual behavior in the human female*. Philadelphia: Saunders, 1953.

————, & Pomeroy, W., & Martin, C. *Sexual behavior in the human male*. Philadelphia: Saunders, 1948.

Kiser, C. V. (Ed.). *Research in family planning*. Princeton: Princeton University Press, 1962.

Klackenberg, G. Thumbsucking: Frequency and etiology. *Pediatrics*, 1949, *4*, 418–424.

Klaus, M. H., & Kennell, J. H. Mothers separated from their newborn infants. *Pediatr. Clin. North Am.*, 1970, *17*, 1015–1037.

————, & ———— *Maternal-infant bonding*. St. Louis: Mosby, 1976.

Kleeman, J. A. A boy discusses his penis. *Psychoanal. Study Child.*, 1965, *20*, 239–266.

———— Genital self-discovery during a boy's second year. *Psychoanal. Study Child.*, 1966, *21*, 358–392.

———— Genital self-stimulation in infant and toddler girls. In J. Frances & I. Marcus (Eds.), *Masturbation from infancy to senescence*. New York: International University Press, 1975, pp. 77–105.

Klein, D. *Kindergarten entry: Its effects on children and their families*. Symposium on going to school presented by the Committee on Mental Health Massachusetts Chapter, American Academy of Pediatrics, 1963.

Klerman, L., & Jekel, J. *School age mothers: Problems, programs and policy*. Hamden, Conn.: Linnet Books, 1973.

Kline, P. *Fact and fantasy in Freudian theory*. London: Methuen, 1972.

Knoblock, H., & Pasamanick, B. (Eds.). *Gesell and Amatruda's developmental diagnosis* (3d ed.). Hagerstown, Md.: Harper & Row, 1974.

BIBLIOGRAPHY

Koch, C. R., Hermann, J., & Donaldson, M. H. Supportive care of the child with cancer and his family. *Semin. Oncol.*, 1974, *1*(1), 81–86.

Koch, H. L. Some emotional attitudes of the young child in relation to characteristics of his sibling. *Child Dev.*, 1956, *27*, 393–426.

——— The relation of certain formal attributes of siblings to attitudes held toward each other and toward their parents. *Monogr. Soc. Res. Child Dev.*, 1960, *25*, 1–124.

Kohlberg, L. The development of children's orientations toward a moral order. I: Sequences in the development of moral thought. *Vita Hum.*, 1963, *6*, 11–33.

——— A cognitive-developmental analysis of children's sex-role concepts and attitudes. In E. E. Maccoby (Ed.), *The development of sex differences.* Stanford, Calif.: Stanford University Press, 1966.

——— Cognitive-development theory and the practice of collective moral education. In M. Wolins, & M. Gottesman (Eds.), *Group care: The educational path of Youth Aliyah.* New York: Gordon & Breach, 1971.

——— A cognitive-developmental approach to moral education. *Humanist*, 1972, *32*, 13–16.

———, & Zigler, E. The impact of cognitive maturity on the development of sex-role attitudes in the years 4-8. *Genet. Psychol. Monogr.*, 1967, *75*, 89–165.

Kohler, L., & Holst, K. Malocclusion and sucking habits of four-year-old-children. *Acta Paediatr. Scand.*, 1973, *62*, 373–379.

Kohn, M. L. Social class and parental values. *Am. J. Sociol.*, 1950, *64*, 337–351.

——— Social class and parent-child relationships, an interpretation. *Am. J. Sociol.*, 1963, *68*, 471–480.

——— Class and conformity: An interpretation. In M. L. Kohn, *Class and conformity: A study of values.* Homewood, Ill.: Dorsey Press, 1969, pp. 189–203. [Also in I. L. Reiss, (Ed.), *Readings on the family system.* New York: Holt, 1972, pp. 331–343.]

Koocher, G. P. Childhood death and cognitive development. *Dev. Psychol.*, 1973, *9*, 369–375.

Koos, E. L. *Families in trouble.* New York: King's Crown Press, 1950.

Kopfstein, D. Risk-taking behavior and cognitive style. *Child Dev.*, 1973, *44*, 190–192.

Korner, A. F. Individual differences at birth: Implications for early experience and later development. *Am. J. Orthopsychiatry*, 1971, *41*(4), 608–619.

——— Early stimulation and maternal care as related to infant capabilities and individual differences. *Early Child Dev. Care*, 1973, *2*, 307–327.

——— Individual differences at birth: Implications for child care practices. In D. Bergsma (Ed.), *The infant at risk.* New York: Intercontinental Medical Book Corp., 1974. [Original article series in *Birth Defects*, 1974, *10*(2), 51–61.]

Korones, S. *High risk newborn infants: The basis for intensive nursing care.* St. Louis: Mosby, 1972.

Korsch, B. M. The child and the operating room. *Anesthesiology*, 1975, *43*, 251–257.

CHILD AND FAMILY DEVELOPMENT

————, & Aley, E. F. Pediatric interviewing techniques. *Curr. Prob. Pediatr.*, 1973, *111*, 3–42.

————, & Negrete, V. F. Doctor-patient communication. *Sci. Am.*, 1972, *227*(2), 66–74.

————, ————, Mercer, A. S., & Freemon, B. How comprehensive are well child visits? *Am. J. Dis. Child.*, 1971, *122*, 483–488.

Kotelchuck, M. The infant's relationship to the father: Experimental evidence. In M. E. Lamb (Ed.), *The role of the father in child development.* New York: Wiley, 1976.

Kraus, B., & Jordan, R. *The human dentition before birth.* Philadelphia: Lea & Febiger, 1965.

Kraus, M. V., & Hunscher, M. A. *Food, nutrition and diet therapy* (5th ed.). Philadelphia: Saunders, 1972.

Kravitz, H. A study of head banging in infants and children. *Dis. Nerv. Sys.*, 1960, *21*, 203–208.

Krogman, W. M. *Child growth.* Ann Arbor: University of Michigan Press, 1972.

Kroll, R. G., & Stone, J. H. Nocturnal bottle feeding as a contributory cause of rampant dental caries in the infant and young child. *J. Dent. Child.*, 1967, *34*, 454.

Krugman, S., & Gershon, N. (Eds.). *Infections of the fetus and the newborn infant.* New York: Alan R. Liss, 1975.

Labov, W. The logic of nonstandard English. In J. E. Alatis (Ed.), *20th annual round table.* Washington, D.C.: Georgetown University Press, 1970.

Ladas, A. K. The relationship of information and support to breast-feeding. In *Psychosomatic medicine in obstetrics and gynaecology*, 3d Int. Congress, London, 1971. Basel: Karger, 1972, pp. 287–289.

Lakin, M. Personality factors in mothers of excessively crying (colicky) infants. *Monogr. Soc. Res. Child Dev.*, 1957, *22*(1) (Series No. 64).

Lamb, M. E. Interactions between eight-month-old children and their fathers and mothers. In M. E. Lamb (Ed.), *The role of the father in child development.* New York: Wiley, 1976a.

———— Proximity seeking attachment behaviors: A critical review of the literature. *Genet. Psychol. Monogr.*, 1976b, *93*, 63–89.

———— Father-infant and mother-infant interaction in the first year of life. *Child Dev.*, 1977, *48*, 167–181.

————, & Lamb, J. E. The nature and importance of the father-infant relationship. *Fam. Coord.*, 1976, *25*, 379–385.

Lambert, W. E., Yackley, A., & Hein, R. N. Child training values of English-Canadian and French-Canadian parents. *Can. J. Behav. Sci.*, 1971, *3*, 217–236.

Lamm, E., Delaney, J., & Dwyer, J. T. Economy in the feeding of infants. *Pediatr. Clin. North Am.*, 1977, *24*, 71–84

Langford, W. S. The child in the pediatric hospital: Adaptation to illness and hospitalization. *Am. J. Orthopsychiatry*, 1961, *31*, 667–684.

BIBLIOGRAPHY

Lansky, L. M. The family structure also affects the model: Sex-role attitudes in parents of preschool children. *Merrill-Palmer Q.*, 1967, *13*, 139–150.

Lansky, S. B., & Lawman, J. T. Childhood malignancy. *J. Kansas Med. Soc.*, 1974, *75*, 91–94.

Lanzkowski, P. Investigation into the aetiology and treatment of pica. *Arch. Dis. Child.*, 1959, *34*, 140–148.

Larsen, V. L. Stresses of the childbearing year. *Am. J. Publ. Health*, 1966, *56*(1), 32–36.

Legg, C., Sherick, I., & Wadland, W. Reactions of preschool children to the birth of a sibling. *Child Psychiatry Hum. Dev.*, 1974, *5*, 3–39.

Leiderman, H. Mother-infant separation: Delayed consequences. In M. H. Klaus, T. Leger, & M. A. Trause (Eds.), *Maternal attachment and mothering disorders: A round table*. Sausalito, Calif.: Johnson and Johnson Baby Products Co., 1975, pp. 67–68.

Leifer, A. D., Leiderman, P. H., Barnett, C. R., & Williams, J. A. Effects of mother-infant separation on maternal attachment behavior. *Child Dev.*, 1972, *43*, 1203–1218.

LeMasters, E. E. Parenthood as crisis. *Marriage Fam. Living*, 1957, *19*, 352–355.

——— *Parents in modern America* (3d ed.). Homewood, Ill.: Dorsey Press, 1977.

Lenneberg, E., Rebelsky, F., & Nichols, I. The vocalizations of infants born to deaf and to hearing parents. *Hum. Dev.*, 1965, *8*, 23–37.

Lesinski, J. High-risk pregnancy: Unresolved prediction problems of screening, management, and prognosis. *Obstet. and Gynecol.*, 1975, *46*, 599–603.

Levine, J., Fishman, C., & Kagan, J. Social class and sex as determinants of maternal behavior. *Am. J. Orthopsychiatry*, 1967, *37*, 397.

Levine, M., & Bakow, H. Children with encopresis: A study of treatment outcome. *Pediatrics*, 1976, *58*, 845–852.

———, & Seligman, J. *A baby is born*. New York: Golden Press, 1962.

Levinger, G. Task and social behavior in marriage. *Sociometry*, 1964, *27*, 433–448.

Levy, D. M. *Maternal overprotection*. New York: Columbia University Press, 1943.

——— *The demonstration clinic*. Springfield, Ill.: Charles C Thomas, 1959.

Lewis, C. E., & Lewis, M. A. Child initiated care workshop. San Francisco: Ambulatory Pediatric Association, April 25, 1977.

Lewis, M. *Clinical aspects of child development*. Philadelphia: Lea & Febiger, 1971.

——— State as an infant-environmental interaction: An analysis of mother-infant interaction as a function of sex. *Merrill-Palmer Q.*, 1972, *18*, 95–121.

——— The latency child in a custody conflict. *J. Am. Acad. Child Psychiatry*, 1974, *13*(4), 635–647.

———, & Lewis, D. O. Pediatric management of psychologic crises. *Curr. Probl. Pediatr.*, 1973, *3*, 3–17.

Liakos, A., Panayotakopoulos, K., Lyketsos, G., & Kaskarelis, D. Depressive and neurotic symptoms in the puerperum. In *Psychosomatic medicine in obstetrics and gynaecology*, 3d Int. Congress, London, 1971. Basel: Karger, 1972, pp. 343–346.

Lidz, T. The family as the developmental setting. In E. J. Anthony & C. Koupernik (Eds.), *The child in his family*. New York: Wiley, 1970, pp. 19–39.

────── *The person. His development throughout the life cycle*. (Rev. ed.). New York: Basic Books, 1976. (Excerpt reprinted with permission.)

Liebernecht, K. Helping the battered wife. *Am. J. Nurs.*, 1978, *78*, 654–656.

Liebert, R. M., Neale, J. M., & Davidson, E. *The early window: Effects of television on children and youth*. New York: Pergamon Press, 1973.

Lindemann, E. Symptomatology and management of acute grief. *Am. J. Psychiatry*, 1944, *101*, 141–148.

────── , Rosenblith, J., Allensmith, W., Budd, L., & Shapiro, S. Predicting school adjustment before entry. *J. School Psychol.*, 1967, 6, 24–39.

Linder, C. Breath holding spells in children. *Clin. Pediatr.*, 1968, *7*, 88–90.

Litman, T. J. An analysis of the sociological factors affecting the rehabilitation of physically handicapped patients. *Arch. Phys. Med. Rehabil.*, 1964, *45*, 9–16.

Livingston, S. Breathholding spells in children: Differentiation from epileptic attacks. *JAMA*, 1970, *212*, 2231–2235.

Lourie, R. Studies in bed rocking, head banging, and related rhythmic patterns. *Clin. Procedures Child. Hosp. Washington*, 1949, *5*, 295–309.

────── , Layman, E., & Millican, F. Why children eat things that are not food. *Children*, 1963, *10*, 143–146.

Lovell, K. E. The effect of postmaturity on the developing child. *Med. J. Aust.*, 1973, *1*, 13–17.

Lowrey, G. H. *Growth and development of children* (6th ed.). Chicago: Year Book Medical Publishers, 1973.

Lubic, R. W. Developing maternity services women will trust. *Am. J. Nurs.*, 1975, *75*, 1685–1688.

Lucey, J. F. Hazards to the newborn infant from drugs administered to the mother. *Pediatr. Clin. North Am.*, 1961, *8*, 413–419.

McBride, W. G. Thalidomide and congenital abnormalities. *Lancet*, 1961, *2*, 1358.

McCarthy, D. Language development in children. In L. Carmichael (Ed.), *Manual of child psychology*. New York: Wiley, 1946, pp. 476–581.

Maccoby, E. E. (Ed.). *The development of sex differences*. Stanford, Calif.: Stanford University Press, 1966.

────── , & Jacklin, C. N. *The psychology of sex differences*. Stanford, Calif.: Stanford University Press, 1974.

────── , & Masters, J. C. Attachment and dependency. In P. H. Mussen (Ed.), *Carmichael's manual of child psychology* (Vol. 2, 3d ed.). New York: Wiley, 1970.

McCord, W., McCord, J., & Zola, I. K. *Origins of crime*. New York: Columbia University Press, 1959.

McCracken, B. H. Etiological aspects of obesity. *Am. J. Med. Sci.*, 1962, *243*, 99–111.

McDermott, J. F. Parental divorce in early childhood. *Am. J. Psychiatry*, 1968, *124*(10), 1424–1432.

Mace, D. R. The employed mother in the U.S.S.R. *Marriage Fam. Living*, 1961,*23*, 330–333.

McFarland, M. B., & Reinhardt, J. B. The development of motherliness. *Children*, 1959, *6*, 48–52.

MacFarlane, J., Allen, L., & Honzik, M. *A developmental study of the behavioral problems of normal children between twenty-one months and fourteen years.* Berkeley and Los Angeles: University of California Press, 1962.

McGanity, W. J., Little, H. M., Fogelman, A., Jennings, L., Calhoun, E., & Dawson, E. B. Pregnancy in the adolescent. *Am. J. Obstet. Gynecol.*, 1969, *103*(6), 773–788.

McGraw, M. B. *Growth: A study of Johnny and Jimmy.* New York: Appleton-Century-Crofts, 1935.

—— Later development of children especially trained during infancy: Johnny and Jimmy at school age. *Child Dev.*, 1939, *10*, 1–19.

—— *The neuromuscular maturation of the human infant.* New York: Hafner, 1943.

McKay, J., & Lucey, G. Medical progress: Neonatology. *N. Engl. J. Med.*, 1964, *270*, 1231–1236.

McKevitt, R., Nader, P. R., Williamson, M., & Berrey, R. Reasons for health office visits in an urban school district. *J. School Health*, 1977, *47*(5), 275–279.

McKigney, J. Economic aspects. *Am. J. Clin. Nutr.*, 1971, *24*, 1005–1012.

McLean, J. A., Schrager, J., & Stoeffler, V. R. Severe asthma in children. *Michigan Med.*, 1968, *67*, 1219–1226.

Maddi, S. R. *Personality theories: A comparative analysis.* Homewood, Ill.: Dorsey Press, 1976.

Madsen, C. H. Positive reinforcement in toilet training of a normal child: A case report. In L. P. Ullman & L. Krasner (Eds.), *Case studies in behavior modification.* New York: Holt, 1965.

Madsen, W. *The Mexican-American of south Texas.* New York: Holt, 1964.

Maier, H. W. *Three theories of child development* (Rev. ed.). New York: Harper & Row, 1969.

Makinen, K. K. The role of sucrose and other sugars in the development of dental caries: A review. *Int. Dent. J.*, 1972, *22*, 363.

Malone, C. A. Some observations on children of disorganized families and problems of acting out. *J. Am. Acad. Child Psychiatry*, 1963, *2*, 22–49.

Maresh, M. Changes in tissue widths during growth. *Am. J. Dis. Child.*, 1966,*111*, 142–154.

Marston, M. V. Compliance with medical regimens: A review of the literature. *Nurs. Res.*, 1970, *19*, 312–323.

Martin, D. *Battered wives.* San Francisco: New Glide Publications, 1976.

Martin, H. P. Nutrition: Its relationship to children's physical, mental and emotional development. *Am. J. Clin. Nutr.*, 1973, *26*, 766–775.

———, Beezley, P., Conway, E. F., & Kempe, H. C. The development of abused children. In I. Schulman (Ed.), *Advances in pediatrics* (Vol. 21). Chicago: Year Book Medical Publishers, 1974, pp. 25–73.

Martinez, C., & Martin, H. Folk disease among urban Mexican-Americans. *JAMA*, 1966, *196*, 161–164.

Masters, W. H., & Johnson, V. E. *Human sexual response.* Boston: Little, Brown, 1966.

Mattsson, A. Long-term physical illness in childhood: A challenge to psychosocial adaptation. *Pediatrics*, 1972, *50*, 801–811.

Mayer, J. Some aspects of the problem of regulation of food intake and obesity continued. *N. Engl. J. Med.*, 1966, *274*, 670–672.

Mead, M. *Male and female.* New York: Mentor, 1955.

Meadow, K. P. Parental response to medical ambiguities of congenital deafness. *J. Health Social Behav.*, 1968, *9*, 299–309.

——— The development of deaf children. In M. Hetherington (Ed.), *Review of child development research* (Vol. 5). Chicago: University of Chicago Press, 1975.

Mehl, L. E. Home delivery research today—A review. *Women Health*, 1976, *1*(5), 3–11.

Meier, J. *Developmental and learning disabilities: Education management and prevention in children.* Baltimore: University Park Press, 1976.

Melamed, B. G., & Siegel, L. J. Reduction of anxiety in children facing hospitalization and surgery by use of filmed modeling. *J. Consult. Clin. Psychol.*, 1975, *43*(4), 511–521.

Melear, D. Children's conceptions of death. *J. Genet. Psychol.*, 1973, *123*, 359–360.

Mercer, R. T. Responses of mothers to the birth of an infant with a defect. In *ANA Clinical Sessions*. New York: Appleton-Century-Crofts, 1975, pp. 340–349.

Meyer, H. F. Breast feeding in the United States. Report of a 1966 national survey with comparable 1946 and 1956 data. *Clin. Pediatr.*, 1968, *7*, 708–715.

Meyerowitz, J. H., & Kaplan, H. B. Familial responses to stress: The case of cystic fibrosis. *Social Sci. Med.*, 1967, *1*, 249–266.

Michaels, R. H., & Mellin, G. W. Prospective experience with maternal rubella and the associated congenital malformations. *Pediatrics*, 1960, *26*, 200–209.

Milio, N. Values, social class, and community health services. *Nurs. Res.*, 1967, *16*, 23–31.

Millar, T. P. The hospital and the preschool child. *Children*, 1970, *17*, 171–176.

Miller, D., & Norris, R. Entrance age and school success. *J. School Psychol.*, 1967, *6*, 47–60.

Miller, F., Courth, S., Knox, R., & Brandon, S. *The school years in New Castle upon Tyne 1952-1962.* London: Oxford University Press, 1974.

Miller, I. Maternal attitudes. In A. Clark, M. Brunnell, & E. Henning (Eds.),

BIBLIOGRAPHY

Parent-child relationships: Role of the nurse. New Brunswick, N.J.: Rutgers University, 1968, pp. 18–25.

Miller, L. G. Toward a greater understanding of the mentally retarded child. *J. Pediatr.*, 1968a, *73*, 699–705.

Miller, R. W. Delayed effects occurring within the first decade after exposure of young individuals to the Hiroshima atomic bomb. *Pediatrics*, 1956, *18*, 1–17.

Millichap, J. G., & Fowler, G. W. Treatment of "minimal brain dysfunction" syndromes. Selection of drugs for children with hyperactivity and learning disabilities. *Pediatr. Clin. North Am.*, 1967, *14*, 767–777.

Milunsky, A. *The prevention of genetic disease and mental retardation.* Philadelphia: Saunders, 1975.

Mindlin, R. L., & Densen, P. M. Medical care of urban infants: Continuity of care. *Am. J. Publ. Health*, 1969, *59*, 1294–1301.

————, & ———— Medical care of urban infants: Health supervision. *Am. J. Publ. Health*, 1971, *61*, 687–697.

Minuchin, P., Biber, B., Shapiro, E., & Zimiles, H. *The psychological impact of school experience.* New York: Basic Books, 1969.

Minuchin, S., Montalvo, B., Guerney, B. G., Rosman, B. L., & Schumer, F. L. *Families of the slums: An exploration of their structure and treatment.* New York: Basic Books, 1967.

Money, J., & Ehrhardt, A. A. *Man and woman, boy and girl.* Baltimore: Johns Hopkins Press, 1972.

————, Hampson, J. G., & Hampson, J. L. Hermaphroditism: Recommendations concerning assignment of sex, change of sex, and psychologic management. *Bull. Johns Hopkins Hosp.*, 1955a, *97*, 284.

————, ————, & ———— An examination of some basic sexual concepts: The evidence of human hermaphroditism. *Bull. Johns Hopkins Hosp.*, 1955b, *97*, 301–319.

Monte, C. F. *Beneath the mask.* New York: Praeger, 1977.

Moore, K. L. *The developing human* (2d ed.). Philadelphia: Saunders, 1977.

Moore, T. W. Effects on the children. In S. Yudkin & A. Holme (Eds.), *Working mothers and their children.* London: Michael Joseph, 1963.

————, & Ucko, L. Night waking in infancy: Part I. *Arch. Dis. Child.*, 1957, *32*, 333–342.

Moorrees, C. *The dentition of the growing child: A longitudinal study of dental development between 3 and 18 years of age.* Cambridge, Mass.: Harvard University Press, 1959.

————, Sisson, W., Peckos, P., Christie, R. G., & Baldwin, D. Need for collaboration of pediatrician and orthodontist. *Pediatrics*, 1962, *29*, 142–146.

Moos, R. H., & Tsu, V. D. The crisis of physical illness: An overview. In R. Moos (Ed.), *Coping with physical illness.* New York: Plenum, 1976, pp. 3–21.

Moreland, J. Racial acceptance and preference of nursery school children in a southern city. *Merrill-Palmer Q.*, 1962, *8*, 271–280.

Morely, M. E. *The development and disorders of speech in childhood.* London: Livingstone, 1957.

Morris, M. G. Maternal claiming—Identification processes: Their meaning for mother-infant mental health. In A. Clark, M. Bunell, & E. Henning (Eds.), *Parent-child relationships: Role of the nurse.* New Brunswick, N.J.: Rutgers University, The State University of New Jersey, 1968, pp. 26–35.

———, & Gould, R. *Role reversal: A concept in dealing with the neglected/ battered-child syndrome* (Monograph G-17). New York: Child Welfare League of America, 1963.

Morrison, I. The elderly primigravida. *Am. J. Obstet. Gynecol.*, 1975, *121*, 465–470.

Morrison, J. R., & Stewart, M. A. Bilateral inheritance as evidence for polygenicity in the hyperactive child syndrome. *J. Nerv. Ment. Disorders*, 1974, *158*, 226–228.

Moss, H. Sex, age, and state as determinants of mother-infant interaction. *Merrill-Palmer Q.*, 1967, *13*, 19–36.

———, Robson, K. S., & Pederson, F. Determinants of maternal stimulation of infants and consequences of treatment for later reactions to strangers. *Dev. Psychol.*, 1969, *1*, 239–246.

Moss, J. J., & MacNab, M. M. Young families. *J. Home Econ.*, 1961, *53*, 829–834.

Moynihan, D. P. *The Negro family: The case for national action.* Washington, D.C.: U.S. Dept. of Labor, Office of Policy Planning and Research, 1965.

Murphy, D. P. Maternal pelvic irradiation. *Congenital malformations* (2d ed.). Philadelphia: Lippincott, 1947.

Nadelson, C. "Normal" and "special" aspects of pregnancy. *Obstet. Gynecol.*, 1973, *41*, 611–620.

Nader, P. R., Bullock, D., & Caldwell, B. School phobia. *Pediatr. Clin. North Am.*, 1975, *22*, 605–617.

Nagera, H. Children's reactions to the death of important objects. *Psychoanal. Study Child*, 1970, *25*, 360–400.

Nagy, M. The child's theories concerning death. *J. Genet. Psychol.*, 1948, *73*, 3–27.

Nakushian, J. M. Restoring parents' equilibrium after Sudden Infant Death. *Am. J. Nurs.*, 1976, *76*, 1600–1604.

National Academy of Sciences, Institute of Medicine. *A strategy for evaluating health services.* Washington, D.C.: National Academy of Sciences, 1973.

National Foundation for Sudden Infant Death. *Facts about sudden infant death syndrome.* Pamphlet published by National Foundation for Sudden Infant Death. 1501 Broadway, New York, New York 10036.

Neligan, G., & Prudham, D. Norms for four standard developmental milestones by sex, social class, and place in family. *Dev. Med. Child Neurol.*, 1969, *11*, 413–431.

Nellhaus, G. Head circumference: Birth to 18 years. *Pediatrics*, 1968, *41*, 106–114.

Neumann, C. G. Obesity in pediatric practice: Obesity in the preschool and school-age child. *Pediatr. Clin. North Am.*, 1977, *24*(1), 117–122.

———, & Aplaugh, M. Birthweight doubling time: A fresh look. *Pediatrics*, 1976, *57*, 469–473.

Newberger, E., Newberger, C. M., & Richmond, J. B. Child health in America: Toward a rational public policy. *Milbank Mem. Fund Q., Health Society*, 1976, *54*, 249–298.

Newson, J., & Newson, E. Parental roles and social contexts. In M. Shipman (Ed.), *The organization and impact of social research*. London: Routledge & Kegan Paul, 1976.

Newton, M. Mammary effects. *Am. J. Clin. Nutr.*, 1971, *24*, 987–990.

Newton, N. *Maternal emotions*. New York: Hoeber, 1955.

——— Psychologic differences between breast and bottle feeding. *Am. J. Clin. Nutr.*, 1971, *24*, 993–1004.

——— Forward. In T. Thevenin. *The family bed: An age old concept in childrearing*. Minneapolis: Tine Thevenin, 1976, p. xiii.

———, & Newton, M. Lactation—Its psychologic components. In J. G. Howells (Ed.), *Modern perspectives in psycho-obstetrics*. New York: Brunner/Mazel, 1972, pp. 385–409.

———, Peeler, D., & Rawlins, C. Does breast-feeding influence mother love? In *Psychosomatic medicine in obstetrics and gynaecology*, 3d Int. Cong., London, 1971. Basel: Karger, 1972, pp. 296–298.

NICHD National Registry for Amniocentesis Group. Midtrimester amniocentesis for prenatal diagnosis. *JAMA*, 1976, *236*(13), 1471–1476.

Nilsson, A. Para-natal emotional adjustment. *Acta Psychiatr. Scand.*, Supplement, 1970, *220*, 9–61.

——— Paranatal emotional adjustment. A prospective investigation of 165 women. In *Psychosomatic medicine in obstetrics and gynaecology*, 3d Int. Congress, London, 1971. Basel: Karger, 1972, pp. 157–160.

Norton, S. J., & Glick, P. C. Changes in American family life. *Child. Today*, 1976, *5*(3), 2–4.

——— Emerging and declining family roles. *J. Marriage Fam.*, 1974, *36*, 238–245.

Nye, F. I. Marital interaction. In F. I. Nye & L. W. Hoffman (Eds.), *The employed mother in America*. Chicago: Rand McNally, 1963, pp. 263–281.

———, & Berardo, F. M. *Emerging conceptual frameworks in family analysis*. New York: Macmillan, 1966.

———, & ——— *The family. Its structure and interaction*. New York: Macmillan, 1973. (Excerpts reprinted with permission.)

———, & Hoffman, L. W. The sociocultural setting. In F. I. Nye & L. W. Hoffman (Eds.), *The employed mother in America*. Chicago: Rand McNally, 1963, pp. 3–39.

Obrzut, L. A. J. Expectant fathers' perception of fathering. *Am. J. Nurs.*, 1976, *76*, 1440–1442.

O'Dell, S. Training parents in behavior modification: A review. *Psychol. Bull.*, 1974, *81*, 418–433.

Ogburn, W. F. The changing family. *The Family*, 1938, *19*, 139–143.

Olshansky, S. Chronic sorrow: A response to having a mentally defective child. *Social Casework*, 1962, *43*, 190–193.

O'Meara, W. V. Fluoride administration in single dose: A survey of its value in prevention of dental caries. *Clin. Pediatr.*, 1968, *7*, 177–184.

Orden, S. R., & Bradburn, N. M. Working wives and marriage happiness. *Am. J. Sociol.*, 1969, *74*, 392–407.

Orlansky, H. Infant care and personality. *Psychol. Bull.*, 1949, *46*, 1–48.

Osofsky, H. J. Antenatal malnutrition: Its relationship to subsequent infant and child development. *Am. J. Obstet. Gynecol.*, 1969, *105*, 1150–1159.

Osofsky, J. H. *The pregnant teenager*. Springfield, Ill.: Charles C Thomas, 1968.

————— Poverty, pregnancy outcome and child development. *Birth Defects*, 1974, *10*, 37–50.

Otto, H. A. Criteria for assessing family strength. *Fam. Process*, 1963, *2*, 329–338.

————— A framework for assessing family strengths. In A. Reinhardt & M. Quinn (Eds.), *Family centered community nursing*. St. Louis: Mosby, 1973, pp. 87–94.

Owen, G. M., Kram, K. M., Garry, P. J., Lowe, J. E., & Lubin, A. H. A study of nutritional status of preschool children in the United States, 1968–69. *Pediatrics*, 1974, (Part II), *53*(4), 597–646.

Paige, D. M., Cordano, A., & Huang, S. Nutritional supplementation of disadvantaged elementary-school children. *Pediatrics*, 1976, *58*(5), 697–703.

Paine, R. S., Werry, J. S., & Quay, H. C. A study of minimal cerebral dysfunction. *Dev. Med. Child Neurol.*, 1968, *10*, 505–520.

Pajntar, M. Obstetrical complications—Personality changes and emotional tension during pregnancy. In *Psychosomatic medicine in obstetrics and gynecology*, 3d Int. Congress, London, 1971. Basel: Karger, 1972, pp. 131–136.

Pan American Health Organization. *Maternal nutrition and family planning in the Americas*. Report of a technical group meeting. Washington, D.C.: Pan American Health Organization, 1970.

Parcel, G. S., & Nader, P. R. Pilot experience with a school health education program that specifies target population and evaluation procedures. *J. School Health*, 1977, *47*(8), 453–456.

Parke, R. D. Effectiveness of punishment as an interaction of intensity, timing, age, nurturance, and cognitive structuring. *Child Dev.*, 1969, *40*, 213–235.

————— Father-infant interaction. In M. H. Klaus, T. Leger, & M. A. Trause (Eds.), *Maternal attachment and mothering disorders: A round table*. Sausalito, Calif.: Johnson & Johnson Baby Products Co., 1975, pp. 61–63.

Parkes, C. M. The nature of grief. *Int. J. Psychiatry*, 1967, *3*, 435–438.

Parmelee, A., Wenner, W., & Schulz, H. Infant sleep patterns: From birth to 16 weeks of age. *J. Pediatr.*, 1964, *65*, 576–582.

Parsons, T. Family structure and the socialization of the child. In T. Parsons & R. F. Bales (Eds.), *Family: Socialization and interaction process*. New York: Free Press, 1955.

—————, & Bales, R. F. *The family: Socialization and interaction process*. Glencoe, Ill.: Free Press, 1955.

BIBLIOGRAPHY

————, & Fox, R. Illness, therapy, and the modern urban American family. *J. Social Issues*, 1952, *8*, 31–44.

Patterson, G. R. *Families: Applications of social learning to family life*. Champaign, Ill.: Research Press, 1975.

————, Reid, J. B., Jones, R. R., & Conger, R. E. *A social learning approach to family intervention: Families with aggressive children*. Eugene, Oreg.: Castalia, 1975.

Pavenstedt, E. (Ed.). *The drifters*. Boston: Little, Brown, 1967.

———— An intervention program for infants from high risk homes. *Am. J. Publ. Health*, 1973, *63*, 393–395.

Pearlin, L. I. *Class-context and family relations: A cross-national study*. Boston: Little, Brown, 1971.

————, & Kahn, M. L. Social class, occupation and parental values: A cross culture study. *Am. Sociol. Rev.*, 1966, *31*, 466–479.

Pederson, F. A., & Robson, K. S. Father participation in infancy. *Am. J. Orthopsychiatry*, 1969, *39*, 466–472.

Perinatal Perspectives. University of Rochester Strong Memorial Hospital Perinatal Center, 1977, *3*(4), 1–7.

Perkins, S. A. Malnutrition and mental development. *Except. Child.*, 1977, *43*, 214–219.

Perry, D. G., & Parke, R. D. Punishment and alternative response training as determinants of response inhibition in children. *Genet. Psychol. Monogr.*, 1975, *91*, 257–279.

Pervin, L. A. *Personality: Theory assessment and research*. New York: Wiley, 1975.

Peters, J. E., Davis, S., Goolsby, C. M., Clements, S. D., & Hicks, T. J. *Physician's handbook: Screening for MBD*. Summit, N.J.: Ciba Medical Horizons, 1973.

Pfouts, J. H. The sibling relationship: A forgotten dimension. *Social Work*, 1976, *21*, 200–204. (With permission.)

Piaget, J. *The moral judgement of the child*. Glencoe, Ill.: Free Press, 1948.

———— *The child's conception of the world*. New York: Humanities Press, 1951.

———— *The origins of intelligence in children*. New York: International University Press, 1952.

Pilowsky, I. Psychological aspects of complications of childbirth. A prospective study of primiparae and their husbands. In *Psychosomatic medicine in obstetrics and gynaecology*, 3d Int. Congress, London, 1971. Basel: Karger, 1972, pp. 161–165.

Pineo, P. C. Disenchantment in the later years of marriage. *Marriage Fam. Living*, 1961, *23*, 3–11.

Pisacano, J., Lichter, H., Ritter, J., & Siegel, A. An attempt at prevention of obesity in infancy. *Pediatrics*, 1978, *61*, 360–364.

Pitkin, R. M., Kaminetsky, H. A., Newton, M., & Pritchard, J. A. Maternal nutrition—A selective review of clinical topics. *Obstet. Gynecol.*, 1972, *40*, 773–785.

Pless, I. B., & Pinkerton, P. *Chronic childhood disorder—Promoting patterns of adjustment*. London: Henry Kimpton, 1975.

————, & Satterwhite, B. Health education literature for parents of handicapped children. *Am. J. Dis. Child.*, 1971, *122*, 206–211.

Plummer, G. Anomalies occuring in children exposed in utero to the atomic bomb in Hiroshima. *Pediatrics*, 1952, *10*, 687–693.

Pomeroy, M. Sudden infant death syndrome. *Am. J. Nurs.*, 1969, *69*, 1886–1890.

Popich, G., & Smith, D. Fontanels: Range of normal size. *J. Pediatr.*, 1972, *80*, 749–752.

Powell, G. J., & Powell, R. N. The infant in the black culture. In D. Bergsma (Ed.), *The infant at risk*, 1974, *10*(2), 141–152. (Original article series in *Birth Defects*, National Foundation.)

Presser, H. B. Early motherhood: Ignorance or bliss? *Fam. Planning Perspect.*, 1974, *6*, 8–14.

Preventive Medicine USA: *Health promotion and consumer health education*. A Task Force Report sponsored by the John E. Fogarty International Center for Advanced Study in the Health Sciences, National Institute of Health, and The American College of Preventive Medicine. New York: Prodict, 1976.

Proshansky, H. The development of intergroup attitudes. In L. Hoffman & M. Hoffman (Eds.), *Review of child development research* (Vol. 2). New York: Russell Sage Foundation, 1966, pp. 311–371.

Protheroe, C. Puerperal psychoses: A long-term study, 1927-61. *Br. J. Psychiatry*, 1969, *115*, 9–30.

Prothro, E. T. Socialization and social class in a transitional study. *Child Dev.*, 1966, *37*, 219–228.

Provence, S., & Lipton, R. *Infants in institutions*. New York: International University Press, 1962.

Prugh, D. G. Emotional problems of the premature infant's parents. *Nurs. Outlook*, 1953, *1*, 461–464.

————, Staub, E. M., Sands, H. H., Kirshbaum, R. M., & Lenihan, E. A. A study of the emotional reactions of children and families to hospitalization and illness. *Am. J. Orthopsychiatry*, 1953, *23*, 70–106.

Pugh, W. E., & Fernandez, F. L. Coitus in late pregnancy. *Obstet. Gynecol.*, 1953, *2*, 636–642.

Quinton, D., & Rutter, M. Early hospital admissions and later disturbances of behavior: An attempted replication of Douglas' findings. *Dev. Med. Child Neurol.*, 1976, *18*, 447–459.

Quirk, B., & Hassanein, R. The nurse's role in advising patients on coitus during pregnancy. *Nurs. Clin. North Am.*, 1973, *8*, 501–507.

Rabin, A. I. *Growing up in the kibbutz*. New York: Springer, 1965.

Rabkin, L. Y., & Rabkin, K. Children of the kibbutz. *Psychol. Today*, 1969, *3*(4) 40–46.

Rainwater, L. *Family design: Marital sexuality, family size and contraception*. Chicago: Aldine, 1965.

———— Crucible of identity: The Negro lower class family. *Daedalus*, 1966, *95*(1), 172–216.

BIBLIOGRAPHY

Ramey, J. W. Communes, group marriage, and the upper-middle class. *J. Marriage Fam.*, 1972, *34*, 647–655.

Rapoport, L. The state of crisis: Some theoretical considerations. In H. J. Parad (Ed.), *Crisis intervention: Selected readings*. New York: Family Service Association of America, 1965, pp. 22–31.

Rapoport, R. Normal crisis, family structure and mental health. In H. J. Parad (Ed.), *Crisis intervention: Selected reading*. New York: Family Service Association of America, 1965, pp. 120–130.

————, Rapoport, R. N., & Strelitz, Z. *Fathers, mothers and society*. New York: Basic Books, 1977.

Ratner, H. Introduction. In T. Thevenin, *The family bed: An age old concept in childrearing*. Minneapolis: Tine Thevenin, 1976.

Raush, H. L., Goodrich, W., & Campbell, J. D. Adaptation to the first years of marriage. *Psychiatry*, 1963, *26*, 368–380.

Redman, B. K. *The process of patient teaching in nursing* (3d ed.). St. Louis: Mosby, 1976.

Reiss, I. L. *The family system in America*. New York: Holt, 1971.

Rendina, I., & Dickerscheid, J. D. Father involvement with first-born infants. *Fam. Coord.*, 1976, *25*, 373–378.

Riccardi, D. & Robinson, A. Preventive medicine through genetic counseling: A regional program. *Prev. Med.*, 1975, *4*, 126–134.

Ricciuti, H. Malnutrition and psychological development. In J. Nurnberger (Ed.), *Biological and environmental determinants of early development: Proceedings* (Vol. 51). Baltimore: Williams & Wilkins, 1973.

Richards, M. (Ed.). *The integration of a child into a social world*. London: Cambridge University Press, 1974.

Richards, N. D. Methods and effectiveness of health education: The past, present and future of social scientific involvement. *Social Sci. Med.*, 1975, *9*, 141–156.

Richardson, S. A., & Guttmacher, A. F. (Eds.). *Childbearing—Its social and psychological aspects*. Baltimore: Williams & Wilkins, 1967.

Richmond, J., Eddy, E., & Garrard, S. The syndrome of fecal soiling and megacolon. *Am. J. Orthopsychiatry*, 1954, *24*, 391.

Rittlemeyer, L. F. Thumbsucking: A preventable problem. *G. P.* 1955, *11*, 555–560.

Ritvo, S., & Solnit, A. J. Influences of early mother-child interactions on identification processes. *Psychoanal. Study Child*, 1958, *13*, 64–85.

Roberts, K. E., & Schoellkopf, J. A. Eating, sleeping and elimination practices of a group of two and one-half year old children. *Am. J. Dis. Child.*, 1951, *82*, 137–152.

Robertson, E. K., & Suinn, R. M. The determination of rate of progress of stroke patients through empathy measures of patient and family. *J. Psychosom. Res.*, 1968, *12*, 189–191.

Robertson, G. G. Nausea and vomiting of pregnancy. *Lancet*, 1946, *251*, 639–668.

Robertson, J. *Young children in hospitals*. New York: Basic Books, 1958.

—— Mothering as an influence on early development. *Psychoanal. Study Child.*, 1962, *17*, 245–264.

Robins, L. N., & Tomanec, M. Closeness to blood relatives outside the immediate family. *Marriage Fam. Living*, 1962, *24*, 340–346.

Robinson, S., & Naylor, S. R. The effects of late weaning on the deciduous incisor teeth: A pilot survey. *Br. Dent. J.*, 1963, *115*, 250–251.

Robson, K. S. The role of eye-to-eye contact in maternal-infant attachment. *J. Child Psychol. Psychiatry*, 1967, *8*, 13–25.

——, & Moss, H. A. Patterns and determinants of maternal attachment. *J. Pediatr.*, 1970, *77*, 976–985.

——, Pedersen, F. A., & Moss, H. A. Developmental observations of diadic gazing in relation to the fear of strangers and social approach behavior. *Child Dev.*, 1969, *40*, 619–627.

Rodgers, R. H. Improvements in the construction and analysis of family life cycle categories. (Ph.D. dissertation, University of Minnesota, 1962.) Kalamazoo, Mich.: Western Michigan University, 1962.

—— *Family interaction and transaction—The developmental approach.* Englewood Cliffs, N.J.: Prentice-Hall, 1973.

Roehner, J. Fatherhood: In pregnancy and birth. *J. Nurs. Midwifery*, 1976, *21*, 13–18.

Rogolsky, M. D. Screening kindergarten children: A review and recommendations. *J. School Psychol.*, 1968–69, *7*, 18–27.

Rollins, B. C., & Feldman, H. Marital satisfaction over the family life cycle. *J. Marriage Fam.*, 1970, *32*, 20–28.

Rosenwaike, I. The influence of socioeconomic status on incidence of low birth weight. *HSMHA Health Rep.*, 1971, *86*, 641–649.

Rossi, A. S. Transition to parenthood. *J. Marriage Fam.*, 1968, *30*, 26–39. [Reprinted in I. L. Reiss, (Ed.), *Readings on the family system.* New York: Holt, 1972.]

Ross Laboratories. *A study in maternal attitudes.* Columbus, Ohio: Ross Laboratories, 1959.

Rothbart, M. K., & Maccoby, E. E. Parents' differential reactions to sons and daughters. *J. Personal. Social Psychol.*, 1966, *4*, 237–243.

Rothenberg, M. Effect of television violence on children and youth. *JAMA*, 1975, *234*, 1043–1046.

Rowe, G. P. The developmental conceptual framework to the study of the family. In F. I. Nye & F. M. Berardo (Eds.), *Emerging conceptual frameworks in family analysis.* New York: MacMillan, 1966, pp. 198–221.

Roy, S. C. Role cues for the mother of the hospitalized child. *Nurs. Res.*, 1967, *16*, 178–182.

Rubin, J. Z., Provenzano, F. J., & Luria, Z. The eye of the beholder: Parents' views on sex of newborns. *Am. J. Orthopsychiatry*, 1974, *44*, 512–519.

Rubin, R. Basic maternal behavior. *Nurs. Outlook*, 1961, *9*, 683–686.

—— Maternal touch. *Nurs. Outlook*, 1963, *11*, 828–831.

—— Attainment of the maternal role. Part 1. Processes. *Nurs. Res.*, 1967a, *16*, 237–245.

———— Attainment of the maternal role. Part 2. Models and referrants. *Nurs. Res.*, 1967b, *16*, 342–346.

Ruderman, E. A. *Child care and working mothers: Study of arrangements made for daytime care of children.* New York: Child Welfare League of America, 1968.

Rugh, R. X-Irradiation effects on the human fetus. *J. Pediatr.*, 1958, *52*, 531–538.

Russell, C. S. Transition to parenthood: Problems and gratifications. *J. Marriage Fam.*, 1974, *36*, 294–301.

Rutter, M. Normal psychosocial development. *J. Child Psychol. Psychiatry*, 1971, *11*, 259–283.

———— Tizard, J., & Whitmore, K. (Eds.). *Education, health and behavior.* London: Longman, 1970.

Saarni, C. I. Piagetian operations and field independence as factors in children's problem-solving performance. *Child Dev.*, 1973, *44*, 338–345.

Safer, D. J., & Allen, R. P. *Hyperactive children: Diagnosis and management.* Baltimore: Baltimore University Park Press, 1976.

————, ————, & Barr, E. Depression of growth in hyperactive children on stimulant drugs. *N. Engl. J. Med.*, 1972, *287*, 217–220.

Salber, E. J. The effect of sex, birthrank, and birthweight on growth in the first year of life. *Hum. Biol.*, 1957, *29*, 194–213.

Samamiego, L. R., Caldwell, H. S., Nitschke, R. et al. Exploring the physically ill child's self perceptions and the mother's perceptions of her child's needs. *Clin. Pediatr.*, 1977, *16*, 154–159.

Sameroff, A., & Chandler, M. Reproductive risk and the continuum of caretaking casualty. In F. Horowitz, M. Hetherington, & S. Scarr-Salapatek (Eds.), *Review of child development research* (Vol. 4). Chicago: University of Chicago Press, 1975.

Samora, J. *LaRaza: Forgotten Americans.* South Bend, Ind.: University of Notre Dame, 1966.

Sampson, E. E. Birth order, need achievement and conformity. *J. Abnormal Social Psychol.*, 1962, *64*, 155–159.

Sandidge, S., & Friedland, S. J. Sex-role-taking and aggressive behavior in children. *J. Genet. Psychol.*, 1975, *126*, 227–231.

Sandler, A., & Haynes, V. Non-accidental trauma and medical folk belief: A case of cupping. *Pediatrics*, 1978, *61*, 921–922.

Saslow, H., & Harrover, M. Research on psychosocial adjustment of Indian youth. *Am. J. Psychol.*, 1968, *125*, 224–231.

Saunders, L. *Culture difference and medical care: The case of the Spanish speaking people of the Southwest.* New York: Russell Sage Foundation, 1954.

Sayre, M. The need to ban competitive sports involving preadolescent children. *Pediatrics*, 1975, *55*, 564 (letter to editor).

Scarr-Salapatek, S., & Williams, M. The effects of early stimulation on low-birth weight infants. *Child Dev.*, 1973, *44*, 94–101.

Schachter, S. Birth order, eminence and higher education. *Am. Sociol. Rev.*, 1963, *28*, 757–767.

Schaefer, E. Parents as educators. Evidence from cross-sectional longitudinal and intervention research. *Young Child.*, 1972, *27*, 227–239.

CHILD AND FAMILY DEVELOPMENT

Schaeffer, B., & Callender, W. Psychologic effects of hospitalization in infancy. *Pediatrics,* 1959, *24,* 528–539.

Schaffer, H. R., & Emerson, P. E. The development of social attachments in infancy. *Monogr. Soc. Res. Child Dev.,* 1964a, *29,* 1–77 (3, Serial No. 94).

———, & ——— Patterns of response to physical contact in early human development. *J. Child Psychol. Psychiatry,* 1964b, *5,* 1–13.

Scherp, H. W. Dental caries: Prospects for prevention. *Science,* 1971, *173,* 1199–1205.

Schlesinger, H. S., & Meadow, K. P. *Sound and sign: Childhood deafness and mental health.* Berkeley: University of California Press, 1972.

Schmitt, B. D. School phobia—The great imitator: A pediatrician's viewpoint. *Pediatrics,* 1971, *48,* 433–441.

Schooler, C., & Scarr, S. Affiliation among chronic schizophrenics: Relation to intrapersonal and birth order factors. *J. Personality,* 1962, *30,* 178–192.

Schulman, S. W., Earl, J., & Guerro, R. S. *Mexican-American youth and vocational education in Texas: Summary and recommendations.* Houston: Center for Human Resources, University of Houston, 1973.

Scott, C. Health and healing practices among 5 ethnic groups in Miami, Florida. *Publ. Health Rep.,* 1974, *89,* 525–532.

Scott, J. P. Critical periods of social development. In R. C. Smart & M. S. Smart (Eds.), *Readings in child development and relationships.* New York: Macmillan, 1972, pp. 74–84.

Sears, R. *Survey of objective studies of psychoanalytic concepts.* New York: Social Science Research Council, 1943.

———, Maccoby, E., & Levine, H. *Patterns of child rearing.* New York: Row, Peterson, 1957.

Sebastian, C. B. *Teachers' understandings of the behavior of Mexican-American children.* Los Angeles: University of Southern California Press, 1972.

Seltzer, C. C., & Mager, J. An effective weight-control program in a public school system. *Am. J. Publ. Health,* 1970, *60,* 679–689.

Selye, H. The pathophysiology of stress. *Postgrad. Med.,* 1959, *25,* 660–665.

Sewell, W. H. Social class and childhood personality. *Sociometry,* 1961, *24,* 340–356.

Shaffer, D., McNamara, N., & Pincus, J. Controlled observations on patterns of activity, attention and impulsivity in brain-damaged and psychiatrically disturbed boys. *J. Psychol. Med.,* 1974, *4,* 4–18.

Shainess, N. Motherhood: A tempering experience. *Child Fam.,* 1965, *4,* 3–12.

——— Psychological problems associated with motherhood. In S. Arieti (Ed.), *American handbook of psychiatry* (Vol. 3). New York: Basic Books, 1966. pp. 47–65.

Shapiro, S., Schlesinger, R., & Nesbitt, R. *Infant, perinatal, maternal, childhood mortality in the U. S.* Boston: Harvard University Press, 1968.

Share, J., & Veale, A. *Developmental landmarking for children with Down's syndrome.* Dunedin, New Zealand: University of Otago Press, 1974.

Sheikh, A. A., Prasad, V. K., & Rao, T. R. Children's T. V. commercials: A review of research. *J. Commun.,* 1974, *24*(4), 126–136.

Shere, M. O. Socio-emotional factors in the family of twins with cerebral palsy. *Excep. Child.*, 1956, *22*, 197–199, 206.

Sherman, M. Physiologic bowing of the legs. *South. Med. J.*, 1960, *53*, 830–836.

Shirley, M. M. *The first two years: A study of twenty-five babies*. Minneapolis: University of Minnesota Press, 1933.

Shulman, J. L., Kaspar, J. C., & Throne, F. M. *Brain damage and behavior*. Springfield, Ill.: Charles C Thomas, 1965.

SIECUS. Sexuality and the life cycle. In J. L. McCary & D. R. Copeland (Eds.), *Modern views of human sexual behavior*. Chicago: Science Research Associates, 1976.

Siegel, A. The great brain robbery. *Johns Hopkins Magazine,* March 1974, 19–23.

———, & Haas, M. B. The working mother: A review of research. *Child Dev.*, 1963, *34*, 513–542.

Silber, E., Stewart, E. P., & Bloch, D. A. Patterns of parent-child interaction in a disaster. *Psychiatry,* 1958, *21*, 167–195.

Sillman, J. H. Finger-sucking: Serial dental study from birth to five years of age. *N.Y. State J. Med.*, 1942, *42*, 2024–2028.

Simmons, K. Physical growth and development. *Monogr. Soc. Res. Child Dev.*, 1944, 9(1, Serial No. 37).

Simpson, N., Dallaire, L., Miller, A. et al. Prenatal diagnosis of genetic disease in Canada: Report of a collaborative study. *Can. Med. Assoc. J.*, 1976, *115*, 739–748.

Sinclair, D. *Human growth after birth*. London: Oxford University Press, 1969.

Singer, J. E., Westphal, M., & Niswander, K. R. Relationship of weight gain during pregnancy to birth weight and infant growth and development in the first year of life. *Obstet. Gynecol.*, 1968, *31*, 417–423.

Skeels, H. M. Adult status of children with contrasting early life experiences. *Monogr. Soc. Res. Child Dev.*, 1966, *31*(3, Serial No. 105).

———, & Dye, H. B. A study of the effects of differential stimulation of mentally retarded children. *Proc. Am. Assoc. Ment. Defic.*, 1939, *44*, 114–136.

Skipper, J. K., Jr., & Leonard, R. C. Children, stress, and hospitalization: A field experiment. *J. Health Social Behav.*, 1968, *9*, 275–287.

Skolnick, A. *The intimate environment. Exploring marriage and the family*. Boston: Little, Brown, 1973.

Slovic, P. Risk-taking in children: Age and sex differences. *Child Dev.*, 1966, *37*, 169–176.

Smart, M. S., & Smart, L. S. *Families developing relationships*. New York: Macmillan, 1976.

———, & Smart, R. C. *Children: Development and relationships* (2d ed.). New York: Macmillan, 1972.

Smith, E. W. Transition to the role of grandmother as studied with mothers of pregnant adolescents. In *ANA clinical sessions*. New York: Appleton-Century-Crofts, 1971, pp. 140–148.

——— The role of the grandmother in adolescent pregnancy and parenting. *J. School Health*, 1975, *45*, 278–283.

Smith, M. B., & Brahce, C. I. When school and home focus on achievement. *Educ. Leadership,* 1963, *20,* 314–318.

Smith, P. B., Mumford, D. M., Goldfarb, J. L., & Kaufman, R. H. Selected aspects of adolescent postpartum behavior, *J. Reprod. Med.,* 1975, *14,* 159–165.

Smith, R. H., Downer, D. B., & Lynch, M. T. The man in the house. *Fam. Coord.,* 1969, *18,* 107–111.

Snyder, R. D. Congenital mercury poisoning. *N. Engl. J. Med.,* 1971, *284,* 1014–1016.

Soderling, B. The first smile: A developmental study. *Acta Paediatr.,* 1959, *48* (Supplement 17), 78–82.

Somers, A. R. Violence, television and the health of American youth. *N. Engl. J. Med.,* 1976, *294,* 811–817.

Sontag, L. Differences in modifiability of fetal behavior and physiology. *Psychosom. Med.,* 1944, *6,* 151–158.

Soule, A. B. Clinical uses of the Brazelton neonatal scale. *Pediatrics,* 1974, *54,* 583.

Spargo, C. J. *Attitudes of mothers using day care centers toward their employment.* Unpublished master's thesis, University of Wisconsin, Madison, Wisconsin, 1968.

Spaulding, M. R. Adopting postpartum teaching to the mother's low income style. In B. Bergersen, E. H. Anderson, M. Duffey, M. Lohr, & M. Rose (Eds.), *Curr. Conc. Clin. Nurs.* (Vol. 2). St. Louis: Mosby, 1969, p. 280–291.

Spinetta, J. J. The dying child's awareness of death: A review, *Psychol. Bull.,* 1974, *81*(4), 256–260.

———, Rigler, D., & Karon, M. Anxiety in the dying child. *Pediatrics,* 1973, *52,* 841–845.

Spiro, M. E. Ifaluk ghosts: An anthropological inquiry into learning and perception. In R. Hunt (Ed.), *Personality and cultures: Readings in Psychological Anthropology.* New York: Natural History Press, 1949, pp. 89–94.

——— Is the family universal? *Am. Anthropol.,* 1954, *56,* 839–846.

Spitz, R. A. Hospitalism. *Psychoanal. Study Child,* 1945, *1,* 53–74.

——— Autoerotism reexamined. *Psychoanal. Study Child,* 1962, *9,* 16–75.

———, & Wolf, K. Autoerotism: Some empirical findings and hypotheses on three of its manifestations in the first year of life. *Psychoanal. Study Child,* 1959, *3/4,* 85–120.

Sprott, W. J. H., Jephcott, A. P., & Carter, M. P. *The social background of delinquency.* Nottingham: University of Nottingham, 1955.

Stack, C. B. Who owns the child? Divorce and child custody decisions in middle class families. *Social Prob.,* 1976, *23,* 505–515.

Starfield, B. Measurement of outcome, A proposed scheme. *Milbank Mem. Fund. Health Society,* 1974, *52*(1), 39–50.

———, & Borkouf, S. Physician's recognition of complaints made by parents about their children's health. *Pediatrics,* 1969, *43,* 168–172.

———, & Mellits, E. Increase in functional bladder capacity and improvements in enuresis. *J. Pediatr.,* 1968, *72,* 483–487.

Steele, B. F., & Pollock, C. G. A psychiatric study of parents who abuse infants and small children. In R. E. Helfer and C. H. Kempe (Eds.), *The battered child.* Chicago: University of Chicago Press, 1968.

Stein, A. H., Pohly, S. R., & Mueller, E. The influence of masculine, feminine and neutral tasks on children's achievement behavior expectancies of success and attainment values. *Child Dev.,* 1971, *32,* 195–207.

Stevenson, H., & Stewart, E. A developmental study of race awareness in young children. *Child Dev.,* 1958, *29,* 399–410.

Stine, O. Content and method of health supervision by physicians in child health conferences in Baltimore. *Am. J. Publ. Health,* 1962, *52,* 1858–1865.

Stolz, L. M. *Influences on parent behavior.* Stanford, Calif.: Stanford University Press, 1967.

Stone, L. J., & Church, J. *Childhood and adolescence* (3d ed.). New York: Random House. 1973.

Stott, D. H. Follow-up study from birth of the effects of prenatal stresses. *Dev. Med. Child Neurol.,* 1973, *15,* 770–787.

———, & Latchford, S. A. Prenatal antecedents of child health, development, and behavior. *J. Am. Acad. Child Psychiatry,* 1976, *15,* 161–191.

Strauss, A. Medical ghettos. In A. Strauss (Ed.), *Where medicine fails.* Chicago: Aldine, 1970.

Strean, L. P., & Peer, L. A. Stress as an etiologic factor in the development of cleft palate. *Plastic Reconstruct. Surg.,* 1956, *18,* 1–8.

Stuart, H., & Sobel, E. The thickness of the skin and subcutaneous tissue by age and sex in childhood. *J. Pediatr.,* 1946, *28,* 637–647.

Sultz, H., Schlesinger, E. R., Mosher, W. E., & Feldman, J. G. *Long-term childhood illness.* Pittsburgh: University of Pittsburgh Press, 1972.

Super, C. Environmental effects on motor development: The case of "African infant precocity." *Dev. Med. Child Neurol.,* 1976, *18,* 561–567.

Sussman, M. B. Family systems in the 1970s: Analysis, policies, and programs. In D. P. Hymovich & M. U. Barnard (Eds.), *Family health care.* New York: McGraw-Hill, 1973.

———, & Burchinal, L. Kin family network: Unheralded structure in current conceptualizations of family functioning. *Marriage Fam. Living,* 1962, *24,* 231–240.

Sutton-Smith, B. Children at play. In A. Kilbride (Ed.), *Readings in human development 76/77.* Guilford, Conn.; Dushkin Publishing Group, 1976, pp. 151–157.

Szasz, T. S., & Hollender, M. H. Contribution to philosophy of medicine; Basic models of doctor-patient relationship. *A.M.A. Arch. Internal Med.,* 1956, *97,* 585–592.

Tagliacozzo, D. M., & Kenji, I. Knowledge of illness as a predictor of patient behavior. *J. Chron. Dis.,* 1970, *22,* 312–323.

Tanner, J. M. Physical growth. In P. Mussen (Ed.), *Carmichael's manual of child psychology* (3d ed.). New York: Wiley, 1970, pp. 77–155.

Tanner, L. M. Developmental tasks of pregnancy. In B. S. Bergersen, E. H. Anderson, M. Duffy, M. Lohr, & M. Rose (Eds.), *Current concepts in clinical nursing* (Vol. 2). St. Louis: Mosby, 1969, pp. 292–297.

Tarnapol, L. Delinquency in minimal brain dysfunction. *J. Learning Disabil.,* 1970, *3,* 200–207.

Tasch, R. J. The role of the father in the family. *J. Exp. Educ.,* 1952, *20,* 319–361.

Taussig, H. B. Thalidomide and phocomelia. *Pediatrics,* 1962, *30,* 654–659.

Taylor, A. Institutionalized infants' concept formation ability. *Am. J. Orthopsychiatry,* 1968, *38,* 110–115.

Taylor, B., & Howell, R. The ability of three, four, and five year old children to distinguish fantasy from reality. *J. Genet. Psychol.,* 1973, *112,* 315–318.

Taylor, R. L. Psychosocial development among black children and youth. *Am. J. Orthopsychiatry,* 1976, *46*(1), 4–19.

Teberg, A., Hodgman, J. E., Wu, P. Y. K., & Spears, R. L. Recent improvement in outcome for the small premature infant. *Clin Pediatr.,* 1977, *16*(4), 307–313.

Templin, M. C. *Certain language skills in children. Their development and their interrelationships.* Minneapolis: University of Minnesota Press, 1957.

ten Bensel, R. W., & Berdie, J. The neglect and abuse of children and youth: The scope of the problem and the school's role. *J. School Health,* 1976, *46*(8), 453–461.

Tennes, K. H., & Lampl, E. E. Stranger and separation anxiety in infancy. *J. Nerv. Ment. Dis.,* 1964, *139,* 247–254.

Terman, L. et al. *Psychological factors in marital happiness.* New York: McGraw-Hill, 1938.

Thain, W. S., Castro, G., & Peterson, A. What's wrong with my baby? *Am. Fam. Physician,* 1977, *15,* 90–96.

Thevenin, T. *The family bed: An age old concept in childrearing.* Minneapolis: Tine Thevenin, 1976.

Thoman, E., Leiderman, P., & Olson, J. Neonate-mother interaction during breast feeding. *Dev. Psychol.,* 1972, *6,* 110–118.

Thomas, A., Chess, S., & Birch, H. G. *Temperament and behavior disorders in children.* New York: New York University Press, 1968.

————, ————, ————, & Hertzig, M. E. A longitudinal study of primary reaction patterns in children. *Compr. Psychiatry,* 1960, *1,* 103–112.

————, ————, ————. ————, & Korn, S. *Behavioral individuality in early childhood.* New York: New York University Press, 1963.

Thomson, A. M., Hytten, F. E., & Billewicz, W. Z. The energy cost of human lactation. *Br. J. Nutr.,* 1970, *24,* 565–572.

Tisza, V. B., & Gumpertz, E. The parents' reaction to the birth and early care of children with cleft palate. *Pediatrics,* 1962, *28,* 86–90.

Tompkins, W. T. National efforts to reduce perinatal mortality and morbidity. *Clin. Obstet. Gynecol.,* 1970, *13,* 44–56.

Torres-Matrullo, C. Acculturation and psychopathology among Puerto Rican women in mainland United States. *Am. J. Orthopsychiatry,* 1976, *46,* 710–719.

Torrey, E. F. *The mind game: Witch doctors and psychiatrists.* New York: Emerson Hall, 1972.

Touliatos, J., & Lindholm, B. W. Behavior problems of Anglo- and Mexican-American children. *J. Abnorm. Child Psychol.*, 1976, *4*, 299–304.

Traisman, A. S., & Traisman, H. S. Thumb and finger sucking: A study of 2,650 infants and children. *J. Pediatr.*, 1958, *52*, 566–572.

———, ———, & Gatti, R. A. The well baby care of 530 infants. *J. Pediatr.*, 1966, *68*, 608–614.

Trethowan, W. H. The couvade syndrome. In J. G. Howells (Ed.), *Modern perspectives in psycho-obstetrics.* New York: Brunner/Mazel, 1972, pp. 68–93.

Tronick, E., & Brazelton, T. B. Clinical uses of the Brazelton Neonatal Assessment Scale. In E. Z. Friedlander, et al. (Eds.), *Exceptional infant* (Vol. 3) *Assessment and intervention.* New York: Brunner/Mazel, 1975.

Tropauer, A., Franz, M. N., & Dilgard, V. W. Psychological aspects of the care of children with cystic fibrosis. *Am. J. Dis. Child.*, 1970, *119*, 424–432.

Tryon, C., & Lilienthal, J. W., Jr. Child growth and development. *NEAJ.*, 1950, *39*, 188–199.

Tulkin, S. R., & Kagan, J. Mother-child interaction in the first year of life. *Child Dev.*, 1972, *43*, 31–41.

Turner, E. The syndrome in the infant resulting from maternal emotional tension during pregnancy. *Med. J. Aust.*, 1956, *1*, 221–222.

Uchida, I. A., Holunga, R., & Lawler, C. Maternal radiation and chromosomal aberrations. *Lancet,* 1968, *2*, 1045–1049.

Udry, J. R. *The social context of marriage* (2d ed.). Philadelphia: Lippincott, 1971.

U.S. Bureau of the Census. Mobility of the population of the United States: March 1967 to March 1968. *Population characteristics,* Current Population Reports, Series P-20, No. 188. August 14, 1969.

U.S. Department of Agriculture. Consumer and Food Economics Division. Family Food Budgeting. *Agr. Res. Serv. Home Garden Bull.*, 1969, *94*, 6.

U.S. Department of Health, Education and Welfare. *Ten-State Nutrition Survey 1968-1970.* DHEW Publications No. (HSM) 72-8130. Atlanta: Center for Disease Control, 1972.

U.S. Department of Health, Education and Welfare. National Center for Health Statistics. *Vital statistics report,* 1975.

Van Arsdale, W., Roghmann, K. J., & Nader, P. R. Visits to an elementary school nurse. *J. School Health*, 1972, *42*(3), 142–148.

Van Stolk, M. Beaten women, battered children. *Child. Today*, 1976, *5*, 8–12.

Vaughn, V. C., & McKay, R. (Eds.), *Nelson: Textbook of pediatrics* (10th ed.). Philadelphia: Saunders, 1975.

Veenker, C. H. A critical review of research in health education. *Int. J. Health Educ.*, 1965, *8*(4), 179–187.

Vernon, D. T. A., & Schulman J. L. Hospitalization as a source of psychological benefit to children. *Pediatrics*, 1964, *34*, 694–696.

———, ———, & Foley, J. M. Changes in children's behavior after hospitalization. *Am. J. Dis. Child.*, 1966, *111*, 581–593.

Vollman, R. R., Ganzert, A., Picher, L., & Williams, W. V. The reactions of family systems to sudden and unexpected death. *Omega*, 1971, *2*, 101–106.

von Bertalanffy, L. *General systems theory.* New York: Braziller, 1968.

Vorherr, H. Drug excretion in breast milk. *Postgrad. Med.*, 1974, *56*, 97–103.

Waechter, E. H. Children's awareness of fatal illness. *Am. J. Nurs.*, 1971, *71*, 1168–1172.

———— Developmental consequences of congenital abnormalities. *Nurs. Forum*, 1975, *14*(2), 108–129.

Wagner, M. G., & Arndt, R. Postmaturity as an aetiological factor in 124 cases of neurologically handicapped children. *Clinics in developmental medicine* (No. 27) *Studies in infancy*. London: Heinemann, 1968.

Wahler, R. G. Oppositional children: A quest for parental reinforcement control. *J. Appl. Behav. Anal.*, 1969, *2*, 159–170.

————, Winkel, G., Peterson, R., & Morrison, D. Mothers as behavior therapists for their own children. *Behav. Res. Ther.*, 1965, *3*, 113–124.

Walder, L. O., Cohen, S. I., Breiter, D. E., Daston, P. G., Hirsch, I. S., & Leibowitz, J. M. Teaching behavioral principles to parents of disturbed children. In B. G. Guerney (Ed.), *Psychotherapeutic agents: New roles for non-professionals, parents and teachers*. New York: Holt, 1969, pp. 443–449.

Waldman, E. Children of working mothers, March 1974. *Monthly Labor Rev.*, 1975, *98*, 64–67.

————, & Glover, K. *Marital and family characteristics in the labor force*. Special Labor Force Report 144, U.S. Dept. of Labor, Bureau of Labor Statistics, April 1972.

Wallace, H. M. Factors in mortality and morbidity. *Clin. Obstet. Gynecol.*, 1970, *13*, 13–43.

———— The health of American Indian children. *Health Serv. Rep.*, 1972, *87*, 867–876.

Wallerstein, J. S., & Kelly, J. B. Parental divorce—The preschool child. *J. Am. Acad. Child Psychiatry*, 1975, *14*(4), 600–616.

————, & ———— The effects of parental divorce: Experiences of the child in later latency. *Am. J. Orthopsychiatry*, 1976, *46*(2), 256–269.

Wallston, B. The effects of maternal employment on children. *J. Child Psychol. Psychiatry*, 1973, *14*, 81–95.

Walter, L. M., & Margolf, S. S. The relation of sex, age and school achievement to levels of aspiration. *J. Educ. Psychol.*, 1951, *42*, 285–292.

Warkany, J. Etiology of congenital malformations. *Adv. Pediatr.*, 1947, *2*, 1–63.

Warrick, L. H. Family centered care in the premature nursery. *Am. J. Nurs.*, 1971, *71*, 2134–2138.

Watson, E., & Lowrey, G. *Growth and development of children*. Chicago: Year Book Medical Publishers, 1967.

Watts, A. S. Helping children to mourn. *Med. Insight*, 1971, *3*(8), 57–62.

Weil, R. J., & Tupper, C. Personality, life situation, and communication: A study of habitual abortion. *Psychosom. Med.*, 1960, *22*, 448–455.

Weiner, I. B., & Elkind, D. *Child development: A core approach*. New York: Wiley, 1972.

Weiss, R. R., & Pexton, M. R. *The expectant father*. North Quincy, Mass.: Christopher Publishing House, 1970.

BIBLIOGRAPHY

————, & Trithart, A. Between meal eating habits and dental caries experience in preschool children. *Am. J. Publ. Health*, 1960, *50*, 1097.

Werner, E., Bierman, J., & French, F. *The children of Kauai*. Honolulu: University of Hawaii Press, 1971.

West, D. J. *Present conduct and future delinquency*. London: Heinemann, 1969.

White, B. L. *The first three years of life*. Englewood Cliffs, N.J.: Prentice-Hall, 1975.

————, & Watts, J. C. *Experience and environment* (Vol. 1). Englewood Cliffs, N.J.: Prentice-Hall, 1973.

Whiting, J., & Child, I. *Child training and personality*. New Haven: Yale University Press, 1953.

Widdowson, E. Mental contentment and physical growth. *Lancet*, 1951, *1*, 1316–1318.

Wilkins, L., Jones, H. W., Holman, G. H., & Stempfel, R. S. Masculinization of the female fetus associated with administration of oral and intramuscular progestins during gestation: Non-adrenal female pseudohermaphrodism. *J. Clin. Endocrinol. Metab.*, 1958, *18*, 559–575.

Will, J. A., Self, P. A., & Datan, N. Maternal behavior and perceived sex of infant. *Am. J. Orthopsychiatry*, 1976, *46*(1), 135–139.

Will, S. I. Nursing's role in affecting positive maternal attachment to a child with an anomaly—A case study. In *1974 ANA Clinical Sessions*. New York: Appleton-Century-Crofts, 1975, pp. 359–369.

Willemsen, E., Flaherty, D., Heaton, C., & Ritchey, G. Attachment behavior of one-year-olds as a function of mother vs. father, sex of child, session, and toys. *Genet. Psychol. Monogr.*, 1974, *90*, 305–324.

Williams, R. L., & Cole, S. Self-concept and school adjustment. *Personnel Guidance J.*, 1968, *46*, 478–481.

Williams, T. M. Childrearing practices of young mothers: What we know, how it matters, why it's so little. *Am. J. Orthopsychiatry*, 1974, *44*(1), 70–75.

Williams, W. V., Polak, P., & Vollman, R. R. Crisis intervention in acute grief. *Omega*, 1972, *3*, 67–70.

Willoughby, J., & Haggerty, R. A simple behavior questionnaire for preschool children. *Pediatrics*, 1964, *34*, 798–805.

Winick, M. (Ed.). *Nutrition and fetal development*. New York: Wiley, 1974.

———— Maternal nutrition. In R. L. Brent & M. I. Harris (Eds.), *Prevention of embryonic fetal, and perinatal disease*. DHEW Publication (NIH) 76-853, 1976, pp. 97–117.

Winnicott, D. W. The theory of the parent-infant relationship. *Int. J. Psychoanal.*, 1960, *41*, 585–595.

Winokur, G., & Werboff, J. The relationship of conscious maternal attitudes to certain aspects of pregnancy. *Psychiatr. Q.*, Supplement, 1956, *30*(1), 61–73.

Wise, H. B., Torrey, E. F., McDade, A., Perry, G., & Bograd, H. The family health worker. *Am. J. Pub. Health*, 1968, *58*, 1828–1838.

Withers, R. F. J. Problems in genetics of human obesity. *Eugenics Rev.*, 1964, *56*, 81–90.

Witkin, H. A., Goodenough, D. R., & Karp, S. A. Stability of cognitive style from childhood to young adulthood. *J. Personal. Social Psychol.*, 1967, *7*, 291–300.

Wolfenstein, M. Death of a parent and death of a president: Children's reactions to two kinds of loss. In M. Wolfenstein & G. Kliman (Eds.), *Children and the death of a president*. New York: Doubleday, 1965.

Wolfer, J. A., & Visintainer, M. A. Pediatric surgical patients' and parents' stress responses and adjustment. *Nurs. Res.*, 1975, *24*(4), 244–255.

Wolff, J. R. The emotional reaction to a stillbirth. In *Psychosomatic medicine in obstetrics and gynaecology*, 3d Int. Congress, London, 1971. Basel: Karger, 1972, pp. 330–332.

Wolff, P. H. Observations on the early development of smiling. In B. M. Foss (Ed.), *Determinants of infant behavior II*. London: Methuen, 1963.

Wolkind, S. N., Kruk, S., & Chaves, L. P. Childhood separation experiences and psycho-social status in primiparous women: Preliminary findings. *Br. J. Psychiatry*, 1976, *128*, 391–396.

Wright, B. A. *Physical disability—A psychological approach*. New York: Harper & Row, 1960.

Wright, J. D., & Wright, S. R. Social class and parental values for children: A partial replication and extension of the Kohn thesis. *Am. Sociol. Rev.*, 1976, *41*, 527–537.

Wyatt, G. Speech and language disorders in preschool children: A preventive approach. *Pediatrics*, 1965, *36*, 637–647.

Yalom, I. D., Lunde, D. T., Moos, R. H., & Hamburg, D. A. Post-partum blues' syndrome: A description and related variables. *Arch. Gen. Psychiatry*, 1968, *18*, 16–27.

Yamazaki, J. N., Wright, S. W., & Wright, P. M. Outcome of pregnancy in women exposed to the atomic bomb in Nagasaki. *Am. J. Dis. Child.*, 1954, *87*, 448–463.

Yankauer, A. Child health supervision—Is it worth it? *Pediatrics*, 1973, *52*, 272–279.

————, Goss, K. G., & Romeo, S. M. An evaluation of prenatal care and its relationship to social class and social disorganization. *Am. J. Pub. Health*, 1953, *43*, 1001–1010.

Yarrow, L. J. Maternal deprivation: Toward an empirical and conceptual revaluation. *Psychol. Bull.*, 1961, *58*, 459–490.

———— Research in dimensions of maternal care. *Merrill-Palmer Q.*, 1963, *9*, 101–114.

———— The development of focused relationship during infancy. In J. Hellmuth (Ed.), *Exceptional infant I: The normal infant*. New York: Brunner/Mazel, 1967.

Yarrow, M. R., Scott, P., DeLeeuw, L., & Heinig, C. Child-rearing in families of working and nonworking mothers. *Sociometry*, 1962, *25*, 122–140.

Yates, A. J. *Theory and practice in behavior therapy*. New York: Wiley, 1975.

Yudkin, S., & Holme, A. (Eds.). *Working mothers and their children*. London: Sphere Books, 1969.

BIBLIOGRAPHY

Zax, M., Sameroff, A. J., & Farnum, J. E. Childbirth education, maternal attitudes, and delivery. *Am. J. Obstet. Gynecol.*, 1975, *123*, 185–190.

Zeilberger, J., Sampen, S. E., & Sloane, H. N., Jr. Modification of a child's problem behaviors in the home with the mother as therapist. *J. Appl. Behav. Anal.*, 1968, *1*, 47–53.

Zigler, E., & Child, I. L. *Socialization and personality development.* Reading, Mass.: Addison-Wesley, 1973.

Zimmerman, C. C., & Cervantes, L. F. *Successful American families.* New York: Pageant Press, 1960.

Zita, A. C., McDonald, R., & Andrews, A. Dietary habits and the dental caries experiences in 200 children. *J. Dent. Res.*, 1959, *38*, 860.

Zuk, G. Religious factors and the role of guilt in parental acceptance of the retarded child. In R. Noland (Ed.), *Counselling parents of the mentally retarded.* Springfield, Ill.: Charles C Thomas, 1970.

Zwerdling, M. A. Factors pertaining to prolonged pregnancy and its outcome. *Pediatrics*, 1967, *40*(2), 202–212.

Index

INDEX

INDEX

INDEX

INDEX

INDEX

INDEX

INDEX